I0188823

Published in 2022 by Connor Court Publishing Pty Ltd.

Connor Court Publishing Pty Ltd.
PO Box 7257
Redland Bay QLD 4165
sales@connorcourt.com
www.connorcourt.com

ISBN: 9781922815231

Cover design by Ian James.

Front cover photo, Brendan Nelson with US Ambassador to Australia, Caroline Kennedy. Photo courtesy of Australian War Memorial, Canberra.

Printed in Australia.

Gillian

For love, friendship and support through thick and thin

My parents, Des and Pat

For gifts of intelligence, emotion and the power of expression

Tom, Emily and Bec

For sacrifices made, absences endured and unconditional love

The Jesuits

For others

Contents

Foreword

It's with a touch of irony I find myself being asked to write a foreword for the ultimate wordsmith and storyteller. While our skill sets don't exactly match, I do believe they align and complement each other, as evidenced by the delivery of bipartisan support for one of Australia's largest public works projects for an institution.

I'm speaking of course about our partnership on the major extensions of the Australian War Memorial. With Brendan's role as then Director and mine as Chair, we managed to achieve something that will be for me, one of my proudest accomplishments.

I like to think of Brendan as a man for all seasons. Prepared to address any challenge with the strength of his convictions, able to read a room or situation, applying not only appropriate responses but ones that inspire us to want to do more, and that reflect his moral compass and conscience.

Our paths first crossed in the early 1990s after my friend and colleague, Ken Parker, told me I needed to meet "a great new young fella in the Party" who'd been selected for Parliament. Being the youngest President of the Australian Medical Association (AMA), he already had a profile, but that's a journey best left for Brendan to tell you about here in this book.

Having taken a different pathway to become a Doctor, Brendan immersed himself into the prosecution of public health and its outcomes. His personal efforts and commitment to equal access to medical care, especially to those most vulnerable, reflect his character.

Being Brendan, he didn't just 'talk' about it, he went and 'lived' it and still does. In the course of that commitment, he made lifelong friends in the Indigenous community and the community at large, who still admire and respect him today.

We live in a world where at times conflict and lack of human kindness take over in the rush to go forward and achieve material objectives. Brendan's life shows us humanities in the full broadness of their meaning. Armed with a strong sense of family and putting others first, he shows us the value of regarding kindness and caring as being equally important as ambition and drive.

Underlying these emotions is a wonderful memory that allows him to recall names, places, facts and figures more adroitly than anybody else I've ever met. It was for good reason he earned his nickname 'rain man'.

He was always destined for public service. I have known and been involved with hundreds of politicians in my time, many of whom have an agenda of their own which is more about power than public service. Brendan's ambitions have always been shaped by his desire to create public benefit.

From the value of an education, to changing the ways universities thought about learning, his simple philosophies created lasting measurable benefits.

John Howard, a former Prime Minister and a personal friend, whom Brendan and I both admire and respect, did not select Brendan to the portfolio of Defence by accident. I'm sure he saw the young man whose intellect and dedication would ensure a stronger Defence force.

But Brendan also brought to the role benevolence and empathy as only a doctor could, agonising over decisions of putting anyone's life in harm's way. His commitment to care would filter through every level, ensuring that benefits flowed to the lowest ranks, from better food to better equipment. He cared passionately about every soldier, every airman, and every sailor.

When Brendan became Leader of the Opposition, he introduced changes to the Party, and helped revive it. He was a man who brought factions together and helped formulate cohesive policy that became the foundation of the Opposition's platform. It was a sad day when he was overturned by those in the party whose values stood poles apart from his.

Following his gracious exit from Australia's political stage Brendan went on to serve in an equally important role, connecting our country with the EU and NATO. No easy task given the conflicts we'd had with trade with the EU and the limited understanding and respect they had for our part of the world. By the time Brendan had finished his term, he'd changed that perspective. We were highly regarded by the EU and NATO, we had a seat at the table, and were participating.

During all of this, Brendan made time for his most passionate love: embedding himself in the detail of the traditions of those who have fought for us in the First World War.

If you've been fortunate enough to listen to Brendan talk on this period of Australian history, you'll know just how much he loves those men and women and their stories. The names on the Menin Gate, the tombstones in Flanders, always become so much more when he talks of them.

Brendan came to the War Memorial with fresh eyes and fresh ideas with the experience he observed in Europe and their commitment to Australian Remembrance. At the conclusion of his term as Director, he'd not only raised the profile of the Memorial and its work, but he'd also taken us on a journey of recognising a modern generation of service men and women.

With Government support, the AWM is in the process of a long-term expansion ensuring there's enough space devoted to 'all' our service history and contemporary service. Stories of our original diggers, veterans of the Second World War, Korea, and Vietnam, will sit alongside modern conflicts, humanitarian and peacekeeping missions.

No doubt Brendan will add to many initiatives he introduced but now in the guiding role as Chairman. He will continue to ensure the Memorial is a place of respect, of healing and unification, where we are reminded of the values of what it means to be Australian.

If you want to understand Brendan's moral code then you need look no further than a video made under the AWM's Giving Campaign (funded by Mike and Kate Ribot de Bressac). Called 'The Hall of Memory', it outlines the virtues that provide a strong code of ethics to which we should all aspire.

Today, with the luxury of hindsight, it's interesting to reflect on how our political landscape may have evolved with Brendan Nelson in the mix.

Whether read through the eyes of a patriotic Australian or political junkie, you're about to share in a wonderful descriptive narrative that reminds us not only of the values of what it means to be Australian, but of the importance of storytelling in getting messages across.

This book is more than a life story, it's actually a fingerprint of our cultural and moral journey.

KERRY STOKES AC

Chairman, Australia Capital Equity.

Chairman, Seven Media Network Australia.

Chairman, The Australian War Memorial (2015-2022).

Preface

None of it was planned. Had I done so, as with any life, some of it – but little – would be different.

My wife, Gillian finally persuaded me to do this. "You have to get this down. You have to record this for your kids, before you forget it and you are gone", she emphatically intoned. It was a road trip, returning from Corowa, after delivering the 2021 Tim Fischer Oration, that finally did it. Each memory, the experiences and the people that are the landscape of my life began falling out. Here are the people who made me, helped me strive to be a better person and to try to make a difference. You only have one life, one chance to use it in a way that makes a difference to the lives of others.

I have learned a lot. Some of it the hard way and often when I least expected to learn anything.

Although an entire industry is dedicated to the task, leadership can't be taught, but it can be learned. The qualities that inform good leadership can be discovered through observation of, reflection upon and absorption of the leadership qualities we find in others. The power is in the story. This is my story.

I have focused on people, events and experiences that are especially meaningful to me and from which I think readers will be prompted to reflect. Some are amusing, others deeply moving. Just writing and reliving these experiences has been emotional.

Beyond my parents, Des and Pat, I thank a number of people especially who made me. The nuns and Christian Brothers laid a solid foundation; Modbury High School in Adelaide whose teachers cared; the Jesuits whose values informed all I have attempted to do since. Words cannot do justice to the influence on my life of Dr Bruce Shepherd, Doug Thompson and Rhondda Vanzella, each truly loyal, steadfast and central to my life.

To Don Glover, Robert Longstaff, Lee Hall, Warren Entsch, Bob Baldwin, Joanna Gash, Tony Smith, Bruce Billson, Joe Hockey, Peter

Reith, Sir John Carrick, Catherine Murphy, Maria Fernandez, Simon Berger, Rear Admiral Ken Doolan (Retd) and Kerry Stokes, thank you.

Nervously, I asked Kerry Stokes if he would be prepared to write the foreword. That he readily agreed and what he wrote, is a great gift which I treasure. His own life journey, from the most humble and challenging circumstances, his intellect, emotional empathy, generosity of spirit and contribution to our nation, make him the man I admire.

Trish Burgess proof read and edited the book for me as a labour of love.

I am also indebted to the men and women of the Australian Defence Force, veterans and their families. My interactions with them throughout much of my life, directly and indirectly, continue to have a profound influence on me.

I owe an immense debt to the members of the Australian Medical Association (AMA) for their belief in me, especially when I was young. To the Liberal Party I owe all that I was able to achieve in public life, beyond medicine. I will never lose sight of Robert Menzies' vision and philosophical foundation for the Party, of which I will be a member until my death.

The experiences and stories told in this book have been made possible through the support given to me first by the medical profession and then by Australian taxpayers. As such I cannot, in conscience, profit from it. All royalties from this book will be shared equally by Lifeline and Legacy, two charities literally saving lives and supporting people, veterans and families.

Aboriginal and Torres Strait Islander readers are cautioned that deceased Indigenous Australians are named and featured throughout my story.

Finally, I had been married and divorced twice when I met and then married Gillian Adamson in 1999. To 'Lady Nelson', as I affectionately call her, thanks is not enough. She made my life.

At the 2021 Lifeline 50th anniversary in Canberra, two young doctors asked me, "How did you go from being a doctor to the President of Boeing in Australia?" This is how.

1

Context is everything

Married in 1957, my parents Des and Pat came from vastly different backgrounds. That the marriage survived more than three decades is a credit to them both.

Adopted into an Adelaide family of Orange Lodge Methodists in the late 1920s, Dad grew up through the great depression. Living with his sister Dorothy, his parents were necessarily frugal, to the extreme.

His adopted father, Alex, was a clerk. A founding member of the Clerks Union of Australia, he was a communist until 1956. Always meticulously dressed, including hat, notwithstanding their circumstances. The family politics were left – hard left. Yet he and Beatrice, having housed and fed their family and taken the young boy in as their own, would always give what they had left to the church charities. Life was hard but framed by a value system my father took into his life. At 18, in 1945, Des volunteered for war service with the RAAF, but the war ended before he could get there.

Des made a decision that would frame his entire life – he went to sea. He worked as a steward on domestic and international ships, serving on some of the world's largest, most prestigious passenger liners.

My mother, Pat, born in 1935, grew up in Launceston with her younger brother Geoff, her mother Molly being a Roman Catholic of Irish descent. One of seven children, her maiden name was Molly Maguire. When she and Arthur Beecroft married, he converted to Catholicism. Faith was the bedrock of their lives and the framework was military service.

Pat's grandfather was a Gallipoli veteran. A mechanic from Launceston, Bob Beecroft enlisted early – number 24. A member of the 12th Battalion and veteran of the landing on 25 April, he evacuated from Gallipoli in October 1915 with severe enteric fever. In Palestine he joined the Australian Flying Corps (AFC) as a mechanic in 1 Squadron and survived the war. My grandfather, Arthur, was one of six Beecroft sons who would wear the uniform in both peace and war. Arthur enlisted for war service in 1940, serving in the major campaigns of Balikpapan and Labuan. When he returned from the war, my mother didn't know who he was. After the War, Arthur ran his own grocery store and small, mixed business on Kings Meadows Road, Launceston.

My mother was bright. A student of Sacred Heart College in Launceston, she excelled. Her interests were in medicine but 'girls' did not study those subjects, being directed instead into arts and humanities. Winning a scholarship to the University of Tasmania, she undertook a Bachelor of Arts. Arthur and Molly had a baby, Christine, who understandably was doted upon – an unexpected 'gift from God'.

Then came devastating news that upended everyone's world and changed the trajectory of my mother's life. Christine, at the age of three, was diagnosed with a cancer of the kidney. Arthur and Molly were consumed by their much-loved child's illness, from which they knew she would die. My mother was recalled from university to run the family shop. She would never return to it. Christine's death became the source of deep and enduring sorrows.

It was into this environment my father arrived. Working on a ship that arrived in Tasmania, eight years older than my mother, a handsome 'man of the world', Des was a shining light to the future.

When they married in a Catholic church, my mother was 21. They moved to Melbourne and were living in Coburg when I was born in August 1958. Dad was away at sea as my mother struggled with a baby and a small network of friends, away from her family. Arthur and Molly's first grandchild might as well have been on the other side of the world. Air travel and long-distance phone calls were beyond the means of everyday Australians.

My parents moved to Launceston in 1959. My sister, Tracey, was born in November that year and my brother Philip in 1961. They built a modest weatherboard house in Cornwall Crescent, Launceston. Within that home, and in that community, we three children had the best childhood.

My mother was a stay-at-home mum for the first decade of my life. Dad secured a job as Chief Steward on the MV *William Holyman*, a 2,000-ton cargo ship. The *Holyman*, as we called her, sailed weekly, between Launceston and Melbourne. From our home we could see the ship slowly wind her way past our part of the river. My mother would know when to take the 15-minute drive to Kings Wharf to pick up Dad.

A condition of their marriage was that the children would be Catholics. At the top of our street the Presentation Sisters opened a school – Our Lady Help of Christians. Shortly after followed a church next door complete with parish priest. Into that modest environment we three kids began our educational journey under the tutelage of the nuns: warm and generous teachers.

Music was a big part of family life. Dad pulled out his piano accordion for family singalongs in which the neighbours were frequent participants. At other times he would have his records playing constantly and loudly. When he discovered Johnny Cash in the late 60s, everything went country. Dad always went 'big time' with his passions.

I was introduced to fishing when my parents decided to have a go off a jetty on the Tamar River. A short time later Dad bought a small tinny in which we kids had some of the best fishing experiences – and dramas – of our formative years.

In 1968 I was moving into Year 5. My parents enrolled me at St Patrick's College in the Launceston CBD. Here I was introduced to the Christian Brothers, literally, by my father. We drove to the school and, having got out of the car, Dad checked I was presentable. He placed his hands, one on each of my shoulders: "Son, this is very important. You have to look Brother McInerney in the eye and shake his hand firmly". He then tested my handshake several times before we entered the grounds.

The Christian brothers were hard taskmasters. They had to be. There were 54 kids in my Year 5 class. Anyone that misbehaved – talking in class, laughing and other misdemeanours – was in trouble. Brother Caldwell kept his leather strap in a jar of methylated spirits on his desk at the front of the class. He knew how to use it. I regularly received two or four cuts across my open hand. The trick was to hyperextend your wrist just before impact in an attempt to deflect the blow and then immediately return to your desk and press the pulsating palm against the steel base of your desk.

Every month we had exams. "Life is tough", Brother Caldwell proclaimed. "You boys need to learn early on that you have to work hard if you want to get anywhere. My job is to get the best out of you".

So, every month we would be tested. The results would be formulated and transmitted to our parents in plain language. On this basis every student would be ranked from top to bottom – 1 to 54. For the ensuing month we would be seated in that order. A competitive spirit was instilled in me. I was never top of the class, but nor was I at the bottom. Decades later as Australia's education minister, teacher unions were advocating smaller class sizes, ratios being less than half those of my youth, I often thought back to those years at St Pat's.

These were happy years. Great neighbours, Cubs, friends and doting grandparents. Long summer holidays were spent away with my family: the caravan, boat, Dad's widowed mother, two big dogs and four weeks of sun, swimming, fishing and adventure. To this day, Adventure Bay on the south eastern side of Bruny Island remains my most loved place in Australia. I have asked Gillian to spread my ashes there when I am gone.

My brother and I discovered tennis in Launceston. My mother decided to get Tracey interested. Philip and I grabbed the racquets and started hitting balls around the back yard. We went on to coaching, and competition tennis. Basketball and football were my other passions and my team, St Kilda.

Dad's ship, the *William Holyman*, was an important part of my childhood. When it berthed, Dad would take us to work with him where we were treated to ice cream and fishing off the stern. I was also exposed to endless discussions of politics, all left wing, anti-establishment, of the union culture. Dad was a delegate for the Cooks and Stewards Union, serving on its council for four years.

Throughout those years, time in my grandparents' home in Basin Road, Launceston, was shaping me in ways I would learn later in life. Stories of war service were accompanied by black and white photographs of young men and women in uniform. My great-grandfather died from a heart attack in 1939, so I did not know him nor hear of his Gallipoli and Middle East wars directly. But I did hear my grandfather, Arthur, in conversation with his brothers and friends: Tobruk, Alamein, New Guinea, Borneo and life at sea. Though all had survived the war, Bob, who had been a POW, had escaped and been recaptured three times and Jack, who saw his horrors from the deck of HMAS *Hobart*, returned with their own lived traumas.

I was about 10 years old when one of Arthur's mates came over. Bert had been in Bomber Command. After a few beers, he described the Lancaster in which he had been the rear gunner, hit by 'flak' over Turin. Tears welling up, he said, "I was sure I was dead Art. The plane was violently twisting, burning and hurtling to earth. The last thing I remember was a giant boot kicking me in the back. I woke up in the air … none of the boys survived".

Anzac Day was important. My mother would dress us up and make sure we were there to see 'grand pop' march.

In the late 60s, my mother decided to put her considerable intellect to work. Our GP (General Practitioner), Dr Frank Madill, offered her a job as his receptionist. Frank was warm and engaging. Mum loved the new challenges, finally exposed to the medical life denied her because of gender.

In 1970 I went from the St Patrick's junior school in the city to the senior school. This meant two buses there and two back at the end of the day. A long trip, but it was somewhat liberating to spend quite a bit of time travelling on the ridiculously overloaded bus at a time when hormones were kicking in.

At St Pat's senior school, I joined the school cadets. We all had our uniforms and .303 rifles. The school had a rifle range. We paraded as if at RMC Duntroon. Each week soldiers would come to the school to teach us a new skill. I have not yet had to pull a machine gun apart and put it back together in rapid time – but at least I know how!

Dad made a big decision in 1970 that would later have other, significant, consequences. He left Holymans and with it a cocooned work life. The winds of change were blowing through the shipping industry. He moved to the government-owned Australian National Line (ANL).

My parents – like all parents – wanted the best they could provide for their children. In 1971, my father did something which for him was rare. He took me for a walk. We walked from our home down Cornwall Crescent. He told me to look at the houses. To a 13-year-old boy who had seen these houses thousands of times before, this was strange, very strange. But only a couple of months earlier he had attempted to explain 'the facts of life' to me in the boat on the Tamar River while fishing – you never knew what weird stuff you were going to get.

"Son, your mother and I don't have any money. We don't know powerful, influential people. The only way you are ever going to live in a better house is if you work as hard as you can at school". I didn't know what on earth he was on about at the time. But later in my life, I thanked him and said, "Dad, there is never a better house to live in than one in which you are loved and wanted, no matter how big the house or expensive the cars in the drive".

A short time later they put that Launceston home up for sale. They wanted to move to a city in which there was a university, to give their children opportunity. Adelaide had family and more affordable housing. When my mother returned from Adelaide to announce they were buying a three bedroomed Jennings display home in Modbury with a swimming pool, we couldn't wait to get there.

Just before the move, early in 1972, things took a turn for the worse in the shipping industry. It was a period of immense change, rationalisation and reform. As Dad had only recently joined ANL his employment was tenuous. The union rule was 'last on, first off'.

The house in Modbury quickly became a home. It was an area that had settled many British migrants with young, aspirational families like ours. My parents had a mortgage and heavy financial commitments. Dad's employment was marginal, without work for prolonged periods as he struggled to get on the roster at Port Adelaide. My mother landed a job as a medical receptionist for Dr Philip Game, another doctor who sowed seeds of ambition in me.

Given their financial circumstances, my parents enrolled us in the local public schools. I arrived at Modbury High School wearing the school blazer and tie. I noticed few of the boys were dressed as I was. My first day was the commencement of term two. I was the new kid from Tasmania. First lesson was French. Midway through, the female teacher asked me a question. Consistent with what the Christian brothers had drilled into me, when a teacher – let alone a woman – spoke to you, you stood up. I immediately sprang to my feet. The class erupted in laughter. The teacher blushed and quietly said, as things settled, that standing was not required. I knew then things would be different here. I enjoyed Modbury High School. My classroom was one of six, temporary demountable buildings at the back of the school. Years later, when I returned as Opposition leader, it was still there – with many more.

My brother, Philip, and I made a bee-line for the Golden Grove tennis club when we arrived in Adelaide, playing two seasons of competitive tennis.

In 1973 I wanted to join the Navy. That was it. I could leave school and join as a midshipman, complete my education and pursue a respectable career in the military. Like my father, I would spend it at sea. My parents were troubled by this. They would of course have been proud to have a son in the Royal Australian Navy, but not at the age of fifteen. They went into overdrive to ensure that the key influencers in my life would talk me out of it. My Year 10 teacher spoke to me in very caring terms about my further potential in life. "You've got more in you than that. If you still want to join the Navy when you have done Matric, then okay". I dropped it.

In 1974, I started what was then School Certificate. Today it is Year 11. This was the sharp end of secondary education and at year's end, a public exam. At the end of the third week I was struggling with disruptive troublemakers. I was missing something that I felt I had with the Christian Brothers. It wasn't the weekly mass nor the broader offerings of cadets and rowing. Something I couldn't put my finger on. Whatever it was, I knew that for all its strengths, Modbury High School would not quench my restless thirst for it.

Dad was back in fulltime work with ANL now. My sister and brother by this time were back in Catholic schools. In my brother's case, St Ignatius College at Athelstone. I asked my parents if I could join him there with the Jesuits.

My father of course was not a Catholic, but he did have a great respect for those of faith. He went to the school twice. They refused me on the basis that the College was full and the term was well advanced. Something happened. They changed their mind and to my delight – and my lifelong salvation – I passed through the gates into St Ignatius College.

Years later the then Headmaster of the College, Father Phillip Hosking SJ, told me that my father had written him a letter begging him to accept me into the school. There was "something special about this boy. If you take him, he won't let you down. You won't regret it".

Starting at St Ignatius wasn't easy either. Most of these students had known one another for years. I was an outsider. More than a few were in cliques, reluctant to welcome the new and unfamiliar. That year was both challenging and liberating. I studied hard, played tennis and generally threw myself into the life of the school. A memorable highlight was the end of year school formal. One of the organising committee members said that he had a really good new band booked. They were "quite cheap". "What sort of music do they play?" I asked. Hard Rock was the response. We booked *Cold Chisel*. They pumped out *Deep Purple* and *Free*. The lead singer was energetic, agro with attitude. We loved them. The rest of the country was about to discover them.

At year's end I had excelled in English, Economics and Biology but received poorer results in physics, chemistry and mathematics. I changed subjects for Matric (Year 12), dropping the highest level maths for a composite and replaced the sciences with biology and European History. In doing so, I assumed I had closed off certain careers such as medicine.

In 1974 I was playing tennis at the Modbury tennis complex one hot Saturday afternoon. Two girls sat watching. One especially took my attention. She was the most beautiful girl I had ever seen. I was sixteen. When I later met her mother, I learned Deanna Lee was 13 years old. Nonetheless, we began a friendship that would become love and marriage at a very young age. It brought us both immense joy but also deep, wounding sorrows.

To my astonishment, at the commencement of Year 12, I was made a prefect – chosen by staff and students. I was honoured, taking to my new responsibilities with earnest enthusiasm. The much-loved drama teacher at St Ignatius was Richard Flynn. School policy was that all students in Year 12 had to be involved in the school play. To me, this was madness. Especially in the second half of the year when I would be concentrating on the make-or-break exams. Why on earth would I want to be distracted by being in the school play? Richard Flynn, however, was one the most persuasive influencers in my formative years. "There are essential life skills to be learned here Brendan. You might just enjoy it young man", he exhorted with his indefatigable enthusiasm.

I was cast as the Mayor in Friedrich Durrenmatt's *The Visit.* I put a lot into it. The rehearsals, working with others, taking direction from Richard, embracing a character and learning tales of morality in this tragicomic play. I loved it. And, as with everything that happened to me in those two years with the Jesuits, I was a better person.

For those unfamiliar with the Jesuits, they are a seriously above average IQ, militant faction of the Catholic priesthood. It was often said of the Pope that he was constantly wondering what the Jesuits would say next, having a history of questioning Catholic orthodoxy. In 1556 the

University of Paris had censured the Jesuits. It was said that "they had no rules, were at odds with the bishops, parish priests and the university itself".

The Jesuits made me. I learned life values from those men – Fathers Hosking, Dennett, Strong, O'Kelly, Olsen and others. They informed all that I have attempted to do every day since.

A life of success would be built on four things:

- Commitment. You must consistently apply yourself to the people and causes to which you commit. Don't give up.
- Conscience. Every decision you make in your life has a question beneath it – what is the right thing to do? In relation to decision making, "no such thing as big or small decisions", they said. Every decision you make has consequences for you and for others. In leadership, I have observed those who agonise over some decisions in the belief that they are important, trivialising other decisions with perfunctory consideration. Inevitably they get into trouble.
- Compassion – to share another person's pain. In leadership, it also has an essential meaning and relevance. Knowing what another person thinks, is important. But far more important, is to know how another person thinks. Once you understand how another person forms his or her world view, what and who influences and shapes them, you are more than halfway there to working out how to change their mind. You need to be imbued with what historian Stuart Macintyre described as the imaginative capacity to see the world through the eyes of others.
- Courage. Nothing of value in life is achieved without risk. Not a cavalier, reckless courage but an audacity motivated by the best interests of others. A spirit that challenges doubt and enables us to break through fear.

Six weeks before the big, final Year 12 exams we had trials in the school hall. I bombed out badly in maths – 25%. My mother stepped in and 'saved me'. She paid the son of a family friend to tutor me. I did little else for six weeks.

When my matriculation certificate arrived in the mail, I couldn't believe what I was reading – close to a perfect result. I had already decided that I wanted to go to university. I was good at economics, so enrolled at Adelaide University.

Father Hosking's father died in 1975, leaving him a small sum of money. He spent it taking three boys away with him for four weeks on a driving holiday. We travelled in his Holden Kingswood through remote South Australia, weaving our way across western New South Wales up to Queensland. We camped, stayed in motels and with Catholic families. Having mass twice a day for a month, I called time on being a regular church goer.

The Jesuits, Christian Brothers and nuns who educated me are accorded a special place in my life. I have immense respect for them and the sacrifices they made for their faith and vocation, their lives given for others. Fortunately, and thankfully, I was neither subjected to, nor aware of the shocking sexual abuse perpetrated by some against children. Notwithstanding this reprehensible, heinous violation of everything that Christ's life and the Church represents, my admiration for most remains steadfast.

Early in 1976 I walked into Adelaide University as an economics undergraduate. But I soon knew I was on the wrong track. I could not see myself committing my life to micro or macro-economic pursuits. I thought I would end up being an accountant or a public servant. Neither captured my imagination. At the end of the first term, I told my mother I was going to drop out. I wrote to my father. To say they were deflated is an understatement – devastated more likely. I compounded their pain by having an ear pierced. My mother consoled herself, "at least it's not a tattoo". The earring would become a major character test in the years ahead.

I landed a job at Harris Scarfe in Adelaide Mall, in the basement selling doors and curtain fittings. There I worked with three mature ladies of the *Are you being served?* genre. I loved them, and I think they liked me. I learned how to deal with rude, unreasonable and demanding people – and the joy of a fortnightly pay packet.

That training came in handy years later when I was out canvassing for votes and kissing babies. Having knocked on one woman's door in Campbelltown to a tirade of abuse, I complimented her on her beautiful Sorrento door. Then, noticing she had a jammed draw string on the window curtain, I fixed it, delivering a vote for our candidate!

Weekends were filled with tennis, Deanna and labouring for a builder. I bought my first motorbike, a Honda 400/4 Super Sport, and, with it, a lifelong love of bikes.

It was this year that the troubled nature of my brother's life revealed itself more fully. Having been a quiet, almost perfect child, it was clear at the age of 15, his would not be a conventional life. He couldn't settle at school and left for a bricklayer's apprenticeship. The police turned up at home with him. Unlicensed, he had been riding an unregistered motor bike on the road. It was a portent to a troubled life, the cause and meaning of which would not be revealed to us until 1990.

Constantly on my mind was what to do with my life. It seemed those most fulfilled with their lives spent it, in some way, in the service of others. The Jesuits had proselytised on the subject when I was at school. Now it was real. I briefly considered the priesthood but there were certain banned activities for which I had already acquired a taste.

Then, a stroke of pure luck. My entire life changed.

2

Medicine – A doctor in the house!

Late in 1976, I was thumbing through the Flinders University of South Australia handbook, reading with interest that a medical school had been established in 1974.

Medicine traditionally required an outstanding Year 12 result in mathematics, physics and chemistry. But Flinders was taking a new, innovative approach. Essentially, "we don't care what subjects you have done at school as long as you have excelled". Students who had not done these subjects were required to use their elective time, 25% of course contact, to do physics and chemistry.

I had never considered doing medicine. Once I dropped the heavy science subjects after sub-par Year 11 results, I thought it not an option. I applied immediately. My mother's response when I was accepted into medicine was not what I expected. "Thank goodness, now you'll have to take the earring out!"

The year that I began my journey into medicine, my mother commenced training to be a registered nurse at Modbury Hospital. We had both found what we wanted.

Medicine at Flinders was a six-year undergraduate degree when I enrolled in 1977. The intake was small, sixty-four. When you have an earring, you forget it's there. I had intended to remove it before enrolment, but simply forgot. The first academic I met simply said, "Get that thing out of your ear son". When the second said exactly the same thing, I said, "Look I am here to study medicine, not to be judged in a fashion parade. The earring stays". And so, it did, right through a lot of tumultuous changes in my life.

The adjustment back into study was difficult but I got through it, including Physics and Chemistry. The medical school was collocated with the then new teaching hospital in Adelaide's southern suburbs. Gus

Frankel, Andy Rogers and those who pioneered the Flinders Medical School did a great service to medicine and Australia. My first-year community medicine tutor was Dr Rosemary Crowley. Our paths would cross years later in politics.

In second year, I teamed up to share a flat in Bedford Park with Derick Hedges. Older than me, he was a thoughtful, bearded auto electrician from Elizabeth. It was a dodgy block of flats. Derick drove an old HR Holden wagon beneath which he placed an ice cream bucket to collect the oil dropping from the motor. In the morning he would pour it back into the engine. I rode a Kawasaki Z900 with a raked frame and extended chrome forks. Back from Uni close to midnight, I rode it through the back door and chained it to the stairwell.

After Uni all week, I was back home to Modbury. I worked at the Clovercrest Tavern Friday or Saturday night and Saturday mornings in the bottle shop. I learned a lot about life and working Australians at the Clovercrest Tavern, especially in the front bar.

I shared with Tim Manners in third year – a top bloke and son of a Port Broughton fisherman. Salt of the earth! We were foundation members of the Flinders Investments Group of Companies, better known as F.I. Annoyed at paying compulsory union fees, a small group of us designed F.I. to be a club that would challenge the nonsense emanating from the Student Union – counter-culture of sorts. It allowed us to pursue our common interests – beer and horse racing. Plenty of laughs, including the annual dinner where every member gave a speech, a club tie and secret handshake. Our home brew, 'Toongabbie Gold', was brewed wrapped in an electric blanket in one of the study cubicles. Dignity prevents me going into further detail.

I hit something of a wall in third year. It all seemed overwhelming. It was our young local GP, Gil Blicavs, who persuaded me to stick with it. I am grateful to him for saving my medical career, but he saved something far more important – my father.

My mother happened to call home to my father who was feeling very unwell. Uncharacteristically, he didn't resist her insistence that he go to the doctor. Sitting in Gil Blicavs' waiting room twenty minutes later, he collapsed with a full cardiac arrest. Gil successfully resuscitated him, but cardiovascular disease haunted my father literally to his death in 2004. He smoked, drank and did no exercise. I cannot remember him running, walking, kicking a ball, or swinging a bat. In that I resolved to be different.

Amongst the inspiring teachers I had at Flinders, neurologist Professor Rick Burns and surgeon, Professor Jim Watts, stand out. I turned up for a fourth-year neurology lecture one day delivered by Rick Burns. He spent an hour telling us about the clinical mistakes he made, why he had made them and what he learned. Few people in life would ever do such a thing. Yet here was this preeminent neurologist describing a woman presenting six months after her best friend had died with a rare cerebellar tumour. She had exactly the same symptoms as her late friend. Rick diagnosed a Facsimile Grief illness. She deteriorated and later died from precisely the same cancer.

I learned the importance of humility and knowing that although we think we are right, we are fallible. Sharing failure with others is as important as success. A lesson John Howard would reinforce in me twenty years later.

Jim Watts was the Professor of Surgery. He had power and commanded respect. During a ward round with his rather obnoxious registrar, we stopped at the end of a patient's bed. The conversation was about her treatment and delayed diagnosis of bowel cancer. The registrar made some disparaging remarks about her GP. We continued the round, finally turning from the ward into the corridor. Suddenly Professor Watts rounded on the registrar in a tone I will never forget: "If you ever criticise and demean a patient's GP in front of them again, I will personally see to it that you do not have a career in surgery in this hospital – ever!"

Another lesson. So many young trainee doctors manage up, treating their seniors with deferential respect and all others with disdain. Every person is important.

Deanna and I were married that year, 1980. I had attempted to break off the engagement, simply because I thought we were too young. I was 21, she was 18. It went ahead in May. My dear friend Damian Meade and his brothers performed Jim Croce's *Time in a Bottle* at the wedding. My deep regret is that we had not been a decade older when we met. I ended the marriage eighteen months later. A pain that I cannot forget.

I spent my elective course time in third year doing something different – two nights a week with the Adelaide Crisis Intervention Unit. These extraordinary men and women, social workers, were on call for a broad range of crises. Most of us live sheltered lives, oblivious to the deprivation, despair and depravity lived by too many among us. From a central office at an undisclosed location, calls would come in from police, ambulance and directly from the public. A trained social worker/psychologist would assess what was required and if considered appropriate, a social worker would be dispatched to visit the home. Armed only with their professional training, a comprehensive knowledge of Adelaide's emergency support services and a two-way radio in the pre-mobile phone days, off they went into the night. Twice a week I was assigned to one, observing, learning, trying to be helpful and stay out of the way. They appreciated the company.

Domestic violence, child abuse, suicidal ideation, incest, acute psychosis, alcohol and drug ravaged lives – they saw it all. One call was to the aftermath of a woman complicit in her partner raping her six-year-old daughter. There are no words for how it impacted us all. Things like that never ever leave you.

One call, all too common, was domestic violence. The male de-facto partner was a 'regular', well known to the service. Just after midnight, we opened the screen door of the severely neglected public housing tenement and knocked. The social worker introduced himself. A tirade of expletives erupted from the other side of the door. We stepped back and let the fly screen door close. I stood in the unlit stairwell. The door burst open. A gun. A double barrel shot gun pointing at us. Neither of us needed to be told a second time when the dishevelled man holding the gun bellowed for us to "Fuck off – now!"

Back in the car and having driven quickly, I was tremulous. The social worker radioed for the police who arrived within minutes. An hour of negotiation later, he was disarmed and arrested. When asked, they replied, "Yes, it was loaded".

Money was tight as a student. Medical research was one avenue for earning a few dollars. Neuroscientist, Professor Laurie Geffen was recruiting healthy, paid volunteers for a drug trial. Subjects would receive intravenous methamphetamine in varying doses over a six-week period. After each dose, one of which would be a placebo, you then had to sit in a booth and play the equivalent of video games for an hour and a half. I had never used illicit drugs before this and I have not done so since. But I know why some people do.

I turned up in the neuroscience laboratory faithfully each Wednesday afternoon. As I lay on the hospital bed, an intravenous canula was inserted by Professor Geffen's assistant. I noted the resuscitation trolley nearby and briefly pondered the wisdom of what I had volunteered to do. Professor Geffen injected the drug. An immediate, exhilarating rush, intense excitement, energy and supreme sense of well-being. I could do anything. I was helped to the booth for my tasks which I believed I had managed brilliantly. The results were otherwise.

After the first week, I rode my push bike the 45 minutes to home. Within hours, as the drug wore off, I felt bad, really bad. Flat and depressed. The key was to get home, go straight to bed and sleep to avoid that dreadful feeling. I completed the study, grateful for the week I had the placebo. No illicit drug would knowingly enter my body again. But I would also, more than anger, have sympathy for users.

The further I advanced through my medical degree into clinical medicine, the more I enjoyed it. We all worked hard – damned hard. The hours were horrendous but I enjoyed my fifth year at the conclusion of which were our big, final exams. As always, I studied furiously for the written exams and felt reasonably confident I had passed. A week would lapse before we had to front for oral exams. Three specialists would ask questions for 60 minutes on any topic at all. How do you prepare for such a thing? Some of my mates did so by partying for a few days. I refrained, thinking I needed every brain cell. In the final hour before my viva, I was sitting in front of the 'bible' – Harrison's *Principles of Internal Medicine*. I opened it at random – Hydatid Disease. Formerly a reasonably common tapeworm infection that affects major body organs. Interesting but obscure, I thought.

With sweaty palms and trepidation, I walked into the room to find I had an obstetrician, a paediatrician and a pathologist. The latter, Professor Doug Henderson, was a very serious, deeply scholarly intellectual, enthused by the pathological dimensions of disease, a man who did not suffer fools easily. It might be said of Doug that he 'needed to get out a bit more'. Professor Henderson asked the first question, adjusting his very thick, black rimmed glasses. He reached over to a trolley from which he removed a pathological specimen in a Perspex container, "Mr. Nelson, please describe what you see and if possible, what you think this is".

I had no idea. But I did know that Doug Henderson was into the slightly obscure and sorted his students out with quirky little tests. It looked like grossly distorted lung with an enormous cavity. As I described what I saw, I thought I would take the plunge with an educated guess based on Doug's character and the cavernous nature of the disease. "This is a Hydatid Cyst in a section of lung", I confidently proclaimed. Doug Henderson literally jumped forward in his chair with an enthusiasm I had never seen in him. I had nailed it. I passed my finals much closer to the top of my year than I had ever thought possible.

My sixth and final year in 1982 was pure joy. All clinical, no exams but learning lots. The Flinders Medical Centre was short of interns, so I was asked if I would work as a surgical intern for six weeks, although not yet graduated. Then I worked several months at the Repatriation General Hospital. 'The Repat' was built specifically to care for veterans after the First World War. A barracks-like ambience with large wards. They were men, mostly veterans, some from the Great War. All kinds of diseases ailed them, the more common being smoking induced lung diseases. A sputum cup on every bedside table.

I was performing a manual removal of faeces from a severely constipated elderly man: "This is worse than bloody Pozieres". It went over my head. A veteran of the place that our official historian, Charles Bean, described as "more deeply sown with Australian blood than any other place on earth", and I just moved on to the next patient. Therein lies one of my great regrets. I was running around caring for these men. Yet I failed to appreciate that I was among men who were leaving us, who had fought and suffered through the First World War. Shame on me.

I met Kate that year of 1982. We moved in together.

When I started my medical degree, there were 64 of us. Graduating six years later in 1982, we were reduced to 54. Overwhelmingly I was proud of what I had been able to achieve with the support of my parents as the first member of our family to complete a university degree.

We medical students assembled in the main lecture theatre in the medical school for our sendoff. Of all that was said, one piece of advice transcended everything. Ross Kalucy was the Professor of Psychiatry. Much admired and respected, he had a significant influence on us all. His lectures were peppered with stories from his own life experiences. To illustrate what he was teaching, whether eating disorders, depression or substance abuse he had powerful anecdotes. Unlike many psychiatrists, he was of our world. After speaking to us in terms you would expect, he told us that statistically two of us would be dead within a decade. Those lives would be lost to suicide. We should never see ourselves as infallible, beyond the vulnerabilities of those for whom we would care, nor immune to despair. We should always care for ourselves and for one another. We should always be aware of and respond to the warning signs from within. A decade later I thought back to what he had said. I still do.

We all stood, took the Hippocratic Oath and were gone.

I threw myself into my intern year at the Flinders Medical Centre. I didn't know what to do with my career. But to have the choice of discipline you had to seriously impress in your intern year in a major teaching hospital. The hours were inhumane. In those days we officially worked from 8am until 6pm. Every fourth night your 'unit' was on call. This meant you started at 8am, worked all day, all night and then until 6pm the following day. We worked six days a week and were often there on the seventh.

Theoretically you would go to bed in one of the hospital rooms when you had done all your work. Invariably we were responding to ward calls or to see and admit patients presenting to the emergency department. The registrar, a few years more senior, would decide to admit the patient, the intern doing the 'leg work'. If you were the surgical or obstetric intern you could also find yourself in the operating theatre for hours overnight. In all, an 85-hour week.

I think back to surgical registrars working all day and all night – out of bed to the emergency department and often in theatre operating. Then front at 8.30am the next day for an elective operating list that could include anything from a colectomy (bowel resection) to a mastectomy. Frightening when I look back on it, these sleep-deprived young men and women literally having people's lives in their hands. Add to this that they were studying for the most difficult exams possible to gain entry to their specialist careers. The toll was heavy. It was in this context that I received one of my most valuable life lessons.

It was a Saturday afternoon. I was on call for the paediatric surgical ward, called to see a baby. The charge sister had called. A three-month-old baby was showing all the signs of pain. A Nissen Fundoplication had been performed to strengthen the point at which the oesophagus (swallowing tube) joins the stomach. In doing so, the risk of inhaling stomach contents into the lungs is prevented. The nurse asked me if I would write the baby up for a pethidine infusion. Pethidine is a morphine-like drug, a narcotic. My basic training at that time told me that you did not give narcotic infusions to children under the age of twelve months. I hesitated. I knew what senior nurses thought of interns. I knew that they could make your life hell. I also looked at her, probably thirty years' experience in paediatric nursing and thought to myself, "She's forgotten more about this than I will ever know".

So, against my instinctive better judgement, I dutifully signed the drug order and rushed off to my next call. My beeper went off. An outside call. I found a phone, "Yes, Dr Nelson I will put the call through", said the operator. A thunderous tirade of abuse exploded into my right ear. So loud, it is a wonder I don't have permanent ear damage. It was John Freeman, the surgeon who performed the operation. "What … what were you thinking? What on earth made you think giving pethidine to this baby was a good idea, you imbecile?" My only feeble response was, "The charge sister told me to do it".

From that day, I was determined I would never place myself in that position again. Instead, I would make my own decisions. I would seek and consider advice but, in the end, they would be my decisions. In hindsight, looking back over my life, some decisions have been wrong. But they have been mine. I was able to explain the basis of the decision I made.

1983 was a big year for me, but a much bigger year for Australia. We won the America's Cup. The entire nation was gripped with yachting fever when the final, seventh deciding race was held on 26 September. America had successfully defended the Cup for 132 years. The Australians, funded by Alan Bond, inspired by the engineering genius of Ben Lexen and under the leadership of John Bertrand, were in with a chance having fought back to 3 all in the series.

At the time I was doing my stint in the Accident and Emergency Department as it was then called. I had fixed shifts from 8pm until 8am the following day. There were only two medical staff who worked that shift – an intern and a registrar. The registrar was one of the finest doctors and human beings I have known. Dr Chris Baggoley was the personification of good humour, decency, sharp intellect and a brilliant clinician to boot. Perhaps being a vet before medicine helped!

During our 12-hour shift we would expect to see 50 to 60 patients. The nursing staff would triage the most urgent. Ambulances would drive up the ramp with the stretcher cases, walking wounded through the front doors. A common summation of the problem was 'PFO', Pissed and Fell Over. I took more than my fair share of those.

It is a reflection on human behaviour and the use of major teaching hospital emergency departments that on the night of that last race, only two people presented for treatment. One had a dissecting aortic aneurysm. The second was dead on arrival. Chris and I spent the night watching the race, barely interrupted.

I did it again that year. Kate and I married in October.

Notwithstanding upsetting John Freeman, I had a good year. I knew I had options. John Chalmers, professor of medicine said, "Why don't you go somewhere else for a year, do something else and think about it?"

I did. We went to Tasmania, to Hobart. I could return home to fishing, Bruny Island and new adventures. We packed up the Kombi and off we went to the Royal Hobart Hospital. I was a Resident Medical Officer, Kate a registered nurse. That year, 1984, was one of the best of my life, though not without some tears.

Richard 'Dick' Buttfield was the deputy medical superintendent of the Royal Hobart Hospital. A 'committed bachelor' and rugby player, he welcomed me into his office, interviewed me and gave me the job. Kate saw the Director of Nursing. In 1984, 'The Royal' was still doing things the old way. I would do four rotations – anaesthetics, emergency medicine, obstetrics and radiation oncology. The visiting specialists' semi-circular car park and rose garden, right in front of aged hospital buildings, were clues to what I would find inside. From a modern tertiary teaching hospital, I had come to one harking back to an earlier era.

My first attachment was to the anaesthetics department. The head was a gentlemanly Scot, Dr Stuart Lamont. I was assured that I would be well taught and supervised. For the first two weeks I would assist the anaesthetists after which I would take on more direct responsibility. I learned quickly and I learned a lot. I was soon intubating patients, anaesthetising low risk patients and a member of the 'crash' resuscitation team. I was able to assume responsibilities that at Flinders would be at least another year away.

On the 'fifth floor' was the RMOs' Lounge: a bar, fridges, lounges, a pool table and newspapers. The latter ranged from the broadsheets to the highly coveted, *Melbourne Truth*. Pewter beer mugs hung above the bar. Each doctor was expected to buy his or her mug, have it engraved and hang it above the bar ready for quenching what appeared to be heavy thirsts. Your mug would remain at the bar in perpetuity as a reminder to others that you had proudly worked at 'The Royal'. I often wonder what happened to mine.

Just a month into the job, I made lifelong friends. "You're always safe with stout mate". So, said the bloke when I asked what on earth he was drinking. One of the registrars had thrown a party at his home perched high up in South Hobart. Lots of doctors, but also normal people. Tony Kube was one of them. Red hair, ample girth, the face and ears of a rugby player, he went on. "You drink stout, you're in control. They call me Kube".

"They call me Brendan, Kube". By night's end when three guys helped carry Kube out to lay him in the back of his Ute, I made a mental note to avoid stout. Not so 'safe' it seemed. So, began an enduring friendship. Tony a picture framer, Vietnam Veteran, stalwart of the Tasmania University Rugby Union Club, loved and respected by everyone who knew him. His wife Linda – 'Lil', a registered nurse, larger than life and heart of gold.

Dr Robert, 'Rob' was a colleague. In medicine you have many colleagues but fewer friends. Politics even more so. Rob was also doing his resident year. A whip smart man, inquiring mind and in 1984, of a view that being a doctor was a big deal. He also had an endearing naivety about him. We were in the lounge on the fifth floor and struck up a conversation about the 'Heart Balm' column in the *Melbourne Truth*. Rob asked me where I was living. We were moving into a house we bought at Kingston Beach. "I had a hell of a time getting a bank loan though. Terrible". Rob fired up. "I went to the Commonwealth Bank. I told the guy I was a doctor. Basically, told me to clear off! Can you believe it?" He went on, "But I've got the loan now. I'm buying a place up in South Hobart from my mate Peter Sexton".

"A private sale Rob?" "No", he replied. "I'm buying it through the agent". I pressed him for detail which he happily imparted. "There's only one potential problem with it though – it's next door to the tip".

"You're buying a house next to the South Hobart tip? Are you mad?" "No mate. It's all sorted. The tip's closing next year". Enquiring as to why he was so certain, "The agent told me. I signed the contract yesterday".

For years when I went to the tip, I would always call in and see Rob. He loved the sound of seagulls in the morning.

Kube's wife, Lil, was working in the paediatric ward. Rob was called to assess a boy with haemophilia. The boy's parents were not impressed with Rob. Lil described the boy's father poking his finger into Rob's chest yelling, "Now look here prawn, I'm not taking this!"

When Rob reported this to me, I told him we needed something better than 'prawn'. "What kind of an insult is that?" Days later, I was four people behind him in the bank queue. "Hey, scum!" Rob turned, "Yeah?" And so 'scum' it became.

I loved my obstetrics rotation. Deliveries, episiotomies, obstetric emergencies, assisting with caesarians and with time, forceps deliveries. Some shifts started Friday morning working continuously, being on call in the hospital until Monday night. The logic of these hours was firstly that young doctors needed to be exposed to the full, continuous course of a patient's condition. The second was manpower and cost.

One of my responsibilities during my emergency medicine term was to run the clinic for Sexually Transmitted Diseases (STDs). It was open from 6pm until 9pm, Tuesday and Thursday nights. Known to the young medical staff as 'The Stick Clinic', when I arrived for my first session, I got the picture. Almost all men, they sat on a long wooden bench seat, restless, furtively looking askew at one another. In the midst of a Hobart winter, more than a few sat wearing sunglasses. To alleviate their unease and whatever discomforts they had brought with them, the senior registered nurse assigned to work permanently in the STD clinic was a man. A very worldly man, 'Sister' Tony Bennett.

Patients would be called by Sister Bennett. They would be brought into a large room in the centre of which was a table. In each corner a curtained space for consultation. As I was writing up patient notes,

Tony Bennett, who had an unfortunate way of speaking – a staccato drawl – was leading an obviously nervous, reluctant man into the room. He said to the hapless man, “Don’t worry mate, we’ve all been through it”. Turning and inviting me to readily agree to the statement, “Haven’t we, Dr Nelson? And we know it’s hell!” Laughter bellowed from behind the screened areas as I murmured I could not comment.

I was also witness to death and tragedy.

In radiation oncology we dealt with life, hope and death. The twice daily ward rounds led by Dr Ken Macmillan included a priest. Frequently he was the most valuable member of our team.

It was perhaps here that the idealism, love and decency of the everyday person was fully revealed to me. The courage of men and women facing certain death. I learned the importance of a ‘good death’, one that is shared with those whom you love. A death in which doctors know that withdrawing intervention is often more important than initiating it. I learned that the fear of death is worse than death itself. I learned there are worse things than death.

My brother Philip called for the second time in three months. He had a somewhat troubled life, much of it spent unemployed by choice. The loves of his life were his chopper (motor bike), dog ‘Spike’ and tennis. Having moved from Adelaide to Sydney, Port Hedland and back to Sydney, he was now living in Mullumbimby. “I’ve got that thing called shingles again. Should I be worried?”

Concerned, I replied, “You need to see the doctor and make sure he examines you thoroughly and takes some blood tests. Young people getting shingles twice can be a sign of an underlying problem … let’s hope you haven’t caught that new disease, AIDS”. He didn’t speak about it for another six years, embracing a vegetarian lifestyle and heading to Thailand to live with monks. But he was always different.

3

Not a person suited to representing the interests of doctors

At year's end I had to make a decision. I applied for the paediatric training programme back at Flinders Medical Centre. I was accepted, so back we went, leaving many fond experiences and friends.

I started in the Neonatal Intensive Care Unit. It was intense. Desperately ill, fragile, tiny babies – most born prematurely. Incubators, open ventilated beds, lots of technology but in 1985, limited computerisation. The same long hours and when not working, my head was in a text book. I attended the 'at risk' births and emergencies. The stresses trying to intubate (place a breathing tube through into the wind pipe) tiny babies, find veins and resuscitate them.

Then there were the disasters.

A woman with twins had an obstructed labour requiring an emergency caesarian section. Relatively routine in a major teaching hospital. As I stood to the side of the theatre accepting the first baby, the anaesthetist rang the alarm on escalating, malignant hypertension. Completely uncontrollable along with her heart rate. The second baby was distressed but okay. Their mother would not survive the birth. A rare, undiagnosed pheochromocytoma had erupted, spilling its adrenaline-like hormones uncontrollably into her bloodstream. Two babies, an inconsolable father, traumatised medical and nursing staff. I am emotional even now, years later thinking about it.

I lived on adrenaline and caffeine. Each morning I would manually calculate the feeding formula to be delivered intravenously, terrified of making a mistake.

After six months I transferred to the paediatric wards. Dealing with older children, their illnesses and parents, and on call for the emergency department – hard but rewarding work. One of the scarring events was a six-year-old in extremis in the emergency department.

Frantically trying to intubate and resuscitate the child while I could hear his mother screaming outside. Things like that don't leave you. They never should.

I started to re-think what I was doing. Was this the rest of my life? I observed the consultant paediatricians a decade or so ahead of me. That would be me at the age of 35. Most mainly dealt with a dozen diseases and feeding problems in babies, unless sub-specialising. That was not for me. If I invested any more in this I would regret it.

I took the plunge at the end of 1985 and resigned.

Three of my mates had established a locum service in Adelaide which was booming. I rang David Bartlett and asked if I could have some shifts. I needed a car and medical bag and would do home visits all over Adelaide, day and night. Additionally, I could do locums for GPs. A good way to earn an income, work flexibly and think about what next.

I enjoyed the work but the drug users, socially dysfunctional and the filthy circumstances in which some people lived, took me back to the Crisis Intervention Unit five years earlier. And yes, another gun, though not pointed at me. A security guard in a motel room late at night, who wanted pethidine for a 'bad hip'. When the gun appeared, my resistance quickly dissipated. I couldn't get out of there quickly enough.

Early one morning I was called to see a young woman vaguely unwell. I arrived to the neglected house in the Adelaide foothills. In response to my knock on the door, a voice called me to come in. Semi-lit darkness, mess everywhere and young woman lying on a filthy bed. An unkempt punk hair style, sallow complexion, jaundiced eyes and beads of perspiration. She was sick. The drug injecting paraphernalia scattered on the bedside table told the story. I felt nauseated and as always in these situations, a touch of fear. They know you are carrying drugs, always the risk of being jumped. But she was alone. The drug use, lifestyle and hepatitis had added twenty years to her appearance. Beneath it all, I could see a beautiful young woman. I concluded she had endocarditis – an infection of the inner heart lining and heart valves. Persuading her that she was close to death, needing urgent hospitalisation was not easy.

I sat there for a long time in which she spoke of her upbringing, life, whom she loved and who loved her. Private school education, wealthy parents and trappings few people I knew ever had. "I was never good enough for them", she cried. I said, "Well, perhaps they were never good enough for you. Let's keep you alive so you can think about that and tell them". She was unconscious when the officers put her into the back of the ambulance. I thought of the tragedy of which I was now a part. Another heroin addict who would surely die. More emotion as I drove to my next call.

We decided to go back to Hobart. When I mentioned this to my accountant, he said, "One of my medical clients has just done that. Dr David Crean. Look out for him, he's a good guy".

In 1986 I started working at the St Helens Private Hospital emergency department. The hospital housed a locum service run by an irascible character, Viv Lancaster. Bearing the unfortunate cosmetic effects of an eye injury in earlier life, Viv was not a doctor but he learned how to make a living from them. We saw patients presenting at the emergency department and, under duress, an occasional home visit might be provided.

I found myself working with David Crean. A likeable man, he was one of Frank Crean's sons, Frank having been Gough Whitlam's first treasurer. David's brother, Simon was making his way up the ranks of the ACTU. Over the years I had the privilege to meet Frank and Mary. Wonderful people. Labor's Joel Fitzgibbon might describe them as "old style labor". My father certainly did.

Kate was pregnant. If you wait until you're ready to have kids and can afford them, you never will. It was time, we were both 27 years old. When Kate told me it was twins, I was speechless. We decided not to find out the genders. There need to be some surprises in life.

My finances were limited at the time, so my choice of car was modest. I loved the old Renaults and had a sun gold Renault 16. My mates thought the car a little 'low-class'. To rebut this, I needed a bonnet emblem like the three-pointed star on a Mercedes Benz. I asked a patient if I could have her old dentures. “Can’t afford your own Dr Nelson?” she asked. I reassured her they were for the car. I superglued the dentures to the bonnet at the front of the car. A sure sign of luxury.

Early Saturday morning, all I saw was a red flash, sudden violence as the car spun around. I had been hit by a car running a red light. Then I was hit by another car travelling behind me. It all stopped, “I’m alive”. I got out of the car which was in a very bad way. I went across to the driver of the sports car that had hit me. In shock, emergency services cut him out. The police officers interviewing me were perplexed when I said I needed to look for my teeth. One noted that they seemed intact. “No, I had a pair of false teeth glued to the bonnet. I have to find them.”

David proposed that he and I establish our own locum service. We should do so in the northern suburbs, providing both after-hours emergency treatment in rooms and a comprehensive home visit service. It seemed like a good idea.

One of the most popular doctors in Hobart’s northern suburbs was Peter Pitt. A charismatic Second World War veteran of Bomber Command, he had returned to study medicine. He made a bee-line for the northern suburbs, establishing his practice in Derwent Park. He worked hard and lived hard in the days when doctors servicing the working class were thin on the ground. He loved horse racing, fishing and farming, investing in all three. Peter’s son, Greg, was a chip off the old block and had joined his father in the practice. Both were friends I admired greatly.

David and I went out to see Peter and Greg to discuss our idea. They liked it, offering Peter’s old surgery. We leased and refurbished it, recruiting staff and notifying the doctors of the service we were planning to open. As we advanced our plans, the twins were preparing to join the world. On 9 January, Jeff Bradfield performed a Caesarian section on Kate. The first out was a boy. I thought – two boys. That the second was a girl floored us in the best possible way. Tom and Emily. Blessed, truly blessed. It snowed on Mount Nelson that day, and Tony and Linda Kube were with us just hours after the births.

The management of St Helen's Hospital didn't like our plans for the After-Hours Medical Service. Its medical director, Dr Peter Beaumont, was secretary of the Tasmanian branch of the Australian Medical Association (AMA). They sent a letter to every GP in Hobart. It suggested David and I were of questionable character and not to be trusted with the undertakings we were making. I was outraged. David engaged a Melbourne defamation barrister. We initiated proceedings. I had to borrow more money, but there was too much at stake. The matter was eventually settled out of court. I made a mental note to 'deal with the AMA', but for now we had a practice to get up and running.

We opened in April 1987. David and I shared responsibilities running the practice. The staff called him 'the treasurer' because he was good with the figures. And he was, later going on to serve successfully in government as Treasurer of Tasmania!

A number of doctors worked with us. The surgery opened at 6pm and closed at midnight after which the doctor on duty slept there taking calls and doing home visits as needed until 8am. From 6pm until midnight a second doctor was doing home visits. It was very busy, popular with both the medical community and their patients. I also did locums for GPs. On many occasions I had little or no sleep, frequently getting out of bed several times a night to drive across town to see a patient.

Only weeks after we opened, with all the financial pressures, the federal government delivered a mini budget. Treasurer Paul Keating abolished all loadings for medical services provided after hours. The same Medicare payment would be paid for a home visit at 9 o'clock in the morning as 3am. David and I were devastated. But we had made a commitment to the community and come hell or high water we would honour it. The GPs agreed to pay a modest service fee to help defray the impact. I was getting out of bed at 3am to drive to Hobart's satellite public housing estates for $15.85 less tax and running costs.

But to Labor's class warriors, I was one of the greedy, overpaid doctors against whom war had been declared. Simultaneously, the nurses' union placed an ambit claim on us. Unbelievable. Yet I looked at the wonderful women who staffed the practice, knowing they appreciated and valued the work, their pay and with it the ability to feed and clothe their kids.

That was it. When the federal election came in July that year, I was very happy to vote for John Howard, my first vote for the Liberal Party. I couldn't bring myself to tell my father.

Our home at Blackmans Bay was two-story. The main bedroom was upstairs. The babies slept downstairs, sharing a bedroom. Late one evening when they were just months old, Kate came racing up the stairs, screaming in a way that said the worst had happened. Emily was not breathing. She was blue. I placed her on the floor, stripped her, checked her mouth and airway and physically stimulated her with a couple of slaps. She coughed and breathed. An aborted cot death. More grey hairs.

The following year I decided do something about the political climate in which we were trying to practise medicine. I had resigned from the AMA over the Peter Beaumont letter but thought I might re-join and see what I could do. A Labor backbencher from Western Australia, George Gear, was building a career for himself attacking the motives and incomes of doctors, one of a growing number. I rejoined the AMA. I also joined another organisation to see what I could do – the Labor Party. Had I been planning a career in Liberal Party politics, suicidal. At the time, though, my only naïve intention was to try to talk some sense into somebody.

I attended five meetings of the Hobart branch of the ALP. I met some good people; I met some nutters, but I didn't meet anyone with sympathy for my views. I gave it away.

The AMA headquarters in Hobart were in Gore Street, South Hobart, in a stately, 19th century building. It had presence but lacked any sense of modernity for a changing world. So too did the AMA which owned and occupied it.

I was at my third AMA meeting at 'Gore Street', as it was affectionately known. I sat at the back of the meeting of about 40 doctors, mainly men from a range of disciplines. I was angry about attacks on the profession and wanted an AMA that effectively represented me and my generation. Yet the agenda was missing anything like this. The chairman, Dr John Liddell, a neurosurgeon, listened with a sympathetic demeanour to my statement.

"I am here because I am angry. I am angry with the federal government for its attacks on the profession and I am angry with the AMA for its inability or unwillingness to stand up for us."

He responded: "Look, I share your anger with the government. But these are just politicians, they come and go. We are here for the long haul, committed to our patients and our profession. Whatever we do, we can't win. We just have to wear it." In one sense he was right, but I was fuming. I turned to the doctor next to me, "If it's the last thing I do, I'm going to change this organisation."

My friends laughed when I told them. I had a crew cut, earring, questionable background for leadership of such a conservative body, I was 28 and I didn't own a suit. The thematic refrain was, "You'll never get anywhere. No one will listen." But in a democratic organisation, I thought, if you have conviction, a sound argument and express it well, you must surely be able to effect change.

Secretary of the southern division of the AMA became vacant. I grabbed it, unopposed. It automatically put me onto the State Council of the AMA. Preparing for my first meeting in Burnie late in 1988, I was cautioned by a senior office bearer not to attend. When I asked why, he said, "Because it is widely held that you are not a person suited to representing the interests of the medical profession". That was it. I was now on an unstoppable mission.

Months later, I called into Gore Street. The clerical secretary, Mary Piles, was an efficient, eternally cheerful woman. She sat behind a desk surrounded by old filing cabinets, a bar heater beneath the desk. She had lots of pink slips of paper on her desk. I asked what was going on. "We're having an election. President of the Branch."

This is exactly what I needed, the opportunity to influence the leadership of the AMA. I naively asked about the candidates. Mary looked at me quizzically. "There's only ever one candidate. Branch Council decides who the next president should be, that person's name goes on the ballot paper, I mail it to the members and they vote."

"Mary, is this a joke? This is Monty Python. You can't be serious."

This is the way it had always been done. I asked who the candidate was. A delightful, mature lady from northwest Tasmania. I had to do something. I called a mate of mine, Dr Michael 'Mike' Wertheimer, a young general surgeon 'on my page'. I urged him to find someone with energy, progressive views and some grey hair to nominate. He took to the task with enthusiasm, but called two days later, "No one wants to rock the boat."

As I drove from one home to the next that night, I thought about it. In the morning I called a lawyer friend. I dropped a copy of the AMA's constitution off, "Is there anything which would prevent me from running for President of the AMA?" He called me that night, "You're good to go." I was now in an election contest.

The conservative elements of the leadership were beside themselves. I was asked if I would drop out. I said I would in favour of the right candidate. I didn't want to be president, I just wanted change. The following day two candidates entered the field. One, a psychiatrist who had been involved in public controversy, the other a highly respected, aged surgeon. I saw my life pass before my eyes. No, I would not withdraw. We would have a contested election, four candidates.

The President was elected by the membership who, until then, had never had to exercise much energy, doing so with a single candidate. I thought I should write to the voters. My two-page letter set out what I saw as the AMA's challenges, what had to be done about them and articulated a vision that embraced not only professional and industrial issues, but a social policy agenda. Branch Council then discussed a censure motion against me for "bringing the Association into disrepute". I communicated this to the membership.

The ballots would be counted and the result announced in June 1989 at the Gore Street offices. This was my first AGM. The room was packed, an unprecedented turnout. After what seemed an eternity, the scrutineers returned with the result. "Dr Brendan Nelson has been elected President." I was president-elect and would be president a year later.

The incoming president was an impeccably scrupulous anaesthetist, Mike Hodgson. I was blessed to serve as his 'apprentice'. I had to learn about the AMA, leadership and procedure as quickly as I could. I had one year. I didn't own a dinner suit so skipped the annual dinner the night of the AGM, buying a suit first thing Monday morning.

Australia's balance of payments crisis was starting to bite, with more of our patients unemployed. David told me he would run for Parliament in Tasmania's Lower House. The Pitts embraced his candidacy as did their considerable working-class patient base. Posters appeared everywhere – "*Go for the Doctor*".

He was elected into the minority Labor government with the Greens. It was a disaster. David managed to juggle medicine and parliament, switching to the upper house in 1992. Soon, too, I was juggling my growing AMA responsibilities with the demands of the practice and our young family.

There were some light moments though.

I was called to see a lady living in a unit around the corner from the practice. I was met by her husband, Ted. Photos and models of trains everywhere, Ted was a retired train driver with a pitch perfect Welsh accent to match. He led me down the short corridor to his wife, Phyllis. Entering the poorly lit room, I was immediately aware of groaning. An invalid's triangle hung from a perpendicular timber anchor attached to the wall. A morbidly obese woman, her abdominal flanks extended to each side of the single bed. A multitude of tablets and medicine bottles sat on the bedside table, spilling out onto the floor. Next to them stood six bottles of lemon soft drink and a glass containing her false teeth. I introduced myself. A thick guttural Welsh accent emerging deep from within. She clutched her stomach, both hands slowly coming up towards her neck. "I'm in incredible pain Dr Nelson … it starts here in my stomach, comes all the way up to my throat, pierces into my back and beyond." Then, suddenly thrashing her head from side to side, beating her chest to a crescendo, "You've got to help me Dr Nelson!"

I asked a range of questions until, "Mrs. H, have you seen a specialist?" Slowly, confidence growing in her voice, "I was seen by a Dr Millingen. He did so many tests, poked and prodded me like no one before." Keith Millingen was Tasmania's preeminent neurologist. I was getting somewhere. "And what did Dr Millingen say, Mrs. H?"

Turning to face me, pausing for dramatic effect and maximum impact, "He said I were a malignant hypochondriac!" Ted quipped, with a sense of pride, "Worst case he's ever seen Dr Nelson." I could only smile. The joys of medical life.

Those many visits to people's homes were shaping me in ways I didn't appreciate at the time. How do you console a family told by the police at their door that a much-loved son is dead, killed in a car accident? The wife and mother who has discovered her husband has hung himself in the garage? The woman severely beaten by her partner, two kids and nowhere to hide from him? These and more.

I was also noticing the photographs. Especially then for anyone in their seventies and beyond, black and white photos of young men and women in uniform. On mantle pieces and walls. Many looked out from their youth to lives not lived. One memorably in North Hobart. An elderly lady still lived in the modest family home. Her mother had outlived her father and then died. But one room had remained untouched for seventy years. Her brother had enlisted for the First World War in 1915, killed in the bloodbath at Bullecourt two years later, his body never found.

And there were joys. In medicine as in life, those uplifting moments come when you least expect. One Saturday afternoon, from the packed waiting room, I called a child's name. A woman stood with a baby. I smiled as she entered. We sat. I turned to ask what had prompted her to seek help. They were from Adelaide. So was I of course, but too busy for chit chat. I looked at the mother's face, vaguely familiar. A face like hers was hard to forget. I couldn't quite place it. Having established the basis and treatment of the child's feeding problem, she looked at me, "We've met before. Five years ago. You saved my life."

I knew immediately, "I thought you would die." She confirmed that was the prognosis of the doctors when admitted to ICU. The heroin addict from the Adelaide Hills. We both hugged, tears, lots of tears.

She said that although she carried Hepatitis, she was well, certainly off drugs and reconciled with her family but with the wisdom to know their failings. Married, happy and working. The privilege it is to make a difference to the lives of others, let alone save some.

The work days were long and when I finally arrived home, there would be multiple phone calls to return. Mobile phones had arrived. I would have one fitted in my car. It revolutionised my life in ways I could not have imagined. I could make and receive calls as I drove. Amazing!

4

Joining Shepherd's flock

As I spent a lot of time in the car, I carried a Dictaphone. I would dictate AMA letters for Mary Piles to type up for me in the office, trying to be as efficient as I could with the limited hours in the day.

I very publicly led a campaign against the establishment of a chain of glittering, corporatised 24-hour bulk billing emporia in Tasmania. These were of the genre of the Edelesten clinics in Sydney. Popular with the public – anything that's free usually is, but having a corrosive impact on the behaviour of doctors. I was making progress in my efforts.

One morning, just after 2am, I had just got into my car in the northern satellite suburb of Bridgewater. My car phone rang. It could only be trouble. A thickly accented eastern European voice came through the speaker. Confused at first, I turned on my Dictaphone to record it. A death threat. I would be beaten and killed if I continued to publicly oppose the medical clinics:

> I am from the black cat mafia. Unless you shut up you will disappear … money is no problem, $50,000 will be paid to see you disappear … you are being watched, we have a file on you and your family.

Shaken, I rushed home to check my family. I took the recording to the police later that morning. The matter was investigated, the caller found, charged and tried. I thought long and hard about whether it was worth it. I knew though that I had be true to myself and what I had committed to do for the AMA's members who had elected me.

Later that year, I met a man who changed my life.

Dr Bruce Shepherd had led the surgeons out of the New South Wales hospitals in the mid-eighties in a bitter dispute. Until then specialists treated public patients in public hospitals for nothing and trained the young doctors. In return, they were able to admit and treat their private patients. The Wran Labor Government in New South Wales, supported by the Hawke Government and its health minister, Neal Blewett, were determined to get control of the medical profession. Neville Wran had said to Bruce, "Dr Shepherd, you represent the last independent group in society and as such, I move to control you."

In 1989 Bruce Shepherd was travelling the country to establish the Australian Doctors Fund: money to support the profession in its battles with government. A reception was held at the Hobart Wrest Point Casino. Dr Shepherd set out the profession's challenges and what needed to be done. The AMA was also in his sights. He was engineering a takeover of its New South Wales branch. Mike Wertheimer approached me, "Mate, come and I'll introduce you to Bruce." I told him that wasn't a good idea.

Anyway, up I went. "How do you do Dr Shepherd? I don't like you. As far as I am concerned, you have given the profession a bad name. I'm on a reform agenda with the AMA and I'm going to do whatever I can to marginalise you and people like you." I thought he would say two words, the first of which would be 'get'.

Instead, he looked at me and said, "I've been watching you. You're going to go a long way. The medical profession desperately needs people like you. When you get to know me, then tell me what you think about me. In the meantime, you'll find we've got a lot more in common than you think." Then, "The first piece of advice I am going to give you is not to pass an opinion on someone you've never met." I was completely disarmed. Bruce, Mike Wertheimer and I went for a Chinese meal!

Therein lies one of the many lessons from Bruce. Over the years, had I uncritically accepted someone else's view or my own preconceived prejudices, I would have achieved much less and be a diminished person for doing so. Bruce became a mentor.

In 1989 I made the first of many trips to Sydney and with it, my introduction to Bruce in his consulting rooms in Mosman. To Australia's militant surgical community, this was General Central Headquarters.

Dr Bruce Shepherd was our field marshal. His secretary, Anne Smith, was his Chief of Staff. To get to Bruce, you had to go through Anne. Bruce's rooms were a re-purposed house of the 1930s, with apartments springing up around it. I noted a Walkinshaw Group A Holden Commodore under the carport. I was heading into a testosterone-rich environment.

Anne Smith welcomed me, poured a cup of tea and sat with me as Bruce finished seeing his last patient. I noted a sign in the waiting room, *Sexual harassment will not be tolerated.* Anne had worked loyally with Bruce for years and stood with him through the doctors' dispute and the death of his much-loved wife, Annette. A devout Catholic, Anne prayed for forgiveness, not so much for her own very few sins, but for Bruce's many. Anne handed me a book. She said that if I was to have a good relationship with Dr Shepherd, I should read it, advice offered in a tone that suggested this to be of the utmost importance: *The Network: a guide to anti-business pressure groups* by Bob Browning.

Bruce emerged from his office and welcomed me in. The décor was striking – dark maroon textured wall paper, a large black leather chair behind a very big desk. There were books, family photos, political cartoons and awards for surgical excellence. I noted several copies of *The Network* on his desk and reassured Bruce that Anne had already given me a copy with advice to read it. He smiled, "Good man". So, began our journey together through to his death in a Bowral nursing home 28 years later.

Having discussed the medico-political landscape for an hour or so, Bruce said, "Mate, I am about to give you the most valuable thing I have." Knowing him to be a man of considerable wealth, my heart skipped a beat as I leaned forward in my chair. Bruce opened the top drawer in his desk, removing a large, black leather-bound book. "I am going to introduce you to my network. I am going to open doors for you." I made a mental note – some networks are good, others are not.

With that, Bruce said, "I'll take you for a spin in the car. You'll love it." And I did. We got in the race car, testing the boundaries of Mosman's road rules. Above the roar of the engine, Bruce yelled, "I saw this racing at Bathurst and rang the Holden guys the next day!"

At Bruce's family home, *The Network* was on the table in the foyer, another in the sitting room and two copies on my bedside table in the guest room. With close to a bottle of wine on board when I went to bed, I started reading it. As an aspiring acolyte of Bruce's, I had to digest its contents.

I assumed the presidency of the Tasmanian branch of the AMA in 1990. Thanks to Mike Hodgson, I felt ready. There was no shortage of issues to be addressed, but already I was convinced that the profession's influence lay entirely in the extent to which it was a voice for those who had none. I could see that power can be used in certain ways to make a difference to the lives of those who have neither power nor influence.

The national conference of the AMA that year was the first I attended. Many delegates regarded me as a curiosity. Most welcomed me, sensing the need for younger members of the profession assuming leadership roles. The black-tie dinner was held in the Great Hall of Parliament House. The new Minister, Brian Howe, was guest of honour. The speaker was one of the true giants of the medical profession, a man for whom I have the greatest respect. Professor David Pennington was also Vice-Chancellor of the University of Melbourne. He delivered a stunning 40-minute oration, "Government and the Professions" (*Medical Journal of Australia*, Vol 153, 3 September 1990). To the mesmerised audience, Pennington soulfully described the origins, nature and fundamental tenets of the medical profession. He spoke of changes in society, expectations of governments from an increasingly demanding population, and why the two are in conflict.

The profession, he argued should lead public opinion and not follow it. In the same way that we placed our individual patient interests ahead of our own, so too the organised profession must "rediscover its commitments", especially to an ethic of service. To place the welfare of others ahead of our own. Governments would respond to public opinion. The public's trust in the profession would be rebuilt in advocacy, motivated primarily by its best interests, not our own.

I now knew I had found my way to make a difference. I had joined the AMA because I was angry, both with it and the government. But I now understood that I had both an opportunity and a responsibility to harness the power of the profession across a range of health and social issues facing society. Yes, we needed to be a strong voice for health financing, professional and industrial issues. But we needed the same determination to be a powerful advocate for issues shaping health outcomes.

Tobacco control, boxing, road trauma and immunisation rates were among the issues I took up very publicly. The AMA had policies on these and other issues but it needed, what I would describe as, an "activism of caring". We should not just have meetings, determine policy and sleep with them under the pillow, but actually get out into the public arena campaigning for what we believed. I commissioned big banners for the press conferences and a modern AMA logo beneath which was – *Doctors caring for the Community.*

Jean Moore was CEO of the Royal Hobart Hospital, an intelligent, political, tough but caring woman. At her request I visited her. She had an idea. It was one that would later go national. The other disciplines had divisions of medicine, surgery, obstetrics and psychiatry. These created paid opportunities for specialists to spend time working on broader issues in their discipline, covering standards, research, epidemiology, financing and public health. She asked me why we couldn't have a division of general practice?

GPs should be given a voice in the management of patients in the hospital. She envisaged GPs being a part of clinical units contributing to patient management plans, including medications, discharge and community care. She wanted their voice to be heard within the decision-making corridors of the hospital. GPs could play a role beyond that of their own practice in shaping health care in the community. It seemed like an inspired idea to me. She asked if I would consider being the inaugural director and I agreed. Three sessions a week, a small budget and a blank sheet of paper upon which the first Division of General Practice in Australia would be formed. A year later I bowled the idea up to the federal health minister, Brian Howe.

Michael Hodgeman QC was the Liberal member for Denison until 1987. His Canberra nickname was appropriate, "The mouth from the south". I recall in 1987 as I drove through the public housing estate of Bridgewater, Michael was there dressed in a three-piece pin-striped suit, rose in his lapel, head held high, election materials in hand striding down the street. Incongruous as it seemed, he was door-knocking the homes of constituents who literally lived in another world. Yet I also knew that most loved and admired him.

Michael was indefatigable in his defence of boxing. He loved the sport. In 1990 I was invited onto the ABC *7.30* programme to debate him. The AMA's position was that as long as hitting the head remained the object of the sport, boxing should be banned. The programme's anchor, Judy Tierney, adjudicated the debate, skills for which Michael had an unbeatable reputation. We went backwards and forwards until Mr. Hodgeman leaned forward and said straight to camera, "There is not a person in the state of Tasmania that has suffered any brain injury from boxing."

Judy Tierney turned for my reply. I looked across to him and said, "Mr. Hodgeman, I understand that you yourself were a boxer. I rest my case." Judy cracked a smile, Michael quipping, "That's below the belt." But from that day we were friends. Such was the character of the man.

Beyond advocacy, I thought that we should give doctors financial incentives to join the AMA. The National Australia Bank was looking to break into the professionals market when I walked through the door of the state manager. The end result was a deal that would give the AMA's 450 members a NAB Mastercard with the AMA coat of arms on it. It would double as a membership card. There would be a substantial interest rate reduction across business and personal lending. This and a range of other financial benefits saw membership soar.

By year's end we had 700 members and were enjoying a strong public profile.

It was proposed that the AMA's constitution be amended to allow the President to serve a second term. It carried at the AGM without dissent. I would serve as branch President for another year, the first to ever do so. It seems I was a person suited to represent the interests of the medical profession after all.

With booming membership came an income stream that would allow us to appoint an executive officer. I was in the office when Mary Piles said a man wanted to speak to me but did not want to give his name. He told me he was calling about the position, but wanted to know if at the age of 49 he was 'too old'. Emphatically, I said no. Sensing his relief, he introduced himself – Doug Lowe, former Labor premier of Tasmania. I was dumbstruck. Doug was appointed and served the AMA magnificently, professionalising every aspect of the operations. The sceptical, ultra-right-wing specialists later came to appreciate and admire his skills, particularly negotiating industrial agreements on their behalf.

Only a few years later, Doug Lowe would do something even more important nationally. Bruce Shepherd gained control of the New South Wales branch of the AMA. He was branch president when he won a bitter contest against the 'old guard' to become the national president. He wanted an executive team that supported him. Late in 1990, Bruce and his supporters took me to dinner in Canberra. Their plan was to persuade me to run for the National Vice-Presidency of the AMA the following year at the 1991 AGM. I was taken aback. My initial response was to tell them that this was madness. I had a young family, two medical practices to run and I needed to complete the AMA reforms I was overseeing in Tasmania. Unlike them, I was only 30 years old and yet to consolidate the path of my life. Thanks. But no thanks.

We went to Adelaide that year for Christmas with Kate, the kids and the dogs. Unusually, the whole family would be present. My brother, Philip, was coming from Mullumbimby. A pleasant surprise as we hadn't seen much of him in recent years. Philip looked well, although his hair had thinned as had the muscle bulk of earlier years. As always, he was quiet. But he was also more engaged than usual in asking about our lives. We were alone in the car together when he said, "I've got HIV". I was shocked, but at the same time I was not. In a flash, it all made sense. Like most people at that time, I asked how he got it. His answer didn't matter other than to dismiss the question and my insensitive stupidity in asking it.

Until then, it had never occurred to us that he might be gay, this super fit, muscular man who had lived for a period in the biker culture. His bike had screamed, "Don't mess with me" – a Kawasaki Z900, raked and moulded frame, extended forks, chromed rear car wheel, coffin tank and gothic air brushed images. Chromed everything and a four into two exhaust system without baffles. Yet apart from a female friend here or there, we had never seen him with a woman, always men. The troubled teens, insecure and turbulent life made sense. As did his shingles six years earlier.

Amongst the tragedy is that our family would have loved and accepted him. Probably more so had he told us he was gay. My parents would have only lamented he would not have children. He asked me to tell Mum and Dad. I did. So many tears. My parents had separated and divorced after 30 years of marriage only two years earlier. This news was a greater blow to them both.

The next day I booked Philip, Tracey and me to have a studio photograph taken. The last photo of us together.

On the drive back to Tasmania, I turned my attention to Bruce Shepherd's encouragement for me to run for Vice President. There was little point doing what I was without reform of the federal body. I might also achieve a lot. My brother facing his mortality at such a young age made me appreciate that you only have one life. I went back to Bruce early in 1991. I told him what was motivating me and I was determined to win.

Until then, senior AMA office was essentially the gift of the Association, to recognise decades of service. Achieving high office under the age of 50 was unheard of. Bruce wanted the AMA's leaders to be active, with 'fire in their belly', to fight for the profession. He scorned the AMA's failure to support him and his colleagues through the doctors' dispute and to 'roll over' on Medicare's introduction.

Juggling all these balls, I campaigned for the vice-presidency. The incumbent was Dr Mike Jones, a long-standing AMA representative and respected Perth GP. He was no fan of Bruce who was at war with what he called the AMA's 'travelling dinner club'. Bruce saw me as a way to head them off. He was impressed by what I had achieved in Tasmania, including my response to the death threats when fighting the medical 'entrepreneurs'.

Bruce enlisted the support of the most energetic person I have ever met. Stephen 'Steve' Milgate had been a Liberal candidate for Nick Greiner's successful tilt at government in New South Wales. Steve was working with Greenwood Challenor in management consulting. Bruce engaged him to oversee and help with the campaign. Steve gathered the names and contact details of all the delegates to the AMA national conference in late May. These 110 delegates would hear the candidates speak and then vote. The 1990 conference had been my first, I had seen how it worked. I felt ready. Ignorance is bliss.

I spent three months working on the campaign, managing everything else including leading the Tasmanian branch. To the conservative proceduralists and ophthalmologist grouping, I said that I could run their agenda better than they could. As someone who understood the rigours of specialist training, the sacrifices made and the legitimately high incomes they should earn, I could effectively prosecute their case. In return, I asked for their support in driving a public health and social policy agenda, spanning issues as diverse as the environment, tobacco control and child abuse.

We had a deal.

The 1991 AMA national conference was held at the Shine Dome (Academy of Science) in Canberra. We had worked the numbers and were quietly confident we had 67 votes. I set out my vision for the Association: what I would seek to achieve in the role and as difficult as it was, why change was so needed. It was not the last time I would mount such an argument to topple an incumbent.

The result was declared in my favour – 67. A clear majority. Steve Milgate had taught me how to count.

5

"You'll have to change the government"

Bruce was elated that I was now his vice-president. I joined a first-rate executive led by him, including Professor Priscilla Kincaid-Smith as Chairman.

We escalated our campaign on public hospital waiting lists, emerging crisis in private health insurance coverage, runaway costs in Medicare bulk billing, the rural doctor work force, cuts to medical research, unsustainably low general practice Medicare rebates and patients who could not access mental health services for love or money – literally. Brian Howe had commissioned a National Health Strategy Review in 1990, placing it in the hands of the equally left-wing economist and researcher, Jenny Macklin.

I ramped up the campaign against the tobacco industry and their apologists. The next frontier was to get tobacco out of sport. The evidence was overwhelming. Almost 19,000 Australians were dying every year from tobacco-related diseases. There is no safe level of consumption for the product. I was leading protests against tobacco sponsorship at cricket matches and rugby games.

Rothmans was a major sponsor of the Sydney to Hobart Yacht race. As the yachts made their way up the Derwent River, I sat before a bank of television cameras with pathological specimens – amputated foot, cancerous lung and haemorrhaged brain. Confront them with the reality. Nothing glamorous about disease and death. I reminded the nation of that from the oncology ward of the Royal Hobart Hospital where people were dying from the tobacco induced cancers. It gave them no comfort to see the fluttering Rothmans spinnaker.

When I proposed that I lead a group of doctors to carry a coffin representing the death of Labor's public health credibility on tobacco, Bruce Shepherd arced up: "Mate, you have to remember the dignity of the profession."

In 1991 I was presented with the award for "Outstanding Contribution to Public Health Promotion" by the Victorian Health Promotion Foundation. We still had a long way to go – higher tobacco taxes and explicit health warnings on the packets.

The Federal health minister, Brian Howe, was of Labor's left. He was also deputy prime minister. A former Uniting Church minister from Victoria, an earnest, doctrinaire man. To Bruce he was up there with the anti-Christ. Brian Howe wanted to help general practice. But he was constrained by the government's budgetary position in the midst of the recession. He sensed that I was someone with whom he could deal.

Bruce was understandably sceptical of government. At one point he exploded, thundering, "You're spending too much time at Parliament House. You're getting too close to government. Our job is to fight them, not talk to them!"

I reminded Bruce we had been to hell and back to move the AMA's headquarters from Sydney to Canberra. Within 'mortar shot' of Parliament House from Barton, our members expected us to engage our enemy. And we did.

We had ideas for General Practice and sought to sensibly guide the Minister. Howe spoke of general practices near his Melbourne office, solo or two partner operations. "This is all so inefficient and I am funding it. Why can't they all merge and provide a wide range of services?" The corporate entrepreneurs had similar ambitions.

I proposed Divisions of General Practice to the AMA Council, the first of which I was leading in southern Tasmania. It would give GPs opportunities to work beyond individual patient care and be paid for undertaking broader roles in the community. For example, I had GPs working with a pharmacist on the effective treatment of Urinary Tract Infection. It had improved clinical outcomes and reduced costs. We had a dietician educating GPs on how patients could interpret food labelling and make better food choices in the supermarket. Brian Howe liked it. The first ten divisions were funded. Today they are a permanent part of the healthcare landscape.

The AMA had gone hard – I had gone hard, against universal bulk billing. As treasurer introducing the pharmaceutical co-payment in 1990, Paul Keating defended it by saying, "Anything that's free leads to overuse". He was right then and it is right now. The public of course loves it. However, Medicare benefits were increasing at a rate less than half that of inflation, so bulk billing doctors had no choice but to see more patients more often to maintain incomes. A zero-sum game. Explaining it at a press conference, I held up a credit card and a Medicare card: "The government has given every Australian a bankcard in the form of a Medicare card. It has told them to go and use it as often as they like to consume services which they are not in a position to know they need. As it is free, they are also less discerning about the quality".

When it was put to me that 78% of Australians liked bulk billing, I replied: "The only thing surprising about that is the other 22% who don't want something for free."

Brian Howe felt me out on a Medicare co-payment. I had several meetings with Howe and his advisor, Tom Brennan, at which a co-payment was explored. The principles agreed were a small reduction in the Medicare Benefit, but not for pensioners and concessional card holders. GPs would be able to charge the difference.

I asked of the Prime Minister's support for the idea and was reassured Bob Hawke was on board. This would be a major breakthrough for the AMA and a big call for the Labor Party. Bulk billing was a sacred cow. Brian Howe characterised it as reining in unsustainable increases in Medicare outlays.

The AMA Federal Council debated the wisdom of support for the proposition. My argument carried the day. The principle was more important than the money. We had both an opportunity and a responsibility to support the introduction of a price signal for those who could afford it. "Too many patients were treating their doctors like barmen – set 'em up Doc." There would also be other measures supportive of general practice in the budget.

I assured Brian Howe of our support. He would need it. But what Howe had not disclosed was revealed when Paul Keating delivered the budget in August. The Medicare rebate would drop by $3.50 for 'non-cardholders' and GPs could bill for the gap. However, the government was taking $430 million out of health from these savings and redirecting them to Howe's pet project – the *Better Cities Programme.* We couldn't support a reduction in funding for healthcare. We withdrew our support and attacked the redirection of health funds.

All this fed into Paul Keating's campaign to topple Bob Hawke. My first-year medical school tutor and now Labor Senator, Dr Rosemary Crowley, led the charge internally against the co-payment in support of Keating. The co-payment was dropped in a deeply humiliating way for Brian Howe. On 21 November 1991, John Hewson and Peter Reith released *Fightback!* Just before Christmas, Paul Keating replaced Bob Hawke, fatally damaged by the co-payment and unable to gain ascendancy over Hewson.

Bruce Shepherd had been working on his own political campaign. He wanted to change the AMA's constitution. The president should serve three consecutive years, rather than two. This would require an Extraordinary Annual General Meeting (EGM) with more than 95% of eligible voters supporting the proposition. Bruce had more than a few enemies, but overwhelmingly the membership liked what he was doing. The process was guided by the AMA's Secretary General, Dr Alan Passmore. Almost all members voting would do so by proxy.

An hour before the closure of voting, a box containing 1,400 proxies 'appeared' on the front desk of AMA headquarters. The final count was 94.7% in favour – a whisker short of the required 95%. Bruce immediately smelled a rat. He ordered the ballot papers not be destroyed, but they were. However, Bruce's loyal lieutenant, Anne Smith, had copies of four ballot papers. They had been faxed to her by the AMA secretariat days earlier to show Bruce a cross section of votes 'in the box'. She faxed them down to Passmore's deputy, Dr Bill Coote, a man of impeccable integrity. Bill said, "When that first ballot paper came off the fax – Dr Jane Pillow, I recognised the handwriting immediately."

Dr Passmore left the AMA a very short time later. He had certainly been working hard. The building's lift computers recorded him entering the building in the early evening and leaving close to sunrise in the weeks leading up to the ballot. The EGM was run again. This time, 99% in favour. Bruce would lead the AMA for a third year into May 1993 and through the federal election. It would give me another year as vice-president.

The Australian Doctors Fund (ADF) convened a conference in Sydney in May 1992: *AIDS – Have we got it right?* It attracted a large registration and much controversy. The keynote speaker was Professor Fred Hollows. He and Bruce were mates. Bruce's concern was that the 'gay lobby' had hijacked Australia's approach to HIV/AIDS, breaching standard public health practice. Bruce and Bob Hawke's first health minister, Neal Blewett, had a mutual contempt for one another. Bruce had publicly described Blewett as having gone 'soft' on AIDS.

Fred's concern was for Aboriginal people, desperately fearful that remote Aboriginal communities would be ravaged by AIDS. Fred took me aside, "Brendan, the way I see it, you're going to be the next AMA president. There are two things you need to do. First, you have to liberalise the AMA's attitude to Medicare." I said, "Fred, you better give me the second. I hope it's easier than the first." "The second, is to squeeze every last drop out of the AMA presidency and every position you ever hold to help the blacks. Christ knows they bloody need it."

We concluded that Australia got it right on AIDS. Fred died the following year, 1993.

As I worked away at my locums, nightshifts and performing my AMA duties, I was across a wide range of health issues. I offered policy commentary on pretty much everything from health financing to alcohol related deaths. But I was flummoxed when journalist Karen Polglaze rang from AAP: "Dr Nelson, I'm calling to ask what the AMA's position is on ATSIC's environmental health policy."

"I've got a patient with me. I'll call you back."

I called AMA headquarters where a small army worked on a multitude of issues. I spoke to the director of public health, Dr Peter Wilkins. "Peter, what's ATSIC?" He explained: the Aboriginal and Torres Strait

Islander Commission; but had no idea what its environmental health policies were. In response to my next question – no one at the AMA worked on Aboriginal health. So, began a journey of discovery and a commitment to do what I could to honour Fred Hollows' second exhortation. It proved not to be easier than his first.

At the May 1992 Federal Council meeting, Bruce Shepherd proposed Dr Kevin Fagan be awarded the highest honour the AMA could bestow: the Gold Medal for Service to Medicine and Humanity. Kevin Fagan was unknown to a significant minority of the AMA's 28-member council. Bruce's opponents assumed he was up to 'mischief'. Kevin Fagan happened to be Dr Alan Passmore's father-in law. As Kevin Fagan was dying, Bruce wanted to bestow the medal before he died with a bedside presentation. It was a close-run thing, to the eternal shame of those who opposed it.

Kevin Fagan was a Jesuit-educated surgeon, a man of towering character and humility and a surgeon who had suffered the brutality of the Japanese on the infamous Burma-Thai railway in the Second World War where he led a party of prisoners. Russell Braddon wrote in *The Naked Island*:

> Above all there was the extraordinary courage and gentleness, and the incredible endurance of the Medical Officer, Major Kevin Fagan.
>
> Not only did he treat any man needing treatment to the best of his ability; he also carried men who fell.
>
> He carried the kit of men in danger of falling; he marched up and down the whole length of the column throughout its entire progress.
>
> If we marched 100 miles through the jungle, Kevin Fagan marched 200 miles, and when at the end of our night's trip, we collapsed and slept, he was there … to clean blisters, set broken bones and render first aid.
>
> And all this he did with … the ready humour of a man who is not tired at all … he is the most inspiring man I

> have ever met. Some 20,000 British and Australian troops share my view.

In 1946, after the war, Kevin Fagan wrote of his experiences for the *Medical Journal of Australia*:

> It (the war) gave me a great understanding of men. And great appreciation of ordinary things in life: bread and butter, a bit of jam on your toast in the mornings, a glass of beer when you're thirsty. And, the value of human relations.
>
> You know, when it comes to an end, the only thing that really matters are the people whom you love and the people who love you.

I regard voting in favour of him receiving the Gold Medal as one of the things of which I am most proud. He is not a household name, but he should be.

Things were not improving on the political front. Paul Keating was Prime Minister, Brian Howe remained health minister. I had built relationships across the political divide and targeted the government's backbench. There I found some sympathy for our public health platforms but far less when it came to Private Health Insurance, public hospital waiting lists and the growing challenges in General Practice.

I took a call mid-year from the Tasmanian President of the Liberal Party, Eric Abetz. I had not met Eric but knew of him. He asked me to consider being the Liberal Party candidate for Franklin at the forthcoming election. I was taken aback but flattered. I told him I had my practice, a young family and AMA agenda. Thanks. But no thanks. Just before we ended the conversation, I said, "But if I ever do seek to go into politics, it will certainly be for the Liberal Party." Given the nature of his call and my response to it, I joined the Liberal Party.

I couldn't any longer own and run the After-Hours Medical Service. David was serving in the Tasmanian parliament and the AMA was demanding. We sold the practice and I switched to doing locums for GPs and home visit shifts when it suited me. In 1992, Brian Howe said that private health insurance made an "insignificant contribution to health financing." He followed it up by accusing doctors of putting profits before patients. We were livid.

My medical practice was largely concentrated in public housing estates and the blue-collar working-class suburbs of Hobart and Launceston. One patient was Ethel Guy, Labor to her boot straps. A heavy smoker with a disconcerting wheeze, Ethel was president of the Tasmanian Pensioners Union. She was a woman I respected, shaped by a tough life. I said to her, "Ethel, as you know, I get to talk to the heavies in Canberra. What would you say to the health minister, Brian Howe?"

"Brendan, can you tell them in Canberra to help us with private health insurance? I've got members going without food to pay for it?"

Days later, on 13 October 1992, I met Howe in his Canberra office. This meeting played a major role in changing the direction of my life. I got to private health insurance: "Minister, the government really has to offer support to help battlers maintain their private health insurance. One of my patients, Mrs Ethel Guy is president of the Tasmanian Pensioners Union. She told me to tell you that elderly people are going without food to pay for it."

Howe snapped: "You don't get it do you? If you want to change anything this government is doing, you'll have to change the government."

As I left, I resolved to take his advice. The AMA under Bruce and me would do what we could to change the government. Bruce was already well primed. Now I was as well.

Dr Bob Woods, the Member for the inner Sydney seat of Lowe, was developing the Liberal Party's health policy. Bob reached out to the AMA for support in this for the 1993 election. He was well versed in the major health issues. When the Liberal policy was released, the AMA was determined to make a stand in support of it. It included a co-payment for non-concessional card holders, private health insurance to cover gaps up to the AMA fee, means tested support for private health insurance and penalties for higher income earners without it.

Brian Howe had told us to 'change the government' to change policy. Into battle we went.

Back in Hobart, I had just returned to my car in Bridgewater after a home visit. Prime Minister Paul Keating's voice filled the space as the radio came to life. A grab from his latest job creating scheme: "In the next decade, there will be no jobs for people pushing brooms."

I sat in my car, in a street, in a suburb that at the time had 13% employment in the "recession we had to have", surrounded by households in which no one had ever had a job. Here, as George Orwell had written in *The Road to Wigan Pier*, getting a job was as likely as owning an aeroplane. I pondered what such pronouncements would mean, if anything, to these, my patients.

Keating was essentially saying to several million Australians, "there is no place in my future for you". While he meant that we would all need training and advanced skills, the reality is that among us there are men and women whose lives are fulfilled 'pushing brooms'.

A year earlier the editor of the *British Medical Journal*, Dr Richard Smith, had reviewed two large longitudinal studies on the health effects of unemployment. He concluded and explosively wrote: "The evidence that unemployment kills, particularly in the middle aged, now verges on the irrefutable." There is, he said, a 30% overall increase in mortality, illness, suicide, domestic violence, anxiety and divorce.

In 1992, with youth unemployment at 27%, it was a dark, depressing time. Australia is a country built on a strong work ethic. We define ourselves through our work. Within minutes of meeting someone, they ask what sort of work you do. Many of my young patients had never had a job. They felt that they did not belong, had no role in Australia, no sense of belonging or purpose. The final indignity was to be called a 'dole bludger'. So too, women quietly felt shame in saying, "I'm just a housewife", as if it described a life of lesser value.

I brought the AMA's resources to bear on the issue, planning a conference on 'The Health Effects of Unemployment'. It would be held in the AMA headquarters. We brought Richard Smith out to deliver the keynote address. No government minister accepted the invitation to attend and speak. But opposition leader, John Hewson, did.

On the day of the conference, Bruce and I were waiting at the front of the building along with a very large media contingent. My phone rang. It was Hewson's media advisor: "Dr Hewson wants to be met only by you Dr Nelson. He has asked that Dr Shepherd meet him after he enters the building." I knew why he might want that, but thought it an appalling thing to do to the great man. Bruce asked if there was a problem. I hesitated, then told him. He turned and said, "I'll leave all this with you mate. I'll go upstairs and back to Sydney."

I chuckled when I saw John Hewson's rather tired taxi bumping along the road. Incongruous, I thought, for a man who drove a Ferrari.

The conference was a great success, brimming with positive ideas and proposals. One was a national campaign to change attitudes toward the unemployed:

Some call me a dole bludger
others call me unemployed
but my name is Michael.

Another was for structured, supported work opportunities for the unemployed. It would finally come with the Howard Government's *Work for the dole.*

Paul Keating, sensing the danger to him of Hewson addressing our conference on unemployment, launched a missile: "Bruce Shepherd is the ugliest leader of the most rapacious union in the country."

Bruce's public response: "Well, if that's the best he can do then he can get stuffed!"

At Sydney airport a hungry media throng demanded my reaction. "Dr Shepherd has always had the dignity of the medical profession foremost in his mind. The Prime Minister should also." I walked away wearing a wry smile, thinking back to Bruce's rejection of my 'coffin' idea on tobacco policy.

I crisscrossed the country for the final two weeks of the election campaign, addressing many public audiences on the Liberal health policy. I was in Melbourne for a public demonstration in support of private health insurance. I read Paul Keating would be at a bookshop in Toorak, railing against the GST's impact on the publishing industry. The CEO of the Health Insurance Industry Association was Neil Batt. I called him: "Keating is in Toorak this morning, Neil. Let's take the fight up there instead of the hospital." He agreed.

Neil had been a long serving Labor minister and deputy premier of Tasmania. With fifty of our supporters, we arrived at the bookshop. A restless crowd assembled – the Prime minister's advancers, security, Labor supporters, the curious and a spattering of normal people. Two buses stopped from which emerged what were readily identified as union heavies. Keating arrived and the crowd parted for his entry into the shop. Half cheered, jostling for position with their campaign banners. Our group jeered, waving placards. From nowhere, Neil suddenly produced a megaphone:

> Ladies and gentlemen. My name is Neil Batt. I am a former National President of the Australian Labor Party. I am CEO of the Private Health Insurance Association. I now introduce Dr Brendan Nelson, Vice-President of the Australian Medical Association to address you.

He passed me the megaphone at which point the union thugs moved in. I thought it best to begin with the unemployed and communities with whom I worked. "Too many of our fellow Australians are sick and dying because they don't have a job. Many have given up hope of a job. Beyond economic recovery, there is much we can do but this government will not even respond to the AMA's plan." I went on in this vein. They settled. One man even told a woman to shut up so he could hear me.

Then I switched to the affordability of private health insurance:

> Eight hundred and fifty thousand aged pensioners are struggling to keep their private health insurance. Some are going without food to pay for it. Yet Mr Keating, reportedly worth of $5million, has told the nation from the Royal Adelaide Hospital that people don't need health insurance,

> wasting their money because Medicare is all they need. Mr Keating does not have private health insurance.

That was it. It was on. A melee! I was grabbed, spat on and pushed into the crowd. Cameras rolling, a woman screamed, accusing me of being a "Liberal Party stooge". I lost it: "I have never voted Liberal in my life!" An expression my father had used often over the years. In my case, of course, it was untrue but, on the day, it did seem to cool things a little.

By early evening I was in Adelaide to address a dinner at the Royal Adelaide Golf Club. I was in the bar area when I saw myself on television yelling into the nation's living rooms. My heart sank. Bruce called to tell me he was proud of me. I told him it wasn't right. It wasn't and I would pay a heavy price for it, just not yet.

John Hewson spent the last week of the campaign doing mass rallies in capital cities. I was in the crowd at Circular Quay. Hewson had lost his voice, standing on the back of a semitrailer flat tray. John Howard did the talking. The crowd was restless, with a large presence of jeerers. I chanced upon the Labor icon, Tom Uren. He told me it would be the coalition's health policy that would defeat it on Saturday. As we spoke, the Rural Doctors Association was breaking ranks, urging a vote to maintain universal bulk billing.

Paul Keating was re-elected. Hewson lost the 'unlosable election'.

On Channel Nine's flagship *Sunday* programme the morning after the election, Laurie Oakes interviewed Labor's strategist and numbers man, Graham Richardson. Understandably buoyant and predicting two Labor terms from the defeat of Hewson, Laurie asked him about the Liberal leadership. Richardson brought the tone of his voice down a notch: "There's only one person in the Liberal ranks that would come within a bull's roar of worrying us, and that's John Howard".

The family photograph taken on the occasion of my brother Philip's christening at St Finn Barr's church, Launceston 1961. At rear from left, my maternal grandfather Arthur holding Tracey, my mother's brother Jeff beside him. My maternal grandmother Molly and her mother. My father, Des holding me in front alongside his adopted father, Alexander. My mother holding her much loved infant son, Philip.

Year 12 St Ignatius College Adelaide 1975. Centre front row.

My semi-raked Kawasaki Z900A 1978.

AMA Tasmanian President 1991. Fighting the tobacco industry and its sponsorship of sport with pathology specimens and Dr Cliff Kelland (right). Organs and a gangrenous foot removed from smokers. A powerful message.

The young GP. Hobart 1990.

Addressing the media with my mentor, AMA President Dr Bruce Shepherd, 1992 when I was Vice President. Bruce was tough and uncompromising in his advocacy for an independent medical profession.

Address to the National Press Club September 1993 as AMA Federal President. This image finally drove the implementation of uniform, potent national heath warnings on cigarette packets.

AMA Federal President. Docker River 1993 with Aboriginal amputee, Bill Edygima.

6

The Power of Speech in a new world

A victorious Paul Keating nominated three organisations for 'special treatment'. Each had campaigned openly and aggressively for the coalition. It was going to be a long, hard three years for the AMA.

The AMA's national conference was two months away in late May. We wondered whether Brian Howe would continue in health. Paul Keating may not like us, but surely he knew he had a problem.

Doug Lowe knew that not only did the AMA have a problem with Brian Howe, but so too did his beloved Labor Party. The AMA's Tasmanian branch executive officer, I had appointed a couple of years earlier, had proven to be a strategic thinker. Knowing Labor had to wrestle the health portfolio from the Left, he had 'put in some calls' to his contacts in the NSW Labor right. He reassured me that although the AMA was *persona non grata* with the government, "the message had been heard".

When Keating announced Graham Richardson would be the Minister for Health, Bruce said, "Now we've got a bloke that we can work with". Richardson rang Bruce, scrubbed to watch him do a hip replacement and reassured him he was calling a truce in the anti-doctor war.

Our first meeting, my first meeting with the new minister, was memorable. We met in the Minister's Parliament House office. Fresh from his surgical encounter with Bruce, they cheerfully exchanged pleasantries. Graham Richardson was accompanied by his chief of staff, Michael Crawford, and two advisors. They sat on one side of the table, we on the other.

Graham patted his tie as it wound its way around his ample abdominal girth. As he did so, I thought, "Stomach pretty much the same size as Bruce's." He peered across the table at us with the air of a man who had met his enemy whom he nonetheless respected: "The punters have voted for Medicare five times in a row now. Why did you blokes give us such a hard time during the election campaign?"

Bruce said, "Well, where do we start?" I piped up: "Minister, we felt as if we were on a bus running madly out of control down the side of a mountain. We couldn't get the driver's attention so we had no choice but to try and knock him out."

Silence. Then: "Look, it's a new world. You're dealing with me now. Howe, Macklin … every time the Labor Party fucks up the Left's got control of it. You be straight with me and I'll be straight with you. For a start, I think people should have private health insurance."

Bruce exclaimed: "Well … if someone had said that to me a couple of months ago, you would've sidelined us."

It was a new world – a better world, but it would only last one year.

I was unopposed for the presidency at the 1993 national conference in May. In his outgoing address to the delegates, Bruce described what he regarded as the qualities I brought to the AMA's leadership. He said that in many ways I had been something of a son to him. He placed the chains of office on my shoulders. From that day, not once did he tell me what to do. I would be my own person and, as John Freemen had taught me in 1983 over the pethidine order to the baby, I would make my own decisions.

I was blessed with an executive of immense intellect and wisdom: Professor David Weedon, pathologist as Vice-President, nephrologist, Professor Kincaid Smith, was Chairman of Council and Dr Ross Glasson, a radiologist with superb business acumen, was treasurer. Psychiatrist, Dr Yvonne White, and GP, Dr Peter Arnold, rounded out the team. And a team we were.

Just days after my election, I visited the Aboriginal Medical Service in Redfern, Sydney. I met Naomi Mayers and Sol Bellear, co-founders and their staff. I met patients, was briefed on the key health and financial challenges. I told them I would do my utmost to be a voice for them. As I walked through the modest facility, the first AMA president to ever do so, I thought of Fred Hollows. I would 'squeeze every last drop', sensing how power could be used for others.

For my first meeting with Graham Richardson, I thought I would offer him three issues. Even at this stage I had concluded that anyone with more than three priorities doesn't have any. I decided Private Health Insurance affordability, Public Hospital Funding and the third issue to which the AMA was now deeply committed, Aboriginal Health. Richardson was all ears. The difference from Brian Howe was beyond belief.

On Aboriginal Health, the Minister was sympathetic, wanted to offer all the support he could, but I should be warned: "I've spent a lifetime looking at polls, and I can tell you that it's not in to top 100 issues worrying the voters." I would see what I could do about that.

Appearing on *The Midday Show* a short time later, Graham Richardson spoke of the key issues with which he was dealing. Private Health Insurance was top of his list. He confirmed he had private health cover and then floored us all. When asked if he thought Paul Keating should have private health insurance, he said "yes". It was more than a new world, it was a revolution.

Beyond policy, I turned my attention to the AMA's bureaucracy. I had concerns about a senior member of the staff, doubtful he should continue in the AMA's employ. I called Bruce for an opinion: "Mate, he's never fought for anything. You have to surround yourself with people possessed of two qualities. The first is that they believe in something enough to bleed for it, fight for it. That you share their cause is less important than them having one. The second is to look for people that are over-enthusiastic. Much better to hose someone down several times a day than having to stick ginger up their bum to get them moving."

Another valuable lesson in leadership.

My first National Press Club address as AMA President was booked for 29 September 1993. In those days, before an entrenched internet and social media, an address to the National Press Club was a very big deal. It still is. To speak to a live television audience, with the nation's leading journalists seated before you, was the pinnacle of communicating a message. Among those tuning in is the political class.

I knew this was to be an important speech. It remains one of the most significant of my career.

I made an early decision to use my life in ways that would make a difference to the lives of others. I had also learned the power of speech – to inspire, challenge and change the often unyielding attitudes of others. I wrote the speech. More to the point, wrote an outline and dictated it. Mary Piles typed it up.

I put a lot into it. Unsurprisingly, health financing, professional and industrial issues facing the profession, featured. Medical 'over servicing'; informed financial consent for private patients; mal-distribution of the medical workforce; government control of GPs; the crisis in Obstetrics – doctors turning their back on the discipline and, the law in conflict with medical ethics, were included. These were staple fare for the AMA President in 1993.

But I also resolved that I would not be 'safe' as President. I wanted to lead the profession as much as represent it to society. So, I covered what needed to be heard: the health effects of unemployment and how to mitigate sickness and premature death from it. Environmental issues, including degradation of air and water quality, depleted aquifers and unsustainable resource depletion were now health issues. A model of continuous population growth was turning the world into a global feed lot, threatening human health and wellbeing in ways we could not comprehend. The Pope's encyclical would deny women access to contraception, thereby furthering misery throughout impoverished parts of the world.

The de-institutionalisation of people with mental illness into the community had freed up resources that had not followed them. Drug law reform, needle exchange programmes, and even consideration of drug injecting rooms, were needed. A lost sense of meaning and purpose was contributing to escalating existential despair and suicide amongst young people.

I attacked Tasmanian law that made it a criminal offence to engage in a homosexual act, urging legislators to ask themselves how they would feel to be criminals by virtue of sexuality. These laws, I said, "are an indictment of the humanity and understanding that should lie in all human beings".

Although, for many decades, doctors had given of themselves in the care and treatment of Aboriginal Australians, I was "ashamed that the profession's peak body had done so little", recounting my own introduction to the issue. Indigenous Australians had life expectancies and health outcomes equating to Haiti, India, Papua New Guinea and Ghana. Divided responsibility, buck passing, limited expertise and consultation, lost land, devastated culture and forced removal of children from parents, all conspired to create the circumstances in which Aboriginal Australians lived – and died. We had failed them.

The treatment of women in the profession needed to be urgently addressed by specialist colleges: "To be a doctor, wife and mother must be the hardest job on earth. Why are we making it even harder?"

Of course, I also reserved a special place for tobacco control – advertising, sport and arts sponsorship. Formula one cars were little more than racing cigarette packets. The headline issue at that time was health warnings on cigarette packets.

As vice-president, I had worked with public health and QUIT groups for over a year, negotiating new, powerful health warnings for cigarette packets. Explicit warnings such as *Smoking Kills* would cover 30% of the packet's front and back. I dedicated a significant part of the speech to the issue. The deal with the states had been finalised and announced only ten weeks earlier in July by the Victorian health minister, Marie Tehan. The night before my address to the Press Club, the Kennett Victorian Government announced it would withdraw its support for the deal. I was angry beyond words. Of course, it had absolutely nothing to do with my address the following day, but I thought if they were going to scuttle it, at least I would have the perfect forum for a 'right of reply'.

I was nervous when I got up before dawn on 29 September. I decided on the plane to cut tobacco control from the speech in the knowledge I would be asked about the Victorian Government's public health vandalism in questions.

I arrived at the AMA's Canberra headquarters mid-morning. I was pondering maximum impact on the cigarette packets. I needed an analogy, a prop. I asked Executive Assistant, Jean Reed, to go to the supermarket and buy me two items – a packet of cigarettes and a can of Baygon insect killer. She was startled in the extreme. Reassuring her, I said I wanted to point out that poisons carry detailed information about what happens if ingested. In contrast, cigarette packets told you nothing, although two Australians an hour were dying from consuming them. Off she went.

Rohan Greenland was the AMA's media director who did not need 'ginger up his bum' to get moving. A principled man of conviction, he 'bled' for his causes. I said, " I'm worried about the speech. I think it's too controversial. It is what I believe, but I think I should take some of it out." Rohan had served under Bruce Shepherd. "Brendan, you have come this far. You have been elected on the basis of who you are and what you bring to the leadership of the AMA. You need to do this."

Reassured and emboldened, Jean Reed's return from shopping extinguished any residual doubt. "Dr Nelson, I got the Baygon. But next to it was the RATSAK. Have a look at this." A staple of my childhood, I had seen RATSAK many times. But I had never paid close attention to the labelling on the box. RATSAK – *Kills Rats and Mice.* Brilliant!

The Press Club was packed. Lunch attendees and journalists covering the health round along with a smattering of the political. I discreetly placed my props under the lectern before pressing the flesh and sitting down. The much-loved former President of the Press Club, Ken Randall, introduced me. The applause when I finished the address suggested at least those present were happy. But I had not spoken about the public health issue for which I was arguably best known – tobacco. Sure enough, the first question was Michelle Coffey from the *Herald Sun* newspaper. "Dr Nelson, what is the AMA's reaction to the Victorian Government's decision to withdraw from the national agreement for stronger health warnings on cigarette packets?"

I said, "Well, I'll do what many politicians do and duck the question." With which I bent down to retrieve what I had beneath the lectern. They chuckled as I reappeared. I presented a mock-up of the packet that had been agreed by the states. I characterised the Victorian Government as the 'weakest link'. "By day's end, 54 Australians will be dead from a tobacco related disease, 250 kids will smoke their first cigarette today – 56 in Victoria and 10 of those kids will be dead from smoking within 20 years. You tell that to those people in Victoria."

I held up the RATSAK: "This is a well-known brand of a rodent poison. You will notice that it *kills rats and mice*. Plain language, black on gold." In the other hand, I held a packet of Winfield cigarettes: "This product kills 20,000 Australians every year, kills you in the dose recommended by the manufacturer, is not safe to be consumed in any dose and injurious to those in the presence of a person smoking it. What the Victorian Government wants is marginally bigger than the health warning on this packet that you can't read – *Smoking reduces your fitness*. Enough said."

At the conclusion Ken Randall presented me with a book on behalf of the National Press Club. The title, he commented, was a concept with which he believed I was already familiar – *The Power of Speech*.

Although Graham Richardson had publicly supported the states in the new warnings when they signed on in July, privately he was not an enthusiast. But when I arrived back from the Press Club, he was on the phone, "Mate, you got me. Brilliant. We'll use the *Trade Practices Act* to get around the states."

Bruce Shepherd called: "I just watched you on TV. I'm proud of you, bloody well done." A measure of the man.

The AMA's phones went off: doctors calling to express their support, others wanting membership forms which would surge over the coming year. The NSW branch ran off hundreds of copies of the speech and sent it to members.

But there were others. A Sydney gastroenterologist: "Dear Dr Nelson, as you are no longer interested in my income, herewith is my resignation from the AMA."

Mind you, I had finished my address by saying that we had to recommit ourselves to an ethic of service to others. Doctors who joined the AMA and whom I led, would give much more to their AMA membership than they would ever receive.

The government was rightly concerned about Medicare 'over-servicing' by doctors. Every Australian had been given a 'credit card' in the form of Medicare card and been told to use it. Bulk billed services cost the patient nothing. The doctor was accepting payment 25% below what the government believed it to be worth in its own Medicare Benefits of Schedule fees. The basic problem was that patients, as consumers, had no financial reason to question either the quality or need for the service.

We like to think we are reasonably informed when we buy a fridge or a TV. But in healthcare, most people have no idea whether they need a repeat consultation, test or procedure. When I chaired the AMA's Ethics and Professional Conduct Committee in Tasmania, we interviewed an orthopaedic surgeon who botched an operation on a patient's foot. I asked him why the woman had even agreed to the procedure in the first place. His reply spoke the truth: "I can talk a patient into anything." That's the point. It is tempting for doctors to create demand where there isn't any, even more so when there is no price signal. That the overwhelming majority of doctors are not so tempted is a tribute to their commitment to high standards.

In 1993, Graham Richardson wanted action on medical over-servicing. So did we, but preferably through a price signal which had gone with John Hewson's election loss. The Minister's officials had their own plans for new bureaucracy to address the problem. The Health Insurance Commission, with responsibility for Medicare payments, had one as well. I said to the Minister, "Whatever the bureaucrats come up with won't work. If you want a model that will deal with doctors abusing Medicare, we'll do it better than they ever will."

Respecting the profession, unlike his predecessors, he paused: "Okay. You've got a deal. But if you do me over, I'll be coming for you." Vice-President David Weedon took the lead on this for the AMA. He collaboratively conceived and developed the Professional Services Review, at the heart of which was a group of doctors reviewing suspicious Medicare Billing behaviour detected by the HIC's computers.

Graham Richardson had outstanding staff, loyal men and women who made him look good. Patti Warne was his advisor on medical overservicing. Having grown up in Hobart and attended St Michael's Collegiate School, a young Patti had worked for Gough Whitlam. She recounted how at the age of 25 she had gone back to the school reunion. The principal had asked each girl what she was doing.

Patti said: "When my turn came, I stood and said with pride, I am an advisor to the Prime Minister of Australia." The principal had looked at her and said slowly, "Well then … you're not doing a very good job Patti." She was smart, tough and emotionally intelligent. She knew what Richardson wanted and would deliver, come hell or high water.

The Chairman of the Health Insurance Commission was Laurie Willett, an experienced public servant. A meeting had been arranged at the Sydney Airport Qantas lounge with the Minister, Laurie Willett, David Weedon and me, along with relevant staff. It didn't take me long to see that Laurie was not briefed on the Minister's plan. We exchanged pleasantries.

Laurie introduced himself to Patti Warne as Chairman of the HIC, saying he was "looking forward" to working with the Minister on drafting the legislation. He handed her a card. She looked at, tore it in half and put it in the bin: "I won't be needing that." Graham and his staff had a unique way of communicating beyond any doubt what they wanted and where they were going. I made a note to myself, "Don't mess with Patti."

The AMA drafted the legislation.

Bruce had built the foundation for change and I was advancing it, quickly. This was a period of immense change and transformation for the AMA.

It's the little things and small events in life that often mean the most.

Walking through the open AMA office, I stopped to talk to staff. A woman said, "Dr Nelson, I have been working at the AMA for eleven years. For the first time, I feel proud to tell people where I work." The reaction of the others that followed was deeply moving.

7

"I live it every day"

I needed to get to remote Aboriginal Australia and project the issues into the lounge rooms of middle Australia. We planned an extended trip to the Northern Territory, towns and remote communities.

I would be supported in the Territory by two ophthalmologists, a psychiatrist, physician and Dr Paul Bauert, an NT paediatrician and the AMA's Branch President. What he didn't know about Aboriginal health wasn't worth knowing. He was also one of my strongest AMA backers. Rohan Greenland, our AMA media director, travelled with us along with Amanda Meade who would cover the trip for Fairfax Media. The trip was a transformation. I was confronted by what I saw, heard and felt. From it, some things would change.

The Alukura Aboriginal Women's Health Service is about 13 kilometres from Alice Springs. Its programme combines modern obstetric practice with traditional Aboriginal birthing culture. The female director, supported by her all female staff, delivered a twenty-minute briefing outside the facility at a spot where some women chose to have their babies.

We moved to enter the building. Emblazoned across the glass double doors was an enormous sign:

STOP!
NO MEN
STRICTLY UNDER NO CIRCUMSTANCES ARE MEN
ALLOWED BEYOND THIS POINT

I gestured to the sign. The director turned and said, "It's okay Dr Nelson. We don't think of you as being a man." I was simultaneously reassured and deflated!

Over that week I visited town camps, outstations and remote communities. We encountered Aboriginal children and adults suffering from diseases the rest of Australia had forgotten existed. In one community I found up to 54 people living in a three-bedroomed house. We found communities suffering renal disease simply for lack of drinkable water; local stores packed with processed foods but a scarcity of fruit and vegetables; alcohol, petrol sniffing and the consequences of violence.

Everywhere I went and whomever I met, Aboriginal people, their leaders, doctors, nurses – all were suspicious of me and my motives. The startled, thematic response was that they had never seen anyone in my position, let alone wanting to help. In this part of Australia, fully blind people waited months for cataracts, assessment of their diabetes and longer for artificial limbs.

When I asked John Liddle, director of the Central Australian Aboriginal Congress, what I could do to help, he didn't know. "The AMA has no history with Aboriginal people."

He was right. I shared my shame that it was so. "Back in Canberra, we have 40 people working on all kinds of industrial, professional and public health issues. Until very recently, not one worked on Aboriginal health. The organised profession has to do more. I want us to be a voice for you." He was speechless.

We landed at Docker River, 550 kilometres southwest of Alice Springs, just in the nick of time. The photographer was air sick on the way in. I managed to place my Akubra hat in front of him just as he vomited. The welcoming party was perplexed that my priority was water to wash out my hat. Strange fella, they must have thought!

Morbidity and mortality rates were extremely bad. I would learn valuable lessons here. Driving into the settlement I saw a number of tile brick dwellings. On top of each was a large, industrial quality air conditioner. Yet the homes lacked windows, converted into open living which their Aboriginal occupants preferred. When I asked, "Oh, they were built in the Whitlam years."

The district medical officer was Dr Nick Williams. He had spent a lifetime caring for the First Australians. He was pleased to see me but he wasn't. "I am an advocate for Aboriginal people … you can't just fly in here for a couple of hours and expect to understand Aboriginal people. It takes years." He went on in this vein. When he finished, I told him he was right: "I will never understand Aboriginal people and their needs like you. But I want to change the way the medical profession thinks about places like this. For example, we've got teams of eye people running around doing trachoma programmes, totally uncoordinated." The penny dropped.

I went to one of the 'Whitlam' dwellings. Two elderly Aboriginal people, a man and wife, lived here. They sat on a single mattress in a dusty room. Medications, a walking stick and personal effects were neatly placed on a low side table. Both had diabetes and its complications. Both needed constant care. They had finally agreed to go to an aged care facility in Alice Springs, but after ten days against all advice, returned to Docker River.

I sat on the edge of the mattress. When I asked the man why they had insisted on returning to Docker River, he stood. I stood with him. He pulled back the rudimentary curtain across one of the windows where once had been glass. It revealed magnificent hills and ranges sweeping behind the community. Gesturing to them, he softly said, "Mother … mother. I die here."

Much of Aboriginal life, identity and meaning is bound with land, a bond like no other. The only relationship that comes remotely close, in my experience, is that of farmers.

I was led to another elderly man on the outskirts of the community. In his eighties, Bill Edyminja lived outdoors. An amputee, he sat on a bed and sleeping bag bearing the image of a twenty dollar note. A billy can hung from the tree. A variety of dogs lounged around his 'home'. Dr Williams told me that Bill, a diabetic, had a cataract operation. Discharged early, his foot became gangrenous and the leg was amputated. Prior to all this, Bill was a keen and active hunter. He still looked pretty fit to me, notwithstanding his problems. I sat down next to him and struck up a conversation. Aboriginal people love their dogs. I love dogs too, so I thought it a good place to start. At this point an enormous, lean dog meandered over to us. As I was sitting, I was looking at the dog at eye level. It looked like a Stag hound-Irish Wolf Hound cross breed. I asked Bill if it was 'okay' to pat the dog. He nodded in approval, "He good dog … no bite". I reached out and patted the dog as I would my own. As I did, Bill confirmed that he had eight dogs but this one was his best, proudly telling me, "he chase down Kangaroo and bite his head off – just like that!" His hand Karate chopped my forearm. I carefully removed my hand from the dog's head.

Bill had waited eight months without success to get an artificial leg so he could get back to hunting. I told him that it was on my list of things to do. When I spoke to Graham Richardson back in Canberra, he made a call and the leg was delivered.

At Yuendumu, 300 kilometres northwest of Alice Springs, I met a Dutch medical student. I asked her why she had come all the way to central Australia. "I wanted to see medicine practised in a third world environment." All I could say was thank you and welcome to Australia.

Here, one of the Aboriginal Health workers proudly showed me her art. The paintings were vibrant forms of story-telling of the western desert genre. Jillie Nakamarra Spencer spoke little English so I turned to her friend. "Please explain to her that I am the boss of the doctors in Australia. I have come a very long way, far from here. I want doctors to help her to help heal your people."

I went on to explain I would like her to do a painting for doctors. It should be a big painting that tells the story of doctors working with Aboriginal people to help them when they are sick. I would pay her for the painting. I would also pay for her and a friend to come to Canberra to present it to the big AMA meeting the following May in 1994. I had no idea what was said in the exchange in traditional language that followed. She smiled. I smiled and we said goodbye.

At Maningrida, in the heart of Arnhem Land, we found similar problems and issues. But here also children had contracted Rheumatic Fever. I was shocked. It was a disease I thought we had 'beaten' in Australia. As I was about to board the plane, I turned to the chairman of the Community Council. "Was it always like this?" I asked.

He surveyed the community landscape, "No. We used to grow vegetables, hunt for food and natural tucker. Then Mr Whitlam sent money for nothing. Many people sat down." The first, but not the last, occasion on which I heard the expression.

At Croker Island, I had a remarkable meeting with a then 93-year-old man. Distinguished, polite and shirtless, his torso carried initiation scars from his youth which he proudly showed me. He described how and when each was acquired. His English was good, a product of missionaries. He recalled as a boy, about seven years of age seeing the first sailing boat pass through the strait – white sails and white people. I asked him if life was better or worse now than when he was young. Without hesitation, "Much better. Much better. We've stopped killing each other." When I reassured him I would not hurt him, he looked at me, "No sir. Aboriginal people have stopped killing each other."

Back in Darwin, I walked into the Danila Dilba Aboriginal Community Controlled Medical Service. Its director was an Aboriginal woman, Barbara Flick. She allowed herself only a fleeting smile. "I've been waiting for you", she said, in a tone that suggested this would be an uncomfortable meeting. Laid out carefully and strategically on a large desk was a series of papers, graphs and photographs.

A Yawallyi woman, Barbara systematically explained with the props before her, the nature and extent of the problems; stifling bureaucracy; resources needed and policy settings required. I listened, my staff took notes. As we left two hours later, I turned and said, "We have to find her a job. She is a formidable woman."

A number of key policy initiatives emerged from this trip. The first win was to get responsibility for Aboriginal health out of ATSIC and into the Department of Health and Aged Care. When Karen Polglaze had exposed my ignorance of ATSIC and Aboriginal health two years earlier, it had also revealed a fundamental flaw. Neither the AMA nor the peak professional health bodies had any direct reason to consider funding for Aboriginal health. It was parked in ATSIC and as such was not a part of the health budget proper. Those responsible for the health of the rest of the population were not overseeing health expenditures for Indigenous Australians. Under pressure, the government transferred it to its own health department.

The medical workforce was another major problem. In 1993, there were seven Indigenous doctors in Australia and less than twenty in training. I convened a meeting of the Deans of all the medical schools from which emerged a consensus on entry requirements and support for undergraduates. Some medical schools would build capacity and expertise in training Indigenous doctors. Newcastle University was an early leader.

I announced that the AMA would facilitate creation of the Indigenous Doctors Association of Australia. To a large AMA audience in Sydney, with Barb Flick alongside, I said:

> Indigenous Australians need to be supported and encouraged into medicine, not only for what they will do for their own people, but the difference they will make to the rest of us. Aboriginal doctors should have aspirations no different from any other doctor. Whether they work in remote settings caring for their own people or as surgeons in urban Australia, their greatest impact will be on us. By their presence, they will challenge us every day, reminding us of our own inherent biases and the profession's responsibility to be an agent of change – change to unacceptably poor health outcomes in Aboriginal Australia.

Reform to undergraduate and post graduate medical training was made. Professional structure and training was provided to Aboriginal Health Workers and autonomy, funding and status given to Aboriginal Community Controlled Health Services.

I was sitting in my Canberra office when the phone rang. It was Graham Richardson: "Mate, we're cooking with gas. It's number four. The polls. Aboriginal health, Australians are worried about it." Professor David Pennington had said that politicians follow public opinion and seldom lead it. Richardson was a master of both.

Richardson took the *60 Minutes* television cameras with him to remote communities in late January 1994. Charles Woolley asked him why, after 11 years in government, were the problems still so bad. He said, "Well, I've spent a lifetime reading polls. And I can tell you, concern for Aboriginal people and their health has not been in the top million issues worrying the voters." He and I, in our own way, worked to see that it did 'worry the voters'.

John Newfong was a true pioneer in Aboriginal activism. A Ngugi man of Moreton Bay, the first Aboriginal Australian to be employed in mainstream media. In 1972, he was spokesperson for the newly established Aboriginal tent embassy where he lived in its early days. He famously said, "The mission has come to town." I appointed him to head our new Aboriginal and Torres Strait Islander Health Unit. The AMA now had someone who not only knew what ATSIC was, but how to engage it with influence.

With John's leadership, we convened a two-day national summit on Aboriginal health in the AMA's Canberra headquarters. It was attended and addressed by the ATSIC Deputy Chairman, Sol Bellear, as well as doctors caring for Indigenous Australians, peak specialist medical colleges, nurses, Aboriginal health workers, State and Commonwealth health officials and a number of politicians.

It was uplifting standing before them, realising the importance of what we were doing. I spoke of the myriad diseases afflicting Indigenous Australians, lived experiences of many of those in the room. I praised those doctors who committed their lives to caring for Indigenous Australians. I also reiterated the shame I felt about the AMA itself failing to support them and to be a voice for them to society. We emerged with a template for action. Sadly, John Newfong was not a well man and stayed only briefly. John's departure opened the way for me to recruit Barbara Flick from Danila Dilba.

Graham Richardson resigned from the ministry a week later, after only a year in the job. I was deflated. Carmen Lawrence, the former Premier of Western Australia, would be the new minister. I didn't know what to expect. As always, I took an open mind to our first meeting.

We were met in the minister's office by her advisor, Hal Swerrisen. He welcomed us but soon introduced me to his political views which were disturbingly hard left. I was cautioned not to invite the minister to Aboriginal communities as she was "familiar with the issues". The minister was friendly and professional. No, she would not be entertaining initiatives to support private health insurance: "People who want it should do what I do and pay cash". On leaving, I resolved to reach out to the opposition.

Xavier College in Melbourne is arguably the jewel in the Jesuit crown. I had been invited to address the College's annual major fundraising event. Beyond my admiration for and public gratitude to the Jesuits, I decided on two key issues, Aboriginal health and the reproductive rights of women.

In 1993, the Keating Government suspended Australia's $130 million reproductive aid programme for the developing world. Although the government benches were filled with members opposed to the decision, they needed the wily, Independent Senator from Tasmania, Brian Harradine. Senator Harradine was a devout Catholic whose faith informed his role in public policy.

I looked into the Xavier audience. Members of the board, priests, teachers, parents and students. Given the College's deep sense of social justice, my advocacy of Aboriginal health was well received. I then turned their attention to women, specifically those in the developing world impacted by the funding freeze. I challenged them. A fundamental tenet of our humanity must be that every woman should be free to follow and live in accordance with her faith and religious convictions. But, equally, women have the right to access education about their own fertility and, if they choose, the means to control it. The silence broke with applause that seemed to go on and on.

Returning to my seat, I leaned across to the Principal, Father Michael Stoney SJ, "I hope that wasn't too controversial Father". Softly smiling he said, "We don't want a lot of yes men in the Church my son".

The AMA's 1994 national conference was fast approaching in late May. Only three weeks away, I had not heard from Jillie Nakamarra Spencer at Yuendumu. I assumed my commissioning of the artwork had been lost in translation – literally. My mobile phone rang. A quiet, unintelligible voice. I was about to end the call, when another voice came on: "Doctor Nelson, this is Grace from Yuendumu. Jillie finished the painting last night."

"Jillie started work on the painting the night she met you. She has worked on it every night since. Today it is finished." Another emotional day. The cost, I was told, was $400. I insisted we would pay $1500. Jillie and Grace would be invited to Canberra to present the painting to a "big meeting of doctors". Neither woman had ever been on a plane. I reassured Grace when she asked, "Yes, Canberra is a part of Australia – but some white fellas wish it wasn't!"

These two remarkable women made their way to Canberra with all the new experiences it gave them. Elevators, fancy hotels, a meeting place in the form of a parliament and so many doctors in one place. On that Sunday morning in late May 1994, Jillie Nakamarra Spencer spoke to 140 of the nation's doctors in Canberra's Hyatt Hotel ballroom. Softly she described why she had chosen to be an Aboriginal Health Worker, "It is in my heart", as she held her left breast. Gesturing to her painting, she said it was the story of her people being cared for by doctors who have the "power to heal in their hearts".

I said that her painting would hang proudly in the foyer of the AMA's Canberra headquarters. An image of the painting would adorn our policies and papers on Aboriginal health. It would remind us and future generations of doctors of our responsibility to this nation's first peoples and to always support those with "care in their hearts". My Hobart mentor, Dr Michael Hodgson, said it was the most meaningful experience of his years attending AMA national conferences. He was not alone.

Alexander Downer had assumed the leadership of the Liberal Party days earlier. I enjoyed a good relationship with John Hewson, but his treatment of Bruce Shepherd had left a bitter taste with me. Working with a Downer led Opposition was a positive. When Bronwyn Bishop was appointed shadow health minister I was delighted. She was a warrior of conviction and an ideal person to take up the cause of private health care, choice and support of an independent profession.

However, things got off to an awkward start. Bronwyn said when asked of tobacco advertising prohibition that those with such views had "yet to prove their case". I called Bronwyn immediately it was reported. When she confirmed what she had said, I told her I would have to criticise that position. She said that was not a problem. It quickly proved to be a big problem – for her and for the new leader. Alexander Downer called me to reassure me coalition policy had not changed.

From the conference that year we also advocated decriminalisation of cannabis use or possession of small amounts for first offenders. To the media, I said: "Youth is a period of experimentation. Whatever the pontification of society, young people will continue to experiment in risk-taking behaviour. A quarter of the parents of teenagers in this country have got a child who's used or is using a drug. At times they are coming into contact with the criminal world to engage in their drug use. Cannabis use is more dangerous than smoking, but its criminality for personal use compounds the adverse consequences of doing so."

The day after the conference, the Government announced it was resuming Australia's Overseas Aid Programme for family planning. Something to celebrate.

Queensland's Labor Government wanted to advance the health of its Indigenous population. In June, its health minister, Ken Hayward, called inviting me to join him on a visit to Cape York communities. He wanted my ideas on what we could do and support from the medical profession to assist. In mid-July we made our way through the communities of Aurukun, Coen, Doomadgee, Kowanyama, Lockhart River, Hope Vale, Weipa and up through the Torres Strait.

I was struck by two things. First, irrespective of the political party, everyone now saw addressing Indigenous health and living conditions as a priority – genuinely so. Second, no matter how much these people had endured, without exception we were welcomed.

The Aboriginal ladies at Mapoon were dignified in the quiet way they would speak, carefully choosing every word. This was Mapoon, but there was also 'Old Mapoon'. The history thirty years earlier is tragic. The old settlement had been on bauxite the mining company had wanted out of the ground. After months of negotiation, the authorities arrived unannounced, rounded up the families and burned their dwellings. Far North Queensland in those days was not an easy place for Aboriginal people. Constance Cooktown had been in a boat that day, fishing with her father. They returned to smouldering ruins, her mother and everyone gone. "Things like that never leave you", she whispered. It will be to my eternal shame if sitting there with those women that day should ever leave my memory.

In Cairns I met a woman I will never forget. Rose Colless recounted the efforts to which she had gone over many years to help her people, whom she loved. The Yarrabah Mission had framed her life. She pressed a book into my hand, *Reaching Back,* stories of the Mission and the lives of its people, edited by Judy Thomson. In national discourse, "Aboriginal Reconciliation" was the new catch cry. "Rose, what does reconciliation mean to you?" Silence, then she cried, "I don't know … but I know I live it and I live it every day. It will be a long journey." I cried.

When asked by the media in Cairns what I had learned – "Why are many of the health care facilities for Aboriginal people on the Cape so small and primitive? The toilets in the AMA's Canberra headquarters are bigger" – Ken Hayward bristled. But his government responded with an action plan and resources.

The Royal Australasian College of Physicians invited me to deliver the Arthur E. Mills Oration at its annual congress in 1994. Mills was a pioneer of the specialist college. In the depths of the Hobart winter, I delivered one of the speeches of which I am most proud. The Hobart Town Hall was packed: the Council of the College, its Fellows, those to be inducted and families. These were the men and women who trained, credentialed and oversaw our nation's specialist physicians. My 45-minute oration was titled *The Social Conscience and Obligations of Physicians in Contemporary Australia.* I had carefully researched and written this one. Within it was my guiding, 'north star': the practice of medicine and the influence of the profession cannot be separated from the problems facing society. I doubt it ever could and that is what I told them.

Aboriginal Health; Euthanasia; Unemployment; Youth Suicide; treatment of women in the medical profession; AID programmes for birth control in the developing world; female genital mutilation; population and environment; global warming; boxing; gun control; tobacco advertising; human rights of the mentally ill; nuclear proliferation; illicit drugs; alcohol promotions – I carefully went through them all seeking to challenge them to our broader vision of responsibility.

Earlier in 1994, I had taken Channel Nine's *A Current Affair* to some Sydney hotels at night. The Black Prince Hotel had a Thursday night special – "Half price drinks for ladies". I used my position to confront middle Australia with the exploitation of their daughters. There were five men for every woman in the pub. The mainly young women were intoxicated to varying degrees. To the Hobart audience I said that in these and similar cases, the AMA must represent a profession prepared to stand up and fight injustice. Doctors must be powerful and articulate advocates for people who have neither power nor influence. Gestures of intellectual independence from professional organisations will simply ensure that whatever you stand for will remain in obscurity. None of us should ever accept that the problems we face are too hard, too complex, or that we cannot make a difference. I concluded: "When all scientific problems will be solved, all important questions will remain unanswered." It was one of the most satisfying nights of my public life. The speech was editorialised in the *British Medical Journal.* I now knew I was making a difference to my profession.

A chain of events was about to further change the direction of my life.

8

You have to be in the main game – Sydney

Trish Worth was the Federal Member for Adelaide. A woman with a soft demeanour, strategic brain and intellect to match, she hosted me at her Canberra Parliament House office on budget night, 1994. Trish was of the 'moderate' wing of the Liberal Party. You had to be if you wanted to hold the seat of Adelaide which she had won the year before. To do so in the *Fightback!* election was no mean feat. Her background was health and I liked her a lot.

Trish called me in June, asking if I would like to meet the new leader, Alexander Downer. I was excited. Mr Downer was ascendant in the polls, presented a fresh face and Carmen Lawrence as health minister was taking up where Brian Howe left off. Her description of doctors being of a "privileged class" had reinvigorated the class war.

My media advisor, Rohan Greenland, accompanied me to Canberra's Tang Dynasty restaurant. I was pleased the opposition leader wanted to discuss health policy, which we did. Then conversation turned to another motive for the dinner. Trish suggested to Alexander I would be an ideal Liberal Party candidate for the Adelaide seat of Boothby. He warmed to the idea. The sitting member was Steele Hall, a former South Australian Premier and Senator, now split from the Liberal Party that had given him public life. Alexander wanted him gone. I was startled by the suggestion, but Trish had done her homework. I had lived in Boothby for nine years and knew the electorate well. I thanked them but declined the offer. I lived in Hobart, deeply immersed in my medical practice and AMA leadership responsibilities.

But I saw an opportunity and had nothing to lose raising the idea.

Parliament was then gripped by the legislative response to the High Court's decision in the Mabo Case. Two years earlier, in June 1992, the Court had held that some Indigenous Australians held a legal form of ownership of land – "native title". 'Terra Nullius' was dead. The coalition parties were deeply challenged to represent their farming and mining constituencies.

I said to Alexander: "Before making final decisions on native title, why don't you do what Paul Keating will never do? He won't put his Italian shoes in the Northern Territory's red dust. Come with me. I will show you an Australia rarely seen by our political leaders – impoverished Aboriginal Australians, lives drastically shortened by a crisis unseen by Australians." The AMA would arrange the itinerary and media. He didn't have to say much during the trip, just listen. It offered the opportunity for his humanity to be revealed. I was bowled over when he agreed, then and there.

We would tour remote Northern Territory communities. I invited two print journalists sympathetic to Indigenous issues and the Central Australian Aboriginal Media Association (CAAMA) to cover the trip. Rose Crane, niece of Western Australian Liberal Senator, Winston Crane, covered remote NT issues for ABC Television. Rose was a no-nonsense straight shooter who would give us a fair go. I presented the plan to Mr Downer's office, reassuring them everyone understood the paramount importance of confidentiality. All good, or so I thought.

Two weeks before the trip, Mr Downer's office unilaterally changed the media coverage. Fairfax out, *Herald Sun* in. CAAMA was told they were not coming in two words. We were due to fly out of Adelaide on Monday morning in early August. It was Friday morning. I was driving to work in Hobart listening to ABC radio's current affairs programme, *AM*. Alexander Downer was being interviewed about Native Title. I was shocked when he said, "I am going to remote Aboriginal communities on Monday with Brendan Nelson."

My heart sank. I knew that broadcasting the trip would be bad. It got worse. Unbeknownst to me, Alexander was to spend Saturday at the State Council meeting of the Liberal Party of Western Australia. He used the platform to announce that in government, the Coalition would repeal the *Native Title Act*. All hell broke loose!

Media outlets were suddenly chartering planes in hot pursuit. The Keating Government focused on the alternate Prime Minister's trip to meet Aboriginal people for whom land was 'mother.' Mr Downer would be pressed to explain the coalition's policies on land and native title. As we made our way through the communities, the media constantly wanted to interview him. He readily obliged them. A neophyte myself in the art of politics, I didn't understand why we couldn't simply meet, observe, listen, question and absorb with, perhaps, an end of day interview about what we had learned and seen. The low point was Mr Downer's confusion over the Northern Territory *Land Rights Act* of which he appeared to have little knowledge.

We visited Kintore, Yuendumu, Urapuntja and Amengerternhne. At Yuenedumu I embraced a beaming Jillie Nakamarra Spencer. Alexander asked the community leaders preparing to drive to Darwin for the Collingwood vs Aboriginal all-stars game who they were backing. Incredulous he would even ask, in unison they cried, "Collingwood!"

At one settlement I was interviewed by a television crew in front of an elderly Aboriginal couple living under a piece of corrugated iron. So immune are some Australians to these problems that an Alice Springs print journalist chastised me for "choosing to be interviewed in front of them mouthing the rhetoric of fourth world Aboriginal living standards". The published article went on to say that "after all there were only forty families homeless in this community".

Flying across central Australia in a small plane gives you a lot of time to think. I always looked down in wonder at a breathtakingly beautiful but harsh land. We speak glibly of 60,000 years of Aboriginal life and culture. That these people lived and prospered in it, speaks to a resilience beyond our comprehension.

The final stop was Utopia, 350 km north east of Alice Springs, home of the Alyawarre and Anmatyene people. The Labor Member for the Northern Territory, Warren Snowden, had joined the welcoming committee. Health, housing, lack of services, unemployment and land ownership – issues to which we had become too well accustomed.

Our plane was chartered from an Indigenous owned company. Late in the day our pilot became agitated, insisting it was time to leave. Given his urgency, we jumped into the vehicles. The journalists, however, were more interested in their interviews which I suspected would not be kind to Mr Downer. Finally, the pilot exploded. If we didn't get on the plane, he would go without us. The cars raced off to the airstrip.

We were taking our seats when the co-pilot closed the door and engines roared to life. As the plane taxied, three journalists arrived waving frantically. The pilot ignored our pleas. In a cloud of dust that settled slowly over them, we flew off to Alice Springs. I broke the awkward silence: "At least they'll have plenty of time to write their stories in the three-hour drive to Alice Springs." Already in no mood to be generous to Mr Downer, watching him suddenly leave them at 'Utopia' was hardly going to help. In flight, I asked the pilot why the hurry. "Remember I told you I was doing more study? Well, I'm learning how to land a plane in the dark."

The trip proved to be the first of a series of events that would be Mr Downer's undoing. From those three days with him, however, I concluded he was a good man.

I flew back to Sydney where I was guest speaker at the black-tie NSW Medical-Legal dinner. I changed in the toilets of the Intercontinental Hotel. In attendance were four hundred of Sydney's well-heeled from the medical and legal professions. In addition to the impact of the law and legal interpretations of it compromising the disciplining of unethical, rogue doctors, I would speak to the issues I had confronted in remote Australia. By now I had learned the discipline of speaking without notes which, among other things, allowed me to observe and respond to audience reaction. I called for a national state of emergency to be declared in relation to the health and living conditions of Aboriginal Australians.

Three tuxedoed men approached me. One, who wore a red rose in his lapel, said, "We are orthopaedic surgeons. We are mates of Bruce's. I don't know what the AMA's paying you, if anything. I don't understand what you're doing. But for the first time in thirty years I feel proud of my profession and to be a doctor."

Others felt differently. A physician told me that health problems of Aborigines are "social issues" beyond the scope and responsibility of doctors. A minister warned me that the medical profession was in danger of losing its credibility, saying its increasing outspokenness on social issues had nothing to do with health. I resolved to press on. We were making a difference. I also knew this is what most of the profession and membership wanted. However, the call for an emergency declaration went unheeded until 2007.

The Australian Democrats were led by Senator Cheryl Kernot. Her office called inviting me to dinner with her. The Democrats were closer to Labor than the Coalition but they wielded power, putting a brake on some of the Labor Government's excesses. I readily accepted another dinner with a party leader, the AMA's health agenda in my back pocket. We sat in the parliamentary dining room, just the two of us.

I liked Cheryl Kernot. I saw her as a woman of class and intellect, frequently a voice of reason in the public space of 1994. It didn't take long for her to get to the purpose of the dinner. She asked if I might entertain a career in politics as a candidate for the Democrats. I told her I was flattered that she and her colleagues should consider me a worthy candidate, but no thanks. However, if I did stand for parliament, it would be for a major party. The Democrats played an important role, but they were responding to someone else's agenda: "You're on the side of the field trying to direct the players." In my own mind, of course, it would be the Liberal Party.

Cheryl Kernot looked at me, "I knew you would say that. In your position, I would feel the same way. You've got to be in the main game." I thought back to that dinner three years later when she defected to Labor amidst a raging controversy.

Alexander Downer went into deeper trouble with his "Things that batter" quip in September in which he parodied his party's domestic violence policy. His polling nose-dived. I thought more seriously about his Boothby proposal. I called him. I would have a serious look at it.

Days later I was scheduled to share the podium at the National Press Club with Moira Rayner. She was a barrister, human rights advocate and

Victoria's first Commissioner for Equal Opportunity, and a formidable woman. We spoke about human rights and children, she from a legal perspective and me from the medical. I was asked about speculation I might seek to enter parliament. I said I was not there to speak about such things. We were there for children. Moira Rayner said something I could not avoid and which stayed with me a very long time. "The price we pay for people like Dr Nelson not being prepared to stand for public office is that we continue to be governed by those for whom we have a low regard."

Flying back to Hobart that night I thought about that day. Perhaps I had a responsibility to the profession that had invested so much in me, to do more. In my car, the phone rang. It was the editor of a major daily newspaper: "Brendan, you won't get any more done now unless you get into parliament." I started researching Boothby, in particular the Liberal Party officials. Dr Lehonde Hoare was past President of the South Australian AMA. 'Frosty', as he was known, was also one of my strongest backers. His wife, Betty, was president of the Liberal Party College for Boothby. I couldn't believe my luck. I called her.

Betty was excited to learn that with Alexander Downer's encouragement, I was calling with a view to being a candidate for Boothby. She was cautious: "I'll have to do a bit of research and come back to you, Brendan." She called two days later. The reaction was mixed but, in the majority, positive. I would have to come to Adelaide for "a couple of months" and work on the ground. I thought it tricky but doable.

I took the AMA executive into my confidence, cleared it with my wife, Kate, and was getting ready to make the jump. The President of the Liberal Party in South Australia was Vickie Chapman. On a September Saturday as the Liberal Party Federal Council met in Launceston, Vickie called: "Brendan, I appreciate you wanting to have a shot at Boothby but I'm calling to tell you there is no point. We have an unbeatable candidate." She paused and told me in confidence it was Senator Robert Hill. Given he was a senior South Australian Liberal backed by the state president, I had no hope. The "unbeatable candidate" was subsequently beaten in the pre-selection by a young doctor, Andrew Southcott. His victory strengthened my resolve to follow my own instincts.

Bruce Shepherd invited me to join him and Doug Moran for dinner at Bruce's Cremorne Point apartment. Bruce had remarried that year. His wife, Jenny, was always the perfect host. Joining us was Francis Giacco who won the Archibald prize that year, 1994. Doug Moran was a patron of the arts and, like Bruce, stoutly resisted the political correctness sweeping the art world. Doug instituted his own portrait prize, telling me that he wanted to encourage and reward "real portraitures". Doug was also a strident critic of the Labor Government, in his case of its nursing home policy. It was on this issue that our interests coincided. I had been advocating reform in this space.

The conversation turned to Boothby. I briefed Bruce on the weekend conversation with Vickie Chapman. Notwithstanding Betty Hoare's support and advice, pursuing it was a futile exercise. Bruce said: "Forget about the bloody crow eaters, they're a bunch of hand wringers anyway. Mate, you have to be in Sydney. You should have a look at North Sydney, that's a serious seat." Doug Moran concurred, suggesting he would help me.

I researched North Sydney the following day. A young man called Joe Hockey had spent three years 'locking up the branches.' There was no opening for anyone. The Liberal Party needed a local candidate free of controversy to replace the retiring independent, Ted Mack.

When I reported this to Bruce, he said, "Well, what about the electorate further up the North Shore, Bradfield?" I had never heard of it. Bruce's executive assistant, Anne Smith, thought it a very suitable electorate for me. "It's different up there", she said, "Manicured lawns, well dressed ladies and spacious homes. A lot of doctors live in Bradfield." I asked who the federal member was. Anne said, "David Connolly. He's been there for years, a nice, ineffectual man. But Bradfield is a quiet place and that seems to suit them up there." Bruce said, "Okay then. Let's see what we can do to wake them up."

I was due to deliver the 1994 Occasional Address to the Royal Australasian College of Physicians in Sydney in late September. I made an appointment to see the NSW Director of the Liberal Party the following day. The address to the physicians was quite an event with much formality. At its conclusion, I mingled with members of the audience and found myself chatting with half a dozen doctors. The conversation turned to politics, specifically Alexander Downer's problems as opposition leader. The consensus was that the Keating Government might be returned.

One, Dr John Graham, said he was "heavily involved in the Liberal Party". He was president of the Pymble branch in which there was great controversy. He had written a week earlier to the state director. They wanted a new federal member and had drawn up a list of prospective candidates that should be approached, including Tennis great, John Newcombe.

"Where's Pymble?" I asked. "Brendan, you wouldn't know, but Pymble is in the seat of Bradfield on Sydney's upper north shore. Our federal member for twenty years is a guy called David Connolly. It's a safe seat and we want a change." I couldn't believe what I was hearing. Armed with this intelligence, I met party director, Barry O'Farrell, the following morning. I wanted to discuss being a candidate. He started to reel off seats he wanted to win. I said, "Thank you Barry, but I am interested in only one seat – Bradfield."

Laughing, he told me not to even think about it. I persisted, "No, only Bradfield". He sensed I was serious. I knew he had a letter from the Pymble branch wanting renewal. He paused, "Okay. I will arrange for you to meet a few people." Barry gave me contact details for three people: Don Glover, immediate past president of the Bradfield Liberal Party conference and member of the Pymble branch; former NSW premier, Nick Greiner, and Sir John Carrick, doyen and former long serving general secretary of the Party's NSW division and Fraser Government minister.

I made appointments to see them the following week.

Don Glover was no nonsense. Conservative, he had resigned the Bradfield Liberal presidency in principle over David Connolly's betrayal of both the Bradfield liberals and John Howard. In 1989 when the Peacock–Howard leadership tensions peaked, David Connolly asked each of the eighteen Bradfield branch presidents for whom he should vote. Sixteen urged a vote for Howard. Connolly voted for Peacock. Don was impressed that I was supported by Bruce Shepherd, "had my own mind" and a national profile of potential benefit to the electorate. He undertook to support me. And that he did – in spades.

Nick Greiner was engaging, curious, spoke about the rigours of public life and encouraged me to have a go, warning David Connolly would be hard to dislodge. He wouldn't endorse me, but he would "not get in the way".

I researched Sir John Carrick before our meeting: a remarkable man and life. Revered in Liberal Party ranks, he was a survivor of the infamous Changi prison, the Burma-Thai railway and Hellfire Pass. He had championed the Menzian vision of liberalism and played a role in its nascent development as a research officer in 1946. From 1948 he towered over the NSW division of the party as its general secretary before serving as a Senator and Education Minister. I also knew him to be a mentor to John Howard. What he thought would matter most. I arrived at John and Angela's Killara home mid-afternoon. Both were welcoming and respectful. Angela showed me the garden, we discussed my family and a little of medical politics. Her gastroenterologist daughter was married to Dr Bob Woods. Having lost the seat of Lowe in the 1993 election, Bob had filled a casual vacancy in the Senate just a few months earlier. Angela left me alone with Sir John. We talked about everything, including politics in general. I asked him for advice which he readily gave. Finally, "Sir John, I will be frank with you. It is my intention to challenge David Connolly for pre-selection." He pursed his thin lips, "It will have to be a serious challenge". I assured him it would. Then, "You know he's called David smiles cunningly". I later learned a play on David Connolly's middle name, Miles.

Angela returned with impeccable timing, sensing it was time for me to go. Sir John told her of my intentions. She smiled, "John, Brendan must meet that rather loud woman on the lower north shore

… what's her name again?" "Rhondda Vanzella", he replied. A woman who would change my life.

I left armed with what I needed – implicit support for my rather naïve venture and the name of a powerbroker who might help me achieve it. As the taxi made its way through the streets of Bradfield past the houses, schools and public amenities, my calculation was simple and one based on my experience with people. It was an electorate filled with educated, largely professional and successful people. I had been involved in national affairs for five years, yet the people of Bradfield had a representative of whom I had never heard. Having consistently voted Liberal, they had seen their team lose five tests. They must surely want a change in batsman. They must surely want their aspirations and electorate to have a national profile worthy of them. It was that simple.

Back in Hobart, I put it to my wife, Kate. I wasn't sure how she would take it, moving to Sydney, politics and all it would entail. If she refused, that would be it. Her reaction surprised me: "I knew one day you would say this. It's not something I would want for us and our children, but I know you won't be happy unless you try. As for moving to Sydney, this place is dead, let's go."

We put the house on the market the following day. As the logistic wheels began to turn in uprooting our family, my AMA advocacy continued. Con Sciacca called me early in November 1994. I knew he was the Minister for Veterans Affairs and of the Labor right and a Queenslander of proud Italian heritage, widely respected by veterans.

He asked if I could do him a favour, "a big one". "Two years ago, my only son, Sam, died. He was nineteen – Ewing's Sarcoma." A painful pause. "Tina and I set up a foundation in his honour. We commissioned Mark Ragg to write a book about kids with cancer from a parent's perspective, real stories, dealing with the medical system and where to get help." The Governor General, Bill Hayden, agreed to launch the book at the National Press Club on the evening of 8 November. Unfortunately, Mr Hayden had fallen off his horse, fracturing several ribs and couldn't do it. Would I be willing to step in? I agreed immediately.

On the day of the launch I arrived at Parliament House to meet Mr Sciacca before heading to the Press Club. He emerged from his office, jovial, extending his hand for an equally warm handshake. "Brendan, call me Con. You poor bloody bastard, having to deal with Carmen Lawrence." There was more, but best not for print. I took an instant liking to the man.

He offered me a beer. I accepted a cup of coffee. In an anguished tone, he spoke of his son, diagnosis of the rare bone tumour, their journey through the medical system and then, his death. The Press Club was packed with Labor luminaries peppered with coalition MPs and Senators, foremost among them Senator John Herron. John was a surgeon, former AMA Queensland president and a magnificent human being. He and Con were friends. Cancer support groups and families afflicted by cancer mixed with the powerful and famous.

I reflected on having recently been asked by Richard Carlton from *60 Minutes* what the most difficult experience was that I have had as a doctor. Although I had a loaded gun pointed at me, been assaulted with a dog and stabbed with a hypodermic syringe, I would prefer all three than to try to give sufficient care, comfort and compassion to a family losing a child. Nothing forces you to confront your own humanity and values as much as the death of a young person. The book was a potent reminder that while almost all pain can be relieved, not so all human suffering. Later, sitting in my hotel room, reflecting on the Sciaccas' loss, I knew I had been afforded another lesson. It's not what happens to you in life that determines its value, but how you deal with it.

Our Hobart home sold. We bid our farewells and then, days before Christmas 1994, we set off. I drove my VW Kombi, towing the boat. Kate's mum, Myra came with us. A simply wonderful woman, a Godsend. The twins were excited. My 'crazy-brave' adventure was underway.

9

"Mate, when did Captain Cook get here?"

Days before Christmas I parked the Kombi outside Bruce's apartment in Cremorne Point. We moved our few things in. The next day I flew to Perth to do a media conference with Carmen Lawrence. We announced restrictions on smoking in public places and released the new cigarette packet warnings for which we had fought so hard. In Sydney it was oppressively humid and someone had broken into Kate's car, stealing sundry items. Welcome to Sydney!

The New Year pressures were multiple – find a house and work, get the kids into schools, maintain the AMA work rhythm and begin the preselection campaign. My brother Philip was also becoming more noticeably frail as AIDS began to exact its toll.

The crisis in public hospitals reached fever pitch in Victoria. I had been vocal in my criticism of the implementation of the Casemix funding model. The Premier, Jeff Kennett, gave his health minister, Marie Tehan, a week's 'leave' so he could personally look at the issues. I was sitting on the balcony of the Sydney apartment when my mobile rang: "Dr Nelson, are you able to take a call from the Premier of Victoria?" A familiar voice. "Dr Nelson, Jeff Kennett. Of all the people criticising what we're doing with our hospitals, you seem to be the only one that knows what he's talking about. I would like to meet you."

Two days later I flew to Melbourne. I told the Premier what was wrong, why and offered advice on what he should do. I visited the Royal Melbourne and Alfred hospitals, met with frontline doctors and amplified their concerns to the media. The state government responded well. Ever since, I have been a steadfast admirer of Jeff Kennett, although not of his football team!

Senator Meg Lees was a South Australian Democrats Senator. Deeply committed to advancing the interests of Aboriginal Australians, she attended all the conferences we convened on Indigenous health. She asked if I might join her on a road trip to Aboriginal communities throughout western New South Wales. Over five days in February 1995, we made our way through the towns of Walgett, Brewarrina, Bourke and Cobar.

As always, we saw and heard much to inspire and much to despair. At Brewarrina, the Pastoral Protection Board, exasperated by dog attacks on sheep, had laid poisoned baits around the outlying parts of the town. It was here of course that the Indigenous population was concentrated. Aboriginal people have dogs. There had been no consultation. Dogs ate baits, returned to homes to vomit and die in, around and under houses. Two children as a consequence required hospitalisation. How, I thought, can this still happen in modern Australia? I came away from that trip with a great respect for Meg Lees. Her views differed from mine on a number of key issues, but an intelligent, substantive and caring political figure. It cemented a relationship that would endure, helping me enormously years later when I was driving reform in universities.

We found a house in Lindfield to rent. St Aloysius College enrolled Tom and Loreto Kirribilli, Emily. Father Tony Smith SJ was the principal of 'Alos'. At my parental interview, he asked if Tom liked sport. "Yes, Father. He loves soccer". Father Smith smiled with approval. "That's good. We have rugby". I said, "Terrific father, but Tom plays soccer". "He *will* enjoy the rugby". "Yes father", I meekly replied.

I found work at a practice in the Rocks and another in Merrylands West. The latter was quite a drive, but I needed to gain a familiarity with western Sydney. In the midst of all this the editor of *Woman's Day* called inviting me to be the in-house medical writer. I would have a weekly column and write health features. She didn't have to ask twice. I now had a steady income.

By January 1995 Alexander Downer's leadership of the Liberal Party was finished. Without a change in leadership, the return of the increasingly unpopular Keating Government was a real prospect. I started my campaign. Preselection for Bradfield would be determined in May.

Rhondda Vanzella, to whom the Carricks had referred me, was the Northern Metropolitan party president. She worked from a Liberal Party office in Willoughby. She was familiar with the entire area, having been a successful real estate agent. Rhondda enjoyed a well-earned reputation for being seriously networked throughout the entire New South Wales division of the Liberal Party. She and her husband, Bruce, had lived in Batlow for more than twenty years, where he had been the mayor when he wasn't growing apples. Rhondda had run a small business. She was a woman who uniquely understood farming life, country people, big city Sydney and politics. With an appointment to see Rhondda, I knew this would be 'make or break'. Don Glover told me she was "a force to be reckoned with". I assembled a package of materials and a brochure introducing myself, newspaper cuttings, testimonials and my beliefs. Rhondda listened to my case, looked at my 'handout' and pushed it back at me. She was not sold. I left somewhat deflated, but determined not to give up. I thought I could still win her over. Two days later she called: "I have thought about it. Let's meet again. I'm going to help you. We need change."

We set up a campaign office of sorts in the front room of my Lindfield home. From very modest beginnings, others joined. I started collecting testimonials from people willing to provide one. Bruce Shepherd was pivotal in gathering up his flock behind me.

Appointed an Australia Day Ambassador, I delivered the address at the Manly festivities. Present was the recently elected Federal Member, Tony Abbott. Our paths would cross many times in the years to come. Later that evening, I stood in silence with Lowitja O'Donoghue, then Chairman of ATSIC. As we watched the Darling Harbour fireworks display, I was conscious of the political fireworks and year that lay ahead. I didn't have to wait long.

A journalist called four days later – was I preparing a preselection challenge against David Connolly? I called a press conference to announce that I would nominate for Liberal Party preselection in Bradfield. If successful, I would do my utmost to effectively represent the people of Bradfield, to ensure they had an effective voice in national affairs and to play a role in shaping the future of the nation. Coincidentally, the Liberal Party leadership came to a head the same day. Alexander Downer, to his eternal credit, stepped down on 30 January 1995 allowing John Howard to seamlessly return to lead the Party. His time had come.

Clearly my announcement was entirely coincidental with the leadership change, but must have irritated the Party professionals who wanted 'clear air'. Instead, when John Howard appeared with Ray Martin on *A Current Affair* that evening, he was asked how he would feel if his son got an earring? In hindsight I regret and am embarrassed by my brash, self-confidence. David Connolly was unsettled by the announcement and imminent challenge, but not unduly worried. From his perspective, he had no real reason to be. It is always good to be underestimated.

I nominated for Bradfield. Many of the delegates were predetermined by virtue of holding office in one of the then 19 Liberal Party branches. Others would come from 'State Council', representing standing bodies within the Party and regions from across the state.

In early February the phone rang at home, interrupting my small campaign committee meeting. The caller introduced himself as "Doug Thompson". He owned several nursing homes, including one in Turramurra. "Dr Nelson, I live in Killara and I see all these people attacking you for wanting to be my member of parliament. But I think you're exactly the kind of person we need here. I would like to help. I don't know much about politics, but I do have money."

"Mr Thompson, I will put you on to Mrs Vanzella." Rhondda was especially skilled in the art of fundraising for her causes, persuading people to part with their money. I was now her highest such priority and she did not like to lose. Poor Doug didn't stand a chance. The rest, as they say, is history. Doug and Bruce funded the preselection campaign. Doug also became my best and most loyal friend.

Some of the most hurtful experiences I have had were in those four months through to May. I had brought it upon myself, so nothing I can complain about. The Bradfield Liberals split into three camps. The first was steadfastly pro-Connolly. They abhorred the notion that a carpet-bagging, former Labor Party member should challenge for the party's 'jewel in the crown'. Among them were several who wanted David to keep the seat warm for them. The second, much smaller group, saw me as an ideal candidate well suited to 'put Bradfield on the map'. The third possessed an open mind and liked the idea of a contest. In all, there were almost 200 preselectors who would gather at the Hornsby RSL club on 13 May 1995 to cast their vote.

At first David Connolly seemed somewhat bemused by the challenge. After all, in his 21 years as the Member, he had no reason to believe he was in trouble. But as I methodically made my way through the names on the list and met them, my initial instincts were confirmed. Many were open to a change but doubted I was the person to do it. One noted that it was not until the odium of Connolly voting for Peacock instead of Howard in 1989, that he finally established an office in the electorate. Others observed that despite many years in parliament he had not achieved higher office. Bruce Shepherd's support played both ways. Most admired him, many didn't.

Gary O'Gorman was a respected North Shore lawyer. A conservative man, he was also a preselector. I called him. "Dr Nelson, we haven't met. But from what I have seen and heard, I don't want anything to do with you. However, if Bruce Shepherd is supporting you, then all I can say is, what can I do to help?"

Everyone was important, but three shifts enabled me to be truly competitive. Denise Reid was a barrister and president of the Turramurra branch. She too was planning a challenge and controlled seven votes. She and her husband decided to withdraw and swing their support behind me. Denise and Ross became lifelong friends.

Les Taylor was a name spoken with reverence in the conservative wing of the Party. He was Chief Legal Counsel at the Commonwealth Bank. Rhondda knew and respected him. She advised me to wait a bit before seeing him. In mid-February, I went up to the marbled top floor of the Bank to see Les. A supremely intelligent, balding man with a twinkle in his eye, he reminded me of Bruce Shepherd. I knew he started at the bank when he was fifteen, filling ink wells in Redfern. Only a gifted and loyal man could rise from there to Chief Counsel. He was also a deeply committed admirer of John Howard. Having exchanged pleasantries, I said, "Mr Taylor, the first thing I need to deal with is my past membership of the Labor party." He stopped me. "Brendan, if you weren't popping champagne corks in 1972, you had no heart. If you weren't raising money to get them out in '74, you had no brains. If Bruce Shepherd supports you, then you've got something going for you. I want to find out what it is." When I left an hour later, he called Rhondda and volunteered for the campaign committee.

Tony Hall served on Ku-ring-gai Council. His wife, Lee, was deeply networked throughout the community and along with their son, Andrew, were preselectors. I had already seen them and been rebuffed. Lee did not tolerate men with earrings! Les Taylor said, "There's three votes there and others they can influence. Lee is the key. Try again but speak to her as a mother." I did and she shifted, along with her family. She too volunteered for the campaign. Meanwhile, David Connolly was hosting small groups to his home for dinner. The highlight was him playing a video of me at the anti-Keating rally in 1993 screaming, "I've never voted Liberal in my life!" At least I was able to provide them with a context when they reported back to me.

Then Andrew Parker arrived at the campaign office. He had been John Hewson's media advisor during the *Fightback!* campaign in 1993. Of the Young Liberals and between jobs, he walked in, greeted Rhondda and announced, "I'm here to help". And he did. On one occasion yelling down the phone to a young preselector, "I don't care what you think. Nelson's our man and you're voting for him!"

Feeling the ructions playing out in his neighbouring seat, Tony Abbott called. "Mate … mate, look … David Connolly's not exactly a world beater but he's also not a bad bloke. My advice to you is to have a look at Cook down in the Sutherland Shire. Don Dobie is the Member and to be frank, the walls of Jericho there are ready to fall down." I didn't know much about it but I said to Tony, "Mate, if I pull out now and shift to Cook, wouldn't I be guilty of being the carpetbagger of which I am accused?" I was politically naïve, but not enough to think that a deeply parochial Sutherland Shire would open its arms to a Tasmanian bounced from the North Shore.

In the midst of all this, months earlier I had accepted an invitation from the National Gallery of Australia to deliver a public lecture on a Saturday night in early March. Pru Evans explained that the Gallery was running a series of six speakers across six weeks to speak about art. I told her I knew nothing about art. She reassured me I could do it. Why not, I thought. I arrived at the National Gallery with a view to sorting out the artworks I would show the audience. Literally a broad canvas, I could choose anything. Not being an art critic, it was my first visit to the Gallery. *The Queen's Pictures* were on display: Vermeer, Rembrandt and the great masters. All very interesting, but less so to me. I turned and asked, "You don't happen to have any art depicting the impact of AIDS?"

Though somewhat startled by the question, Pru said, "Yes, upstairs. We have a special exhibition, *Art in the age of AIDS.*"

Slowly I walked past the powerfully evocative works, charcoals, acrylics, photographic portraits and sculptures. Before the image of a mother holding her severely emaciated, dying son, I wept. I told her I would present a number of these works for my lecture.

Cartoons, colonial works of John Glover, Streeton, Boyd, Indigenous western desert works, war art and AIDS. I spoke to them all and what they meant to me in the packed theatre on a Saturday night – *What I Don't Know About Art.* It was therapeutic, deeply so. It strengthened my resolve to get through what was about to happen.

Philip's Karposi's sarcoma of the lung was worse. By now he was oxygen dependent. I offered to take his much-loved motorbike and insisted on him accepting money for it. The farewell for his FJ1200 was an emotional one for him as I rode off from his home in Waterloo. He would not see it again. He was admitted to RPA the next day. I had never attended the Sydney Gay and Lesbian Mardi Gras, but Philip wanted to see it and invited our mother. She told me that they both enjoyed watching it in each other's company. However, as they slowly walked from Darlinghurst through the crowd, two men passed. One loudly scoffed, "Look, he's got mummy carrying his oxygen." My mother spoke of that cruelty again on her death bed 26 years later.

Another phone call. This time from Stephen Smith. I did not know him. General Secretary of the Western Australian branch of the Labor Party, he said he understood I had a brother, Philip. I confirmed that I did, but sadly, expected he would soon die from a fatal disease. He told me that some potentially embarrassing material had come to him about my brother. It related to his earlier lifestyle that contributed to him contracting HIV. When I asked who had given it to him, he said "It's from your side. But I don't trade in this sort of thing. I want you to know I have destroyed it. As much as I would like to frustrate your political career, this is not me." Shaken by the call, I realised I had just spoken to a man of principle. I also now knew the depths to which some people would sink to stop me. At the time, I told no one other than Rhondda and Bruce. Both knew what I was going though.

Philip was convinced he had to try every treatment he could. He heard that a Gold Coast GP was offering peroxide treatments. I knew it was quackery, but his hope was sustained by the belief that he would find a treatment.

Peter and Norma Beckley were literal stalwarts of the Party. They lived in Warrawee. Peter was a Second World War veteran. Both joined the Liberal Party at its formation, fell in love, married, built a house and raised a family. They listened to me for close to an hour, asked some questions and, then, looked at each other. Norma said, "We may be old, but we are realists." Norma became the most devoted and loyal supporter I could ever have wished. True Liberals.

Nick Greiner's father, Nicholas, hosted a fund-raiser at his Killara home, Sunday lunch in the expansive garden. Naturally I attended, managing to part the audience as Moses did the Red Sea. Bill and Betty Flick were of the pest control dynasty. A hard working, no nonsense, self-made couple whose value system had been the architecture for post war Australia. Betty was the key political player of the two. She told you what she thought. The Flicks arrived as I did. Betty said, "I don't know why you're here causing all this trouble. David Connolly's not going to change the world but at least he has good values. With that earring you would be far better suited to the eastern suburbs!"

Days later, on 15 March 1995, I addressed the National Press Club. I began by acknowledging my brother's 34th birthday. Critically ill, he was watching the broadcast from the Gold Coast hospital. I traversed the breadth of issues on the AMA's agenda from general practice to the public hospital crisis. I also spoke of my opposition to euthanasia and the drivers of youth suicide. I was asked about Australia being a republic. Then, as now, I was of the view that Australia's constitutional arrangements have served us well and saw no need to change.

Betty Flick watched the Press Club address. I was told, against her will, she was impressed by what she saw and heard. The following day she had an appointment to see a surgeon. Unbeknown to Betty, Dr Martin Flood was a close ally of Bruce's and a backer of mine. She asked him about me. Apparently he spent quite some time telling her why she should support me. And she did – to the hilt.

On the Sunday after the Press Club address, I visited Philip in hospital. He said he was proud to be my brother. He handed me a card he had especially chosen and written what would be his last message of guidance and love. He urged me to do "good things for humanity":

> I was very proud the (sic) lovely words you spoke about me publicly (at the National Press Club). I was surprised and overwhelmed with joy.
>
> Thanks for being a wonderful brother in this life. I often reflect on the many wonderful fun times we had during our childhood.

> You have always stuck with me through thick and thin, especially during those difficult teenage years. You have been an inspiration to me with your strong determination, perseverance and huge efforts you make. I am very proud of your lovely family.
>
> I wish you the very best with your career. I envisage you doing great things for humanity. Always remember not to do things just for yourself, but for the highest good of mankind.

A devoted and enthusiastic member of the Voluntary Euthanasia Society, not once approaching death did he raise it. Like so many people for whom I cared, it was the fear of death that drove his support for euthanasia, or 'assisted dying' as it is now called. When the time came, four days later in the presence of my mother and father, he died peacefully. He had been treated superbly well, medically and personally. In this busy public hospital, he was a human being. He was not a gay man dying from AIDS.

I returned from the Gold Coast, reflecting long and hard on my brother's life and death. I read the card several times over.

Back in Sydney, I was despondent, close to giving it away altogether. I phoned Don Glover and told him I had serious doubts about what I was doing and putting my family through. He told me to not do anything rash. He would ring around and take the temperature of the Liberal Party conference. He called the next day and told me we had a real chance and to keep at it. I did, reflecting on what Philip had said to me. Then a stroke of luck.

I was soliciting references in support of my bid. I already had Alan Jones, Kathryn Greiner, Michael Yabsley, Ita Buttrose, Father Greg O'Kelly, St Ignatius Riverview Headmaster, and others on board. Dame Leonie Kramer was the Chancellor of Sydney University. I went to see her to ask for a reference. She readily agreed to provide one, but asked what seat I was seeking to win. I told her it was Bradfield. She asked who the sitting member was. "David Connolly", I said. "David

Connolly? But he's leaving politics." "That's the problem, Dame Leonie – he isn't."

She was adamant that Connolly was leaving. In 1994 she had discussed with the Vice Chancellor the need for the University to appoint a development officer. The recruitment process had resulted in the Vice Chancellor coming back to her weeks later with a candidate. "The Vice Chancellor told me that David Connolly was his recommended choice for the job. He said that although he was still in parliament, he was leaving to take up the position."

I couldn't believe what I was hearing. Here was David Connolly portraying me as a carpetbagger. But at the time of Alexander Downer's leadership, he was planning his exit. Armed with this information, I had a spring in my step. I briefed my inner sanctum. Andrew Parker would know what to do with it, but it would need to be confirmed by another party. We couldn't find one.

John Howard, Peter Costello and a number of shadow ministers attended a function in support of Connolly in late April. When asked my reaction by the press, I said I was flattered by the big gun rollout. "Mr Howard's support reflects his integrity and loyalty to the Party, being prepared to back his sitting members in this way. Given Peter Costello defeated a sitting member for preselection, I assume he has a personal view of these things."

My spirits lifted with a brilliant Nicholson cartoon in *The Australian* newspaper in early May. Startled, conservative Bradfield preselectors, sitting around a table with a portrait of The Queen, were shocked that a plane had crashed through the wall. Across the nose of the plane was *Flying Doctors.* Megaphone in hand wearing a white coat, Bruce Shepherd called, "Dr Nelson will see you now". I was portrayed standing proudly, bouffant hair and doctor's bag in hand confronting the audience. It said it all!

Leading into the final week of the campaign, Doug Thompson had booked the Killara Golf Club and at 320 guests, the largest event held at the Club. The guest speakers were Michael Yabsley of the Party's conservative wing and Kathryn Greiner, champion of the progressive moderates. The eight preselectors who attended were either undecided or soft Connolly supporters. Michael and Kathryn were stunning in their support.

Michael said that as a 2GB radio presenter, he had a list of ten people who were to be put to air should they call in to speak on any issue. I was apparently on that list. A long-standing friend of his had called from Melbourne to tell him to "stop rocking the boat". Michael told him that it wasn't possible to rock the boat in New South Wales as the boat was well and truly sunk. "Brendan Nelson", he said, "does not need the Liberal Party. The Liberal Party needs Brendan Nelson."

Kathryn spoke to our interactions across a range of social and health issues. "Brendan", she said, "is as comfortable sitting under a tree talking to Aboriginal people in remote Australia as he is in any corporate boardroom." At night's end, the atmosphere was one of excitement for our cause. It was a turning point, but Rhondda and Les Taylor believed we were still two or three votes short.

Three days before the Saturday preselection, I asked Andrew Parker if we could do anything with the information from Dame Leonie Kramer about David Connolly's job at Sydney University. He gave it to *The Australian* newspaper. Nothing appeared on Friday. Andrew said they couldn't get anyone at the University to confirm the story. The night before the ballot, I joined Tony Abbott at the Manly RSL in a public debate in support of a constitutional monarchy.

The day had arrived, 13 May 1995. My phone rang just after six o'clock. It was Rhondda. "Maaaaate!!! You have to see the front page of *The Australian*. The Connolly story is right across it". To ensure the story was appreciated by preselectors, my supporters dropped 200 copies to the Hornsby RSL, at the entrance to the auditorium.

I called Andrew Parker to thank him. But why, after three days had they finally printed the story we had been sitting on for two months? The journalist had not been able to confirm the story, so in a final attempt, called David Connolly on Friday afternoon and put it to him. Remarkably, he confirmed the story was true. Further, in the middle of the story was this quote, "Of course I was thinking about my own future. Any sane person would." So, there it was. In late 1994, when Alexander Downer was plummeting in the polls and the Liberal Party ship was sinking, David Connolly had been securing himself a life-boat. In contrast, I was trying to get on board to help. So much for 'carpetbagger', I thought.

At the RSL that morning, two Young Liberal supporters of Connolly read the story and left in disgust. They wouldn't vote for him, but they wouldn't vote for me.

The president of the NSW Division of the Liberal Party through all of this was Bill Heffernan. A Junee farmer, wily, smart, husband, father and raconteur, Bill was a man to whom I had taken a strong liking. He had no time for game players and dealt with trouble makers the way he knackered sheep. From the moment I arrived in NSW and met Bill, he 'got it'. He knew there had to be change; after all, the Party held only eight seats in the State. He could see in my candidacy a future for the Party and a person who could help beyond the boundaries of Bradfield. "When Bruce Shepherd rang, I just grabbed the fire bell and went for it". Bill chaired the meeting.

The format was an eight-minute speech from each candidate followed by 12 minutes of questions while the other candidate was out of the room. David Connolly went first.

It was reported that he spoke without notes to his experience, important role on the Opposition front bench where he was shadow minister for retirement incomes, and the need for stability. His first question related to the story published that day in which he was reportedly looking for a career outside of politics less than a year earlier. He tied himself up in knots trying to explain it, especially given his quote about him thinking of his own future. Les Taylor told me he was tapped on the shoulder by a man sitting behind him. He asked if he could have Les's copy of *The Australian.* Minutes later he passed it back, muttering that was it, he was voting for Nelson.

Nervous, I had written a speech and stuck to it. I spoke to the Party's philosophical foundations and future. I canvassed wealth creation, tax and industrial relations reform, health, aged care, a national agenda for youth, reform to programmes for Aboriginal people and respect for national institutions and symbols.

Bill Heffernan gave the first question to Andrew Parker. He asked about my Labor Party background. I told the audience that the past four months of my life would have been much easier if my father had bumped into Sir Robert Menzies when I was a boy and put me into the Young Liberals. Instead, I had come to my belief in the Liberal Party philosophy, not through parental indoctrination, but life itself.

John Gatfield, a Connolly backer, asked how the Party could justify choosing someone like me who had campaigned so forcefully against universal Medicare bulk billing. I reminded the audience that the entire Party had taken that policy to the 1993 election. Everyone in the room, including the questioner, had worked – as I had – for it to be so implemented. "Sometimes you are faced with a choice between what is right and what is popular. You have to do what is right." The room burst into applause.

Another asked, if given the choice of putting the Liberal Party or Australia first, which would I choose? I said, "I will always put the nation's interests above all else." More questions of a similar vein. Surprisingly, they were all in my areas of strength. As my instincts had told me, people here were concerned for the future of the country.

The votes were counted. Bill Heffernan thanked everyone. "Brendan Nelson 96 votes, David Connolly 93".

Multiple emotions ran through me. My life would now change again. An immense privilege had been bestowed upon me, yet I felt sympathy for David and his wife, Monique. The gravity of what had just occurred settled slowly upon both me and Connolly. Don Glover, Rhondda Vanzella, Bruce Shepherd, Doug Thompson, Les Taylor, Denise Reid, Lee Hall and other courageous people had allowed me to stand on their shoulders. I would do my utmost to honour their faith in me.

The media predictably portrayed the result as a snub for John Howard. Arrant nonsense. Had John Howard got on the phones he would have ensured a Connolly victory. He didn't. Les Taylor spoke to Howard days before the ballot, advising him to stay out of it. John Howard's representative on the preselection panel was Tony Abbott. The scrutineer who collected the ballot papers from the 'top table' told me how Tony had voted. He voted for me.

Nicholson provided another brilliant portrayal of it in *The Australian.* With the ALP Armada in the distance, a fully armed 18th century gunship, *Bradfield,* prepares for me to board. A young sailor salutes, "Your ship is ready Lord Nelson." An effigy of David Connolly floats face down in the water, suitcase floating beside him.

I thought it best to get out into the electorate, thinking it might be as divided over my preselection as the Liberal Party itself. Armed with electioneering materials, I headed straight into the heartland, door knocking. Karranga Avenue, Killara, seemed the heart of heartland.

I walked up the driveway to a magnificent home. A man answered the door, looked at me and said, "You're Brendan Nelson". I confirmed that was the case. "Mate, when did Captain Cook get here?" "1770, sir".

He rounded on me. "Well, our family started voting Liberal or the equivalent thereof, not long after. Don't waste your time knocking on doors around here." Reassured, I turned to leave when he came back at me, "You know, we had the two worst prime ministers in succession – Whitlam for stuffing up the country, and Fraser for not fixing it!" I acknowledged the observation, filed it away and soon learned it was a view widely held in Liberal circles at the time.

Several years later, I boarded a plane in Melbourne. I was sitting next to the great man, Gough Whitlam. After pleasantries, I related to him the door knocking exchange in Killara. Without missing a beat, Gough quipped, "Bit tough on Fraser!"

At the AMA's national conference two weeks later, with some emotion, I handed the chains of office over to David Weedon. At the dinner that night, I was presented with the AMA's highest honour, The Gold Medal. Unworthy as I felt to be in the company of Kevin Fagan, I accepted it for all those members of the profession who did so much more every single day for the benefit of humankind.

It was only when I finished leading the AMA that I appreciated just how demanding it had been of my time and intellectual and emotional energy; but also, the sacrifices made by my young family and financial cost it had exacted. One reason why its leaders had traditionally been much older, at the latter end of their careers, is they had built financial security. I had not, then compounded it by moving to the most expensive city in the country. It has never been about money. I had crossed that bridge long ago. I was proud of my profession and to have led it

While building the campaign team for the forthcoming election, my professional life continued. The Royal Australasian College of Physicians invited me back to its annual ceremony and convocation in June. On this occasion I was to be conferred with an Honorary Fellowship of the College for my contribution to public health. When the letter arrived from its president informing me, I had to read it three times.

The Arthur E. Mills orator in 1995 was the recently retired Governor General, The Honourable Bill Hayden AC. He spoke of his support for euthanasia. In my academic gown on the stage of the Gold Coast Arts Centre, I listened carefully. It focused on his rights as an individual, of the inhumanity of allowing people to suffer needlessly. He painted a picture of an elderly, frail Bill Hayden in a nursing home having the 'right' to be assisted to end his life if he so chose.

I had convened a national conference on euthanasia the year before. To it were invited a range of people with different perspectives. Though I had tended to opposing euthanasia, I approached it with an open mind. By the time I heard Bill Hayden, I was settled in my opposition to it. Casting back to the forum, I remembered an elderly man standing in the audience and shouting, "What are you doing about euthanasia? The old people of Australia don't know how they're going to survive without it!"

Euthanasia is popular. It is up there with capital punishment and tax cuts. Of course, it is. When people are polled in daily life, a caller asks if they think someone suffering with a terminal illness should be allowed to be helped to die. Unsurprisingly, most people agree with the proposition. People should have rights – like Mr Hayden – over their own death and, of course, no one should suffer. Death is coming to us all. But it is a largely hypothetical experience. These days few people go intimately through a death. Even fewer see a dead body. Popular language describes people as having 'passed'. We don't even describe them as having 'died'. Whereas in my medical youth, heroics were judiciously applied to the elderly and frail, now everything is expected by families and society. Instead of people dying in general wards, families often demand an ICU bed. Increasingly, by our behaviours at an individual level, we seek to deny death. Yet a wave of euthanasia legislation has all but passed through state parliaments.

Withdrawing treatment is not euthanasia. It is plain commonsense, based on the condition of the patient, prognosis and informed by discussion with family and loved ones. Doctors often fail in not knowing when to stop treatment, more than knowing when to start. Giving a treatment to a patient, the intention of which is to alleviate pain and suffering which contributes to death, is not euthanasia.

Euthanasia is the act of providing a treatment, the specific intention of which is to procure death.

Decision making in this area is like dusk – it's hard to know if it is day or night. Any doctor that says he or she has not given a treatment to a patient that has contributed partly or substantially to death, is either lying or hasn't treated many people. Rarely, there are circumstances in which assisting a person to die may be the right thing to do. It does occur. The doctor and nursing staff work within a legal framework of it being against the law. In exceptional circumstances they may be required to explain themselves before the law which almost invariably finds an act of compassion. I regard this as preferable to trying to define in law the specific circumstances in which one human being is allowed to intentionally end the life of another.

Not every aspect of human interaction can be governed by laws. There are multiple issues at play. Vulnerable people can be manipulated with surprising ease. Doctors are in a powerful position, as evidenced by the orthopaedic surgeon who told me, "I can talk a patient into anything". In some cases, doctors do just that. Adding euthanasia to the list of lawful interventions, irrespective of the safeguards, is fraught with risk.

Doctors can also get it wrong. Have you ever met someone told three years ago by three doctors, all experts in their field, that they had three months to live? Adelaide rheumatologist, Dr Mark Awerbuch, was told just that in 2014 when diagnosed with severe leukemia. All three advised him to "get his affairs in order and go into palliative care". Instead, he didn't give up, found treatment and lived.

We all know cases in which we might champion capital punishment. Notwithstanding its popularity in polls, we don't sanction it. And we don't because we know the legal system can get it wrong. We are not prepared to countenance one innocent death, regarding it too high a price for allowing the execution of others.

Relatives are not always well motivated. Most are, some are not. I have seen clear manipulations of sick, elderly relatives suggesting everything from the early sale of the family home to changing of Wills. If Mr Hayden in his hypothetical nursing home decides he has a 'right' to have his life ended, make no mistake how some relatives will react. One person exercising his/her right in one circumstance can be used to pressure another to 'do the right thing'. As increased user pays contributions necessarily feature in residential aged care funding, some relatives will view it as an erosion of their inheritance. Many of the cases presented as evidence in support of euthanasia, of intractable and prolonged suffering, are in fact cases of poor medical management, absent professional palliative care. Frequently we hear people say, "I watched my mother die in a terrible way. No one should have to go through that."

I ask, for whom is such legislation intended, the dying person or those who cannot deal with it?

There is such a thing as a 'good death'. I have been privileged to be a part of many. Well handled, medically and emotionally, I have seen people emerge from the experience of death having had a spiritual victory. Many everyday people have their own humanity enriched by experiencing the 'good' death of someone they love.

The leading cause of death in Australia from 16 to 40 years of age is suicide. Every one of those deaths is a tragedy, none more so than that of young people. I have yet to hear anyone think that death by suicide is a legitimate solution to unbearable suffering. We do everything we possibly can to prevent such deaths. Over my lifetime, as we reduced the toll taken by disease and accident, we have failed to diminish that exacted by despair. In legislating for euthanasia, we are saying in one circumstance death is a legitimate solution to unbearable suffering, but not in another. The risk of this inconsistency is considerable, legitimising death among some deeply troubled young people. Not all suffering is physical.

As sophisticated as it may seem, society is fragile. A confluence of events can change us in ways not immediately understood. In this, history offers sobering lessons. I told Mr Hayden I did not agree with him.

The global charity, World Vision, was enlisting people who might be champions for the cause. Australia's CEO, Glenda Ormond, asked me if I would visit projects in Africa. In July, I travelled to Kenya with Ita Buttrose. A close friend of Bruce Shepherd's, Ita had supported me in my bid for Bradfield. I respected and liked her. I sponsored a child through World Vision. Like many charities, I sent money believing it would do someone some good somewhere.

Ita and I were largely silent as we went through the slums of Nairobi. The armed guard accompanying us spoke to the inherent danger to strangers, especially white ones. This was a city, a shantytown reeking of destitution, the struggle to survive and daring to dream of a better world. Amid all this people were welcoming, curious and generous. In mid-1995, they had little to inform them of the world from which we had come. But they trusted World Vision.

When I walked into the rudimentary health service, a large sign hung over the desk, "*You will not be seen until you pay*". I asked the African nurse administering the clinic why people should pay in the midst of a slum. Surely, they cannot afford to pay? "Everyone has a little bit of money. They work very hard for it. If they don't pay they don't appreciate what we do for them. We also need money to run the centre". What a contrast. Back in affluent Australia, a doctor displaying such a sign would be subjected to public humiliation.

We found a similar story at a tiny 'school'. An area of bare dirt, surrounded by chicken wire containing a shed with some chairs, stools and two large tables. About forty kids each day were taught by a single teacher who came in and out of the slum. Parents paid US$400 a year for their kids to attend the school. Again, the logic was that when people pay, they value what is being provided. The children we sponsor were so supported in this and similar programmes. Rather than the individual child's family receiving the money donated, it supports these and other initiatives in the village within which the child lives. In villages outside Nairobi, I saw small schools offering education to girls, liberating them from a patriarchal society and offering a future. Smiling, polite, happy girls.

Before leaving Nairobi, we visited Karen Blixen's house, now a museum. Her book *Out of Africa* was dramatised in one of my favourite films of the same name. The home was beautifully maintained, as was the garden and the sweeping fields behind it where once the failed coffee plantation had been. A lingering, special experience.

We travelled in a small convoy of four-wheel drive vehicles down to the Tanzania border. I sat in the front seat of the lead vehicle. Several kilometres from the border, the driver warned me of what lay ahead. "When we get to the border, a guard will come to us wanting passports. I will hand them to him. He will return to his office, come back and give them to us stamped. There will be lots of Maasai beggars there. Whatever happens, do not under any circumstances look at them or say anything. If you do, it will be impossible to move on."

We approached the border: a towering wire fence with central gates over the road and possibly 50 Massai, all wearing what appeared to be traditional dress. They were jumping up and down as if on pogo sticks. As instructed, I turned my gaze away from them as we stopped, a uniformed guard emerging from an office block. He came to the driver's side. Through the half-opened driver's window, he looked at us both, collected the passports and satisfied himself we were legitimate.

After five minutes he reappeared. He handed the driver his passport, then came to my side. As he did, the mob of Massai followed him. I opened the window about 10 centimetres. Massai lunged at the space, one especially loud in his native language as he pushed a colourful, hand painted doll at me. By reflex, I said "Na mate." He shot back, "That Keating, he's a bastard!"

I turned to the driver, "That's worth five bucks and I'm giving it to him." I chuckled to myself long after we passed, admiring the astonishing skill of these beggars. By mid-1995, more than a few Australians agreed with the sentiment.

As in Kenya, the architecture, buildings and infrastructure left by the British was in a state of decline. Sad to see once beautiful buildings crumbling, cracked and discoloured. But I also thought of who had actually built them and the price paid.

In the Arusha region, we stood before the foundation stone of a hospital. Funded from a bequest, it had been laid in 1926. Like many buildings, it needed maintenance and repair. The medical and nursing staff were under immense pressures, but thankful for our interest. They thought I must be a very important man. I assured them I most certainly wasn't, but Ms. Buttrose was. Millions of Australians listened to her. This one hospital served 1.6 million people. Its 350 beds had a 120 per cent occupancy rate. When I asked how that could be, I was told I would soon see. Just 11 doctors looked after 420 inpatients.

The surgical ward was overflowing, literally. Patients were, in some cases 'top and tailed', two to a bed. Others were on mattresses between the beds. Many were being cared for not by nurses, but relatives. One man had undergone a craniotomy. His son was replacing his nasogastric feeding tube. The maternity ward was no different, except for all the patients being women. Though the maternal death rate here was 119 per 100,000 births, it was half Tanzania's then national average.

One memory I carry is that of the disposable gloves hanging on the clothes line to dry. Used, they had been hung to dry for use again, and again after that. So too the syringes and needles would be washed for reuse. No high-pressure autoclave here, just soap and water.

At the time, a quarter of the Tanzanian population was HIV positive. I tried to hide my emotions from our guide.

We visited a small village at the base of Mount Kilimanjaro. As always, people had nothing. Yet they would give us what little they had. Ita and I sat eating a small bowl of goat stew together. The following day I learned how a single cow can change an entire family's life. A smiling man explained how World Vision had lent him money to buy a cow. It supported a family of five. He was now 'rich' enough to afford a bottle of Coca Cola which he insisted we all drink.

I came away in the knowledge that if we become a people who no longer cares about the world, we would abandon our own humanity. The 17th century Prussian philosopher, Immanuel Kant put it best:

> Every human being is an end unto himself, and not a means to be used by others.
>
> Respect for one's own humanity will be found in respect for the humanity of others – and morality is freedom.
>
> In the end, doing the right thing will give us freedom, in every sense of the word.

Back in Sydney and on the campaign trail, Michael Yabsley thought he was doing me a favour: a big fund-raiser at the then ANA hotel in 'The Rocks'. John Howard and Peter Costello were the star attractions. A large crowd of Liberal Party donors, parliamentarians and doyens of the Party were gathering in the midst of growing momentum for our cause. Michael asked me to be the emcee. Naively, I accepted.

Just back from Africa, I had been working all day in The Rocks practice. Late in the day, I pulled my dinner suit from the back of my Kombi and changed at the surgery. I entered the darkened ball room early. I had never been to a Liberal Party fundraising dinner like this and I was the emcee. Michael was the NSW Liberal Party's fund-raiser. I received the run sheet and had prepared introductory notes for John Howard and Peter Costello. Although I had quite a bit of experience in public speaking, I had none in being an emcee. Couldn't be that hard, or so I thought.

At the end of the first segment, I apologised to the audience for not imparting much humour. When I returned to my table which included Bruce and Jenny Shepherd, Kamahl and social commentator, Hugh Mackay, I was nervous. But so far so good. Mike Lynsky was a seasoned journalist who worked for the Hollows Foundation. Mike passed me a card with a joke written on its back. Smutty humour relating to British actor, Hugh Grant.

Anyone that knows me will attest that I am not someone who tells jokes or 'have you heard the one about …' But I looked at the card and remembered reading it in one of the broadsheets a week earlier. I thought on that basis and that Mike Lynsky had passed me the card, it must be okay. When next up, I told the joke. A mixed response. I followed up with a humorous anecdote of a young male patient which I had related the day before at a charity lunch which had been received with raucous approval. This night though, quite the opposite.

When I got back to my table, my friends knew I had just 'blown myself up'. I also discovered that it was not Mike Lynsky offering the joke, he had merely passed the card from Bruce to me. My heart sank. Bruce's sense of humour was not mine. The media response was quick, vicious and understandable. There were calls for me to be disendorsed. Bill Heffernan strongly defended me in the public arena and within the Party, rebutting calls for me to lose my endorsement. I was very low.

Two days later, I was interviewed by Andrew Olle on his Sydney ABC radio programme. He was sympathetic to me, for which I am eternally grateful. Tragically, it would also be his last show. He was diagnosed with the brain tumour that would end his remarkable life just five months later.

Among those unleashed was a Bradfield resident in St Ives. Maurice Sargant was like many who wrote to John Howard on 20 July 1995:

> As a Liberal Party supporter of long standing, I am writing to express my objections in the strongest possible terms to the preselection of Dr Brendan Nelson ... His questionable political record and social behaviour identify him as totally unrepresentative of Liberal voters in this area ... I could never bring myself to vote for this man and I know my views are shared by many others ... for goodness sake find us a more worthy candidate, someone we can identify with and trust.

I rang Mr Sargant. He was incredulous that I was calling. I asked if I could come and explain myself. After some thought, he agreed, asking if he could invite his neighbours and friends. He warned it may be unpleasant. I thanked him the opportunity for me to attend a public stoning. Following my visit, Mr Sargant wrote:

> Many thanks for calling. With my neighbours ... I thought you handled a sensitive situation extremely well. I was impressed, as indeed were they, by your energy, enthusiasm and what you had to say. As for the reservations expressed in my earlier letter; I can only add that I am not a stranger myself to errors of judgement.
>
> I believe you to have a great deal to offer Bradfield and, more importantly, to the Liberal Party of Australia. You have won my support and I will work to persuade others of your worthiness to represent us.

The Bradfield campaign committee was in full swing, but one issue took over an hour to resolve – my earring. Candidates have an introductory brochure. The dilemma was to be photographed with the earring visible or not. In the end, I said that if it wasn't visible, people would think I was hiding it. We went with the diamond earring in the left ear!

Getting voters to send anything back to candidates is not an easy task. In 1995, pre-email, they had to get an envelope, buy a stamp and find a letterbox. Over 900 did just that. A flood of brochures returned to the campaign office. Some had the ear cut from the image, others circled the ear, "What's this?" or, "I'm not voting for a guy with an earring!" Other comments can't be printed. The most memorable advocacy on the issue was just before polling day. Five ladies came to see me. Well dressed, stern faced, all declined a cup of tea. This must be serious. All five sat across from me on the other side of the table. They had an appointed spokeswoman.

"Dr Nelson, we'll get straight to the point. You have an earring". "Yes". "We believe you are a homosexual", she asserted with confident distaste. Struggling to find the words, "Madam, I am not a homosexual. Was I to openly be so, I suspect I would not be here speaking to you in this capacity. I am married and have children. Rest assured, I am not a homosexual". At this point she leaned forward, banged her fist on the table and demanded, "Yes, but can you prove it?"

The awkward silence was broken when one started to giggle. Seizing the moment, I said, "While I understand your desire for proof, there are some challenges in public life to which I will not rise." Tensions defused, they accepted a cup of tea and went on to detail the manifest failings of the Keating Government.

In that period leading to the 1996 election, the mood for change was palpable. It was everywhere. Anyone to whom you spoke, every time you turned on a television, radio or opened a newspaper – change was what the nation wanted. There were two galvanising issues. John Howard was the answer to both.

The first was Paul Keating. Though having his core of electoral supporters, he represented much of what Australians did not like. Mr Keating was regarded as disconnected from the mainstream, both the people and the issues of primary concern to them. He was perceived as being 'above' the day to day concerns of middle, working Australians. His interests appeared to be Australia's place in Asia, the Republic, arts, Indigenous rights and a myriad of issues of interest to 'elites'. Keating had narrowly won 'the sweetest victory of all' in 1993 against John Hewson. He had done so where a change of government had been a certainty. But he had broken faith with the people who had returned him. The 'L.A.W' tax cuts had not been delivered, unemployment – and youth unemployment especially – remained unacceptably high. Business was crippled by red tape as a series of 'make-work' schemes were paraded at great expense to an electorate angry at the state of the nation and the government's inability to fix it. By 1995, a Morgan Poll found confidence in politicians at an all-time low. Cynicism and disillusionment.

The Anglican Archbishop of Sydney, the Most Reverend Harry Goodhew, spoke for much of the nation when he pleaded with politicians "to lead us". "Do not be blind guides", he said. "Represent our highest aspirations as a people. Give the lead and we will respect and support you." He was rebuked by a shrill media choir – churches should stay out of politics. I wondered why genuine moral discourse and discernment should be regarded as out of place in the media's coverage of political debate.

While all this was going on, Paul Keating cut back his parliamentary question time appearances to twice a week. He regularly argued the case for a Republic and took to having the Australian Flag folded so as to conceal the Union Jack. One incident said it all. Timber workers had ringed a protest around Parliament House. As Mr Keating passed, he quipped to the security cordon, "Get those blokes back." A Labor prime minister not only refused to engage his traditional constituency, he was insulting them.

The second key issue was the economy. Australia was still reeling from the balance of payments crisis less than a decade earlier and the crippling use of monetary policy to address it. Home mortgage interest rates had peaked at 18 per cent and business overdrafts at 22 per cent. Unemployment was still painfully slow in coming back off its peak of 11.5 per cent. And all of this was after more than a decade of 'The Accord' – the compact between the ACTU and government for real wage restraint in return for social dividends such as Medicare and family benefits payments. Workers endured all this in a high inflation environment and were not happy. Through all of this, the Keating Government had been accumulating debt. People were worried. They knew the debt was not being used to fund nation building, but instead was feeding recurrent expenditure on pensions, unemployment benefits and welfare.

The Liberal Party's campaign slogan summed it up: *For all of us.*

The foundation for a certain coalition victory had been laid with the transition to John Howard. He had been around a long time, a known and respected entity – even for those who did not like him. He was everything Paul Keating wasn't. He had shown a life-long commitment to the issues that really worried the nation – economic management, small business and reining in union excesses. The Liberal Party's platform for the 1996 election fell on fertile political soil.

It was important to offer policy solutions to real problems but in campaigning, to 'stay out of the way'. The electorate wanted Paul Keating gone and there was no point getting between their anger and the object of it. Nonetheless, knowing what you're against isn't the same as getting what you want. We had to give them a sense of what they would 'get' to build on John Howard's year of philosophical scene setting. John Howard would seek to return Trust, Integrity and Commitment to the leadership of the nation. His would be a prime ministership of substance, not style. His suits Anthony Squires, not Zegna.

Policy was released closer to the 2 March election to allow the electorate to focus not on the opposition, but the government. A debt truck was driven around the country promoting the fact that debt had grown under Labor to $180 billion. Helpfully, it broke down attempting to get up into the marginal seat of Macquarie in the Blue Mountains, drawing attention to a central campaign theme. Its young driver, Simon Berger, would become a big part of my life.

The economy headlined almost anything after trust and integrity on the coalition side. Debt, interest rates, unemployment and inflation were hammered home relentlessly.

The election was not to be won in Bradfield but in the outer suburbs and regions. In marginal seats, the electorate was engaged in the broader economic and cultural debate. Traditional Labor voters saw very little recognisable in the Labor Government before them seeking re-election. John Howard was familiar to them. He reinforced what he would not do – especially having strongly backed John Hewson's radical manifesto, *Fightback!*

Medicare was sacrosanct. Howard would not touch it. And of course, there would "never ever be a GST"! Both issues were touchstones of deep scepticism toward the Liberal Party in many parts of the country. If Howard said he wouldn't do it, they were prepared to believe him. A Howard Government would consolidate the country's finances. It would rein in spending and abolish wasteful, pointless programmes that had young people off the couch for a few weeks and then back on it after a training course.

The Coalition wanted to get business moving. Cut business regulation, exempt small businesses from Unfair Dismissal provisions and increase labour market flexibility with Australian Workplace Agreements (AWAs). An essential commitment though – no one could be worse off. One area of increasing concern to Australians was the environment. We would establish a Natural Heritage Trust which would fund a range of practical environmental initiatives. It would be funded by the sale of one third of Telstra. The carrier's long overdue privatisation could begin with all the proceeds – more than $1 billion, invested in the protection of the environment. Most Australians signed on for it.

John Howard's other lifelong policy passion received a lot of attention – families. Middle Australia sensed that the Keating Government was concerned not for them and their daily struggles, but with minority issues. Practising medicine in western Sydney through 1995 I found many thought the 'rewards' were not for working hard and raising a family, but instead for those seeking or benefiting from government largesse. John Howard announced there would be an increase in the tax-free threshold for families raising children on a single income.

The announcement had a double effect. Hundreds of thousands of families would directly benefit, but there was a wider sense that a coalition government would turn its attention to what John Howard referred to as 'the mainstream'. It was far from plain sailing though.

Pauline Hanson was the Liberal candidate for Oxley. The owner of a fish and chip shop preselected by the Liberal Party for a safe Labor seat. She wrote to the local paper in Ipswich bemoaning the 'special' treatment afforded Aboriginal Australians, foreign aid and Asian immigration. Free Trade, in Mrs. Hanson's view, was destroying jobs and the United Nations had too much money and power.

The Liberal Party under the direction of John Howard disendorsed her immediately, but she was already on the ballot paper. She was elected. That letter opened up a dialogue about issues troubling swathes of Australia. Paul Keating paid the price for it during the 1996 campaign, John Howard and Tim Fischer in 1998.

I learned a great deal during the 1996 campaign.

A vision and a credible plan for the nation are both important. Grand ideas and ideals are well and good but there must be practical measures to which people can relate. There must be a relevant local application of national policies to benefit local communities. Gough Whitlam offered a captivating vision of Australia to the voters in 1972 but had no plan to competently execute it. John Hewson revealed a 760-page detailed plan for the nation in 1993, but was incapable of articulating an inspiring vision for the Australia to which it would give effect.

Candidates need as much as possible to be of the community, champions of the people whom they seek to represent, more important than being representatives of their party or government. Warren Entsch, Jo Gash, Bob Baldwin, Gary Nairn, Danna Vale, Trish Draper,

Kay Elson, Jim Lloyd – all outstanding candidates. They and others would save the government in 1998.

The party had a well-developed plan for the campaign. Each day was carefully planned in advance. Policy was strategically held until its planned release. Every candidate needed to stay on message and to not think he or she knows better than the campaign director – discipline.

At times, what is popular in marginal seats can be the object of criticism in safer seats. I learned that a critical remark made of a policy to your own local media can have national ramifications. Although not guilty of it myself, some candidates would ingratiate themselves to their own electorate, criticising a particular policy only to find candidates elsewhere and the party leadership severely embarrassed.

I learned the importance of repetition.

The media landscape in 1996 was vastly different from today. It was still 'traditional' media, letter boxing, public meetings, debates, corflute advertising, electronic advertising and so on. But even after saturation exposure of people to facts, policies and the failings of our opponents, many voters remained ignorant of even the basics.

The truism is true. When you're sick of saying it, they are starting to hear it.

I was asked by other candidates to visit their electorates and support their own campaigning and fundraising. There would be much more of this in the years to come.

I rang my father days before the 1996 election. I expected he would do what he had done all of his life, and vote Labor. Instead, he said, "Son, I never thought I would say this, but I am voting for John Howard on Saturday. Keating, Brereton – these people don't represent anything I ever stood for." His conversion spoke to a larger movement.

The 1996 election campaign was different in hindsight from all the others faced in 1998, 2001, 2004 and 2007 by the Howard-led team. It was the only one we really felt confident about winning. The closest to it was 2004 after John Howard got Mark Latham's 'line and length'.

10

The right thing to do

Victory was convincing in 1996, the coalition winning 94 seats to Labor's 49. I came into a large back bench. So large was it that for some months I seriously contemplated the wisdom of what I had done. I had left medicine, having also led the Australian Medical Association, to be 'just a backbencher'. I soon appreciated the selfishness of such thoughts. Others had given and endured much more in their journey to the parliament, their tenure fragile and short.

John Howard's long-standing friend, Alan Cadman, was the Member for Mitchell. He was also close to David Connolly. Chief Government whip, Alan was unimpressed that his friend had been deposed by an earring wearing interloper from Tasmania. My punishment was to be seated at the back of the parliament, so far back was I that interjections had to be passed on to be heard. Mind you, Joe Hockey had been allocated a broom cupboard until an office was available. In Joe's case, his sin was to be a player in the 'moderate' faction of the New South Wales Division of the Liberal Party.

Joe and I teamed up with another, now life-long, friend, Bob Baldwin. We rented an apartment in Canberra for parliamentary sittings until Joe's wife, Melissa, bought a house in 1997. When I decided to move into the garage Ross Cameron moved into the house, joining the Member for Deakin, Phil Barresi. There would be lots of Sorority House stories to tell as the years passed.

In the parliament, I found myself seated next to a burley, rugged, larger than life crocodile farmer from Queensland. Warren Entsch also had an earring. He left school at fourteen to clean toilets. After a decade as a RAAF fitter, he drove trucks, worked in nightclubs, sold real estate, caught bulls and cleared scrub. Finally, in his early forties, to use his own words, he'd "had a bloody gutful" and ran for the far north Queensland seat of Leichardt. Alan Cadman thought we would have nothing in common, the doctor from Sydney's upper north shore surely detesting a rough and ready far north Queenslander. Big mistake. We hit it off immediately.

'Entschy' told me about his campaign. John and Janette Howard attended a big fundraiser at the Cairns International Hotel. Entschy bought a suit on special – white linen. "Nervous as hell", he said, standing out the front with hundreds of people seated inside waiting for John and Janette to arrive. Warren has the habit when he's nervous of jiggling the coins in his pocket. He described standing in his white suit, media everywhere but had forgotten he was wearing red underpants. These were visible through his trousers, further accentuated by his failure to zip up his fly. "Mate, I sure had an impact on 'em all!"

The Government Executive was shocked when it was revealed that the budget position was much worse than advised prior to the election. The deficit was $10 billion. The first budget would be much harsher than envisaged from opposition.

The first meeting of the swollen party room heard that sitting hours were to be extended until 11 pm. John Howard told us he didn't want members to 'be at a loose end'. The government's priority would be work. We were encouraged to join government and parliamentary committees. Marginal seat holders were to spend a lot of time 'watering the garden' in their electorates. All were advised by Howard to speak to loved ones at home "twice a day".

The issue that defined the new government and, in the longer term, John Howard himself, was born of tragedy. Only weeks after winning office the massacre at Port Arthur took place. John Howard's response to it was stunning, having an impact well beyond the event itself.

Gun control was an 'easy' issue for people like me, representing a relatively affluent inner suburban electorate. But for about a third of our party room and for all of the National Party, it was the source of severe political pain. The first party room meeting after the massacre would be interesting to say the least. David Hawker was the Member for Wannon representing some of the finest rural areas of Victoria. A thoroughly decent man, who would later go on to be speaker, he was apoplectic about mooted restrictions on semi-automatic weapons. So determined was he to educate the rest of us about guns, he (lawfully) brought one to Parliament House in an effort to prevent an 'over reaction'.

John Howard stood before a very tense party room:

> What I am about to say to you is contrary to everything I have ever believed.
>
> We are going to have to pass laws to control the lives of many people who have never done anything wrong – and who never will.
>
> We are going to have to tell the states what to do, and if they don't we will have to find ways to get around them.
>
> But in my twenty-three years in public life, I have never been more convinced that this is the right thing to do.

And it was.

Many both in the party room and in the wider community, who did not necessarily like John Howard from his response to that issue, respected him. He manifested courage – moral, political and physical. It framed the backbench attitude to him in the most positive way for the remainder of 1996 and beyond. Political courage means standing up to your 'base', your own supporters. This was an exemplar of it. He had proven under extreme pressure to be a leader who would 'do the right thing'.

For MPs who are loyal party members, there are only two occasions in your parliamentary career when you can say what you really think without interruption. Your first, 'maiden' speech and, if you're lucky to give one, your valedictory speech. Whatever may be said of my speeches over 35 years, they were all mine. Not one was written by anyone else. Loyal staff and departmental officers provided me with research and material, but I constructed and delivered what I wanted to say. As a minister, I would always ask the department for a speech which I would read but not use. I was interested to know what they thought I should say, occasionally finding points I wanted to make. But it seemed to me I was elected to offer my own thoughts and ideas, not those of a staff member or public servant.

I thought a lot about my first speech, which I delivered from some hand-written notes. It is the opportunity to present to the parliament who you are, what drives you and the issues that will frame your service to the nation on behalf of your electorate. Most put a fair bit of effort to it, inviting family, friends and supporters to be present when delivered. There are others. One colleague had a staff member write his.

Shortly before I received the Speaker's call, John Howard walked into the chamber. He tried to get to as many first speeches as possible. He knew what it meant to newly elected MPs and their supporters. It was a good way to get a 'feel' for the men and women who had put him into the Lodge and upon whose support he would rely to stay there. I spoke to my journey and motives for seeking to represent the people of Bradfield, paying tribute to those who had made it possible.

Two mistakes were made in the period from election to the budget. In his determination to lift standards, John Howard set a very high bar on ministerial standards. So high, an endless stream of ministers resigned over what were largely trivial matters. Tasmanian Senator, Brian Gibson, was assistant treasurer and had a number of undeclared ANZ shares. A man of impeccable integrity and intellect was gone. The other problem was John Howard's reference to 'core' and 'non-core' promises. The nuance was of course lost. Commitments given pre-election were done so on the basis of what proved to a seriously misleading understanding of the budget position. But the damage was done.

Prior to the budget, John Howard walked six marginal seat holders through its key elements. We learned this after budget night. He was committed to it being regarded as a tough but fair budget, broadly consistent with promises and public expectations. And it was.

Every single area of government spending was targeted and, if possible, cut. The only exception was Defence. I later learned that it was

Howard alone who pleaded for Defence to be left untouched. His then Chief of Staff, Graham Morris, recounted Howard saying to Cabinet in settling the budget, "Look, humour me. I've spent twenty-three years working to get this job, let's not cut Defence." Securing the 1996 Defence budget proved to be John Howard's most prescient decision.

Budget night was a new experience. John Howard and Peter Costello briefed the party room at 7 pm. We were presented with the headline economic data, high level announcements, mostly the good news and the key messaging. The detail of decisions adversely impacting certain groups would trickle out days after the budget. It was only after the budget speech that I discovered budget night events. I heard there was an event for government MPs in the alcove area adjacent to the members' dining room. Rhondda and I headed down there with two of our staff. Approaching, I could hear the unmistakable voice of Tony Abbott addressing the audience, "Well, it's wonderful to have David Connolly here with us tonight. David did such a tremendous job for us over many years…."

Rhondda said to the imposing staffer manning the door, "I'm here with Dr Nelson. We just want to join in. Rhondda was abruptly told, "The event is fully subscribed. You'll have to go somewhere else." Rhondda was about to explode in a way only she can. I intervened, simply saying to the doorman, "My name is Brendan Nelson. I am the Member for Bradfield. I have many failings; poor memory is not one of them."

First thing next morning Rhondda booked the same venue for budget night 1997. We knew one person who would not be welcomed.

In Bradfield the budget was well received, apart from the superannuation surcharge. All sorts of government offices were being closed and consolidated. Immigration Minister, Phillip Ruddock, had called me weeks before the budget to let me know the immigration office in Chatswood would close. I reassured him it wouldn't be a problem. Sure enough, amongst the letters from constituents praising the decision was one asking if it was possible to close the tax office as well.

The real vindication for the budget came barely a month after its delivery. Jackie Kelly had shocked everyone, including herself, by winning the safe western Sydney Labor seat of Lindsay. However, she had failed to renounce her New Zealand citizenship. A by-election was set for 11 September. In the post budget environment of major cuts to a myriad of government programmes and activities, Kelly faced the voters again. These were the very people at the forefront of the new government's 'tough but fair' budgetary strategy. Labor ran its candidate again – former Keating minister, Ross Free. The Coalition gained a 5% two party preferred swing. 'Howard's battlers' had not only stuck, they had grown in number.

As I had grown up in Tasmania and South Australia, rugby was alien to me. When I prepped for my preselection, I studied the game lest I be embarrassed about something unique to New South Wales. A community push was on for a large sporting facility in Pymble. A fund-raiser in the Sydney Town Hall was attended by 1,000 people. I found myself sitting next to a very friendly, conversational man who looked incredibly fit. After an hour of conversation, interrupted by women wanting their photo with him, I asked what sort of work he did. "I work in the finance sector, but I've taken a bit of leave to play rugby." My 'study' of rugby kicked in, "Oh really. What team do you play for?" "The Wallabies".

I desperately worked through my list – Sharks, Eels, Roosters, Panthers, Bulldogs. I couldn't remember Wallabies. "Oh, yes of course. Great team … err … where are you based?"

"What do you mean, where are we based? We're based everywhere, we're the Australian team! I'm the captain of the Wallabies." Eying me closely, he leant over and said softly, "You don't know anything about rugby, do you?" "No", I sheepishly replied. "Please don't tell anyone". So began my friendship with Phil Kearns.

The year would end with the government challenged by the High Court's bombshell decision in the Wik case. Pastoral and Mining leases did not necessarily extinguish native title. By Christmas many backbenchers simply wanted to go into 1997 with a much less ambitious agenda. Warren Entsch told the party room, "Prime Minister, there is only so much people can reasonably digest. They need a rest."

Another group, however, including me, had begun agitating for further reform – tax reform and a GST. After I had raised it in the party room, Peter Costello rose, "If you think it's a good idea to push an agenda like that up and down the country, you've got another thing coming. Anyone who thinks that way should speak to those of us that have. We are not going to repeat that experience."

Although Warren's wish was fulfilled early in 1997, the 'rest' period would prove short-lived.

11

Put your heart in it!

What differentiates leadership from management is vision.

Management is about emptying an in-tray or inbox, making decisions day to day, week to week.

Vision informs leadership. People must be given a comprehensive sense of who they are, where they want to go – and why. Vision has the power to lift people above their own self-interest and short horizon to support ideas that will benefit all. Like sitting around a campfire, it has the capacity to warm us as we reflect on where we have been, where we are and where we are going.

Needless to say, these thoughts were lost on many with whom I worked.

Nonetheless, I articulated my own vision for Australia. I had it framed, hanging in my electorate and parliamentary offices and published in all the materials I distributed to the electorate. My motto for Bradfield was, *PUT YOUR HEART IN IT!*

It stood above my vision for Australia:

> That Australia becomes a country in which we value the health and integrity of human life, as much as we do our economic objectives.
>
> That barriers to the creation of wealth are seen as the enemy of effective social policy.
>
> That the idealism of young people is nurtured.
>
> That Australians live in a society in which their opinions are both solicited and heard.
>
> That every Australian, irrespective of their circumstances, knows they will be cared for – but in return, each is expected to make a contribution to the society from which they derive a benefit.

> That we see ourselves as an outward looking, competitive, compassionate country, imbued with the values of hard work, self-sacrifice, tolerance and courage.

The government's second year in office was messy. Having largely implemented what we promised in the 1996 budget and returned government to focusing on mainstream Australia, it felt like 'drift'. Two issues into which I threw myself were youth suicide and the growing drug problem.

I found that while I could raise issues in the party room and the committees of government, having them published was an effective way to stimulate debate. I was careful not to criticise the government but not afraid to suggest policy prescriptions. In January, *The Australian* published a paper I wrote on youth suicide that prompted a national debate and momentum for response:

> The health and well-being of young people, how well we care for the vulnerable and the extent to which we nurture the ideals of the young are critical measures of a caring society. For a growing but significant minority of young Australians, the celebration of youth has been replaced by a grim determination to survive. Life is one of despair, hopelessness and aggression directed against themselves and others. It is a sad indictment that we have reduced the toll taken by disease and motor vehicle accident, but failed to limit that exacted by despair.
>
> The thematic currency of youth suicide is our failure to transmit a sense of belonging and meaningful purpose to young people. The threshold of resistance to despair has been lowered by a generation that has lost confidence that those who profess to lead both care and understand the problems that they face
>
> The problem is not that young people have not learned our values. It is that they have.

> It has become fashionable to marginalise churches, demean the importance of parenting, push kids to the zeniths of educational achievement and discount voluntary work as the domain of the 'do-gooder'. The price of our shallowness is being paid by our children.
>
> For the first time in many generations, young Australians face a future that does not offer a higher standard of living than that enjoyed by their parents. Under the oppressive weight of the incessant materialist imagery of BMWs, mobile phones and fashionable clothing, many feel that they are being pressured to remain in the education system beyond their natural abilities for jobs they feel are not likely to exist.
>
> It is not the economic indices with which we frequently seem so obsessed that will determine our destiny, but rather our beliefs, values and how we see ourselves in the world. What good will it do us to connect young Australians to the Internet if we are incapable of rebuilding a sense of community, recognising that, in a world of fundamentalist intolerance, uncertainty and instability, what we need most is one another.

Much of what guided me through my public life was encapsulated in this. I spoke to many audiences on such themes.

John Howard regularly hosted small groups of backbenchers at The Lodge. He wanted to know what was on our mind, to be in touch with our concerns. At one such dinner I raised a National Office for Youth. He told me that he had given it some thought but concluded he was better suited to "getting rid of bureaucracy, not creating it". However, I found it struck a chord with many of my colleagues. The foundations for my relationship with them was being built.

The maiden speech in 1996 that attracted most attention was given by the newly elected member for Oxley, Pauline Hanson. She had taken a safe Labor seat on a platform bemoaning free trade, Aboriginal welfare, foreign aid and immigration among many issues. I sat and listened in silence as she unpacked the grievances of several million Australians. Many of them were coalition voters and the traditional, blue collar Labor base. I knew this had to be confronted, not Pauline herself, but the issues. She was, in my opinion, just like so many everyday Australians grieving the loss of an Australia she loved.

Only the year before, Slim Dusty had released 'Natural High' in which he sang of "the Australia no more", of corporate takeovers and selling off Australia. Pauline Hanson had tapped into a simmering resentment of changes people neither understood nor wanted. Though a product of the Keating Government, John Howard was given the 'credit' for her arrival.

In May 1997, *The Australian* published my assessment of things under "Grieving nation open to Hanson":

> Grief is a necessarily painful emotion which, to varying degrees, we have all experienced. When anger at the loss competes for expression, confusion reigns without skilful direction.
>
> Nations, like people, grieve. Pauline Hanson is a lightning rod for grief and anger, the expression of which has legitimacy. Many Australians grieve changes few want and even fewer understand. There is within each of us a constant tension between on the one hand what we want for ourselves, a self-interested resentment of the unfamiliar, and then on the other a need to do what in our best selves we know to be right. Mrs. Hanson has stumbled upon the former, finding to her surprise what a powerful force it is.
>
> Every day brings further evidence of change over which we appear to have little control. Mrs. Hanson is not to be ignored because the issues she raises in her own inarticulate way, go to the very heart of why, so decisively, there was a change of government. The duty of those in public life who profess to lead, is to explain why we have an immigra-

> tion program at all and for whose benefit it is conducted. Why, despite impropriety and waste, do we do anything at all for Aboriginal people? Why, also, should a caring society choose to do anything at all for the world's poor with foreign aid and world peace through the United Nations? Mrs. Hanson's views are to be repudiated, first because they are morally wrong and, second, because they are economically irresponsible.
>
> Grief can be a powerful force for change when harnessed to addressing seemingly intractable problems. Few would have anticipated the decisive action on guns. When parliamentarians merely follow public opinion rather than lead it, when we feel that in some way we need to subscribe to the populist views, then the nation is vulnerable. When facts bow to bias, truth is in danger and evil in all its guises finds an environment in which it may flourish – if not triumph.

Along with Joe Hockey, I was a member of the government's backbench communications committee. The Chairman, Gary Hardgrave, was a broadcaster in his pre-parliamentary life. A likeable man with an engaging personality, he enjoyed the attention of the players in the media landscape. The government and its communications minister, Richard Alston, were of a mind to relax cross media ownership laws. The proposal came to us in late April. Though there was some gain for the Murdochs, the big winners would be the Packers who were allowed to acquire Fairfax, publishing *The Age, Sydney Morning Herald* and *Australian Financial Review.* The arguments were couched in terms of a changed media landscape and the need to move with the times, but I sensed another agenda. In my view, and that of Joe Hockey, it was intended to get Fairfax. Its left-leaning papers were constant critics of the Coalition. If the Packers, who owned Channel Nine and a range of publications, acquired Fairfax, it was argued that a 'more balanced' reporting and analysis of politics would flow. I was no fan of the Fairfax papers but I was not sold on this at all. Nor were a number of the backbench policy committee.

Media moguls started flying to Brisbane to see Gary. When it became clear that the strongest opposition was coming from two standouts, Nelson and Hockey, the pressure ramped up. I received a call from Graham Richardson, now working for the Packers. "Mate, this cross-media ownership stuff is serious. Kerry and James would like to have a chat to you." I told him I was happy to do so. Remembering advice Bruce Shepherd had given years earlier that people should come and see you, "Of course Graham. No problem. My office is in Lindfield, would you like me to make an appointment?"

Graham chuckled as he told me that the Packers didn't operate like that. Perhaps we could meet at the offices of the Channel Nine studios in Willoughby. A reasonable compromise. I arrived alone on the appointed day. Graham and James Packer were in attendance, but not Kerry. James put his well-rehearsed arguments to me, including how his company would ensure 'balance' in reporting. The Fairfax papers were 'editorialising' in their reporting, frequently to the left. The conversation went back and forth until James spoke of his grandfather and father "never interfering with an editor's independence". Graham had not spoken all this time, but James prompted him to agree with Packers' editorial independence. Graham quickly agreed with James, but as an after-thought added, "Except that time Kerry called me about my *Bulletin* column."

I finished by saying, "Mr Packer, I am sorry but I am unwilling to support cross-media relaxation as currently proposed. I am not prepared to allow a future in which you and Mr Murdoch alone are going to tell my children what to think." The next day I was called by the Deputy Editor of *Woman's Day.* My medical column was no longer needed and my writing terminated immediately. Editorial independence is alive and well, I thought.

At the time Kerry Stokes owned *The Canberra Times.* Ken Parker chaired his company, a true gentleman. Ken came to see me. "I heard you stood up to the Packers. People of principle are precious. Thank you." He gave me his card and left. Word got to John Howard and others, neither Nelson nor Hockey were for turning. I attended a huge dinner for 'Friends of Fairfax' at the Museum of Contemporary Art in the Rocks, Sydney. I was one of only four coalition MPs present. I thought as I left that night that I was in for a long tour of duty on the backbench.

In late August John Howard's advisor called to tell me that the government was dropping relaxation of media ownership rules. "There are two reasons, and you're one of them." Bob Katter sent me a handwritten note thanking me. I have long treasured it.

All hell broke loose in May. John Howard announced to the nation that a GST would form part of the Coalition's tax reform agenda for the election, due the following year. Though shocked, most of us were pleased. Pleased that we had a serious policy debate the nation needed and very pleased we would have something worth fighting for. Why John Howard chose to do it on Sunday television remains the subject of speculation. Not an easy decision for Howard. He had ruled it out forcefully only two years earlier as opposition leader with "never, ever".

John Howard attended and addressed a sell-out Bradfield fundraising event on the last Sunday in May. There was a large marquee on the grounds of Ravenswood School for Girls where the crowd of 500 listened approvingly to him speak to tax reform. Australians would vote on a GST at the next general election.

The following day the long-awaited Royal Commission report into forcibly removed generations of Aboriginal children was released. The symbolic centrepiece was a formal Apology to these first Australians. John Howard addressed 1,800 delegates to the Aboriginal Reconciliation conference in Melbourne. As he sought to explain and defend much of what had been achieved since the British arrived in 1788, many turned their backs. He pounded the lectern as he pressed his points. The behaviour of some delegates was regarded by many as offensive. The government's refusal to offer an Apology laid the foundation for a Labor Government to do so a decade later.

Sitting with three of us in the parliamentary dining room several days later, Mr Howard asked what we thought. I said, "Prime Minister, in speaking, tone is often more important than content." His regret was clear and years later he said so.

Warren Entsch had been appointed to chair a parliamentary committee to examine the issues raised by the High Court's decision in the Wik case. Highly contentious, the government had developed a ten-point plan. The High Court, in appeal on a 4-3 majority, determined that native title may not be extinguished by pastoral leases. I attended a meeting in Sydney with some 25 government members on the issue. It lasted all day, at times heated. At one point I stood up to a particularly aggressive colleague with little sympathy for the Aboriginal view. At day's end, Wilson "Ironbar" Tuckey turned to me, "Brendan, the outcome today would have been different without you. Thanks".

In the course of Warren's Inquiry, church leaders called for legislation to extinguish pastoral leases where native title existed. Outraged, Entschy called for people to boycott churches. The day finally arrived for him to table his long-awaited report. I knew that he held a deep affection and respect for Indigenous people. "I love the buggers and they've had a bloody hard time. Mind you, the do-gooders are often more of a problem to 'em."

Perched as we were up the back of the chamber, I was there to support him. He had his lectern on the desk, speech sitting on top. Nervous with minutes to go, he said, "Mate, I'm just gonna have a piss". As he left, I looked at the speech. I couldn't resist. I pulled the liquid paper from my drawer and rewrote the first line. Entschy returned. When he got the call, his left hand by reflex went into his pocket to jiggle the loose change. All eyes turned to him as he looked down to begin, "Bless me father for I have sinned … what the … ?!!!!" He glanced at me with a wicked smile.

My marriage to Kate and our increasingly strained relationship finally reached breaking point. A day of immense emotion began early in the morning. I sought counsel from Bruce, advised Rhondda of what was happening, and, after school, sat down with Emily and Tom to walk them through it. Lots of tears. Finally I explained it to Kate's mother, Myra. All were upset, none were surprised. Kate moved out days later and the slow, painful process of healing began. I had failed at marriage twice. This time with ten-year-old twins.

When parliament resumed, I told Entschy. He turned and said, "Just happened to me mate. It hurts. I love you like a brother." We hugged.

As a backbencher, I had time to focus on areas of interest and concern. One was the drug problem. In the late nineties, it was a true crisis. The ACT Government was talking about establishing heroin injecting rooms. My instinct was to support it. Then, every sixteen hours a parent was feeling the pain of losing a child to heroin. The question to be answered was, if already addicted heroin users administered the drug under supervision, would they be less likely to die, commit crime and shun society?

At that time, I was regularly visiting the staff and volunteers at the Catholic charity Open Family in Cabramatta. Today, this wonderful, vibrant community is a world away from what it was then in the grip of the drug trade. My experience of a visit to Cabramatta at the peak of the heroin epidemic was published in the *Sun Herald* newspaper in July. In part:

> Over the years I have experienced many sickening, heart moving and gut-wrenching things – cot death, suicide, child rape and drug shooting galleries frequented by the near-dead.
>
> Nothing, however, prepared me for a recent visit to Cabramatta.
>
> By mid-morning in the car park behind the bottle shop, just hours after the morning clean-up, discarded needles and syringes were already to be found. The car park, I was told, is used by mothers of young children to shoot up, so desperate are they and others who seek out the heroin trade which resembles Flemington markets.

> As the train pulls into Cabramatta station, several young pushers sprint from one side of the platform to the other, eager to be first to prospective buyers. The footpaths carry empty syringe packets and remnants of balloons in which the heroin is packaged for sale.
>
> Fifty metres from the end of the station walkway, a young teenager and his mate are shooting up, although the second has trouble finding a vein among the red, swollen sores on his arms.
>
> "Where are you from?"
>
> "Cronulla", is the slurred reply.
>
> "If there was a safe place for you to inject, would you use it instead of the toilet?"
>
> "Yeah, sounds good".
>
> An over-worked police officer tells me that an arrest takes an officer off the street for three hours. The dealer returns to his trade by day's end. If he does not, they have "the biggest reserve bench in the country to take his place". If this is 'war', there are many casualties but few survivors, and even fewer victors.

Such views were very much the minority in our party room, but I felt a responsibility to use my position to shine a light on the reality we faced. Within a framework of 'Tough on Drugs' and law enforcement, we must surely be able to keep people alive and remove the detritus of their addiction from the streets of our cities.

With the spate of ministerial casualties piling up over the failure to meet ministerial standards, openings emerged for promotion. To my complete surprise, I was asked by John Howard in October 1997 to chair the House of Representatives Standing Committee on Employment, Education and Training.

The Member for Kooyong, Petro Georgiou, was possessed of a brilliant political brain and social conscience to match. Howard offered him a position as parliamentary secretary. He refused, believing his skills warranted higher office. He remained a backbencher for the rest of his parliamentary career. A pity. The lesson which I have passed on to those seeking my advice, is you do whatever you are asked. Embrace the role as if it is the only job in your life you have ever wanted. Concentrate on the job you've got and the next one will look after itself.

Like everything I threw myself into the new role, conducting four Inquiries in succession, traversing TAFE, Mature Aged Workers, Employee Share Ownership, and Boys' Education. Membership of the committee included Julia Gillard from 1998, for whom I gained a respect that has endured. Although of Labor's left, she was smart, fair and open to a reasonable argument.

One consequence of my marriage breakdown was financial stress. In Canberra, Joe Hockey's classic 'Canberran' home in Furneaux Street had a garage. Adjoining the garage was a room, something of a 'sleep-out'. I put it to Joe that I could move out to the garage, cut my rent in half and he could let my room in the house. Bemused, he readily agreed. It was great out there. A rug on the floor, a bed, a small cupboard to hang clothes and electricity. I could have the light, heater and TV on, but not simultaneously. I needed a fan in summer and three doonas in winter, but I loved it – as did the possums. A fire bucket was on hand for safety.

I had been living alone with the kids and Myra for a few months when Bruce Shepherd's wife, Jenny, broached a subject with me in November: "Brendan, this is a sensitive matter, but don't you think it's time to meet a woman? We know a beautiful woman who lives here in Bowral. She has poise and is about your age."

"Not you too Jenny. Seriously, everyone seems to want to hook me up with someone. I appreciate it, but given what I have been through, I am perfectly happy at the moment. And in my position especially, I have to be very careful." Bruce peered from the top of his newspaper, "Mate, this is a package deal. She is beautiful, your type and she has a wonderful little girl. Do yourself a favour and meet her."

I relented. "Okay, when?" Knowing us both, Gillian's best friend, Sandra Maloney, conspired with Jenny Shepherd for me to meet Gillian Adamson. We did so at a large family barbeque on 5 December 1997. Love at first sight.

Just before Christmas, the *Australian Financial Review* reported me in its 'Rear Window' as 'Quote of the Day': "The problem is not that young people have not learned our values, it is that they have".

Challenged by several senior ministers as to what I meant, I said "Imagine being a 15-year-old growing up in Australia today. As a government, too often we appear to be a bunch of accountants running an economy rather than a group of men and women committed to building a better society. What we say and do plays an essential role in reflecting and shaping our national values".

I seemed to be ever lengthening my backbench career.

12

Bonner is Liberal. I can go now

1998 began with the sensible decision for the kids to move out and live with Kate. I couldn't afford to stay in the house. Rhondda suggested to Doug Thompson, who lived alone in Killara, he might like a flat mate. A lifesaver, Doug welcomed me into his granny flat where I lived for the next eighteen months. We had become good friends, but that period living with him cemented a lifetime friendship.

I discovered we shared a common passion – country music. More specifically, Slim Dusty. Doug had a CD player that loaded 100 CDs. His held 97, every one of them Slim Dusty. Gillian asked Doug if there was any other artist he liked. "I don't mind some of Joy's stuff". Joy McKean was Slim's wife and musical partner. I asked Doug over breakfast if he had ever met Slim. His voice dropped to a reverential tone, "No mate". I asked if he would like me to see if I could arrange it. I thought he was going to burst into tears with excitement at the thought.

I knew Slim was a constituent living in St Ives. I rang my friend, Kamahl, to ask if he would introduce me. A day later Joy called. I told her about Doug and his love of Slim. Doug also wanted to commission acclaimed artist Judy Cassab to do a portrait of Slim. Joy agreed they would come to Doug's home for dinner. Doug swung into action. Only friends who loved Slim's music were invited. Gardeners came in to rearrange everything to meet Joy's tastes. My father travelled from Adelaide, a tragic from way back.

A four-hour dinner turned into a magical six. I knew things were going well when, an hour into drinks and chat about 'the old days on the road', Slim asked Doug if he could go out to the car and get his hat. Judy's portrait was superb. Doug's friendship with Slim blossomed. The two men shared much together.

Having declined the opportunity to meet the *Spice Girls,* John Howard took the government to Thredbo early in 1998. A tragic landslide devastated the tourist resort in the winter of 1997. The Member for Eden Monaro and great friend, Gary Nairn, suggested it as a good way to tell Australia Thredbo was 'open for business.' We held a two-day retreat to reflect on what we had done, where we were and set a sense of direction for the future.

Bonding with colleagues in a relaxed atmosphere was valuable, but also somewhat frustrating. A series of ministers delivered reports on their portfolios. We were briefed on *Work for the Dole* and the notion of mutual obligation. As was often the case, I saw things a little differently. I had advocated some form of structured work for the unemployed from my AMA days, but I questioned the language. "Why call it mutual obligation? That suggests the unemployed don't want to work and we don't want to support them, but we are 'obliged' to do so. On the other hand, if we called it 'mutual responsibility', the unemployed have a responsibility to the society that supports them and in return, we have responsibility to care for them". It was not well received.

A lengthy discussion followed later about 'tolerance'. I asked Philip Ruddock why, in the context of multicultural Australia and ethnic diversity, we applied the word 'tolerance'. I said, "Tolerance implies a reluctant acquiescence to something we don't really like or want. I tolerate my neighbour's lawnmower on Sunday morning but I definitely don't like it." Philip was sympathetic to the argument and suggested I raise it in the party room. Burned once, I decided retreat was the better part of valour.

But I did argue that we needed to articulate a vision for the country that was not only economic but also human and social. When we got the economic settings where they needed to be, people would regard that as our job. They would effectively then ask what we were doing about the things they cared about. We would be shaped as a nation by our values and our beliefs, the way we relate to one another and see our place in the world. I said:

> People are shaped by subtle but powerful forces. They will accept personal hardship if they understand the problem and are convinced that what is offered will deliver a better

> future for their children. I have practised medicine in public housing estates and now represent one of the most affluent areas of the country. People will jump through hoops ten times out of ten if they are convinced their kids will get a better future. To do so, they need to be inspired.

No response. The next speaker went to the contentious Telstra privatisation.

At least I had made my point. I quickly acquired a reputation for being 'different'. And, as one colleague quipped after an intervention, "Brendan, Bradfield is a safe seat, but your campaign to make it marginal continues unabated."

Over the Christmas break, I received a book from a constituent. Entitled *Revelation,* its author a German physicist and philosopher, Bernhardt Philberth. A heavy theological read, it deals with institutional and personal change. One passage stood out:

> Progress leads to chaos if not anchored in tradition.
> Tradition becomes rigid if it does not prepare the way for progress.
> But a perverted traditionalism, and a misguided progressivism propel each other toward a deadly excess, hardly leaving any ground between them.

Therein lies one of the great challenges of leadership. I wished I had read the book before my leadership of the AMA. The 'traditionalists', whose sacrifices and values are the foundation of any organisation, must be known, understood and respected. Once they are confident that their 'traditions' will be the foundation upon which the future will be built, they will respond to good leadership in shaping that future.

At the other end are the 'progressivists'. They seemingly want change for its own sake, neither understanding nor respecting the 'traditionalists' and the past so precious to them. These people need to be led to an understanding of who gave them what they have and made them who they are.

I was thinking of Bernhard Philberth when the Constitutional Convention for an Australian Republic was held in Old Parliament House in February 1998. Malcolm Turnbull and a group of 'progressivists' exuded an air of intellectual and moral superiority on nightly television. More than a few of those supportive of the Constitutional Monarchy, in their conservatism, created the rigid perception of a 'deadly excess'.

I was moved by the passionate defence of the current constitutional arrangements by former Liberal Senator and Aboriginal Australian, Neville Bonner:

> My heart is heavy. I worry for my children and my grandchildren. I worry that what has proven to be a stable society, which now recognises my people as equals, is about to be replaced. How dare you. I repeat, how dare you. You told my people that your system was best. We have come to accept that. We have come to believe that. The dispossessed, despised adapted to your system. Now you say that you were wrong and that we were wrong to believe you.
>
> … I look across this chamber and cannot fail to see the very rich amongst you … what reason do you have now in 1998 to tell the Indigenous people that we must accept what you have decided about our country again. Why are you doing this?

Always a great admirer of this man, his address inspired me. He was right about the educated, well-heeled pushing the republican agenda.

The Convention agreed on the referendum question to be put to the nation the following year. It would be a Republic with a president chosen by a two-thirds majority of the parliament. I have always been a Constitutional Monarchist. I always will be. I respect and admire Her Majesty, Queen Elizabeth ll. But our system of government has little to do with the personalities of the Royal Family. It has everything to do with our constitutional arrangements and the stability it has brought us.

My own instincts were to not change a system that clearly worked and was far from 'broken'. I thought back to April 1994 and two comments that hit me right between the eyes. In those days, the ABC broadcast a Saturday morning television show called *Attitudes*. It canvassed the attitudes of young Australians to a range of contemporary issues. One looked at the Republican debate. Ten young people in their mid to late teens were asked if they supported a republic. All enthusiastically embraced the idea, bemoaning it had not yet happened. Then they were asked to name the prime minister of Australia. Four correctly named Mr Keating. Only two knew the difference between the Senate and House of Representatives. Not one could explain the Australian Constitution's role in our governance.

A week later, on 24 April, the Melbourne *Age* published an interview with a First World War veteran for Anzac Day. In the midst of it he said, "I'm glad I will be dead soon. I don't want to be alive when Australia becomes a republic and the flag changes." This man and his generation felt that way about it as a new generation was at best, oblivious to the 'traditionalists'.

The system of government Australia enjoys, given us by our forebears, has served us well. Here we are 120 years later, free of insurrection, political instability and largely free of the political and judicial corruption endemic in some parts of the world. The Republican push is based on a distortion which capitalises on the constitutional ignorance of most Australians. Australia is totally independent. Sovereignty lies with the parliament and the people. In England, King Charles I lost his head over it – literally.

Under current arrangements, the Governor General has status and a power above the politicians. The political class has power but certainly little status in the eyes of the public. Republicans seem to think you can transfer the powers held by the Governor General to a president and everything is 'fixed'. The Prime Minister chooses the Governor General having an eye to the opposition, public opinion and the capacity of the chosen individual to fulfil the role effectively. He or she so advises the Monarch and the appointment is made. It works well. Many who have excelled in the role would never win a popularity contest.

An elected person, whether elected by the public or a two-thirds majority of the parliament, immediately becomes a politician. The powers of 'the crown', once politicised, can be used for political purposes and not simply 'the common good'. So long as we have a Governor General we have someone who is 'above' the political fray, there to serve only the people, no one else.

An elected person would be seen to have more moral authority and political legitimacy than the prime minister of the day. There have been times when a popularly chosen president would have been most unsuited to such an office. Popularity and leadership of this nature do not always go hand in hand. The power of the Governor General lies not in the power exercised, but in the power denied others. It is a check on power wielded by politicians. I have always been suspicious that many who lead this push want to cut down the power of institutions to elevate their own.

The people who derive the most comfort and sense of 'protection' from the Monarchy and symbols of it, are those who wield neither power nor influence, the everyday Australian. Educated, relatively well-off people are more confident that they don't 'need' these things. Neville Bonner's instincts and observations were correct.

John Howard invested a lot of political capital in 1998. Tax reform was the big one, but the privatisation of Telstra was also politically expensive. Apart from a significant minority of Australians, many of whom were attracted to the slogans of Pauline Hanson and her new Party One Nation, elements of the Coalition parties also had deep reservations.

At the Liberal Party's Brisbane Convention in March 1998, John Howard announced that the full sale of Telstra would be taken to the election later that year. The expected $45 billion in proceeds would flow through to Australians as a 'social bonus'. The world's then second biggest float would, in Howard's vision, make Australians the greatest share-owning democracy in the world. It would also retire some of the crippling debt left by Labor.

The Hawke-Keating Governments, to their credit, had begun the privatisation of large, government owned assets – Qantas and the Commonwealth Bank. They were supported by the Coalition from opposition. Now Labor launched a full throttle attack on us doing the same thing for the benefit of the nation.

The Convention also paid tribute to Neville Bonner. The audience response was emotional as he received honorary life membership of the Liberal Party from John Howard. This man who, in 1983, had been placed in the unwinnable third position on the Liberal Party Senate ticket and then ran as an independent, received an overwhelming, standing ovation. I was proud to be a Liberal.

Throughout my political career I enlisted Rhondda and rolled my sleeves up only three times to work hard to help someone in preselection. Two of them we supported in 1997 – Bill Heffernan and Marise Payne. The third, Scott Morrison, a decade later in 2007.

Bill was the conservative Junee farmer. Tough as the nails he put in his fences, stridently anti-paedophiles and wary of gays, he faced a challenging Senate selection for a winnable place on the Senate ticket. He filled a casual vacancy in 1996 and now had to fight. He had friends and he had enemies. We ran the campaign out of my electorate office. I coached him on his speech and assembled a team to work on Q&A. He would be challenged hard on his attitude to gays. I knew him to be a caring and decent man. His support of me when my brother was dying from AIDS, is something I will never forget.

I said to Bill, "If asked, you express your respect for the innate value of every human being. You have concerns for elements of gay activism, its criticism of mainstream Australia, but in the end homosexual people are our family and friends. However, you won't be campaigning to make it compulsory." He answered thus on the day, they laughed and voted in sufficient numbers to get him up.

Marise Payne was at the other end of the Liberal Party spectrum. Just as we needed Bill, we needed Marise. I said to her critics, "We need to be playing with a full deck. We need a woman of substance, of liberal beliefs and ideals who can speak to and on behalf of younger people." I also remembered the support she had given me just two years earlier along with Andrew Parker for which both attracted criticism. Marise got up. A wonderful woman, she filled the casual vacancy created by the resignation of Bob Woods from the Senate.

Peter Reith had shown extraordinary courage taking on the Maritime Unions. The threats to his safety were real but he pressed on in the belief that Australia's prosperity would increasingly rely on extra waterfront productivity.

By mid-year the tax debate was heating up. Kim Beazley had done a good job keeping the Labor Party together after its resounding defeat in 1996. They were competitive and knew it. They had beaten us on GST in 1993 and wanted to do it again. But this time we had the resources of government available to us. Apart from Telstra and Industrial Relations we didn't have other major controversial political fronts to cover. Also, John Howard was our leader. Many people didn't like Howard, but they respected him. Paul Keating's spiteful description of Hewson as "Dr Strangelove" had penetrated. Howard was different.

Peter Costello argued that 'battlers' could no longer carry the country's reliance on income tax. The ABS told us that over a decade the top 10 per cent of income earners had seen their marginal tax rate drop from 36.5% to 31 %. Their share of income spent on the burgeoning indirect taxes had fallen from 6.3% to 5.7%. In contrast, the bottom 10% of income earners had seen a marginal increase in income tax, but indirect taxes paid by them had skyrocketed from 14.2% to 22.6% of their disposable income. The price of inequity was being paid by those who could least afford to do so. Reform was needed for equity, to fund a nation of collapsing age dependency ratios, abolish redundant taxes and to make us internationally competitive. Labor threw everything at us to stop it.

Even in Bradfield, tax reform was not the easiest of products to sell. Three weeks from polling day 1998, 300 people packed into the Turramurra Uniting Church Hall. The mood was tense. I was just minutes into explaining why a GST would be good for Australia when a man, jammed like a sardine against the back wall, was wildly gesticulating. So concerned was I that he may be having a cardio-respiratory event, I stopped. "Is the gentleman at the back waving all right?" I asked. The man next to him yelled, "He can't hear". A woman stood up in the second row, turned to the crowd and contemptuously proclaimed, "Well I can and I'm happy to swap with you!" No-one laughed.

A week before election day, I asked my father in Adelaide how he was lining up for it. He had crossed his 'Rubicon' in 1996, voting Liberal for the first time in his life. He told me he had been thinking about going back to Labor until he saw Kim Beazley down on the Melbourne docks. "When I saw Beazley with those criminals and stand-over men from the MUA, I knew I had to stick with Howard."

The election, held on 3 October 1998, was a close-run thing. John Howard had been informed by Party Director Lynton Crosby just before close of polling booths at 6pm of exit polling. On the basis of those polled on the way from casting their vote, we had lost. Labor was, with good reason, confident. As the night unfolded though, two things became clear.

Labor had won the popular vote, but we had won a majority of seats. A number of coalition backbenchers had held on against the odds. Many people actually thought they were voting Labor, not appreciating that the MP whom they so admired was the Liberal candidate. Amongst those magnificent colleagues and friends – Trish Worth, Chris Gallus and Trish Draper in metropolitan Adelaide, Jim Lloyd, Jackie Kelly and Jo Gash in New South Wales, and Peter Lindsay and Kay Elson in Queensland. I lost many good friends from the parliament in that election – 14 in all. Among them, Don Randall and Bob Baldwin, who would return in 2001.

I had worked hard through my first term and was hopeful I might be offered a promotion. I wasn't. I was pleased for Joe Hockey who was promoted into the ministry. He was capable, deeply immersed in the politics of the New South Wales division of the Party and deserved it. Tony Abbott, equally deserving and of the conservative wing, provided the balance for factions we deny exist. It was a philosophical balance. Joe Hockey's father, Richard, came to see me. A truly beautiful, gentle man, he tearfully spoke of his disappointment for me. My disappointment was compounded when John Howard asked me to take on the job Joe was vacating – Chairman of the Sydney Airport Community Forum. To this day it remains the worst job I have ever had. Naturally I accepted the task with enthusiasm, concealing how I really felt. Aircraft noise was a major sore point for the government in Sydney.

Peter Pickles had given his name to the auctioneering business he had built. A constituent, a man of deep Christian conviction, he has dedicated much of life and generosity to nurturing and supporting leadership in others. He invited me to attend the National Prayer Breakfast in Washington DC with him. I was honoured to do so. The experience was transformative. I met people who not only dreamed of a better world but also worked behind the scenes without fuss or fanfare to make it happen.

What most affected me though was the visit Peter and I made to the Holocaust Museum in Washington. We lingered in silence before the thousands of shoes, so many of them children's. We wept together watching the footage of the Nazi doctors experimenting on the disabled and mentally ill. We sat in silence together and listened to the survivor testimonies. We stood and looked up to the hundreds of black and white photos of men, women, children and families that looked out onto the world in which they would not live. I resolved when I left that day that I would always visit the Holocaust Museum when in Washington – and I have.

Back home, I turned to my SACF role. In 1995, the Keating Government had opened the third runway at Sydney airport. There were now two parallel runways. Keating's transport minister, Laurie Brereton, said planes would travel with 'laser-like efficiency' up and down the North Shore. He was correct. Suddenly communities were exposed to aircraft noise on an unprecedented scale, including in Labor's inner west heartland. Most of the pain, however, was inflicted on the lower north shore. SACF was tasked with bringing community concerns to government and airport regulatory authorities. It was responsible for developing and implementing noise abatement procedures for Sydney Airport. This ranged from flight paths under the Long-Term Operating Plan to slot restrictions, curfew and a noise insulation programme for impacted homes. A tough assignment! With trepidation I reflected on the emotions unleashed in many public meetings I had attended.

Membership included federal and state MPs, local government mayors, community activists, aviation industry representatives and an assortment of 'challenging personalities'. Air Services Australia and the federal department of transport provided technical support. Some members had lodged apprehended violence orders against one another. Each had strongly held positions on what should be done, little of which could be reconciled. The initial meetings were extremely tense. But, as always, the key is to know the people, how they think and have their world view shaped. I made sure I did so with each one, respecting their view and why it was held. Another technique is humour that can be appreciated by everyone but which relates to a serious point.

John Murphy was the Labor Member for Lowe on the southern side of the Parramatta River. His residents were severely impacted by planes. John was a thoroughly decent, likeable, 'old style' Catholic Labor man. A tireless advocate for his communities, he knew how to talk, and talk. John lacked what in the defence world is known as 'situational awareness'. He was indefatigable in his criticism of our government. Not long into my fourth meeting and by now having the lay of the land, I turned to the secretariat.

"Mr Mrdak, please let the Minutes record the following:

> At 0920, Mr John Murphy, Member for Lowe, moved that: "SACAF condemns the Howard Government in the strongest possible terms for its outrageous mismanagement of Sydney airport and the Long-Term Operating Plan, the politically motivated imposition of aircraft noise

> onto Sydney communities and failure to meaningfully respond to community concerns". The Minutes will further record that the motion was seconded by Mr Barry Cotter, Mayor of Marrickville Council.
>
> It was supported by all SACF members except coalition MPs who voted against it. The two aviation industry representatives abstained.

The meeting was stunned into silence. John, perplexed but excited asked, "How did you know I was going to move that?"

"Just call it intuition John." The meeting broke into raucous laughter. I added, "Tonight I'll take another viewing of Monty Python's *Life of Brian*. Before I had this job, I thought it was a comedy. Now I know it is a documentary!"

The government was working hard to implement its election promises, at the heart of which was the GST. We had a near death political experience to bring the legislation to the parliament and Labor still worked feverishly to oppose it. Kim Beazley outlined an ambitious spending programme for a future Labor government as he steadfastly opposed the tax system we were building to pay for it. John Howard persuaded Meg Lees and her Democrats to support the tax plan taken to the people in 1998. They carved out food and some other items from the GST, but voted it through. Meg Lees did what was right, but it would prove to be the undoing of her party.

One of the most memorable days of my parliamentary service was 20 July 1999.

Tim Fischer, leader of the National Party, Trade Minister and Deputy Prime Minister, rose to the dispatch box just before question time. He announced that he was resigning his leadership and ministry. He would not contest the next election due late in 2001. He explained to the parliament that his family, in particular his autistic son, Harrison, needed more of his time and attention. A remarkable man, Tim had eschewed the considerable power he held, in favour of his family. One of the very few politicians who actually meant what he said in spending more time with his family. Years later his wife Judy revealed Tim had been home only one or two nights a month. A cruel toll.

Many of us were emotional hearing Tim's resignation. To varying degrees, we all knew our families were paying a heavy price for what we did. One lingering memory is of Martin Ferguson, former ACTU president, sitting on Labor's front bench, with tears streaming down his cheeks. Another very good man.

Australia's heroin epidemic returned again to the front pages. Almost 1,000 Australians lost their life to the drug in 1999. The Howard Government was prosecuting a 'Tough on Drugs' agenda. As we did, a debate raged around needle exchanges, injecting rooms, methadone clinics and heroin maintenance programmes. While tough on drugs myself, the policy approach needed nuance.

Although taxpayers are unhappy about their elected representatives taking 'study tours', I booked one. I wanted to visit Switzerland's drug treatment facilities. A confronting experience. I arrived in Zurich early morning. Bleary eyed, I stood in the queue waiting to be processed by customs. "Sir, what is your reason for visiting Switzerland?" I thought it best to be upfront. "I am here to visit heroin injecting rooms." He looked at his colleague and back at me, "Sir, you will need to come with us." I was taken to a small interrogation room and left alone. Soon they arrived along with my luggage. My efforts to explain my interest was academic only were fruitless, until my luggage was fully searched and it was clear I was an Australian parliamentarian now seeking consular assistance.

Swiss drug policy had come a long way since the disaster of the infamous 'needle park' behind the Zurich train station. It needed to. Accompanied by the coordinator of Zurich drug policy, I visited my first injecting room in the red-light district of Kreis 4. We turned from the main street. About 300 metres away, a lone security guard stood in front of a well maintained, nondescript building. The street was deserted. The guard established that those entering were Swiss nationals, neither intoxicated nor aggressive. The door opened to a large room the size of a café. About twenty people sat reading papers, some drinking coffee. Half were dishevelled, fitting the world-weary stereotype of the street addict, the others 'mainstream'.

A matronly woman served coffee and cordial from behind a counter, assisted by an addict rostered for such duties. Behind the entrance door stood an industrial washing machine and dryer adjacent to which were sundry clothes. "A clothing exchange", I was told. "It is very important that these people maintain whatever sense of self-esteem they have. At least if they can rest while they are here and feel good about themselves when they leave, they will use here rather than a park or somebody's garden", said an assistant. Behind the beverage bar were two rooms. On the right was the first aid room. A nurse was dressing the abscess on the arm of a woman aged well beyond her years. The nurse said, "We always talk about living without drugs. This is important. When they are ready, they will listen."

To the left was another room supervised by a registered nurse. The needles, syringes and mixing spoons were laid out ready for a man who entered through the sliding door. Before it closed I noticed resuscitation equipment and hospital standard hygiene.

Back on the street, two police cars were about 800 metres away on the verge of a pedestrian tunnel – arresting a dealer. "Policing around injecting rooms is no different from anywhere else. We track and arrest dealers". The police are also members of the room's management committee along with local government, health and community representatives.

Nauseated is how I felt seeing all this. The sight of human beings engaged in that to which I committed much of my life fighting, was sickening. But the waves of nausea sweeping over me in Zurich would never match those of the desperate futility that enveloped me when I attended my first fatal overdose as a doctor, the young body still warm.

I was impressed. The Swiss had halved their heroin deaths in less than a decade. When I was in Zurich, New South Wales Premier Bob Carr announced that Australia's first supervised injecting room would be opened in Sydney. I backed it. Debate of drug policy is rarely a sane pursuit. We need policy for the world in which we live. We can't stop people from being stupid. But we can stop them from being dead.

I was told I was 'out of step' with the government's 'Tough on Drugs' policies. I was counselled to think of the damage I was doing to my career supporting needle exchanges, injecting rooms and similar policies. Within a framework of prohibition and enhanced policing, I have always believed we can reduce harm. I spoke out publicly in support of what I believed and why, addressing a number of conservative forums, including the Sydney Institute.

On a Sunday afternoon in late 1999, I attended the 75th birthday of a Second World War veteran in Pymble. I didn't know the man or his family. I can only describe the home as a mansion. About sixty people milled around the swimming pool. A string quartet played as canapés were offered to guests sipping champagne. An elderly guest piped up, "You're the bloke wanting all these drugs legalised! What the bloody hell are you up to?" A hush descended on the crowd. The lady whose home it was, jumped in before I could speak.

"We have three sons. Our third is a heroin addict. We love him but we are at out wits' end. In the early hours this morning we received a call from Royal North Shore Hospital. He had been found overdosed in a car parked near the Oaks Hotel. They thought he was dead but managed to get him going. We strongly support what Dr Nelson is trying to do for families like us. Where there is life, we have our hope that this nightmare will end."

Silence had fallen on everyone. One woman spoke up in support of me, to the acclamation it seemed of most people present.

Events in East Timor came to a head after the independence vote won overwhelming support in August 1999. Pro-Indonesia militia wreaked havoc with widespread killing, destruction of infrastructure and displacement of tens of thousands of cowering East Timorese. Under John Howard's leadership and that of General Peter Cosgrove, Australia rose to the occasion. It was one of our finest moments as we led other nations in to bring peace and stability to a newly born nation. Australia managed, just, to get 5,000 troops to East Timor. An independent East Timor and Australia's role in helping the fledgling nation to find security was rightly regarded by John Howard as one of his most significant achievements.

Gillian and I were married in early October on the front lawn of Doug's home in Killara. Family and close friends shared us exchanging vows before Reverend Bill Crews. Weeks before, we went to see Bill at the Exodus Foundation in Ashfield. With my track record, I knew I would not be welcomed back to a Catholic church. Bill was a good friend. We met when I was AMA president and I helped him establish a medical service for the homeless.

Bill was a few minutes into talking to us about the sanctity of marriage when Gillian reached across and touched his hand. "It's okay Bill. We've both been married before. We know what it's like – it's going to be hell." Bill burst with relief, "Thank God, you're in the picture"!

Bruce Shepherd, Doug Thompson, Kamahl, Slim Dusty and Joy, Joe Hockey and Bob Baldwin were among fifty or so who made our day. A lot of emotion.

Over the years, some vile things have been said about me being married three times. Of course I feel a sense of failure. No-one marries wanting anything other than to see it last. The circumstances of my two divorces are vastly different but remain the source of deep disappointment. But in Gillian, I found my perfect partner.

I was pleased to see Australians reject the Republic in the November referendum. I was thinking of Neville Bonner when I saw Malcolm Turnbull and a gaggle of equally well-heeled, inner-city dwellers advocating their cause from the steps of the Sydney Opera House. The imagery and language were alienating to mainstream Australians. Had their cause been fronted by some everyday Australians, respectful of the Monarchy and campaigning from the front bar of a Broken Hill Hotel, they may have had more success. The issue will return.

Neville Bonner died in February 1999 from the cancer he had determinedly fought. He had not lived to see the nation recommit to the constitutional arrangements he so passionately defended.

I was well settled into my backbench role when 2000 arrived. A small group of Liberal Party officials and elder statesmen, including Sir John Carrick, took me to dinner at the Australia Club months after the 1998 election. Led by Robert Longstaff, my Bradfield Electorate Conference president, they reassured me that I had a future on the front bench of the government. Their concern meant a great deal to me.

Working with Rhondda and our electorate office staff, we put together a tribute dinner for Neville Bonner. The Old Parliament House dining hall was booked for 31 May 2000. Capacity was just over 340 people. Doug Thompson agreed to sponsor the event along with a small number of individuals and corporations. About one-third of attendees were Indigenous. I wanted them to pay something but raised money to defray their costs. I suggested to Slim Dusty and Joy that Neville's life could inspire a song. Joy wrote *The Quiet Achiever.* As Slim loved Aboriginal people and they loved him, I asked if he might perform at the event. He readily agreed.

Prime Minister John Howard, Ray Martin, Indigenous Democrat Senator Aden Ridgeway, Flo Grant, Elder of the Wiradjuri Council of Elders and I were among the speakers. Ray Martin read testimonials from eminent Australians. Stan Grant emceed the event and Channel Seven took some of it live to air. As I surveyed the packed room, including the Jaram Dance Group at one end and Slim Dusty's Travelling Country band at the other, I thought this was reconciliation in action. If the room didn't speak to the love and respect for Neville, Heather Bonner's smile and many tears certainly did. Two large, stunning black and white portraits of Neville Bonner looked into the audience from the stage. One has hung in my office ever since to remind me of what is really important in life: the liberating power of even a small amount of education which too often my generation has taken for granted. And, transcending everything else in life, is character.

A few special Australians burrowed into our hearts over the course of the twentieth century. Foremost amongst them is Neville Bonner. His life is a study of not only courage, conscience and compassion in the face of extraordinary adversity, but also one of personal and national reconciliation. He never lost sight of his goal – the fair and just treatment of his fellow human beings irrespective of race, geographic location, socioeconomic background or political affiliation. "I owe a lot to my grandmother", Neville would say toward the end of his life. It was she who insisted he go to school when he was fourteen. In response to the young boy protesting this, she said to him: "Neville, if you learned to read and write, express yourself well and treat people with decency and courtesy, it would take you a long way." It did. Throughout his tenure in the Senate, he was patronised, enduring racism and condescension … but whether it was such incidents or losing the coveted winnable position on the Liberal party's ticket for the 1983 election, he was never consumed by bitterness. His life was one of grace and humility, acknowledged in part by appointment in 1979 as Australian of the Year.

In 1992, Robyn Hughes asked him to nominate his greatest achievement, to which he replied, "It is that I was there. They no longer spoke of boongs and blacks, they spoke instead of Aboriginal people."

When this country is finally reconciled with its Indigenous people, a special place will be accorded to an early pioneer, Neville Bonner, his party and the democratic institutions that enabled him to serve in the Australian Senate.

In my fundraising for the event, I wrote to a number of prominent people. I sought both testimonials and a small financial contribution to assist lower income Indigenous people to attend. I wrote to the two prime ministers throughout Neville's tenure in the Senate. Gough Whitlam returned a beautiful, handwritten letter to me in which he expressed his admiration for Neville and respect for his service. He spoke of their first meeting in the parliamentary dining room where Neville had been looking for somewhere to sit. Gough had called Neville to join him. He enclosed a cheque for $500.

Malcolm Fraser had been Liberal Party leader and Prime Minister from 1975. I had not heard from him, so after three weeks I called his office. His assistant came back to the phone, "Mr Fraser will not be attending, nor will he be donating money." I made a note to never forget this, especially as at the time, Mr Fraser had wrapped himself around causes critical of the Liberal, Howard Government. Mind you, Neville had 'crossed the floor' on 23 occasions.

In the lead-up to the dinner I lobbied for a sculpture or bust of Neville Bonner to be commissioned for display in or around Parliament House. I was told by the director of parliament's art collection that sculptures are "not in keeping with the architectural and aesthetic ambience of the building and surrounds". I should be reassured that a portrait of the late Senator Bonner was in the collection. I was angry. A lot of strange artworks and sculptural pieces were displayed at great cost to the taxpayers in Parliament House. But apparently we were unwilling and unable to have sculptures of great Australians who made us who we are. I took my case to John Howard. He listened carefully, agreed with me but, "Brendan, I'm only the Prime Minister. I have no control over the artworks in Parliament House."

Deflated, I turned instead to a memorial scholarship administered by the Australian National University. The government, supported by Pfizer, the pharmaceutical giant, invested $400,000 in an annual scholarship for two honours graduates in Neville's name.

Four years later during the federal election, Heather Bonner was in hospital dying. 'Bonner', the newly created Brisbane electorate named in honour of Neville, was too close to call on election day. Three days later I called Heather the moment the Australian Electoral Commission declared the result. "Heather, Ross Vasta has won Bonner for the Liberal Party."

Heather whispered, "Bonner is Liberal. I can go now". And she did.

My family. (L) to (R), Emily, me, Gillian, Bec and Tom 2009

The large photograph of Neville Bonner has always prominently hung in my office. A reminder every day of what is really important. The liberating power of even a small amount of education and that transcending all else in life, is character. Education Minister 2002

On stage performing with Slim Dusty, Joy McKean and the Travelling Country band at the State Theatre, Sydney 2002. Education Minister at the time, I had proposed to Slim a song about Neville Bonner's life. He and joy wrote 'The Quiet Achiever'. At the launch of 'Travellin' still, Always will', Slim invited me on-stage to sing it with them.

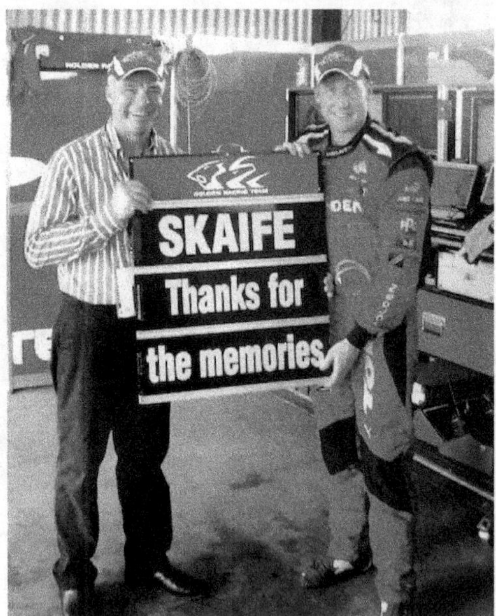

Mark Skaife's last race with the Holden Racing Team. Oran Park 2009. A champion driver and champion man.

At the dispatch box as Education Minister 2003. John Howard and Peter Costello looking on.

Defence Minister. Addressing troops Afghanistan 2006. The best part of the job.

Press conference with US Secretary for Defense, Donald Rumsfeld 2006.

Outside the Pentagon with US Secretary Defense, Donald Rumsfeld. My Chief of Staff Maria Fernandez and media advisor, Nigel Blunden. Following a memorable morning.

13

Taking notes and making cups of tea for Mr Reith

I was happy with my lot in 2000. I enjoyed good relations with my colleagues, felt well supported in Bradfield and was making a difference in my own way.

As Chairman of the House of Representatives Standing Committee on Employment, Education and Training, I had overseen the release of two reports. The third attracted Peter Costello's attention – Employee Share Ownership. Robert Menzies took employee ownership of the companies in which they worked to the 1949 election, safe ground for a Liberal you would think. However, in the course of the Inquiry we discovered $1.5 billion of tax avoidance in Superannuation Trusts. I was suspicious that fraud was also afoot. As the Inquiry concluded, I thought it prudent to brief the Treasurer's office of key findings. These committees are fully independent of executive government, but I believed it wise to ensure 'no surprises'. No one would interfere with what we were doing, but equally key ministers needed warning of impending trouble.

I hadn't had much contact with Peter Costello, although I had been a member of the same government for over four years. He was extremely busy and appeared to have his own group of insiders. After question time, the day after I briefed his staff on my findings, he gestured for me to come down to him. Peter is a tall, imposing man. He referred to the impending report, leaning over to me, "If there is anything in that report to cause embarrassment to the government, you will regret it." To literally press his point home, he pointed his finger at my chest.

The draft had already been written. I spent two successive full weekends anxiously poring over every word, carefully editing anything that might be regarded as criticism of Treasury and government.

A few weeks later, back at the house late at night, Joe and I were engaged in our favourite post-parliamentary pastime, sitting in the lounge room eating Paddle Pops watching Jerry Springer. Ruminating on the day's events, Joe turned the subject to leadership of the Party. Specifically, he felt me out about Peter Costello assuming the leadership from John Howard, presumably a medium term objective.

"Joe, I have been in the parliament for over four years. Peter has barely spoken to me. A few weeks ago, he did, pointing his index finger at my chest threatening me over my report on Employee Share Ownership. He seems close to a small group of people, unaware of the rest of the party room which will decide this. I am happy to stick with Howard". Joe didn't raise it with me again.

I didn't really get to know Peter until we lost office in 2007. Another pity, for both the Party and the country. In December 2000, I was sitting in the waiting room at Bob Jane's Tyre Mart in Artarmon. My phone rang. "Brendan, John Howard speaking". I stood immediately and stepped outside. "Brendan, as you know John Moore's retirement has meant a small reshuffle. I would like you to serve as Parliamentary Secretary to the Minister for Defence. Peter Reith will be the defence minister." I was being appointed to the 'middle bench' as Tim Fischer had described it. The most junior of ministerial positions in a serious portfolio to support a man I admired greatly, Peter Reith. Bill Heffernan called soon after, "You've got lift-off mate". I thanked him.

The announcement went out a short time later. By the time I called my mother in Adelaide, she had heard on the radio that I was to be Parliamentary Secretary to the Minister for Defence. Hesitant, she asked if I was happy. "Yes mum. It is a great job."

Relieved, she said, "Oh, that's good. I wasn't sure if you would be happy taking notes for Mr Reith and making him cups of tea."

This would be the most enjoyable role in my political career. As the junior, junior minister I had responsibilities but did not have to answer questions in question time. I had an experienced senior minister who wanted me to succeed. I was coming into the defence community that had played a significant role in my life and would do so much more in the future.

Peter Reith wanted me to assume more responsibility, including acquisition, management and disposal of defence properties. As I was about to discover, the politics of the latter is fraught. I would oversee defence cadets, IT, Emergency Management Australia and a range of ancillary defence support services. Peter Reith had another special project for me. "Brendan, in my electorate is the Western Port Oberon Submarine Association. Lots of retired submariners. There is a decommissioned sub they want. Your job is to make sure they get it. As the Minister of course, I can't be involved." I had no idea at that stage what it all meant, but sensed its importance to Peter Reith and therein my career prospects.

The politics of defence property in local communities came at me fast. The Fremantle Artillery Barracks, nearby in Western Australia, was a case in point, a cluster of five heritage properties at the centre of which was the 19th century barracks. Local communities, veterans groups and military heritage groups had formed a coalition of the willing to fight the mooted sale. Sir Charles Court, then amongst its defenders, had gone so far as to question my predecessor, Eric Abetz's motives on the basis of his German ancestry. While I knew my job was to dispose of property, turning them into dollars for today's fighting forces, I knew I would get more done if I exercised judicious use of the 'white flag'.

The highest profile properties were those around the Sydney Harbour foreshore. As I noted to John Howard, "They are worth a lot but they are worth nothing". Sale was unthinkable. He and the Environment Minister, Robert Hill, in this the year of the centenary of Federation, established the Sydney Harbour Foreshore Federation Trust. Five iconic, heritage military bases on Sydney Harbour were transferred to the Trust. One hundred million dollars was invested in the Trust to support maintenance and development of the sites.

My introduction to inter-service rivalries and jealousies came at the handover of the Georges Heights Army property. I was up very early on the Sunday morning to treat my lawn. It was dying from a worm infestation. When the Commonwealth car arrived, I was dressed and ready to go. I turned up at Georges Heights ten minutes early. With military people, there is only one thing worse than being late – being early. An army officer came tumbling from his office towards the car, fitting his sword as he walked briskly towards me.

Major General Peter Leahy, Deputy Chief of Army, "You're early sir". "Yes Peter, I am sorry if that upsets you. I was up early this morning treating my lawn. Can you believe I've got this thing in it called Army worm?" "Not possible sir!" he belted out. "Navy worm surely?" He wasn't joking!

To be re-engaged with cadets was a joy. But it had suffered years of indifferent neglect and in some quarters, overt hostility from elements of the political and educational classes. My job was to breathe new life into it. John Howard didn't have to tell me what it meant to him.

The school cadet units were confined largely to the independent schools, the public system having long abandoned them. Knox Grammar, in my electorate, was the exemplar. All the boys were in cadets and offered a parade that would give professional military ones a run for their money. However, most units were in the community and run by volunteers – often ex-military people with meagre resources. Visiting cadet units, the length and breadth of the country, I could see and feel the pride these men and women had in developing the young people in their care. Following a review, I made sure things happened.

Firstly, administrative oversight of cadets would move into the main defence headquarters in Canberra. All cadets would be given a uniform and cadet leaders receive specialised training with money invested in cadet facilities. When aircraft, ships or army equipment were visiting, defence would be required to notify relevant cadet units to enable them to connecr, interacting with equipment and personnel. Controversially, I wanted army cadets to get opportunities to go to civilian rifle ranges and have supervised shooting instruction. We launched the new Australian Defence Force Cadets at RAAF base Richmond.

With the Chief of Defence, service chiefs and cadets from the three services we launched the reform package before C-130 Hercules aircraft parked on the tarmac. The photograph is one for the ages.

In 2014 I received a mounted desk statue of an army cadet. The plaque at its base read:

Be proud of who you are now and in your future
With Respect and Love
27 ACU COFFS HARBOUR
Capt. Rys Herzig C.O.

It came with a card at the top of which was a photograph of Rys Herzig in uniform with his beloved pet boxer. The note from his widow, Linda: "Thank you for helping change the Army and Navy Cadets 12 to 18 year olds' lives for the better – giving them inspiration." To this day that figurine, Rhys' photo affixed to Linda's note, sits by my desk.

Major General Peter Haddad headed Support Command. He was responsible for logistic support to the defence forces. I received advice about a propellant factory at Mulwala on the Murray River. It made gun powder which was then used to manufacture munitions at Benalla on the Victorian side of the border. The Mulwala factory was old, expensive and Defence recommended it be shut down. Australia could import propellants. I asked to see General Haddad. He explained the problem, the basis of their advice and why I should agree to it. I could see that 340 people worked at the factory and that it had been there for decades. I decided I would go to have a look at it first. It was in the electorate of Farrer, held by the retiring Tim Fischer. I thought this would have a bearing on the campaign as no doubt it would on Indi, the other side of the border, where the long-standing MP was also retiring. It would be tricky.

I had never seen anything like the Mulwala propellant factory. It was old and tired. The machinery and 'vibe' evoked images of a Dickensian working environment. One woman in a hair net looked up from her machine, "Minister, I am a single mother with two kids.

Please help us". The environmental issues besetting the site read like the script for an Erin Brockovich movie. It was clear that the entire community needed this factory – badly. Beyond the 340 employed directly, another 350 jobs in the community relied on its survival. Delving further, I discovered that only four ships in the world transported propellants. Australia would rely on booking a ship, it turning up on time and then stockpiling something very dangerous. If there was a disruption to supply, the nation would be vulnerable. Further, the propellants made at Mulwala were of a precise specification for the Army's Steyr rifle. As if that wasn't enough, in an environment where Pauline Hanson's *One Nation* was ascendant, I knew they would run with, "We're even importing ammo!"

The factory had to be rebuilt and modernised. When I put it to Peter Reith, he said, "It'd be cheaper to send all the workers a cheque". Nonetheless, he encouraged me to bring it forward and argue the case. I did. John Howard agreed and $220 million was committed by Cabinet to its redevelopment. I left the Cabinet meeting and went straight down to Albury to make the announcement, then to Mulwala to speak directly to management and the workers. The overwhelming joy spread to the pub afterwards with my appearing on the TV news being feted by the union delegates!

Among the deluge of supportive letters was a drawing of her family from then four-year-old Phoebe Bye from Yarrawonga. Her dad worked at Mulwala and she wanted to show me what it meant to her, drawing her family. I had the drawing photographed with me and John Howard and sent back to her. It appeared in the local papers under the headline *PM has Phoebe's drawing*, people impressed that in Australia a four-year-old's drawing would get to the Prime Minister. Phoebe wrote to me again, eight years later on the announcement of my retirement from politics to tell me I had honoured my promise to her and that her dad was still working at Mulwala!

You go into politics to make a difference. I had made a difference to these people. The decision would be further vindicated by heinous events in New York just months away that would change the world and

Australia's place in it. Australia, like many other countries, would be needing a lot of 'ammo' in the decades ahead.

Meanwhile, I had been working on Peter Reith's submarine, an Oberon class, *Otama*, was decommissioned in 2000. Two Victorian communities wanted it, the Western Port Oberon Association at Hastings and the city of Geelong. A large number of retired submariners were concentrated at Hastings under the leadership of a passionate 'sub tragic', Max Bryant. *Otama* would need to be towed from Western Australia at a cost of $2.5 million. Navy advice recommended Geelong. With studied concern and maritime charts, Navy officers advised me of the complex, significant risk of getting it into port at Hastings. Armed with this knowledge, I went to Hastings to meet the enthusiastic volunteers pining for their beloved submarine. About fifty turned out to make me welcome. All spoke highly of Peter Reith and were dismissive of any suggestion to thwart their dream. At Geelong, I met the mayor, general manager and several councillors. In contrast to Hastings, Navy told me that delivery to Geelong would be straightforward and the proposal to site and display *Otama* was preferred. I knew I had to find a way to land it at Hastings. Mission impossible, it seemed. Then, a stroke of pure luck.

Following the formal discussions, I was in conversation with two of the Geelong councillors. Both were politically aligned to us and spoke beyond the formal briefings. Excitedly, one said, "Brendan, you're going to love what we are planning for the sub once she's in. We're going to paint it yellow. We'll have a yellow submarine magical theme park right through the mall with a Beatles backdrop." I was told to keep it under wraps. Gold, gold, gold is all I could think. Manna from heaven! I feigned only passing interest in the idea. Excitedly I returned to the car and immediately rang my office. I needed another tour of the two bidding sites, but this time I would bring a senior naval submarine officer with me and conduct a full, formal consultation at both. I knew that a 'Yellow submarine' would motivate Navy strongly to get *Otama* to Hastings.

I told no one of the Geelong plans for the submarine, asking Navy to provide me with a senior submarine officer to accompany me to Victoria for consultations. Several weeks later I was introduced to Royal Australian Navy Commander Anthony Vine. I had struck gold again. He had served in HMAS *Otama* and was the last crew member still serving in the Navy. He described himself as "having a passion for the preservation and promotion of Australia's naval history".

Commander Vine, like those before him, held grave concerns for the feasibility of getting *Otama* into Hastings. I listened intently, knowing what lay ahead.

Meeting the Western Port Oberon Association was akin to a reunion. Lots of charts, talk about the life of the submarine and its possible future as a display at Hastings. Max Bryant and his volunteers laboured mightily to convince Commander Vine it could be done. He was noncommittal and focused on the engineering challenges. At Geelong the Mayor welcomed us into the Council chamber. Most councillors were present along with the general manager, chief engineer and staff. We were briefed in detail about the plans for *Otama,* Commander Vine nodding approvingly at what we heard. There would be no technical barriers to getting the sub to the site. I waited until close to the end of formalities.

"Once you have the submarine in place, what specifically do you intend to do with it Mayor? Will you enhance it in any way, breathe new life into it?" He shuffled, looking across to the Shire Engineer. "Minister, it is very exciting. We are going to paint it yellow and play Beatles' music along the wharf. It will be the centrepiece of our Yellow Submarine showcase."

I glanced sideways at ashen faced Commander Vine. The doors had barely shut on the Comcar when he turned to me, "Minister, I think we can have another serious look at getting *Otama* into Hastings. With tides, selective dredging and will, I am confident it can be done." I smiled to myself and thought, "I love the military". Peter Reith got his submarine.

A little piece of bureaucracy – 100 metres of it in fact – was upsetting Warren Entsch in far north Queensland. The Wangetti rifle range north of Cairns was a Defence-owned property. It was leased to the local shooting club. A new firearm used by members required an extension of the rifle range by 100 metres. The 'problem' was that it adjoined the Karanda National Park.

'Entschy' had been lobbying the Environment minister, Robert Hill to make the 100 metres available to Defence. Hill had steadfastly resisted but was prepared to consider relenting if Defence made the application for it. Karanda National Park is millions of hectares. I met with the manager of Defence properties for Queensland in his Brisbane office. I got to the Wangetti rifle range, explaining the need for us to get this done. He advised strongly against it on environmental grounds. I asked him if he knew the Member for Leichardt, Mr Warren Entsch. He confirmed that he did.

I said, "Well, let me paint you a picture of last Thursday in Canberra, outside the chamber after question time. Mr Entsch was standing in front of Mr Howard and very close. He explained why the rifle club needs the extension. He had told the Environment Minister there were 'bloody millions of hectares of National Park and I just want a miserable 100 metres'. I told the official that Mr Entsch reached a crescendo, booming, 'Prime Minister, these are the things that piss people orrfffff!'

"So, do we have an understanding? We are going to get an extension to the Wangetti rifle range?" He nodded in agreement.

The Government had been struggling electorally all year. It began with what was widely regarded as a sleight of hand implementing the GST on petrol. The tabloids labelled it a breach of trust. We had been playing catch-up for months but making progress. After the sudden death of Peter Nugent, we won the Aston by-election in Victoria, confirming the government was competitive. But it was events that unfolded in August that radically altered the nation and political narrative.

An overloaded Indonesian fishing boat carrying 433 Afghan asylum-seekers was stranded in international waters about 140 kilometres north of Christmas Island. The Norwegian container ship MV *Tampa* rescued them. The asylum seekers forced the master of the ship to take them to Australia. John Howard refused entry to the ship, citing the number of 'illegal' arrivals to Australia was already too great. The ship's captain decided to bring the ship into Australian waters on 29 August. John Howard ordered the SAS to board the ship after it crossed Australia's maritime boundary to stop it getting to Christmas Island. He then immediately tabled a Bill in Parliament that would allow Australia to remove a foreign ship from Australian waters. It also authorised boarding of it. The Bill gave retrospective powers to do so. In 48 hours, it was done. So too was Kim Beazley's ambition to be prime minister. He vacillated, but finally Labor voted against it ensuring its defeat in the Senate.

From these tumultuous events was born the 'Pacific Solution'. Asylum seekers would go to Nauru, Papua New Guinea and elsewhere but not set foot in Australia. Some 43 boats filled with 5,000 asylum seekers arrived in 2001. Only 23 more arrived over the remaining period of the Howard Government.

John Howard was in Washington DC with President George W Bush in September. On 11 September, the unthinkable happened. I was watching late night television news. A plane of indeterminate size had crashed into one of the twin towers of the World Trade Center in New York. Nineteen minutes after the first, as coverage of the event continued, a passenger jet crashed into the second tower. The United States of America was being attacked. A third plane crashed into the Pentagon in Washington DC. A fourth, United Airlines Flight 93, we later learned, was on its way to hit the White House. When passengers were alerted by mobile phone calls to their fate, they overwhelmed the terrorists, taking them all to their death in a Pennsylvania field.

Almost 3,000 civilians were murdered that day, including 10 Australians.

The world I knew had just changed in ways that would take months and years to digest. But changed it had.

Lieutenant General Peter Cosgrove was Chief of Army. I was in my electorate office in September working on election materials when one of my staff walked in. "General Cosgrove's office just called. He wants to invite you to a dinner early next month. What should I tell them?" "Look, I love the military people, but seriously? We're on the cusp of an election. Please thank him but I have too much on."

She returned minutes later. "General Cosgrove said to let you know it will be a small dinner for just ten people including Kerry Packer, Laurie Oakes and Lindsay Fox." "What time does it start?"

I was attending an afternoon event for Navy Cadets on HMAS *Kanimbla* at Garden Island on 6 October. The host was then Maritime Commander for Navy, Rear Admiral Geoff Smith. At one point he was called away to take a call from HMAS *Adelaide*. When he returned, he leaned over and said, "Sir, you're not going to believe it. They (asylum seekers) have thrown kids in the water."

Little did I know what that meant until a furore erupted over the coming days. It was clear that the initial advice from Navy was just that, subsequently refuted by forensic examination of the facts. John Howard and senior ministers had passed on the early advice and were excoriated by the media for doing so.

I promised Gillian I would paint our front fence for her birthday on 25 October and took a day off from campaigning to get the job done. My mobile phone rang. Arthur Sinodinos, John Howard's chief of staff, wanted to tell me that the second airport at Badgerys Creek for which I had been campaigning was opposed by Cabinet. He asked what I was doing. "Brushing up on border protection, Arthur"!

I was in Eden Monaro with Gary Nairn three days before polling day. A big van arrived brimming with huge campaign billboards. Gary and I pulled the first one out. We both looked at it and then at each other. A large black and white photograph of John Howard beneath which in bold letters was his quote from the campaign launch – "We will decide who comes to this country and the circumstances in which they come!" I simply said, "You're going to win on Saturday Gary".

The Coalition was returned on 10 November with an increased vote. The only guest at Peter Cosgrove's dinner to have predicted the outcome and margin was Laurie Oakes.

14

"Oh, it's the black stuff that you read!"

I knew John Howard was generally happy with my work as Parliamentary Secretary. I was hopeful I would keep my job and, perhaps, even be considered for the outer ministry. John Howard called a week after the election victory. He thanked me for what I had done and then asked me to come into Cabinet as Minister for Education, Science and Training. Dumbfounded, I managed to say yes, regarding it as an immense privilege to so serve the people and government. He had a couple of things he wanted to say. "Brendan, after the 1998 election, two of your New South Wales colleagues were promoted and you weren't. You must have been very disappointed." "Yes, Prime Minister, I was."

> Well, I gave you that job running Sydney airport and you got on with it. No one knew how disappointed you were. I admire that. I have had a few setbacks in my political life (an understatement). I know how it feels. How people deal with failure says more about them than how they deal with success. The other thing is I want you to bring your views to Cabinet. We have different positions on a number of matters, they need to be heard.

Another lesson in leadership.

My departmental secretary would be Peter Shergold. I was an admirer. He had led Indigenous Affairs. He had a great mind, was thoughtful, curious, pragmatic, with a great sense of humour, treated people well and had a deep social conscience.

New to Cabinet, I asked Peter Reith's former Chief of Staff, Peter Hendy, if he would accept the position with me. He was wanting to move to the private sector but agreed to come and help me on my way. I needed someone skilled in the development of policy, respected and experienced in Cabinet processes. National Party MP, Peter Mc-

Gauran, was my 'junior' minister responsible for science. A safe pair of hands. I always liked the National Party: Peter was one of its best.

After the swearing in at Government House, Entschy managed to get us onto the front page of *The Canberra Times*. So excited was he for me that he hugged and kissed me. He, Joanna Gash, Kay Elson, Danna Vale and others had urged John Howard to promote me for which I am forever grateful. I also learned from Sir John Carrick several years later that Peter Reith had especially taken up my case with Howard. Peter's other 'project' was Tony Abbott. Both of us would become Liberal leader and one, Prime Minister.

The day after the swearing-in, I opened *The Australian* newspaper. A special supplement featured outstanding schools. A photograph of Year 10 students from Salisbury High School in Adelaide's northern suburbs proudly led the feature. Its principal, Helen Paphitis, spoke to the commonsense aspirations of mainstream Australian parents. The students were developing 'values', engaged in broader community outreach and were expected to meet standards in everything from literacy to etiquette. Educating many Indigenous students, the school's academic results spoke to inspired leadership. I asked my staff to get me Ms. Paphitas' phone number. I knew Salisbury well. It was close to where I had grown up in Modbury and I played many games of tennis there. I congratulated Ms. Paphitas and asked if it would be okay for me to visit the school. She was overjoyed by my interest.

I was on a journey. In that first week I reached out to key leaders in higher education, schools, training and science. Denis Fitzgerald was president of the Australian Education Union. School funding was a red hot issue. His Union was a strident critic of our policies that supported the establishment of independent, private schools and funding given to them. We met for a coffee near my Lindfield electorate office. He launched into the "unjust" support given by the federal government to private schools.

I came into the portfolio supportive of choice in education, deeply imbued with the memory of the financial sacrifices my parents had made to educate me in the Catholic system. But beyond the principle of fair support for every student, my mind was open. I presented Denis with data I had read only the day before our meeting. "All of the growth in the independent schools is in the low fee end – Christian, Catholic, Lutheran, Muslim and similar schools. In fact, last year saw a 4 per cent contraction in the prestigious, high fee end of the system."

I asked myself as much as him, "What are these parents looking for? Why are parents on modest incomes, bypassing good public schools they have already paid for, to spend thousands of after-tax dollars educating their kids? What are they getting that the public system is not offering? Answer that Denis and then we can begin to address it." I had my own thoughts. The answer was likely to be in two words – values and standards. Salisbury High School illustrated my point.

And so began a journey of discovery.

Tom Allard was the political writer for Fairfax Media. He put in a request for an interview. Naturally, I was busy but agreed. I had to establish my agenda for the portfolio. I had a scheduled visit to Open Family in Cabramatta, so suggested Tom might like to catch the train out west with me. Three weeks into the job and he asked me for the plan. I couldn't yet give him a plan, but I could give him my vision.

> Our vision is that every Australian, young and not so young, should be supported to find and achieve his or her own potential. While there is much of which to be proud, one of our failings is to have created a culture in which young people feel that their lives are valued by the educational choices they make. Too many young people feel that if they don't achieve an outstanding year twelve result and university entry, they are of lesser value to their families and the country. We should strive to be an Australia in which the educational choices of young people are equally celebrated, whether university, apprenticeships, vocational training or TAFE. For some young people, just getting from school to a job emotionally intact is a far greater

> achievement than anything I have ever done. Some of us are salmon, fighting our way up the fjords of life. Others want a quiet pond in the world.

Early the following morning, driving to my electorate office, a huge banner adorned the Gordon newsagency promoting the *Sydney Morning Herald:*

DON'T BOTHER GOING TO UNI
EDUCATION MINISTER

Much of the day was spent explaining what I had actually said and meant. I stood by my guns though. I knew I was right.

Returning home that night my 15-year-old son Tom, not known as an avid newspaper reader, had carefully placed the *Sydney Morning Herald* on the kitchen bench. He had read every word. "Dad, did you actually mean what you had said to me about this stuff?" Yes, I most certainly had. "Son, I don't mind what you do with your life as long as you do something you love, do your best, keep learning and find happiness." Tom went on to do an apprenticeship in landscaping and has not looked back.

I hoped I had stimulated similar conversations in thousands of households.

Peter Hendy and I accepted a dinner invitation from the Australian Vice Chancellors Committee (AVCC) a week after my swearing in. The AVCC was the peak body for university leadership. Its Chairman was the Vice Chancellor of the University of Western Australia, Professor Deryck Schreuder. The CEO was John Mullarvey, a passionate, indefatigable policy driven advocate for higher education. Yet he was not a university graduate.

At Canberra's Lakeside Restaurant, it became clear from both the conversation and my preliminary briefings on the sector that reform was needed. 'War weary' from their battles with my predecessors Amanda Vanstone and then David Kemp, I sensed a willingness for reform. They spoke of the inevitable 'crisis' in university funding as we consumed a meal beyond the affordability of most Australians. It would be the first of many, a stark contrast to the training sector. In the car on the way back to Parliament House, I told Peter that we had a big job in front of us. I felt we had both an opportunity and responsibility to drive reform, a component of which would be greater government investment in the sector. We would need a discussion with the Prime Minister.

The Department of Education Science and Training held its annual Christmas party at Canberra's Rydges Hotel in early December. The invitation said 'Hawaiian Theme'. Although we were pre-smart phones in 2001, I thought suit and tie would suffice. Given this was my first opportunity to meet the people upon whom I would rely for advice and support, I thought 'boring' would be an appropriate first impression. You only have one chance to make one. The Comcar pulled up outside the hotel. The Departmental Secretary, Peter Shergold, was waiting in a brilliantly coloured Hawaiian shirt, his chest adorned with a Hawaiian lei. I regretted not wearing sunglasses. Next to him was a man wearing an even louder shirt and grass skirt. Peter welcomed me, "Minister, welcome to the staff Christmas party. We have over 400 of our staff here."

Just weeks after the government's re-election, the second man said, "G'day Brendan. My name's Kev. They call me Big Kev. I'm president of the social club. I'm what you call a disappointed voter. I'm also Labor party branch president. I will work my guts out for you over the next three years and then do whatever I can to get you out of office". Shergold's facial reaction said what I was thinking. Kev boomed, "Anyway mate, come on in, have a beer and meet the team."

Over the next four and half years I would come to know this man as an outstanding public servant and Vietnam veteran. When I left the portfolio, Kev arranged an equally large sendoff, presenting me with carefully chosen gifts as we both shed a tear.

As everyone has been to school, and many to university, they think they know about education. I soon learned that much emotion accompanies the advice I received, spilling over to passionate, and at times violent activism. I brought my own life experiences to the task but, as always, with an open mind.

Reverend Bill Crews, of course, was well known to me. His work at the Exodus Foundation was inspiring. When he wasn't feeding the homeless and working poor, keeping drug addicts alive, sheltering refugees and rebuilding the lives of street workers, he ran a remedial reading programme at the back of the church hall.

In 1994, deeply troubled by kids unable to read, Bill had approached Professor Kevin Wheldall at Macquarie University's Special Education Centre. Kevin had a well-earned reputation for an evidence-based approach to reading. *MultiLit – Making up lost time in Teaching* was introduced to Bill's 'Schoolwise' Project. The idea was for the Exodus Foundation to provide pastoral support to the kids and their families while Wheldall's academics and volunteers delivered the didactic reading programme.

I attended the 'graduations' for several years, tissues in hand. Now Australia's Education Minister, I was even more determined to be there. Year 5 students struggling with literacy were collected every week by Bill's mini-bus from Sydney's inner west schools. A team of trained volunteers then spent several hours with them, one to one in a phonics based reading tutorial. At my first graduation as Minister, Bill introduced me to a boy who stood and read a piece of poetry he had written. After his first session six months earlier, he had exclaimed, "Oh – it's the black stuff you read!"

I asked myself, and subsequently large audiences of educators, "How can you spend five years in the education system and not know it's the black stuff that you read?"

As is often the case, it is the informal interaction with the everyday Australian that teaches you the most. I stood chatting with one mother, proud of her son's progress. The conversation was a revelation, so many issues falling out before me. I asked an Indigenous woman who worked at Coles, and whose husband was a delivery driver, when she first thought her son had problems:

> Well, he was in Year 2. I said to my husband that his reading was poor. My husband wasn't sure, but thought his report card was okay so I shouldn't worry. But when he was in Year 3, we both knew he was behind his younger sister. I went to see the principal. The principal told me that he was behind in reading but said he is good at sport. He was put with the other kids in class like him. I asked the principal if she could keep him back in Year 3 to do it again until he could read properly. She said that doesn't happen anymore, all the kids pass to the next year.
>
> Dr Nelson, without Reverend Crews, I don't know where we would be. Rich people can pay for their kids to get a tutor, we can't.

In this single exchange was embedded a series of problems to which I would develop policy responses. I gave her my card and asked if she would send me some of her son's school reports. She did. I spent seven years at university and I couldn't make sense of them – meaningless jargon. I had no idea just how he was actually going from the nonsense in the reports. He was variously described as 'working towards' or 'consolidating'. My instincts were that I had encountered a sweet spot. Good policy was about to meet good politics.

At my request the department undertook research of parents. Specifically, what were parents looking for in the education of their children? It identified the top three issues as values, discipline and standards. It confirmed where I knew I needed to go.

Geoff Masters led the Australian Council for Education Research. He showed me evidence marking high performing schools. Six key features:

> First, leadership is everything. Many principals were enthusiastic, motivated, knew their staff and students, exuding pride. Others were jaded, disengaged and occasionally hostile.

Second, there has to be a culture in which teachers believe that every child can learn, irrespective of their family and social circumstances. One teacher said "These kids come from hopeless backgrounds. We do the best we can". As Dr Ken Rowe said to me that first year, "What kids bring to school determines where they start. But what happens at school determines how far they go".

Third, teachers must be well trained and engaged in their own professional development. No teacher can teach what he or she doesn't know.

Fourth, performance must be measured, published and inform teaching practice. The Braitling School in Alice Springs taught kids of well-heeled business people through to impoverished Aboriginal families. The foyer walls displayed charts. As the principal explained the performance of each class across a range of benchmarks, she drew my attention to Year 4. Reading had sharply deteriorated. "You can see what happened here. We found the teacher had a drinking problem". If you don't measure and report performance, how on earth can it be improved?

Fifth, students must have a sense of belonging in the school community, feeling known, safe and understood.

Sixth, a high level of parental engagement. Too many children are dropped off in Year 1 and picked up in Year 12, parents outsourcing their responsibilities to teachers.

Permeating all of this is values. In *Plato's Republic*, Socrates in 340BC proclaimed that ignorance was the root of all evil. America's third President, Thomas Jefferson, when asked towards the end of his life of his greatest achievement, nominated three things. None included achieving the highest office in the land. His life should be remembered for three things.

First, co-authoring the American Declaration of Independence.

> Second, the Virginia Statute for religious freedom.
>
> The third he regarded as his most significant legacy – co-founding the University of Virginia. When asked why, he said, "Education is the defence of the nation".

Education, perhaps more than anything else, protects us from ideas deeply rooted in ignorance and forged on an anvil of prejudice. But it is more than that.

At the Washington Holocaust Museum, I always pause to reflect on the meeting convened by Reinhard Heydrich at Wansee in the outer suburb of Berlin in January 1942. The German SS officer, chief architect of the Holocaust, chaired the meeting. The thirteen German ministers and senior public servants who signed off on the 'final solution' had the best university education Europe had to offer. Nine had PhDs and Masters degrees. Within a year of the meeting half of the 6 million Jews to be exterminated were dead.

It is more than education. It is the values that inform education. A values-free education risks producing values-free adults.

Benjamin Franklin and Edmund Burke both recognised that our freedoms are in direct relation to the extent to which each of us is willing to 'restrain' our 'moral appetite'. When people refuse to comply with society's mores, governments legislate to remove our freedoms. Values inform character. Beliefs are one thing, values are another. It seemed we should identify key values and explicitly teach them. Values have most meaning when they are lived.

I announced a national consultation would be undertaken to settle on values that should be formally taught in Australian schools. We funded 50 case studies in 69 schools. The results were surprising, only in the extent to which they affirmed my instincts. It found values must be explicit and acted out by teachers.

One teacher confronted me. "My job", he said "is to present young people with choices". He was adamant that it was not his place to "tell them what to do".

I challenged him, "How can anyone be neutral when dealing with young people? These are life choices – drug use, exploitation of others, relationships with authority and sexual activity. Surely it is the responsibility of key adults to take a stand, to abandon the pretence of neutrality, guiding young people in their choices in a non-judgmental way?"

Cabramatta High School found a four-fold increase in boys joining the school choir. More than 90% of students attended Year 10 careers night with a parent, a 10% increase.

Alice Springs High School restructured Year 10 to a team approach, including parents. It changed the students' physical environment and introduced a real justice programme. The results were stunning. Serious behavioural problems dropped 30%. Year 10 retention went to 100% and Year 12 retention to 90%. School attendance jumped from 80% to 96% as incidents requiring intervention plummeted. Student confidence that bullying would be dealt with swiftly jumped and students reported feeling more connected to their school. One student simply said, "We have more freedom".

Far too many young people see tolerance as indifference and freedom as abandonment. Values needed to be taught and acted out by role models every day.

I had one of the highlights of my life in April 2002. Slim Dusty's 103rd album was a collaboration with his daughter, Anne Kirkpatrick. *Travellin' Still ... Always Will* was released in March. Slim, Joy, Anne and the Travelling Country band were performing the album to an invited Sydney audience. The album included 'Bonner' (The Quiet Achiever) which Slim and Joy had written and performed for the tribute dinner two years earlier. They worked through the set when Slim told the audience, "We are now going to sing a song Joy wrote about a wonderful Australian, Neville Bonner. He was the first Aborigine elected to the Parliament back in 1971. I'd like to ask a great mate of mine to come up and sing it with us. Brendan Nelson suggested the song, now we'd love him to sing it as well."

Nervous, I went up onto the stage. A truly magic moment. The 'performance' by Australia's education minister went out on late night television. Early the following morning I flew into Wagga Wagga. As I walked through the small airport with my entourage, a man approached waving his finger. "I know you … I know you. You're the bloke who sings with Slim Dusty!"

Later in the year I had another brush with musical fame. I addressed a large audience at the Park Hyatt Hotel in Melbourne. At 11.30pm I was standing out the front of the hotel waiting for the Comcar. Two Toyota Tarago vans pulled in. The sliding doors opened and several men stepped out. One had a towel over his head. I said "G'day mate. You look like a guy back from a boxing match."

"Kind of. We're musicians. Just done a show". The American accent was vaguely familiar.

I asked what kind of music. He looked at me, "Bon Jovi". I said, "Obviously I need to get out a bit more". He asked me what I did. I told him, he laughed, "Good one man!" And off they went.

Over the years, my staff shuddered when I would say, "I've had an idea".

One idea came to me standing outside a small engineering company in Cairns. I noticed a large street sign displaying information about injuries, days lost, productivity and comparisons with the previous year. I turned to my staff, "Why is it I can get more information about what's going on inside a factory than I can about the performance of a school? School signs tell me about the next P&C meeting, congratulate a sporting team or wish me happy harmony day." Recalling the Braitling School in Alice Springs, I was excited.

Schools would be required to display a sign and promulgate information to parents and prospective parents about school performance across a range of key indicators. In time, we would require information be provided publicly as a condition of Commonwealth funding including such things as literacy and numeracy performances for

Years 3, 5 and 7; Science and ICT and what are ICT benchmarking outcomes; teacher participation in professional development at the school level; student and teacher absenteeism;. teacher retention rates; school leaver destinations – work, vocational training and university.

When I released the mock-up school sign in Sydney and went onto Channel Nine's *A Current Affair* to explain it to the public, the overwhelming support from parents was exceeded only by the hostility from teacher unions and state governments.

One woman wrote to me enclosing copies of correspondence she had with schools in South Australia. Planning to move to Adelaide, she had written to three private schools and two government high schools. The private schools each provided a detailed breakdown of academic, sporting, cultural and social outcomes. One went into some detail about the school values and ethos. The two government high schools provided information only about sporting achievements and advised that further information could not be provided as it was policy not to compare one school with another. She enrolled the two children at a private school.

I asked my department if I could be provided with templates of nationwide school report cards. The mother at Bill Crews' Exodus programme had told me her son's report cards were okay, even though she and her husband were convinced he had a problem. I wanted to satisfy myself that her son's nonsensical report card was not an 'outlier'.

Days later, I received the advice. Brace yourself for reading this. "Minister, none of the states are willing to provide their report cards to you as it is a privacy matter, their responsibility alone". Incredulous, I said, "The Commonwealth government provides billions of dollars to them to support the education of children, yet the federal minister for education is not allowed to see a de-identified school report card?" "Yes, Minister". "Okay, could you then consolidate the email addresses of the principals of government schools across the country?" Anticipating the question, I was told that the states and territories would not allow me to communicate directly with school principals!

I spoke to my media advisor, the super savvy Ross Hampton. I asked him to get me onto my 'go to' programme to speak to Australia's parents – *A Current Affair.*

Some days, you really enjoy your work. This was one of them.

I told the audience I was concerned about school report cards filled with unintelligible jargon. Busy parents too often believed their kids were doing well when in fact they weren't. Instead of teachers telling it how it really is, they were choosing from a menu of descriptors in the computer.

> Some reports say that a student is *working towards* or *consolidating.* What on earth does that mean? If Ian Thorpe's mother calls in half way through the 1500 metres final and asks how he's going, she doesn't want to be told he is 'working towards'. When Skaifie (Mark Skaife) is four hours into the Bathurst 1000, his anxious wife doesn't want to be told he is 'consolidating'. In both cases they want to know how fast they are travelling and where in the pack they are placed – in plain language.

I put the call out to Australia's parents. "State governments won't give me report cards, so please remove your child's name and send me what you have." In under a week we had 400 report cards. All confirmed my suspicions.

The increasingly bitter debate around schools was funding. The Coalition had come to office in 1996 committed to the Liberal principle of choice. Every Australian must contribute through taxes to a well-funded public school system. But, equally, having paid for their children to attend public schools, if they then chose to send their children to a Catholic or Independent School, they should be supported. Their children should receive some financial assistance from government broadly in accordance with the socioeconomic circumstances of the families from which they come.

Every child in the non-government system would receive less funding than those in the public system, but they would all receive something. The government support to students in the non-government sector ranged from 30% to 87% less than those in public schools. Parents paid fees, donated to building funds and bought a lot of raffle tickets to meet and exceed the gap.

State schools are owned, operated and largely funded by State governments. As federal education minister, I was not allowed to enter a state school without the permission of my state counterpart.

Liberal Prime Minister Robert Menzies introduced limited federal funding for both government and non-government schools in 1964. In doing so, he opened the way for parental choice. Historically, the federal government provides most of the government funding for non-government schools while the states fund their own public schools with some commonwealth support.

The Labor Party and Teacher Unions were ramping up their rhetoric against the independent school sector. Disingenuously, they would express outrage that the federal government was giving more money to 'private' schools than public schools. This ignored the fact that the primary funding responsibility of the federal government was that of the non-government sector. The States are the primary funders of their schools, a fact conveniently neglected by our critics. Whereas the Commonwealth's funding was indexed to Average Government School Recurrent Costs, the states were increasing their funding at a fraction of the CPI, thereby compounding the problems in their own schools.

In 2002, the 2.25 million students in public schools received $19.9 billion from government. The 1.05 million in the Catholic and Independent schools received $6.2 billion. Parents paid a further $3.6 billion in fees to educate their kids. As the Americans would say, "Do the math." Those parents are saving taxpayers billions of dollars a year.

Most parents know they will probably never be able to send their kids to the Kings School in Sydney. But they would like to think that they live in a country where, if they sacrificed everything, they might be able to do so. I discovered in such schools parents with second mortgages on their homes, grandparents paying fees, two parents with four jobs and even some who had sold their house to pay school fees.

Ironically, it was the Labor Party and advocates of public schools that were turning parents off. Incessant talk of public schools needing to be 'saved', under-resourced, stressed teachers and crowded classrooms. Non-government schools on the other hand, promoted success and values, as did outstanding government schools such as Salisbury High School and Aberfoyle Park High School in Adelaide, Rossmoyne Senior High School in Perth and Noumea Public School in western Sydney.

It was interesting to delve into the income profile of parents sending their kids to non-government schools. Parents on modest incomes were bypassing 'free' schools to pay fees for something they wanted for their kids. The Australian Bureau of Statistics in 2002 told me that two in every five parents with their children in a Catholic or Independent School were earning less than $20,900 a year. In contrast, 48% of parents sending their kids to government schools were earning more than $104,000 a year. The latter parents sat comfortably in front of their televisions watching the ABC telling them of the injustices of school funding. Labor was driving its social justice truck through the working poor to escalate a war on parental choice. Its driver was shadow education minister, Jenny Macklin.

The Australian Council for Education Research was an endless source of evidence. Dr Ken Rowe was its finest exponent of rational, evidence-based thinking. Ken and his collaborators published research finding that socioeconomic status (SES) had only a 10% predictive effect on educational outcomes. In contrast, quality teaching had a 59% predictive effect. The greatest variation is within schools, not between them.

One of the big challenges was the funding system itself for the non-government sector. My predecessor, David Kemp, had introduced the SES funding model. Postcodes with pooled data on income and occupation profiles contributed to an SES score upon which funding would be applied to the school. When introduced, independent schools were assured that none would be worse off. The other big commitment was that the 1,610 Catholic schools could remain outside the SES based funding model. The Catholic education system traditionally distributed money amongst its own schools. I knew that with just under half the schools being funded entirely on the basis of the SES score, I had to get the Catholics in. I asked the department to model what Catholic schools would receive if they were in the system. It would be $362 million more over the four year funding cycle. It wouldn't be easy. I made an appointment to see Archbishop George Pell. I knew that whatever the Catholic Education Office thought, nothing would happen without his consent.

Prior to meeting Archbishop Pell, I spoke at length with Professor Peter Tannock, former head of the Catholic Education Commission and then Vice Chancellor of the University of Notre Dame in Western Australia. I placed Peter in the same category as Dr Ken Rowe – eminent commonsense, free of dogma, exuding decency and a 'smart operator'. He regarded Catholic schools joining the SES model as both inevitable and desirable. In his view the Government's commitment to Catholic education now needed to be reciprocated. He foreshadowed a visionary ambition for Notre Dame harboured by Archbishop Pell – a campus in the city of Sydney.

The meeting with Archbishop Pell went well. I raised the prospect of Catholic Schools coming under the SES funding system. The 978 Catholic schools that would otherwise attract less funding would remain untouched, their funding 'maintained'. The remaining 632 schools would attract more funding, considerably more and in doing so, lift the Government's support for the sector. Critically important, the Catholic Education Commission would continue to pool and distribute the money to its schools as it saw fit. He was 'comfortable' with the proposed arrangements.

Archbishop Pell outlined his vision for the University of Notre Dame in Sydney. He would redevelop Church owned property and move towards its accreditation. It would require government political and financial support of four million dollars. I was confident John

Howard would like the idea. I certainly did. I agreed, knowing Archbishop Pell regarded this as his legacy for the Sydney Archdiocese. I left the meeting uplifted. This would be a major reform. A private university would also develop in the middle of the turf war between the University of New South Wales, the University of Technology Sydney and Sydney University. Good policy and good politics again.

Concerned about my agenda on school report cards, the Australian Primary Principals Association surveyed parents nationally. The results were disappointing – for them. A third of parents thought reports were inadequate. Fifty-five per cent wanted improvements. Over half of respondents wanted to know how their kids ranked against others in the class. Staggeringly, 59% of principals agreed that school reports were 'teacher orientated', 'full of jargon'. Vindication!

The dichotomy between public and independent schools hit me in the northern suburbs of Adelaide. I visited a state high school. The principal could barely conceal his disengaged and resentful attitude towards both his job and me. I was shown neglected infrastructure and transportable buildings accompanied by a staccato of complaints about funding, the indifferent state education department and failings of government. The Year 12 students had been primed by their teachers – private school funding inequities and mooted higher education reforms that would 'lock them out' of university. Less than a kilometre away, I was warmly welcomed to the Lutheran school just five years old. The place was pumping. An energised, enthusiastic principal showed me around the campus with new buildings and more in construction and students in uniform and engaged parents. Of the same community, but completely different attitude.

In the government system, I would learn from a study of primary school funding, that 25 cents in every dollar intended for the education of students never gets to the schools. Instead, it funds the education department. Public school principals have limited autonomy, whether over teacher selection or building programmes. As one said to me, "How can I guarantee a good education if I can't hire my own teachers?" Nothing got done on buildings and infrastructure until someone turned up from the education department with a clipboard to approve it.

In contrast, every dollar coming to an independent school, whether government or fees paid by parents, is spent at the school level. The school council determines how monies will be managed and projects in which it will be invested. Like us buying a house, they take out a mortgage to build and improve the school. The school council hires and fires the principal who, in turn, decides who teaches at the school.

I was visiting a new government high school in south west Sydney. The principal took me through the buildings, facilities and playing fields. I was impressed. As we approached the foyer prior to my departure, I asked if the school had a motto or vision statement. I was told that was a "dated' concept. I then asked if the school flew the Australian flag. "No Minister, we can't fly the Australian flag here. This is a multicultural school. We have students here from more than fifty different cultural backgrounds." Dumbstruck, I asked, "Well, if that's case, why not be like the UN and fly 50 flags with the Australian flag higher than all the others. In the end, we're all Australian." I was met with a blank stare.

Another idea. I couldn't wait to get in the car and share it with my media advisor, Ross Hampton. "That's it. We will require every school in the country receiving commonwealth money to fly the Australian flag. We'll put it in the quadrennial funding legislation." Ross smiled so hard it hurt. Labor went into meltdown over the flags. Its spokesman, Jenny Macklin, fulminating at the dispatch box in question time, ridiculed the idea. She finished the tirade with a throwaway line, "Anyway, not all schools have a flagpole!"

I did a quick calculation and returned to the dispatch box after her next attack question. The federal government would pay for flagpoles in schools that didn't have one. Almost 1,500 schools applied for a flag pole. This meant backbenchers delivering flag poles to the schools in their electorates. They spoke at installation ceremonies, receiving accolades from grateful parents who liked the emphasis on powerful, values driven symbols. One lingering image is that of Tony Smith, Member for the Victorian seat of Casey. In work clothes, Tony borrowed a Ute. With flag poles tied to the racks, he personally delivered them to his local schools – smiling principals and kids. Pure gold!

In an attempt to improve the gender balance of primary school teachers, we developed a proposal for scholarships to attract more men into teaching. Only 16% of primary school teachers in 2002 were men and the numbers were falling. Labor opposed it on the basis scholarships had to be offered to women as well!

The Prime Minister's science prize was looming. Among the pile of 'briefs' from the department was one for dinner in the Great Hall of Parliament House. The $300,000 prize would be awarded by the Prime Minister before an audience of 600 academics, scientists, ministers and politicians. The taxpayers were footing the bill. Normally, I would read the main body of the brief, satisfy myself that it was in order, sign it and move on. However, I went to the guest list to get an idea of who was actually attending. Pages and pages of names and titles. I could not find a single school teacher. When I got to Canberra, I called the Secretary, Peter Shergold. "Peter, this Prime Minister's Science Prize dinner. Not a single school teacher. Any of us only achieves what we do as a consequence of parents and teachers. We should have at least two tables of school teachers. In fact, why don't we have a Prime Minister's science prize for an outstanding science teacher in primary school and another for secondary school? Let's make it $50,000." Peter liked the idea. And so it was inaugurated.

The more I moved into the portfolio, the schools agenda developed into a ten point plan: Parental choice; Teacher Quality; Attracting the best teachers; National Consistency in Schooling – starting ages and curriculum; Principals' Autonomy; Intolerance of Poorly Performing Schools; Provision of Information to Parents; Values; Safe Schools Framework; Indigenous Education; Transitions – careers advice and employability skills.

My brother-in-law was the Agricultural Science teacher at Corowa High School. Bryon Adamson went into a witness protection programme for the four and half years I was Education Minister. But observing and speaking with him, I gained insight into the problem. Despite an obstinate principal, Bryon successfully campaigned to have viticulture introduced to the school. "For God's sake we're in the Rutherglen wine making region. We need to stimulate these kids to think about science. The wine industry is the future for a lot of them." Just the kind of man you would want teaching your kids, he had been teaching for twenty years. He was up in Sydney doing courses at weekends, took a keen interest in the welfare of his students and worked hard. I could see that the dedicated teacher, immersed in professional development, in to work early, home late, on the phone to parents was being paid exactly the same as the disengaged, indifferent teacher.

I accepted an invitation to address a thousand teachers at the New South Wales Teachers Federation Conference in Sydney. Certain it would be a hostile audience, it offered the opportunity to confront them with the key professional challenges facing them. A very small number applauded when I was introduced. The senior, long-standing Federation official, Angelo Gavrielatos, was polite, appreciating my attendance.

I spoke of my own profession, medicine. Medical schools required accreditation from a national body comprising senior members of the profession. A medical school that lost accreditation was no longer able to train doctors. Of those that taught me as an undergraduate, half were not academics but clinicians with a university appointment. Doctors were required to be registered and for it to be renewed annually. I was a member of the AMA which offered professional and industrial representation along with public interest health advocacy. But doctors are also fellows of a learned College. They have to maintain formal engagement in professional development, continuing medical education and quality assurance. Failure to do so results in de-registration. Doctors subscribe to a code of ethics. They can be excluded from the profession if they do not meet high standards set.

I then presented the contrast for teachers. Teachers were taught by academics. Many of those training teachers had told me that they did not regard themselves as being members of the teaching profession. One had described herself as "a social change agent". Working school teachers did not have university appointments and the profession had little control over the training of the next generation of teachers. Entry requirements into education faculties were disturbingly low. There was no agreed code of ethics, nor did they have a capacity to exclude teachers from the profession. There was no nationally agreed standard for teaching and obviously no way to police and enforce a standard not set and agreed. Teachers had strong industrial representation but weak support for professional bodies from teachers themselves. Teachers were paid not on the basis of performance, but time served in the classroom. Higher remuneration came from being promoted out of what they loved – teaching – to be a principal or departmental official. As I stood at the lectern unpacking all this, speaking directly to them about their professional challenges, increasing numbers actually started listening. Others held up score cards, some accompanied by offensive words and jeers.

I wondered what parents would make of this. I resolved to advance the issues, even if many preferred that I leave them to their own devices. The other "note to self" was to raise dress standards for teachers. Tee shirts and bare midriffs seemed incompatible with higher standards, let alone respect for teaching.

The university education faculties seemed little more than quasi sociology departments. There needed to be an accreditation model akin to the medical profession. Minimum entry levels for teacher training could be set. Students were entering teacher training with tertiary entrance scores from Year 12 of less than 50.

Born of this was the National Institute for Quality Teaching and School leadership. Established at the Australian National University, it would comprise principals, working teachers from both the public and private sectors and researchers in the fields of teaching and school leadership. States, the Deans of Education and peak professional groups would also be represented. It would be of the profession for the profession. With $10 million, its task was to develop the national standards for teaching. It would also develop the professional development and quality assurance programmes that would, in my vision, inform the basis of ongoing teacher registration from which the case for higher teacher incomes could be made.

Flying back from an electorate visit in regional Victoria, I was haunted by the words of the Chairman of an early learning centre in the electorate of McEwen. He had told me that of the 43 kids enrolled to begin that year of 2003, "only five have any concept of a book". There were households in which reading had no place and no books.

In this context I was thinking about the states refusing to report literacy benchmark results to parents. They regarded it as an 'invasion of privacy' to report test results to parents. Teacher unions saw testing as a basis for comparing one school with another. Seriously, you can't make this stuff up. With this in mind, I again recalled the graduation at the Exodus Foundation, the Aboriginal mother whose boy had been left behind: "Rich people can get a tutor".

Another idea – and a bloody good one I thought. Off the plane, I called the Secretary of the Department, now Jeff Harmer. I told him I would like to offer vouchers to parents whose children had not met the Year 3 reading benchmark. I asked him to look at every hollow log of discretionary funding in the portfolio. We would divide it by the number of students who had not met the benchmark and know how much we could offer. He liked the idea. The beauty was that in order to be eligible for the voucher, parents would obviously have to know their child had not met the national testing benchmark. He informed me of the figure. We could offer a $700 voucher. Parents could use it at the school attended by their child or take it to an authorised private tutor.

We ran the story out on the front page of Melbourne's *Herald Sun* newspaper. Victoria was one of the states refusing to make the test results available to parents. John Howard called me early. "Brendan, this is an excellent initiative. Let me know if you need more money".

Within days, Victoria and Queensland caved in to public pressure to release the results to parents, making them eligible for a reading tutorial voucher. By late 2005, evaluation of students provided with vouchers found a rapid improvement in reading age of between 12 and 18 months.

By 2004 the 10 point plan for schooling was fully developed and had been socialised with the states. Comprehensive, it would be embedded in the quadrennial schools funding legislation and take effect from 2008. Everything was there, from principal autonomy and nationally consistent starting age for school to plain language report cards. It passed through the parliament just before the 2004 election. Some elements took effect in different years of the four year agreement. Teacher Unions and Labor states would work hard to have us out of office and reverse what Labor, then in opposition, had no choice but to support. Schools needed the money.

Early in 2004, I told John Howard that although we had a powerful school funding story, I felt we needed to put more money into public schools. The election campaign would be hard enough, but without a 'story' in state school funding to which Australians could relate, it would be harder. Howard was sympathetic but reminded me that if we put more money into public schools the states would simply cut that amount from their own budgets. He was right.

How to get around the states? I was driving past the Roseville Public School in my electorate. The typical school sign, with which we are all familiar, was emblazoned with details about Friday night's P&C trivia night. Next to it was a fund-raising thermometer. A light bulb moment. I can donate money to the P&C raising money for school essentials. It could be play equipment, IT support or library books. They held bank accounts, knew what the school needed and raised the money for it. I called John Howard.

"Prime Minister, I have had an idea. Why don't we develop a programme of Commonwealth contributions directly to P&Cs and P&Fs? You and I are always buying cakes and raffle tickets at schools for worthy projects identified by parents themselves. Why can't the government donate to parent identified priorities?"

He liked it – a lot.

The Investing in Our Schools Programme (IOSP) was born of the conversation. One billion dollars was committed in direct grants of $150,000 to schools. These funds would go to the parent body to fund or co-fund school projects identified by the peak parent group. In many cases the money would be supported by in-kind and cash contributions from parents themselves. Parents loved it. Backbenchers loved it even more.

Some schools preferred the state department of education manage the grant. This revealed what I suspected, with states immediately charging an 18% project management fee. A school in Hornsby illustrated more – gouging. Parents wanted a perimeter fence for the school. They approached a local fencing contractor who quoted $54,000. The New South Wales State Department of Education insisted that as it was 'major infrastructure', they should manage the project. Their preferred contractor quoted $85,000.

One public school in western Sydney wanted to spend its $150,000 on air conditioning. The State Department of Education refused the school access to the upgraded electricity grid. Complete madness but excellent political ammo!

IOSP was a winner on so many fronts. It supported parents, put power and money at the school level in their hands and exposed the failings of education funding and administration at the state level.

John Brogden was leader of the Liberal Party in New South Wales. A good man, sharing many views I held myself, he took me aside at a Liberal event. I was taken aback when he said that I was making his life hard: "Look Brendan, the reality is we need the teachers' unions onside to win an election. All this stuff you're doing with schools is working against us."

When conservative *Herald Sun* columnist, Andrew Bolt, asked me why I was the one "banging on about standards, flagpoles and report cards" when it was a state government responsibility, my conversation with John Brogden offered insight.

The most potent attack on Catholic and Independent Schools came from Labor's education policy for the 2004 election. Although not unveiled until September, I concluded earlier in the year that its policy must cut funding to a number of Catholic and Independent schools. Labor's education spokeswoman, Jenny Macklin, had been advocating a change to the way funding was distributed between schools. A benchmark of fees charged of $9,112 or more was set by Macklin. These "high fees", she said, were "not being taken into account when federal Government funding was allocated". It was my media advisor, Ross Hampton, who said, after she and Mark Latham had visited a low fee Christian school in Western Sydney, "they must have a hit list". He was right. Based on the fees nominated by Macklin, we established that 127 schools would have their federal government funding cut by Labor. We released the "hit list" of schools to be cut.

When Latham was speaking about a "Ladder of Opportunity", I was telling parents he was planning to remove a couple of rungs. Everyone knew that among parents sending their children to these high fee schools were those making enormous personal sacrifices. I knew many parents dreamed of sending their kids to them. Others not on the "hit list" would be nervous about what else Labor would do. I went to work on this, Macklin telling anyone who would listen that I was "making it up".

When Labor's policy was released in September 2004, it confirmed I was right. Money was to be taken from some schools and given to others: the politics of envy and reinvigoration of the class war.

15

"Pigs might fly"

Convinced from my early briefings and interaction with the Vice Chancellors that reform of universities was needed, I went to see John Howard. Peter Hendy and I met him in Sydney, early in 2002. I discussed it with the Secretary, Peter Shergold, beforehand to make sure he understood the issues. Howard listened carefully and, as always, asked penetrating questions.

I proposed a creative process that would be owned by me but arm's length from the government. I would publish a series of ministerial discussion papers canvassing the key issues. The process would educate them and broader audiences about the challenges and canvass policy options. Some of it would necessarily be controversial. Howard understood, but warned that I should not "raise expectations". He was of course referring to money. Looking at Peter Hendy, he further emphasised the need to remain closely aligned with the Liberal Party. I took this to mean that I should not frivolously expend political capital.

The prospect of pulling this off was daunting, but I had gone into politics to make a difference. Peter Shergold suggested a team, handpicked by him and approved by me, to draft the discussion papers. They would be progressively released over the course of the year, followed by broad consultation. I established a reference group drawn from the university, business, schools and vocational training sectors to guide my thinking in the response to the discussion papers. It would be a unique process, fraught with risk.

I wanted a mature, open and informed debate. The consultation process would be exhaustive, collaborative, framed with a sense of historical purpose looking to the future. In my many speeches on universities, I drew on Churchill and Menzies.

Winston Churchill addressed Harvard University in September 1943, in the depths of the Second World War. Receiving an honorary doctorate, Churchill said that when the war ended, "The Empires of the future would be Empires of the mind".

In 1939, Prime Minister Sir Robert Menzies delivered the Canberra University College commencement address. The first function of a university was "to be a home for pure culture and learning". He stood up to those who belittled "academic learning". He spoke of academia as being "one of those civilized and civilizing things which the world needs as never before".

> Let me defend a so-called useless scholarship on the great grounds that it represents a sanity badly needed in an insane world ... that it points to the moral, that the mere mechanics of life can never be the sole vocation of the human spirit. (Menzies, R.G. 1939. *The Place of a University in the Modern Community: An Address. Delivered at the Annual Commencement of the Canberra University College, 1939.* Melbourne: Melbourne University Press.)

I used Menzies to set the tone. I shared his view, strongly so. Science is hard. But how human beings understand and adapt to it is much harder. I quoted these two leaders extensively for two reasons. I wanted the university sector to know that I respected academia and knowledge for its own sake. I neither saw nor wanted a university sector having little more than a utilitarian purpose. As a medical graduate, I frequently described myself as having had a lot of training, but much less education. The latter provides resilience for life.

It was also essential that my colleagues, and Liberal Party members hostile to the university sector, be reminded that two heroes of our movement were themselves deeply committed to higher education. That both did so in the context of the greatest cataclysm in human history speaks even more to the value of a university education.

I set out the challenges in releasing the discussion papers, reminding audiences that Australians have inherited an economic and cultural legacy built largely on the exploitation of natural resources in agrarian, land and labour intensive industries. But each day brings evidence of change that foreshadows a future as much based in knowledge as industries so critical to our past. The Australia in which the next generation would live, to a large extent, would depend on Australia's institutions of higher learning – universities. The future would be informed less by what we know than what we do not. Our challenge was to conduct public discussion in a transparent manner free of the highly emotional and politicised language of the past. I put a series of questions to the sector.

- What defines a university? Who attends and why? Should Australia aspire to have one or two universities ranked in the world's top fifty? If so, how can that be achieved within a policy framework that recognises simultaneously the increasingly onerous community service obligations placed on regional institutions? Can funding arrangements appropriate to strengthening the role of smaller regional universities enable innovation and specialisation within the sector?
- How to improve governance arrangements that best serve the needs of students, staff and society generally?
- To what extent is the commercialisation of intellectual property conducted in a rigorously efficient manner to the benefit of institutions, researchers, industry and Australia's competitive potential?
- How could government policy encourage specialisation among universities without penalty to them?

Another priority for me was the importance of humanities, social sciences, languages, fine arts, literature and philosophy. It was hard for them to source non-government funding though they play a key role in moulding our values, beliefs, the way we relate to one another and see our place in the world.

It was a unique model and politically 'high wire'. The challenge was to get the universities to lift their horizon beyond the short term, combative, 'crisis' driven approach to public policy. Some regarded themselves as too important to have their outlook altered by me or anyone else. The irascible Scottish mathematician Vice Chancellor of Sydney University was one of them. He responded to my remarks when opening the Graduate Management School. From the lectern, turning his gaze to me: "Minister, you can do what you wish, but we will just keep on doing what we do." Others were outstanding in their response, seeing opportunity and a new vision.

Over a six month period we sequentially released seven ministerial discussion papers under the *Crossroads Review*. The title of each spoke to the issues and possible policy responses:

- *Higher education at the crossroads: an overview paper.*
- *Striving for quality: learning, teaching and scholarship.*
- *Setting firm foundations: financing Australian Higher Education.*
- *Varieties of excellence: diversity, specialization and regional engagement.*
- *Achieving equitable and appropriate outcomes: Indigenous Australians in higher education.*
- *Meeting the challenges: the governance and management of universities.*
- *Varieties of learning: the interface between higher education and vocational education and training.*

Just a few months into 2002, my Chief of Staff, Peter Hendy, told me he was leaving. I expected this and wished him well. Casting around for a successor, I knew the appointment would make or break me. Catherine Murphy was John Howard's legal and constitutional affairs advisor. A seriously impressive woman of stature, I had dealings with her through euthanasia legislation, the republic referendum and native title. Just the person to negotiate with the higher education and scientific communities. She might be up for a new challenge. After a number of meetings, she agreed to 'take the plunge'. That we were undertaking major reform across the portfolio made it the job she sought.

At the time, there was not an Australian top 100 university. I challenged them on why every university in the country has to do research. Why couldn't some universities specialise in learning and scholarship? Why did just 12 of the 39 universities account for 78% of the competitive research funding? Without critical mass, how can we be sure of research quality? Why aren't lecturers trained to teach? Why can't academics be promoted for being good teachers instead of research output?

At a time of significant unmet demand for places, the first year attrition rate was 22%. I asked why Australians enrolling in private universities and independent higher education providers couldn't get access to a HECS style loan. Why could overseas students pay full fees but Australians couldn't when they were academically eligible? I told audiences of my visit to the Australian Institute of Music in Surry Hills, Sydney, a vibrant institution then teaching music and performing arts courses to 900 students. The Director, Peter Calvo, put everything in the frame. "Minister, we have kids come here from low income families all over Sydney. Having been accepted academically, they disappear for two years and suddenly pop up again. They work their two or three jobs, save the money and come in to start. How is that fair when they could get HECS to go to Uni to do a course they don't want?" On leaving, I told Dr Calvo that I would do my utmost to see that no Australian would be locked out of his and similar private institutions for lack of money.

The same funding model applied to all, places were underfunded and business investment in universities was frowned upon. I found multiple courses with five or fewer students enrolled: the Southern Cross University offered a degree in surfing; Griffith another in the paranormal; and Swinburne, Makeup Application for Drag Queens. They all have a place, but in a serious institution of higher learning?

The Governance of many was a prescription for paralysis. Council sizes ranged from 12 to a staggering 37 at Sydney University. Worse, many council members were not there to exercise judgement on behalf of the university. They were delegates for sectional interests. Regional universities carried significant community obligations, expected to meet demands for which they weren't funded. They were well in front on recognition of prior learning and providing pathways from TAFE to university.

Generations of young Liberals had bitterly resented compulsory membership of student unions. It was – and remains – an 'article of faith'. I asked the Australian Liberal Students Federation and the Young Liberal Movement to give me 'space' to first address the substantive issues facing the sector. Pursuing Voluntary Student Unionism (VSU) at this time would provoke a major backlash, distracting us from the main game. To their eternal credit, they accepted this. I reassured them I would turn my attention to VSU once the reform process was complete – irrespective of the outcome.

The media, ever helpful, tried to split the Vice Chancellors who were uncharacteristically unified on the big issues. Professor Kerry Cox, an immunologist, was Vice Chancellor of the University of Ballarat (now Federation University). When asked why he was supportive of both the process and issues canvassed, he said: "If I white ant everything not directly helpful to the University of Ballarat, I will put in jeopardy the capacity of Australia as a whole." A true statesman.

My first taste of violence came in July 2002. I was visiting Perth's Curtin University. Standing in the Curtin Library, I could hear drum beats and muffled shouting from the grounds outside. From the corner of my eye, two police officers were talking into their shirt cuffs. Then, with a sense of urgency, I was told we had to leave immediately, through a back corridor and stairwells to a waiting police SUV. A mob of shouting, placard waving protestors ran to the small vehicular convoy. The police were out-numbered, unprepared for what was unfolding. One officer leapt from the car and stood in front of it ordering people back. But they kept at him, screaming, pushing him at which point he produced pepper spray. It was on for young and old when police reinforcements finally arrived to quell the growing violence. The police showed more restraint than I would. Unnerving though it was, Mrs Howard told me back at Kirribilli House that I was now very much a part of the political family!

Following the Curtin riots, I was assigned close personal protection from the Australian Federal Police. I would need them. But there were some light moments. Back in Perth, Glen the younger of the two AFP officers protecting me, was standing outside a restaurant where I was speaking. As I walked out, a vision impaired woman approached him tapping her long, cane stick, sweeping it from left to right in front of her. It hit something solid – Glen's leg. She stopped. Glen said, "I'm on points, maam". She persisted, repeatedly tapping the leg, progressively elevating the stick until dangerously close to his groin. "I'm on points, maam!" he forcefully repeated with increasing anxiety. The otherwise demur lady then sternly barked at him, "I don't give a damn what you're on. Can't you see I'm bloody blind?" Glen stepped back, knowing where the next blow from the solid ball on the end of her cane would land.

Engineers Australia invited me to deliver the Chapman Oration in honour of one of the pioneers of their profession. It involved a dinner format for 500 engineers and their partners in the Great Hall of Parliament House. I put a bit of work into this. I read Herbert Hoover's biography by way of background, spoke of the Roeblings and the Brooklyn Bridge and, of course, General Sir John Monash.

Engineers are serious people – they need to get out a bit. Over the formal dinner, I did what had been asked of me. When I returned to my table, the earnest Chief Executive leaned over, "Dr Nelson, I do apologise for continuing to eat while you began your speech, but your wife said I should enjoy something while you were speaking."

Days later as I was about to leave the Braitling school in Alice Springs, I told the Year 1 children I was going to Canberra to see the Prime Minister of Australia, Mr Howard. I asked, "What is one thing you want Mr Howard to know?" "We're having pizza for tea!"

As I was head down in my portfolio responsibilities, major events were unfolding with significant consequences. Australia had sent troops to Afghanistan after the 11 September attacks in 2001. In January 2002, President George W Bush described an "Axis of Evil" – Iran, Iraq and North Korea. In August, as Iraq's Saddam Hussein played cat and mouse with UN weapons inspectors, John Howard said that Australia would be called upon to help deal with him.

The Cabinet meeting at which it was agreed Australia would commit to the 'Coalition of the willing' was sombre. All of us were aware of the gravity of the decision. It had already been canvassed at length in the National Security Committee of Cabinet. John Howard reminded us at the beginning of the meeting, our kids would be reading about it in 30 years' time. I would not divulge what others said, but I supported it.

The United States had been attacked a year earlier. Almost 3,000 civilians, everyday people just like us, including 10 Australians, had been murdered in New York, Washington and a Pennsylvania field. The United States was not going to wait for the next attack. It was going out to likely state actors capable of launching a large scale attack.

Saddam Hussein had been responsible for 70,000 deaths in two wars. He had used gas against his own people in 1988 at Halabja, killing almost 5,000. Seared into my mind still is the image of the gassed father frozen in death holding his infant child. Hussein was refusing to cooperate with the UN weapons inspectors who wanted to confirm he no longer possessed weapons of mass destruction.

We had a British Labour Prime Minister, Tony Blair, 'on the phone' prepared to topple Saddam, asking which side we were on, and an American Republican President asking the same question. If our values were to mean anything, it was time to act. I believe that if Kim Beazley had been prime minister receiving those calls he would have done what we did. We will never know.

The university public consultations completed, we moved to the next phase. Dr Carol Nicoll led the team tasked with drafting the policy I would take to Cabinet for the 2003 budget process. She represented the finest of the public service. Intelligent, knowledgeable, determined to do her best for universities and her minister. Loyal and steadfast. We were about to go through an extraordinarily difficult period with a complex set of reforms. At its heart was deregulation of universities, differentiation, and specialisation along with increased government and student contributions. The one size fits all model would have to end.

I called a special Ministerial Council meeting to consider thematic issues emerging from the consultations. New South Wales Education Minister, John Watkins, was miffed when I said we should meet at a regional university. I nominated Ballarat University (now Federation University). I invited the Australian Vice Chancellors Committee (AVCC) to attend and address the ministers, led by its President, Professor Deryk Schreuder. The AVCC's proposed changes largely aligned with my own thinking.

Politics throws up a wide variety of personalities. The education ministers were all Labor and, with two exceptions, all women. I invited Professor Schreuder to the head of the table, supported by his CEO, John Mullarvey. Seated alongside was Professor Kerry Cox, Vice Chancellor of Ballarat University, our host. Dr Peter Shergold, my Departmental Secretary, sat behind me with Dr Carol Nicoll.

Professor Schreuder spoke to the AVCC policy paper in terms of the challenges, what was needed and would be broadly supported by the universities' peak group. It included limited fee de-regulation and competitive funding pools for excellence in teaching and scholarship.

The Tasmanian minister, Paula Wreidt, was first out of the blocks. "I knew what we were in for when I drove in here today and saw a big sign in the main street of Ballarat – *Nelson's funerals.*" Tasmania would not support any fee changes.

John Watkins, of Labor's left, was next: "I don't get this. Professor Cox, you are running a regional university. Why on earth would you support any fee increases? Surely your students couldn't afford anything like that?"

It may be said of Kerry Cox that he speaks softly but carries a very big stick – between his ears. With infinite patience, he addressed the ministers: "Yes Minister, you are right. We would be reluctant to increase our student fees even though they are supported by government income contingent loans. Many of our students are the first in their families to ever attend a university. But we are more than competitive in the quality of our teaching. If we can access a funding pool on the basis of quality teaching and in recognition of challenges uniquely facing regional universities, then we would support a deregulated fee market."

Watkins came back again: "I don't get it. Makes no sense". Professor Cox lifted his shoulders: "Well then, let me put it another way. Albert Einstein was a man of considerable intellect and scientific repute. He once said, I now know why people like to chop wood – it is so easy to see the outcome."

Watkins turned to his departmental secretary, perplexed, seeking advice. Inwardly, I laughed and laughed.

Lynne Kosky, Victoria's Education Minister, was also of Labor's left. A strong, principled, intelligent and caring woman, she got all this. She recorded her concerns, engaged the issues intellectually and reserved her position. Of all the state ministers I dealt with at that time, she was the best, notwithstanding my considerable policy disagreements with her – a good example of a political opponent whom you could respect.

The day after the meeting, terror struck in Bali. A bombing. Tragedy on a scale to confront any doubters of the 'war on terror' with the brutal truth. Eighty-eight Australians were killed along with 114 others. Everyday Australians murdered by three men who had trained with Al-Qaeda under the protection of the Taliban in Afghanistan. Our vital interests were at stake. Its repercussions would be felt for decades in many Australian homes beyond those directly shattered that day.

The final higher education reform meeting convened in the Great Hall of Parliament House in November 2002. Fifty participants sat at tables in rectangular formation, their supportive entourages in rows behind. Vice Chancellors, academics, unions, business and industry groups, TAFE, VET providers, States, peak science and engineering groups, humanities and social sciences and more. This group comprised what would be the final consultation and summation of likely reform before the 2003 budget.

Peter Shergold introduced me to speak. Having delivered an overview to the meeting and its purpose, Peter invited his audience to "think about the Minister". I sensed people looking in my direction. He then pulled his tie from behind his jacket and held it prominently in front of him. He walked, while speaking, around the rectangle to ensure everyone could see the images on his tie. Lots of pigs with wings. "I call this my pigs might fly tie".

> I am wearing this to reflect my assessment of the Minister's chances of actually getting his reforms supported, funded and passed. Whatever your opinion of what has been discussed over the past year and the reforms to emerge from the process, this has a long way to go. The Minister has to convince his backbench colleagues. He has to get it through the Expenditure Review Committee, then the Cabinet. The legislation must pass through the House of Representatives. Then, he has to get it through the Senate. With Labor, the Democrats and Greens indicating their opposition, the Minister has to persuade four independent senators to support him.
>
> Pigs might fly!

The impact of his words was sobering, not only to the audience, but also to me.

At day's end, most left in good spirits with a sense of common purpose.

The foundations for the reform package had been laid when John Howard called me in January 2003. He was moving Peter Shergold to head his own department. Although disappointed, I was excited for Peter and pleased that the new Secretary of Prime Minister and Cabinet (PM&C) believed in 'flying pigs'. He was replaced by Jeff Harmer, a decent, consummate public servant.

The Expenditure Review Committee of Cabinet is no place for the faint-hearted. It can be ruthless, unforgiving and, for some, the source of ongoing lived traumas. I arrived with my reform package in all its complexity on the appointed evening in March 2003. I had my chief of staff, higher education advisor Peta Lane and numerous departmental officials in the Cabinet ante room. I was then told only one person could accompany me into the room. I chose Carol Nicoll. Restricting the minister to one advisor or being alone is a technique designed to make it harder. As minister, if you aren't across the detail, able to competently argue every point in arm-to-arm combat with Treasury and finance officials, you have no chance of getting what you want.

Entering the room, I saw people in conversation, others entering to cover my agenda item. As I was settling my papers onto the table and pulling my chair out, I overheard a side-remark from across the table. A colleague made a snide comment to his advisor about Carol. I was enraged, offended beyond words at what had been said. I glanced back to Carol who was taking her seat behind me. Thankfully, she was oblivious to it. I pretended not to have heard. Now was not a time. It would wait.

I made note of two things. The person who made the remark would be reminded of it in the future. I would also nominate Carol for the Public Service Medal in recognition of what she had done, intellectually and professionally, to get us to this point. Two hours later, Carol and I emerged from the room. There had been some relatively minor changes to the package, but it was through. Our team was exhilarated when I shared the news.

I did nominate Dr Carol Nicoll for the Public Service Medal. It was awarded the following year. That medal meant more to me than she would ever know.

Our Universities: Backing Australia's Future was unveiled in the May 2003 Budget. A more diverse, equitable and higher quality higher education sector beckoned. Over a decade, almost $11 billion more would flow into the sector, comprising $6.9 billion in new government funding and $3.7 billion in financial assistance to students in new student loans.

Universities would be partially deregulated. Capitalising on their individual strengths and responding to student demand, they could increase fees by up to 30%, or they could reduce them. No increases allowed though for nursing and teaching. At the same time, government would increase its funding to all universities. An additional 25,000 government funded places and, entirely at the discretion of individual universities, they could offer full fee paying places to eligible Australian citizens. Those students would be supported by an income contingent loan. We also dealt with the 'perennial student' by limiting government support to seven years of equivalent fulltime study – the Commonwealth Learning Entitlement.

Regional universities would receive a Commonwealth loading. There was additional money for them to provide practical 'on the job' experience for nurses and teachers in training in addition to more places.

We renamed the student loan programme from 'HECS' to 'FEE-HELP'. The new acronym standing for 'Higher Education Loan Program'. Students could access government provided, income contingent loans for study in a public university and, for the first time, as a full fee paying student in a public or private institution of higher learning. Loans would also support overseas study – 'OS HELP'. The income threshold for loan repayment increased by 25%, meaning that once graduated, loan repayment would not kick until income was higher. The package included 7,000 new Commonwealth Learning Scholarships annually for rural, remote, regional, low income and Indigenous students.

Two competitive funding pools would be established. The first would be accessed by universities on the basis of excellence in learning and teaching. Criteria would include the novel idea of students assessing the quality of teaching they received and the teaching qualifications of lecturers. The second fund would reward workplace productivity reforms. The *Workplace Relations Act* would be amended to protect students from industrial action by academics.

Indigenous participation, people with disabilities and equity groups also benefited. Under university governance reforms there was money for collaboration, mergers, rationalisation, structural reform and consolidation of universities. The humanities and social sciences communities needed a voice, a peak body. The reforms established the Council for Humanities and Social Sciences. It would shape relationships with policy makers and the broader community, a forum for teachers, researchers and professionals in these fields. The applied scientists were well represented, humanities and social scientists were not.

Four Centres of Excellence would be established – Mathematics, Asia-Pacific Studies at ANU, Water Resource Management and Immersive Languages.

Like clockwork, the Labor Party opposed the reform package, lining up with the Greens. The Australian Democrats had been split since Meg Lees had supported our GST in 2001. Natasha Stott Despoja bitterly resented the support given by her party to the introduction of the GST, against which she had voted. Meg Lees left the Democrats to form her own party, the Australian Progressive Alliance. Natasha assumed the Democrats leadership but by 2003 Andrew Bartlett was leader. Natasha was now the Democrats education spokesman, yet she did not accept my offer of a briefing on the reforms.

I knew and respected Meg Lees from my AMA days. I also knew she would be disposed to political 'pay back' on Natasha Stott Despoja. What better area to do it than higher education? The stars were aligning.

There were three other Senate Independents I would need: Tasmania's wily Brian Harradine and another Tasmanian from the north west of the state, disaffected Labor Senator Shayne Murphy. Former CFMEU Secretary and shearer, Murphy had left Labor over its logging policies. And the last was One Nation's Senator Len Harris, a gold miner and businessman. This would be tricky.

My first meeting with Meg Lees on the university reforms gave me reason for hope. She had read the package, knew the detail, asked many questions and, to my mind, had decided she was not only going to support most of it – she would work to bring the other three on board. She even advised me in relation to dealing with Brian Harradine. Her Chief of Staff was former *Redgum* front man, John Schuman. Whereas Meg Lees did not speak of Natasha Stott Despoja, John was less restrained. He was going to be an asset to my efforts.

Labor's Jenny Macklin got up most days and asked questions of the reforms, railing against fees and the private sector. If it wasn't private schools it was private universities. Her problem was that I was across the detail. Anthony Albanese called me 'Rain Man'. *The Australian* newspaper's much loved journalist, Matt Price, was described as having a 'special interest' in me – and not because he liked me. On the ABC's *Insiders* programme, just after the Budget, he spoke begrudgingly of the Press Conference I had given on the university reforms, "Nelson spoke for 45 minutes on the entire package without a piece of paper. He quoted all kinds of statistics. Back in the office, we checked every one of them and not a single error."

Macklin sprang to her feet in question time after the budget, framing her outrage about increased student fees and full fee paying Australian students in universities. Some days, you love your work.

I started by telling the Parliament a story. I was standing outside the Queensland University of Technology waiting for an advisor. A woman carrying her groceries recognised me. "Are you going in there?" gesturing towards the university. I confirmed I was. She said, "Well, could you please tell them something for me? I haven't been to university, but I know that I pay for what goes on in there. Tell them to remember that when they come out and apply for a job, they will get it before me."

I went on. Australian taxpayers just like her, who had never seen the inside of a university, were contributing 75% of the cost of a university education. Students paid the other 25% with an income contingent loan. Under the new plan, the government would pay more and students would pay more once they were graduated and working. Those university graduates would earn a lot more over a lifetime than many who paid for the majority of the degree.

For theatrics I turned from Simon Crean, Leader of the Opposition, to the government backbench. Entschy (Warren Entsch) was in my line of sight. "Take the Member for Leichardt. There he was at the age of 14 cleaning toilets at the Mareeba train station to pay for the university education of the Leader of the Opposition. So too, the member for Hume (Alby Schulz) was working in an abattoir paying for all those Labor members to get through Uni."

Explaining full fee paying Australian students, I said:

> Let me explain to members in plain language what we are doing. Imagine for a moment that a university is a bus. It is old, tired, packed to the rafters with passengers. The driver is cranky. We are giving the nation's students a new bus – a bigger bus with more seats, more space and a more comfortable, enjoyable experience. Only those who have a ticket can get on the bus but now there are lots more tickets. Taxpayers are paying three-quarters of the cost of the ticket. However, there's more.
>
> We are allowing those who want to pay the full price to get on the fully articulated trailer towed by the bus. It is equally comfortable and will get them to the same destination. The government will lend the full cost of the ticket to the passengers in the trailer – full fee paying students. In Labor's world, only foreign students can get into the trailer. You can fly in from Beijing but God help you if you want to get on from Brisbane!

Uproar, but I knew it worked. John Howard advised me not to tell the stories from the street in the parliament again. I acceded to his experience in this, although I still believe that stories allow people to understand complex issues.

Typical of what I faced in driving reform was an appearance on

SBS *Insight*, hosted by Jennie Brockie. A young woman in the audience asked a question: "Dr Nelson, I live in Wahroonga in your electorate. I am a second year medical student at Sydney University. You have destroyed my life. How am I expected to pay $50,000 to follow my dream?"

The audience applauded. I replied:

> Well, I'd like to live in Wahroonga. Under these changes, the taxpayer, most of whom have never seen the inside of a university, will pay $150,000 for your medical degree. They will also lend you the $50,000, all of which will be spent on your education. The loan is interest-free and you don't have to pay anything back until you work and earn more than $30,000 a year. If you never work, you never pay it back. As you know, I am a doctor myself and a former President of the Australian Medical Association. I know a bit about the medical profession. Once you graduate, your lifetime earnings will be somewhere between $7 million and $13 million depending on what you choose to do with your degree. Not a bad return for $50,000. Most people watching this cannot even dream of having your problems.

No applause. One less vote for me in Bradfield, but they got the point.

Labor was further upset with me when I rejected seven research grants recommended by the Australian Research Council (ARC). The first year I was in the job my science advisor, Tom Barlow, sent me a huge brief to sign. It was to approve the ARC research grants. He told me when questioned that I had to sign off on them, approving millions of dollars for research. I scanned the hundreds of grants, some of which concerned me. "You mean I approve these but have no say in whether they should be funded?" Having confirmed that, I told him that 2003 would be different. This year Tom drew my attention to a number of questionable merit. I rejected seven grants.

Jenny Macklin was highly animated when she thundered across

the dispatch box. I calmly replied that she should think very carefully about asking the question again. If she did, I would answer it and name the grants and researchers. Wisely, she dropped it.

To this day I could still not explain to Australians why they should fund "Queer Tokyo", an examination of the behaviours of homosexual Japanese citizens in its capital city. Similarly, I could only imagine the reaction of devoutly Christian Pacific Islanders – let alone *Daily Telegraph* readers – to spending hundreds of thousands of dollars researching "Transgender sublimation in Pacific Island populations". Sometimes people have to be protected from themselves.

My science advisor, Dr Tom Barlow, had fallen in love with another scientist. Tom was a super-intelligent, tall, lanky man with the unsettling demeanour of Rowan Atkinson's 'Mr Bean'. Tom handed me a brief. He was quite distressed. It was the list of outstanding scientists recommended to receive the highly prestigious Federation Fellowship. I asked him what was wrong. "Michelle has been recommended for a Fellowship". Tom was in love with Michelle Simmons, a British immigrant and quantum computing genius. Of course, he had nothing to do with her being so deservedly recommended for the award of $1 million. But you didn't have to have Tom's IQ to know what the Labor Party might do with it. I said to Tom, "You worry about Michelle and science, leave this to me."

My shadow science minister was Victorian Labor Senator, Kim Carr. His indefatigable advocacy for science was exceeded only by his relentless attacks on the government. So prolific were his attacks, at one Senate Estimates hearing, Peter Shergold pushed in a trolley overloaded with documents departmental officials had produced to answer his questions. I called his office and made an appointment. When I arrived, Kim and his advisor were intrigued. I was offered wine and crackers.

I carefully explained the dilemma, Tom's background and of course, Michelle. I told him neither I nor Tom had anything whatsoever to do with the process. "This remarkable woman should not have her career suffer because her husband has offered himself to work with me. Do your research Kim, I will make the department available to you. If you find any evidence whatsoever that I have deceived or misled you in any way, call for my resignation."

Two days later, he called. There would be no issues with Michelle Simmons receiving the Federation Fellowship. To this day, I thank Kim Carr for what he made possible. She would be awarded a second Federation Fellowship and then, Australian of the Year in 2018.

Slim Dusty was increasingly frail, dying. Joy came to see me in my electorate office about the Slim Dusty Centre planned to tell his story. Slim and Joy had worked with architects on a design that would do justice not only to Slim, but to the lifetime partnership between him and Joy. It was an emotional meeting. We hugged as she left, in the knowledge it would not be long.

The cancer which Slim had fought, finally took him from us on 19 September 2003. Doug Thompson cried when we spoke. Slim had become a close friend and confidant. Doug had helped Slim and Joy buy back the old family dairy farm at Nulla Creek. It was there that Slim had grown up and where he was inspired to write *The Rain Tumbles Down in July.* Slim had shared his love of Henry Lawson with Doug. He had even taken to inviting him up to his studio in St Ives to listen to songs he was thinking of recording. I had to take Slim aside at one stage and tell him that Doug had no objectivity in this whatsoever. As far as he was concerned, anything Slim sang was pure perfection.

As Education Minister, I frequently referred to Slim when addressing audiences about literacy, much to the chagrin of leftist elements in the sector. In 1954, Joe Daly wrote a song for Slim called *Jacky.* Slim renamed it *Trumby* after the creek that flowed through the family farm. It was the story of a much admired and respected Aboriginal stockman. One day Trumby was returning to the homestead when he stopped to drink from a water hole. It had been poisoned for foxes and signed as such. But Trumby couldn't read, so drank the poisoned water. In the song, back in 1954, Slim asked why, after all that we have achieved, a man should die because he couldn't read. In 2003, I was still asking myself the same question.

Slim Dusty's State Funeral was at St Andrew's Cathedral in Sydney on 26 September. It was attended by 3,000 people from all walks of life, from all over the country, many holding photos and much treasured memorabilia. I felt an overwhelming sense of loss. This man had told the story of Australia for six decades across 107 albums with the same record company. He sang of the everyday Australian, of our triumphs and failures. He sang of our heroes, villains and the adversities we have endured. He sang of our landscape and wildlife. He burrowed deep into our hearts. It was surreal, sitting in the front of the Cathedral, next to John Howard, singing *The Pub with No Beer.* A special day of my life, with Joy, Anne and David – Slim's family – sharing him with us.

At the Cabinet meeting the following week, I took the model for the Slim Dusty Centre for my colleagues to see. It needed a $1.5 million investment to get it going. Most, I am ashamed to say, were not enthusiastic. One asserted that fifty years on, no one would remember Slim Dusty. John Howard cast his ten votes in support of it and we were on the way.

One of my other mainstream interests was V8 Supercars. In August, thinking about the promotion of apprenticeships, I asked my media advisor to contact the Holden Racing Team. I was interested to know if it was possible to buy some advertising space on one of the cars. Ross Hampton came back, "Mate, you're not going to believe it. They've got space on the rear bumper and side skirts of each car. And wait for it – the cost is $50,000!"

I was super excited. We could get signage on the Holden Racing Team led by Mark Skaife all weekend, including the seven hour televised race. This went right into the demographic we were targeting. I would be welcome trackside all weekend and do trackside television commentary promoting apprenticeships. That two automotive apprentices could work with the team all week was icing on the cake. Mark Skaife is a class act. A true champion, engaging, treats people well, focused and highly skilled. Teamed that year with Todd Kelly, he had me cleaning his car with the apprentices!

On the Saturday night after final practice and the 'shoot out', I suggested to Ross Hampton that we cross the road and take a look at 'sideshow ally' and soak up some entertainment. There was everything from 'Miracle Hangover Cures' to instant tattoos and Peter Brock dolls. We found ourselves standing behind the stalls in the midst of a crowd watching an AC/DC cover band belting out *Highway to Hell* from the back of a flat tray truck. Ross and I were lapping it up when the bloke next to me shouted, "Bloody good stuff!" I agreed.

"Where ya' from mate?" "Sydney", I said. "What sorta work ya do mate?" Shouting, I told him he wouldn't believe me. He persisted, so I told him. "I'm Australia's Minister for Education, Science and Training". He erupted into raucous laughter, his two mates similarly went into hysterics. He grabbed two cans of VB from the Esky, handed one each to me and Ross, "That's a bloody beauty mate. Wrap yourself around this!"

Race day entertainer was Lee Kernaghan. Out on the grid with the teams fussing over their cars before the race, Lee was waiting to go on to do *Boys from the Bush.* We struck up an immediate rapport, firstly over Slim, his life, music and the funeral. Lee had recorded with Slim and was, like me, emotional talking about his loss. So, began a friendship from which, over a decade later, *The Spirit of the Anzacs* would be born.

The horse trading with the Independent Senators on higher education continued. Tasmania University's Vice Chancellor, Daryl Le Grew, was magnificent in his advocacy for the package with Brian Harradine and Shane Murphy. The University was well rewarded. Among the benefits, a University campus in the north west of the state. The principal of Smithton High School told me only a third of her Year 10 students had been east of Devonport. We had to bring educational opportunities to them.

In the end, all four Independents agreed to support the package. Then, in the final week of Senate deliberations in December 2003, a very large spanner was thrown in the works. A Cabinet meeting was called to consider changes sought by the Independents, specifically more publicly funded places. The flexibility on fee changes was cut from 30% to 25% higher. Just as we were about to leave the table, Tony Abbott said that if we were going to put all this money into universities, we should insist they offer Australian Workplace Agreements (AWAs) to all staff. Cabinet members thought it an excellent suggestion, ending the meeting without debate. My heart sank. The legislation at that point said universities 'may' offer AWAs. It would now say 'shall'.

Sure enough, Meg Lees and the others dug in. A bridge too far.

John Howard was on his way to CHOGM in Nigeria. John Anderson was acting Prime Minister. Alexander Downer saved me. I called him in desperation. We had invested too much getting this far to let it fail now. He got it, telling me he supported calling for another Cabinet meeting. We met on Wednesday, 3 December. I put the case, the disposition of the Independents and reminded them we had already been voted down on the Medicare Safety Net threshold. We needed a win. They agreed. I spoke to John Howard in-flight to Nigeria. He too agreed and was excited at the prospect of the reforms passing.

The following evening my advisor, Peta Lane, and I camped outside the Senate Chamber as the legislation was debated. I was negotiating with the Independents, responding to their concerns and advising of any concessions and amendments to our Senate leadership team. A night of high drama!

A rowdy party was taking place in the courtyard outside the Senate chamber. I was dealing regularly with our Senate Whip, Jeannie Ferris. Late that night she told me of a major 'blow-up' with the Democrats leader, Andrew Bartlett. He had allegedly "stolen five bottles of wine from the Liberal Christmas party". She had dispatched staff to retrieve them and then, in a seriously over-refreshed state, he grabbed and intimidated her in the chamber. My quick calculation was no impact to my Bills but Jeannie was shaken. She reassured me she would see our Bills through the committee stage. And she did. Finally, just after midnight when the vote was taken and the four Independent Senators voted down opposition amendments, I knew we were there. The Senate would resume in the morning to formally vote on the final legislative package.

Tired though I was, I immediately went to each of the four Independent Senators' offices to thank them.

One Nation's Len Harris was packing up to go home. He said he knew he had done the right thing. I told him the morning vote would be "historic". Then, "Oh, sorry Brendan but I'm off to Cairns in the morning. I have to get my car serviced." Panicked, I almost asked him if he had a pair – an agreement for an opposition senator to have leave to ensure no change in a vote. However, asking for a pair is so basic, I didn't want to insult him by asking if he had arranged for one, so let it go.

Up early on Friday morning, *The Australian* newspaper led with – 'Nelson wins big Uni shake-up'. My upbeat mood was shattered when I went to see Len Harris. His son confirmed that he had gone to Cairns. But when he showed me his application for a pair, he had nominated the wrong date – Thursday instead of Friday. I was speechless. The package would go down. Back in my office, I asked one of my staff to go around to John Faulkner's office, Labor's Senate leader. I said, "Just case the place out, see if there's much activity there." Simon Berger returned, "Boss, all lights are on with heaps of grim faced people going in and out."

"They're on to it. We're sunk." I discussed it with our Senate Leader, Robert Hill. He said we should bring it on and let the sector see Labor vote it down. As senators filed in and sat on their respective sides with division bells ringing, I was depressed. John Faulkner, however, looked even sterner than his natural disposition. When the numbers were counted, I knew why. Labor was two votes short! Believing I had the numbers, two Labor senators had left early Friday morning to go back to their electorates, oblivious to Len Harris' unpaired absence.

Among the deluge of correspondence was a letter from Dr Peter Calvo, Director of the Australian Institute of Music:

> Dear Minister,
>
> It worked; you have done it; you have triumphed over all odds.

> This legislation will be the greatest living monument in the march of our nation into the 21st century. It will lay the ground for reinvention of higher education, and the spread of new opportunities across the whole community. Above all it will be a ringing bell for the freedom of education for everyone.
>
> On behalf of the Institute and its one thousand students and staff, I thank you for all the effort and titanic struggle you have put into this task. We salute you.

It meant so much to me. I made a promise to him and so many others upon which we had delivered.

A bromide copy of *The Australian* newspaper arrived for me, compliments of its editor, Chris Mitchell.

Peter Shergold appeared in my office the following week. He presented me with the 'Pigs Might Fly award 2003'. His 'Pigs might fly' tie was framed. He told me he did not believe we would get it through. Typically, of course, he downplayed his own role in it. Pigs do fly, it seems.

16

"I had a cat called Nelson – but he died"

The year 2004 started with some unexpected drama. Gillian and I always went to Nelson Bay, NSW. We took the kids, dogs, boat and hooked up with friends and family. Thanks to a great mate, we stayed in a unit at Corlette. The walk to town is through a bushland esplanade, just off the beach. We were walking through a relatively isolated stretch one morning when a somewhat agitated man and woman emerged walking towards us. "Do you know CPR?" the breathless woman blurted. "Yes, I do". "Well, there's a man back on the track who's had a heart attack!"

Alarmed, we hurried on. About 40 metres further along the track a man lay moribund, alone. Blue. No pulse, no respirations. I told Gillian to run until she got mobile phone range and call an ambulance. She offered to help with the CPR as I checked his mouth for foreign objects, "just run!" I started working on him, Gillian returning some five minutes later. The ambulance finally arrived and took over.

Later that day, word got out that the Education Minister had resuscitated a man at Port Stephens. Bob Baldwin, Member for Paterson, called me. "Mate, what the bloody hell are you doing? The bloke you saved is president of the Nelson Bay branch of the Labor Party!"

I called the man at the John Hunter Hospital the following day. Hoarse from all the interventions, he said "I've got a bloody bone to pick with you Dr Nelson. I'm on a morphine infusion with two broken ribs!" I said, "Well, that means I did it properly". "That's what the doctor here said. Thank you so much." "My pleasure. All I have to do now is change your politics!"

On the cusp of the Senate's consideration of the higher education reforms, Simon Crean resigned as Labor leader. We were shocked when Labor narrowly chose Mark Latham over Kim Beazley. They knew Latham better than us, but we thought he was mad, volatile, intemperate, hardly an alternative Prime Minister. Yet there he was.

Prosecuting the Values in Schools agenda in Question Time, I referred to Mark Latham's aggressive bahaviour. "When Simon Crean was leader, Labor's challenge in which it failed, was to see that the real character of the man was revealed. Its challenge with Mark Latham is to see that it isn't."

Initially Mark Latham had John Howard off balance. Younger, he sought to speak to a younger demographic. Instead of probing the government on the economy, defence and security, it was all about reading to kids and the safety of strollers.

The electorate was sizing up Latham. They were open to change and had rejected Kim Beazley twice – just. Those angry with the war in Iraq, detention of David Hicks and border protection policies had already left us. The fight is always for middle Australia, no more so than in 2004.

Sir John Carrick agreed to allow his name to be given to *The Carrick Institute.* This was the first time he agreed to be so recognised. A giant of the Liberal Party, Sir John had served as Malcolm Fraser's Education minister. Much of his post political life he committed to early child education. He was for me, as for many Liberals, a source of wisdom and guidance.

The university reforms included a new and necessary focus on the quality of teaching and learning. The *Carrick Institute* would receive $1.4 million in establishment costs and $22 million annually to identify and support national priorities in teaching and learning. The quality of teaching is at the heart of everything.

I often reminded people of two Australian scientific giants who attributed everything to their teachers. Sir John Cornforth, on receiving his Nobel Prize for chemistry in 1975, immediately thanked his high school chemistry teacher. The great Lennie Basser had taught chemistry for 28 years at Sydney Boys High. Cornforth said of him, "In my opinion, Len's most valuable gift to his pupils was an attitude to science as an immensely important cultural activity. I can't remember a single chemical fact he taught me, but I know that without him I would not be the scientist I am today."

Physicist, Sir Mark Oliphant, asked of his success, replied: "I was lucky. I had a teacher back in Adelaide, Dr Ray Burdon. He started me off with enthusiasm on this subject and taught me the exhilaration of even small discoveries in the field of physics".

As we focused on teaching, mathematician Professor Garth Gaudry, from the International Centre for Excellence in Mathematics established and funded out of the University reforms, presented me with sobering data. His work told me that of the 31 primary education degree courses in 2003 offered in Australian universities, only four required any Year 12 mathematics. Eight required only Year 11 maths for entry and, nineteen, none at all. Only one university tested and required a pass in mathematics before graduating as a teacher.

I settled on a number of things that needed to be done. But we would wait until we had the schools quadrennial funding Bills through the parliament later in the year, before the election. Opening up another front at this point would not be wise.

In addition to setting a minimum tertiary entrance rank for entry into a university education degree, education faculties should be accredited by a national body, just like medical schools. The Commonwealth could use the Individual Funding Agreements with the universities to drive it. Every undergraduate teacher should be required to pass an exit exam in fundamentals before graduation.

High performing classroom teachers should have university appointments. There is no reason why teachers could not be Associate Professors spending one or two days a week training the next generation of teachers. It would improve incomes for quality teachers, bring practical skills and experience to undergraduate teaching and raise the status of the profession. Is it beyond the wit of man to make this happen?

The university and science sectors were consuming a lot of time and increased government investment, but the politics approaching an election were all around schools and trades. The $8.3 billion decade-long increased investment in science, innovation and commercialisation was essential to the nation's future. But I did not meet a single person who told me they couldn't wait to vote for me because of it. In fact, one of the mathematicians with whom I worked to deliver it, was at the Turramurra booth on polling day, manning it for the Labor Party. I love democracy.

Too often school students were receiving careers advice from well-meaning but poorly trained teachers. Professionalising and funding a national network of careers advisors was a priority. I found dedicated careers advisors toiling away, neglected in public policy. One, Judith Leeson, I nominated for an Award in the Order of Australia. Her joy at receiving her AM was a great tribute to unsung heroes.

An Institute for Trade Skills Excellence and Commonwealth Trade Learning Scholarships were complemented by Tool Kits for Apprentices. The 'Tool Kits' were an $800 voucher which apprentices could access after their three month probation. They loved it, their parents even more. The crowning policy in trades we would take to the 2004 election was to establish 24 Australian Technical Colleges (ATCs). They would be 'private' colleges providing both academic and vocational training in Years 11 and 12. Each would be linked to industry, be run by a principal reporting to a board, partner with other schools and offer performance based pay for teachers. Commencing in 2006, the ATCs would be overseen by a reference group of peak industry bodies.

Labor didn't like it. But their voters did.

To illustrate Labor's problem, I referred in the parliament to the address given by its education spokesperson, Jenny Macklin, to the ACTU congress. Through 11 pages of the speech, the word 'university' was mentioned 23 times. 'Apprentice' appeared once.

As we settled policy and headed towards the 2004 election, trouble erupted in the Sydney Liberal held seat of Wentworth. Peter King QC had only been elected in 2001 to represent the eastern suburbs. A Rhodes Scholar, he was challenged by Malcolm Turnbull for pre-selection in February. Although I knew and respected Peter, given I too had challenged the sitting member for Bradfield, I thought it hypocritical to publicly criticise Mr Turnbull. I didn't know Malcolm Turnbull, only of him. Like most Liberals though, I was appalled by what remains the biggest stacking of branches in the history of the Party.

Whereas I had simply challenged David Connolly after two decades in the seat, Mr Turnbull put over 3,000 new members into the Wentworth branches, including James Packer. My reference for Peter King of course had little impact facing this onslaught. Tony Abbott simply said, "Malcolm is a force of nature".

My campaigner and electorate office manager, Rhondda (Vanzella), was asked by John Howard to run Turnbull's Wentworth campaign. She was ethically challenged by this. The idea that such behaviour should be rewarded was bad enough for Rhondda, but now to help him be elected was galling. But as team players, we agreed she had to do it. In September 2004 I found myself handing out materials for Turnbull at a supermarket in Double Bay with Bill Heffernan, unaware of the character of the man who would, come October, join our ranks.

I only have two regrets from my early life. The first is that I didn't go to a school that offered rowing. It seems like a great team sport. My second is that I didn't learn to play the guitar. I was in the Chatswood Music Centre speaking to the owners. They were very pleased with me as I had put a lot of money into school music education, funding schools to buy instruments. I noticed a beautiful guitar. It marked the 50th anniversary of the Fender Stratocaster, a work of art. I made a pact, "If we win the election, I'm coming back to buy that Strat and sign on for lessons."

Labor maintained its lead over us in the published polls all year, but it felt 'soft'. People were ready to change, but when the campaign was called on 29 August, they wanted Mark Latham tested. Newspoll published on 31 August had Labor in front on the two party preferred vote, 52% to us at 48%. John Howard framed the election immediately as being about 'trust'. He invited Australians to consider whom they could trust with their jobs, security and mortgages.

The country was divided on Iraq, suffering through drought, uneasy about terrorism and deeply polarised around border protection policies. Labor finally released the list of non-government schools that would receive less money under their policy, affirming what I had been saying for months. They had a 'hit list'. Its tax policy stoked further electoral unease. There was a sense of Mark Latham being a political 'punisher', reinforced by colourful language and past aggressive behaviour.

The election campaign is carefully planned months ahead. Strategists decide what ministers will go where and when. I received my instructions. In week two I headed up through far north Queensland. Paul Neville was the National Party member for Hinkler, a man possessed of a warm, generous personality. I loved him. Paul had a large abdominal girth and the endearing habit of always adjusting his pants around the hips to keep them up. In Bundaberg, I was to promote training policies and announce the $800 apprenticeships tool box initiative.

To the assembled media, I spoke to the policy detail, cost and eligibility. Paul was then asked why, the previous day, he had agreed to accept preferences from the conservative Christian Party, Family First. Paul lunged at the question. He was "strong on family values". When you are standing next to someone at a press conference and they speak of family values, your anxiety levels redline. But nothing prepared me for what came next.

"Well yes, as I said, I am very strong on family values. I'm a family man. For example, marriage is not between a man and his dog." As if to emphasise the point, Paul instinctively adjusted his pants further up around his stomach. The journalists turned to me, "So Doctor Nelson, what's the government's response to that?" "Should I lock up my Jack

Russells?" With that, I grabbed Paul, turned and walked away. As we did, Paul said "It's something like that isn't it Brendan?"

I said, "Well Paul Keating once said that marriage wasn't between two jokers and their Cocker Spaniel." Annoyed with himself for 'getting it wrong', Paul wanted to return to the startled media. Emphatically, I told him we were done for the day.

My next stop was Leichardt to campaign with Warren Entsch. The announcement here was $40 million to establish a veterinary school at James Cook University. The event was at the Cairns Airport Veterinary Clinic. Media arrived in numbers and the vets had carefully chosen props. Entschy and I were filmed with a constipated tree frog, a bird that wouldn't eat and a Kelpie in a post-operative stupor.

The subjects to camera were in the waiting room. I announced the government commitment to build the vet school, "We need more vets with their arms up the backsides of cows in Cairns instead of treating budgies in Brisbane. North Queenslanders, their pets and farm animals need vets."

The principal of the practice, a woman, then spoke eloquently about the demands of veterinary practice. As she did, Entschy suddenly stepped in front of the TV cameras. Wrapping one arm around her: "This woman is the mother of my love child!" I momentarily lost it, gesturing for my media advisor to get control. Entschy laughed, kissed the vet and said, "Relax all of yous … only joking!"

Unlike Paul Neville, Warren Entsch had been campaigning for same sex marriage. Genuine, heartfelt, it put him at odds then with most of the party room. I respected him, as I did Paul Neville. Always respect people who believe in something. However, many of his conservative constituents did not share Entschy's enthusiasm for the cause.

I noticed many of his campaign posters had been defaced. Someone had put pink lipstick around his lips. When I stepped into my early morning taxi for the airport, the driver had no idea who I was. I asked him about the election and if Warren Entsch's support for gay marriage was an issue. He turned to me with an incredulous look on his face, waved his tattooed, nicotine-stained hand dismissively, "Maaaaate … Entschy's gonna shit it in!"

My father suffered a stroke two weeks into the campaign. I went straight to Adelaide. Hospitalised, he readily agreed to receive the last rites from our friend and Jesuit priest, Father Greg O'Kelly SJ. A deeply emotional farewell. I knew I would not see him again. There was nothing I could do and had to get back to my job. I called in frequently: stable but in very poor shape.

On Sunday, 3 October, just six days from polling day, I arrived in Launceston to address a campaign dinner. As I was about to leave my room for the event, my phone rang. My mother called to say that Dad had just died. I sat on the bed in the room for ten minutes absorbing it. I had to speak to someone. I called Rhondda in Sydney. No flights out of Launceston. I pulled myself together and went to the dinner, telling no one of Dad's death.

Just before midnight, as I was drifting off to sleep, my phone rang. "Brendan, John Howard. I understand your father died earlier this evening." He had been at the Rugby League grand final night in Sydney. Rhondda must have let his office know of my circumstances. He spoke to me for more than ten minutes, including the loss of his own father. No talk of politics, just loss and emotion.

When political pundits and people in my own electorate were perplexed why so many of us, including me, stuck with Howard, this was a major reason. Here he was, Prime Minister of Australia, days away from an election, phoning me at midnight, man to man. It spoke to Howard's character.

Our Jakarta embassy was bombed that week in September. A grim reminder of the security threats and, with it, that Howard was strong on terrorism. He could be trusted. In that final week, Mark Latham's imposition of inner-city Labor views on the Tasmanian logging industry saw John Howard cheered in Launceston by unionised forestry workers. The symbolism spoke to working people across the country – you could trust Howard.

On the final day of the campaign, John Howard and Mark Latham encountered each other in an ABC studio. Latham's aggressive handshake, standing menacingly over Howard pulling him closer, crystalised doubts about Latham. He was a bully.

We won, increasing our majority by 5 seats. But we had dodged a bullet. Latham had saved us. Remarkably, we also gained a Senate majority.

Sunday morning, the media reported that Kevin Rudd's mother had died on election day. I felt immense sympathy for him. Polling day is frantic, visiting booths, smiling at people being rude to you and going into the early hours of the morning. To have your mother die in the midst of it, I could only imagine. I made a note to reach out to him when parliament resumed.

On Monday, I went into the Chatswood Music Centre and bought the Stratocaster, Fender amplifier and guitar lessons.

17

I don't do deals

Reappointed to Education, I happily continued the reform agenda. Our priorities were teacher training; reading; University Workplace Relations reform; standardised core curriculum for Year 12; a multi-billion dollar research and innovation package; rollout of the Investing in Our Schools Programme and establishing the Australian Technical Colleges. With a Senate majority, I naively thought we could finally deliver on an article of faith – Voluntary Student Unionism.

I farewelled Jeff Harmer as my Department Secretary and welcomed Lisa Paul. Like Jeff, Lisa had a 'can do attitude'. She was also hungry to do her best, newly promoted from Deputy Secretary where she excelled overseeing Australia's domestic response to the Bali bombings. My Chief of Staff, Catherine Murphy, also left to go to the private sector. I greatly appreciated the 'risk' she took leaving John Howard's office to come to lead my team. We had been through much together.

I started by taking my key advisors away to the Blue Mountains, with Lisa Paul and senior officials, for a retreat. We needed to set our vision, policy priorities and resource allocation. Lisa asked if I had found a new chief of staff. "No Lisa, I had plenty of applicants, almost sixty. Not one of them a woman. All men." She asked why "men" was a problem. "Lisa, in my experience, the best people to have in these roles are women. Even better if they are married with children." One of the Deputies, Wendy Jarvie asked why. "Because nothing at work is as complex as what they are juggling at home. They are also accustomed to dealing with the histrionics of men and demanding, infantile, irrational people!"

Somewhat surprised, Wendy asked if there was anyone in the department that might fit the bill. I was mid-sentence, dismissing the suggestion outright, when I interrupted myself, "Yes, yes … that woman, the one Jeff Harmer brought to see me who worked on economic modelling for the higher education reforms … the short one who argued with me, what was her name?"

"Maria Fernandez", Wendy said. "Yes, I like her. Someone with the courage to debate the Minister. I listened to her, but agreed we would require the universities to publish minimum academic entry scores before offers were made. She opposed me and then did a great job implementing the policy with which she didn't agree. Maria."

Maria was nervous when we met in my office, unaware why the Minister would want to see her. Flattered by my request to consider being my Chief of Staff, she asked many questions and, two weeks later, agreed. I told her I would look after her and that no matter what we went through, she would emerge from working with me, her integrity intact. "Yes, I am proudly a Liberal Maria, but I am neither a spear carrier nor partisan hater. It will form a part of your CV, but working for me will neither define nor brand you." She accepted the job. As it turned out, Maria was married. She and Brett had two boys.

By this time I had the great fortune to work with several people who would go on to provide great service to the Liberal Party and to Australia. Alan Tudge joined as my schools advisor, Simon Berger, a superb strategic thinker and communicator, and Andrew Hirst in communications. Yaron Finkelstein basically hosed down people I upset and 'cleaned up' my mistakes! Andrew and Simon would eventually lead the Liberal Party federal organisation. Yaron would be Prime Minister Morrison's principal private secretary. Alan would later become an MP and cabinet minister himself, including being Education Minister. We were a great team.

Malcolm Turnbull introduced himself to the party room by immediately seeking to de-stabilise Peter Costello. He commissioned a tax reform paper to 'stimulate debate'. Phil Barresi related an experience to portend what would lie ahead for us all. "Malcolm kept saying if I needed any help at all I should let him know. So, I went around to his office. He sat at his desk, me on the other side, like a constituent. I started talking to him and he just worked away on his computer as if I wasn't there. Said he was listening and just kept typing".

Mark Latham walked away from the Labor leadership and parliament in January 2005 and Kim Beazley returned as Labor's leader. Normality – for the moment at least. On resumption of parliament, I sought out Kevin Rudd. I didn't know him well but offered my condolences. I shared my own father's death six days out which was hard enough. We had a mutually supportive conversation about grief and the political environment. It would be several years before I would appreciate the impact that conversation had on him.

Late in 2004, I had commissioned Professor Ken Rowe to lead a National Inquiry into the Teaching of Literacy in Australian Schools. I appointed to it educators, researchers, designers of Bill Crews' MULTLIT, teachers, principals, academics and a journalist, Miranda Devine. I asked them to examine the research evidence relating to the teaching of reading and the extent to which current practices were evidence based.

Thomas Jefferson wrote, "Once you learn to read, you will be forever free. Information is the currency of democracy."

Yet, 'freedom' for many young Australians was at serious risk. It still is. I was told by the Australian Council for Education Research that 30% of Australian students in Year 9 were 'functionally illiterate'.

In 2004 I read research published by Queensland University of Technology academic, Ruth Fielding-Barnsley. A survey of 340 final year, early career and special needs teachers found a staggering 56% did not know what a syllable is. Staggeringly, 75% could not count the sounds in words. Referring to this in an address to the National Press Club, I asked rhetorically how on earth these teachers could be expected to explain how written language works.

Ironically, speaking to her research, Dr Fielding-Barnsley told the media, when challenged, "Teachers know what a syllable is – they just can't explain it." That of course, made my point. They are teachers, more than anyone else, they are supposed to be able to "explain it".

Faddism in education had led to a 'whole language' method of teaching reading. It assumes that learning to read is like learning to speak without any specific teaching of the alphabetic system and letter sound relationships.

Apologists often blame failure to read on parents or poverty rather than poor teaching. Kids from well off backgrounds in educationally well-off families would learn to read irrespective of teaching failures. Those from disadvantaged families have disadvantage compounded by ineffective teaching methods and poorly trained teachers.

I asked Ken Rowe to tell me if mastery of the alphabetic code is essential to proficient reading. We needed to know if methods to teach that code directly are more effective than those that don't. As I was also Science Minister, I knew that the education faculties lacked scientific rigour, attracting a paltry 2% of competitive Australian Research Council grants.

The 'Rowe Report' was clear:

> Whether from research, good practice observed in schools, advice from submissions to the Inquiry, consultations, or from Committee members' own individual experiences, that direct systematic instruction in phonics during the early years of schooling is an essential foundation for teaching children to read. Findings from the research evidence indicate that all students learn best when teachers adopt an integrated approach to reading that explicitly teaches phonemic awareness, phonics, fluency, vocabulary knowledge and comprehension. This approach, coupled with effective support from the child's home, is critical to success.

Handing me the report, Ken said that every classroom primary teacher could be taught how to teach reading in two days. Our challenge was to build capacity in teachers toward evidence-based teaching practices. "Teaching standards and student achievement", he said "are interlocking fundamentals to the determination of reading outcomes".

This wonderful man, Ken Rowe, was killed in the Marysville fire tragedy in February 2009.

Highfields Preparatory School was in my electorate. A private prep school in West Lindfield, I was invited to officially open the new library. Two weeks later, about 30 handwritten letters arrived from the Year 2s. One, 'James', a seven-year-old:

> Dear Dr Nelson
>
> Thanks for turning up at our school. You didn't have to come, we already had the key. You're a real comedian, but gee your speech was long.
>
> I had a cat called Nelson, but he died.

At the bottom of the letter was a drawing of a cat in extremis. I framed the letter for my office. Months later, on a flight from Perth to Sydney, I approached the bathroom. The pilot emerged from the cockpit with the same objective. I stepped back to let him in. He said, "No, I'll go after you". I deferred again to him. But he said, "No, I'll go after you. You're much more important, you're my federal member of parliament."

"You're flying the plane, I'll go after you!" He went on, "You're my son's hero." As I didn't get much of that, I asked him how old his son was. "He's seven. He's got this enormous photo of you on his bedroom wall. Next to it is a letter you wrote him. We framed it."

Touched, I asked what I had written to him about. "You wrote him the most moving bereavement letter – he had a much loved cat called Nelson who died."

Another primary student made her assessment. There was an air of great excitement at Pultney Grammar, Adelaide. I was opening the Early Learning Centre. As the state minister, officials, staff and parents casually interacted before formalities, the kids running around, I noticed one little girl alone, unhappy. Extricating myself from the crowd,

I went over, got down on one knee and introduced myself. After a few minutes, I asked her why she seemed sad. "Every time somebody comes to my school wearing a uniform like yours … there is a lot of talking … and I get very sleepy!"

Professor Denise Bradley was Vice Chancellor of the University of South Australia. She came to see me about a library for the University. It would honour former Labor Prime Minister, Bob Hawke. I agreed immediately. My view is that a 'library' should be established to tell the story of the contribution made by each of our Prime Ministers to our nation. We diminish ourselves by failing to do so. I told her it would be 'sensitive' with some of my colleagues. I would arrange for $5 million to be made available to the University in two tranches over two years from the Capital Development Pool. By any standard, Bob Hawke is one of Australia's giants of the 20th century and yet I had to support it quietly. When it opened in 2007, I did not receive an invitation. Keeping it 'quiet' I presumed.

Another initiative I was proud to support came from Chairman of the American-Australian Association, Malcolm Binks, and former Australian Consul General to New York, Michael Baume. The narrative coming from Australian universities about the United States disturbed them. Mostly critical, unbalanced, offering a slanted, narrow view of the US. I shared their concerns. They proposed the establishment of a United States Study Centre based in one of Australia's universities. It would undertake research, providing analysis of American politics, economic, trade, security and social issues. It would educate Australians about the importance of the United States to Australia. They sought $25 million from government.

I agreed immediately, but such a sum could not be magically conjured up within my portfolio. I would need supplementation. They went to see John Howard's Chief of Staff, Arthur Sinodinos, who was also supportive. We had three universities shortlisted, Melbourne, Sydney and the Australian National University. I chose Sydney as I thought it was less likely to be 'captured'.

Student demonstrators in Perth sealed the fate of compulsory student unionism, strengthening my resolve. I had personally intervened to support the development of an Indigenous Education Centre at Perth's Edith Cowan University. The *Kurongkurl Katitjin* Centre received $5 million in Commonwealth funding. It reflected our commitment to Aboriginal education and was a personal priority for me. It would provide excellence in teaching, learning and research in a culturally inclusive environment. Its name meant *Learning Together.*

I was welcomed to the official opening by the Vice Chancellor, Professor Millicent Poole. As cocktails and canapés were served, the familiar beat of drums began to permeate proceedings. By the time speeches began, an unruly mob of chanting protestors surrounded the building. Hard core, militant, angry people determined to get me. The police attempted to cordon off a path to the car but were overwhelmed. They called in riot police and mounted horses. We tried again. This time, an absolute melee. As I finally lunged into the car, one protestor held my foot. I kicked him forcefully as the car sped off.

Stopped to regain composure away from the campus, a lone protestor was determinedly running towards us. The Comcar driver panicked but with three police cars with us, this was not likely to be a grenade attack. The breathless young man leaned on our car, "Brendan, how good was that? We gave it to you for sure!" He asked if I could sign his tee shirt as a memento. I gestured for the police to take him away.

Before taking on voluntary student unionism, I went to see John Howard. We had a bigger industrial relations agenda running and political sores festering on a number of fronts. Before opening up another one, I sought his view. "No Brendan, it's always been an important issue to us. Away you go."

The structure of student unions was opaque. Yet no student could enrol in an Australian university – full-time, part-time or online without paying a compulsory union fee. Central Queensland University and the University of New England each had respectively 80% and

79% of their students enrolled externally. Less than half the university unions publicly reported their finances and balance sheets. They were multi-million dollar operations.

Opponents of VSU argued that sporting organisations would collapse, child care would disappear, food prices skyrocket and campus life be destroyed. But as one student said, "All we need on campus is a 7-11 and an ATM. Anything after that, pay for it yourself."

My field research revealed that I could buy a sausage roll with sauce from the Sunnyside bakery next to Sydney Uni for 80 cents less than at the student cafeteria. The person serving me at the bakery also wore a smile. Where child care was offered, many places were reserved for staff, including those union subsidised. In four cases, child care was dearer on campus than outside.

Two prominent businessmen came to see me in my Lindfield electorate office, doyens of the Sydney University Rugby Club. Having exchanged pleasantries, they went on to mount a strong defence of compulsory student union fees. The impact on the Sydney University Rugby Club of VSU, I was told, would be devastating. To illustrate the case I was told of a young man from country New South Wales studying medicine. The Rugby Club had given him a scholarship so he could play rugby and not need to work part-time to support himself. Such support "would disappear" with VSU.

I asked them why a single mother studying nursing should be forced to pay a union fee to subsidise him and the Rugby Club, which was the beneficiary of wider largesse. As both were constituents, I knew my campaign to make Bradfield a marginal seat was gaining momentum!

If that wasn't enough, Tony Abbott approached me after Question Time. Similarly concerned for Sydney University Rugby Club under VSU, he urged me to re-consider the Bill. "Tony, I can't believe I am getting this from you of all people. This is an article of faith for us."

Activist antagonism to VSU on campuses was growing, as was the frequency of demonstrations against me. To this day, though, I continue to be inspired by the conviction and courage of the Liberal students. In my office today is a photo of twenty students from the Sydney University Liberal Club. Holding handmade signs in support of VSU, they stood across William Street, Sydney, with 3,000 angry, anti VSU protestors coming at them. Courage.

Peter Costello said of our Senate majority that we held it "on a good day". His reference was to Barnaby Joyce, the newly minted National Party Senator for Queensland. Barnaby joined our ranks in July 2005. Some called him a renegade, others were less polite. Barnaby was his own man. However, he was flakey on VSU. A graduate of the University of New England in Armidale, he regarded student union fees as the lifeblood of sport, especially rugby he had played at university. Liberals of course, deeply resent compulsion.

The legislation passed the House of Representatives and went into the Senate. The vote was scheduled for Thursday, 8 December 2005. I had been doing my best to keep Barnaby in our 'tent'. The Nationals Senate Leader, Ron Boswell, whatever misgivings he had, understood the importance of VSU to the Liberal Party. If the junior coalition partner failed to deliver its Senators there would be war.

On Wednesday, after several meetings, Barnaby said he could not support the Bill and would vote against us. I anticipated but accepted it with bitter disappointment. There was no point getting angry with him. Though improbable, he might change his mind. Barnaby had amendments to the VSU Bill he wanted debated. He needed my support for him to do so. I quickly agreed. But in turn, he would have to support all the Government's procedural motions to limit the debate. He could then move his amendments which we would oppose. Neither of us realised that we had unwittingly just sealed the fate of VSU.

Barnaby's backbench Senate office was next to that of the Family First Senator, Stephen Fielding. I had held a number of meetings with Senator Fielding over weeks in relation to the VSU. He always listened, asked questions but said nothing of his disposition. I made an appointment to see him after Barnaby. Although non-committal, his body language spoke to anxiety when I informed him that Barnaby Joyce was going to vote it down.

Debate progressed through Thursday. I asked Robert Hill to get senators to filibuster and make sure we didn't get a vote until I could assess Senator Fielding. John Howard called a party room meeting for 6pm at which he said, "Brendan is still working on it and we may not get a result until tomorrow, Friday." Anger in the room towards Barnaby Joyce was palpable.

I saw Steve Fielding again. He was adamant, he "would not do deals". There was nothing that he wanted in return for his vote. He would not declare his position. But in the course of conversation, he mentioned that as one of sixteen children, at university he "never understood the student union fee". I let it go through to the keeper as if I had not heard it. He ended the meeting with an Apology, he couldn't help me. There was no point in any further meetings, he said, we shook hands and I left.

Back in the office, despondent, I had an idea. I said to Maria (my Chief of Staff), "let's have a look at Fielding's maiden speech. What did he come here to achieve?" Among his priorities was a medical school campus for Monash University in Gippsland, drug education and family support.

Up early on the Friday morning, I sat alone in my office. "Bugger it, I'll have one more go". I went to Fielding's office unannounced. I arrived at 8.30. There was no receptionist, instead a CCTV camera in front of which I waved. Minutes later, Senator Fielding opened his internal door. Smiling nervously, the underarms of his shirt were wet from perspiration. I immediately knew he was stressed, extremely so. He was pleased enough to see me even though we had agreed to no further meetings. We spoke of family, the stresses of our job and again, I thanked him for the considered, decent way in which he had dealt with me. Then, "Senator Fielding, I know that you don't do deals and that nothing I say or do will prompt you to tell me how you will vote on VSU. But irrespective of how you vote, we are planning to establish a medical school campus for Monash University. I also intend to recommend to the government that we fund a major drug education prevention program across Australian universities and provision of support services and counselling for university students". He listened approvingly.

I asked if he would consider meeting the Prime Minister before the vote later in the morning. He agreed. Knowing Barnaby had amendments he wanted moved and the commitment I had made to him, I informed Senator Fielding we would have a series of procedural motions to facilitate Barnaby's amendments. Fielding said that he would vote against any procedural motions but reserved his position on the substantive issue.

I knew then that I was certain to get Senator Fielding to the trough. I now needed to convince him to 'drink'. Barnaby of course didn't realise then, that without the support he had guaranteed on procedural motions, we wouldn't get it up.

Senator Fielding and I met with John Howard at mid-morning. Coalition Senators spoke endlessly in the chamber of their university days until we either directed the Bill be withdrawn or to proceed. Fielding reiterated to Howard that he did not do deals. John Howard said that he understood I had proposed a number of new policies and confirmed the government would implement them. Senator Fielding agreed they were worthy initiatives.

When Fielding had left, John Howard asked me what I thought. I told him that in my judgement Fielding would support us. He would vote against all procedural motions but I had Barnaby locked into us on those because he had his amendments. I had guaranteed Barnaby we would allow these to be moved and debated. Howard asked for Senate leader, Robert Hill, to join us.

"Robert, Brendan thinks we should test this on the floor. I am inclined to agree with him." Robert protested on the basis that we couldn't afford to put something so important into the Chamber without knowing the outcome. I said to them both, "if we fail, it will be my responsibility, no one else's. I will wear it with our colleagues and publicly".

True to their word, Barnaby supported all procedural motions and Fielding joined the opposition in voting against them. But when Barnaby's amendments came to the vote, for the first time, Senator Fielding voted with the government to defeat them. My heart jumped. Sitting in my office, on the edge of my seat, with our staff we watched Senators come into the Chamber for the final vote. Fielding stood talking with a colleague in the centre aisle for what seemed an eternity. Then, when the order was given to 'shut the doors', he slipped into a seat on our side of the Chamber.

It was done. After decades, voluntary membership of Australian student unions, guilds and associations was voluntary.

That day delivered one of the enduring memories of my public life. After sharing the moment with my staff and going to thank Senator Fielding, I went to John Howard's office. Mrs Howard was jumping for joy, her excitement exceeded only by that of loyal advisor, Gerry Wheeler. Mrs Howard hugged me. John Howard's face spoke for us all. What a way to end the year!

Earlier in the year, John Howard had asked me casually over dinner after a Cabinet meeting if I had an interest in going to Health at some stage. I told him that I would. It was health that had driven me to politics. However, I would only like to do it if I could take on reform and what needed to be done.

The conversation came back to me when, just before Christmas, Robert Hill announced his retirement as Defence Minister and from the Senate. There would be a re-shuffle. Gillian asked me if I might be moved to Defence. I said, "No, of course not. That will go to one of John Howard's inner sanctum, maybe Tony Abbott or Nick Minchin."

Barnaby's Christmas card simply said, "Sorry for the heartache".

18

Minister, the only thing I can guarantee you is – we will let you down.

Private Jake Kovco – age 33

Captain Mark Bingley – age 35

SAS Trooper Josh Porter – age 28

Trooper David 'Poppy' Pearce – age 41

SAS Sergeant Matthew Locke – age 33

Private Luke Worsley – age 26

SAS Signaller Sean McCarthy – age 25

Lance Corporal Jason Marks – age 27

These eight men died as a direct result of decisions I made, supported or administered during my tenure as Australia's Minister for Defence. This, more than anything else, is what I carry with me. They are real. They are very real. I recall them, their families and the services I attended as if they were yesterday.

Those decisions, carried most heavily by prime ministers, are also ones for which we all bear shared responsibility.

I was mowing the lawns in late January 2006, emptying the catcher, when my phone rang. John Howard. Would I move to Defence? Having thanked me for my work in Education, he said, "Brendan, I take a bit of an interest in defence matters, please keep me informed." An understatement if ever one was made.

Days later I was driven from Government House, Yarralumla, having been sworn in. A daunting feeling.

Written briefings arrived immediately. My approach was to treat it as a pyramid. Start at the top – key people, civilian and military leaders; budget; size, structure and composition of the defence force; key priorities, especially urgent decisions. And of course, the deployments. We had ten operations in train when I came into the portfolio, four were big – Afghanistan, Iraq, East Timor and the Solomon Islands.

Sadly, I had to leave some of my ministerial staff and acquire people familiar with defence, security and intelligence. I asked Maria if she would remain Chief of Staff. She readily accepted. John Howard called to caution me when he heard this. Her public service background concerned him, reminding me the Government had major issues when communication between the Minister's office and Defence failed. I told him it was a 'package deal'. I would take full responsibility.

It was chaos back at Parliament House. My staff had single-handedly moved my office. Jennifer Ratcliffe had photographed my ministerial education office and painstakingly recreated it. Amazing woman. Amidst the chaos, "Brendan, there's a woman from the Air Force who insists she has to see you". We were flat out, but in she came. A slim young RAAF Flight Lieutenant, Sharon Cooper. She told me that she was my 'ADC'. I had no idea what that meant. "Your aide de comp, sir. It is an appointment to show respect for your office from Defence. I will act as a special liaison for you with Defence and assist in numerous ways. I have been selected for the role by the Chief of the Australian Defence Force."

I did not know then that Sharon was the first nurse to be so chosen for the role. Nor did I know that only 18 months earlier she had been pulled from the wreck of a United Nations Bell Helicopter in East Timor, covered in aviation fuel. She had sustained multiple fractures of her vertebrae, fractured jaw and other injuries. We would go through a lot together. She changed my life and I would change hers.

Nigel Blunden joined me from Channel Nine as media advisor, neither of us knowing what we were about to go through.

Defence remains the hardest job I have had. It was also an immensely rewarding experience that would change me. It would change my view of what is really important in life, the value of life and what it means to be an Australian: decisions to deploy men and women to kill or be killed; geopolitics, strategic thinking and communicating it to the Australian people; enormous sums of money to be spent equipping the ADF, knowing those decisions would reverberate through Defence for decades; the grinding detail of complex Cabinet submissions to be taken through the National Security Committee. Then of course, ensuring John Howard was comfortable with what I was doing and to stay out of Alexander Downer's way on foreign policy.

I was blessed to have as my 'junior' minister, Bruce Billson. Bruce was Minister for Veterans Affairs and Minister Assisting the Minister for Defence. No Minister for Defence Industry in those days.

'Big Kev', the Labor stalwart who ran the social club for the Department of Education, organised a send-off for me. Three hundred turned out. Kev was emotional as he thanked me for what we had done over the four years in the portfolio. I was moved by his tribute.

I received a card which I kept. The left-wing Victorian Labor minister, Lynne Kosky, wrote to congratulate me:

> ... no more hand grenades at ministerial council or missiles across WA's bows ... Good luck. I have really enjoyed working with you because you are prepared to have the discussion and work through issues ... I'm sure our paths will continue to cross ...

Lynne would go on to be transport minister, enduring controversies before succumbing to breast cancer. We are poorer for her passing.

The Chief of the Australian Defence Force (ADF) was Air Chief Marshall Angus Houston. A tall, thoroughly decent, highly intelligent helicopter pilot and former Chief of Air Force. Angus has the reassuring, calm demeanour of an Anglican priest. I knew Angus and liked him. We were about to work closely in the interests of the ADF and our nation.

The Secretary of Defence was Ric Smith. A doyen of the Department of Foreign Affairs and Trade, Ric was a giant of Australia's diplomatic corps, a towering figure of Australia's public service, with a superior intellect, humility and with a great sense of humour. Goodness only knows what he thought of my appointment, but I felt fortunate to have him as Secretary. I knew he would always be straight with me. He didn't disappoint.

Maria and I sat down for our first meeting with Angus and Ric, the 'diarchy'.

We canvassed all the issues you would expect. Budget preparations, my priorities for it and arguments for the Expenditure Review Committee only six to eight weeks away. We worked through the complexity of the deployments. As the meeting was about to conclude, Ric leaned forward with the look of a man who has the weight of the world on his shoulders: "Minister, the only thing I can guarantee you is – we will let you down".

We stood, shook hands and they left. I turned to Maria, "What do you think he meant by that?" It took only a week to find out.

Three days of briefings in 'Russell', Defence headquarters in Canberra with voluminous information about operations, ships, planes, tanks and multibillion dollar decisions to be made. During the morning tea break on my second day, I asked about a story I remembered seeing three weeks earlier. *The Herald Sun* had reported some kind of problem with soldiers' equipment that had caught my attention. I wanted to know more.

Silence. A senior official said, "Minister, nothing to worry about. You have bigger issues to deal with in aircraft replacement and ship building". Reluctantly, I let it go. I was awoken on Saturday morning just before 6am. Nigel Blunden: "Mate, we're being hammered across *The Australian's* front page and News Limited mastheads. A story about soldiers' equipment. Everything from leaky sleeping bags and ill-fitting boots to cracked body armour."

As I was about to learn, a lot of the job was finding things out the hard way. It also reinforced my view that in leadership, you have to trust your instincts.

The Defence budget then was $26 billion. Yet here was a line item of $133 million causing immense grief. My suspicions were that a group of ex sergeant majors was running this area. The businesses that missed out on contracts were unwilling to accept the outcomes with the grace of larger, defence industry Primes. Once I got three outsiders in to look at it, I found it was that and more.

The Service Chiefs, as always, were very high quality. When I walked into the office of the Chief of Air Force, Air Marshal Geoff Shepherd, the models were impossible to ignore – planes he wanted to buy. Most prominent were what I would soon learn was a Boeing C-17 heavy air lift and a Lockheed Martin F-35.

Lieutenant General Peter Leahy was Chief of Army. He was forthright, telling me the army's job was to apply lethal force when I told it to do so. He was right of course. In the end we outsource responsibility to the men and women under his command to kill – or be killed – on our behalf.

Vice Admiral Russ Shalders was thoughtful, focused on the big ships he needed. Navy was also reeling from problems in naval aviation following the crash of the Sea King Helicopter in Nias with the death of six Navy personnel.

The most dangerous period in a new portfolio is the first few months. You aren't yet fully across the detail and clever departments can slip things past you. I threw myself into the detail of the budget, preparing again to do battle in ERC. The two big items were C-17 heavy lift aircraft and a decade long 3% real compounding annual increase to the Defence budget. By the end of March, it was done with wins on the planes and the money. Reflecting the value and importance of sound economic management, when the C-17s were agreed at a cost of $2 billion, Peter Costello asked, "Brendan, could you find out if we can pay cash before 30 June?"

General Leahy was not without a sense of humour, as in 2001 when he had referred to the infestation killing my lawn as 'Navy Worm'. Reading *Army News,* I noticed that he was running a competition to name the first M1A1 Abrams tank. We had ordered 59. I cut the story out and wrote to General Leahy. I had a Jack Russell terrier called

'Sniff'. I had named her after a Slim Dusty song, *Sniff the one-eyed digger's dog.*

My handwritten note proposed that 'Sniff' would be a great name for a tank, given their ability to sniff out trouble. In late March a formal brief arrived attached to a hand written letter from General Leahy:

> Dear Minister
>
> Thank you for your entry in the 'Name the Tank' competition. I am pleased to inform you that you have won second prize – naming rights of Army's newest Explosive Detection Dog. He is now known as 'Sniff'.
>
> Sniff is currently undergoing training in Sydney. You are invited to visit him at any time. During your visit we might be able to discuss your Sniff visiting to commence a breeding programme.

A photograph of a kelpie-cross was attached!

In early March, we celebrated the 10th anniversary of the election of the Howard Government. The Great Hall of Parliament House was packed. All the government members, elder statesmen of the Liberal and National Parties, officials, diplomats, business leaders, donors, supporters and all those who had helped us into government and kept us there.

As John Howard was speaking, I received an urgent message. Seated in the centre of the room, I tried as discreetly as possible to leave. I made my way past a few tables when Paul Neville caught my eye. He approvingly smiled, raising his glass and a little too loudly called my name. He was over-refreshed. As I passed his table, smiling at him, he rose to his feet speaking across other guests. I instantly thought the best thing was to bring Paul with me, take him outside. Paul put his arm around my shoulder to steady himself. Greg Hunt, on the next table and attuned to what was going on, stood and came to Paul's other side. Paul wrapped his other arm around Greg's shoulders and we made our way down the centre aisle towards the doors. We must have looked like a couple of footy players helping a wounded mate from the field.

John Howard continued to speak of our considerable achievements in office.

With his arms elevated around our shoulders, Paul's pants suddenly dropped to his ankles. Panicked, he tried to bend over to pull them up. With one free arm each, Greg and I deftly stooped down and managed to get them back up to his waist. As we moved past the tables, Paul said rather loudly, "Strewth! I can't believe I gave the PM a brown eye in the middle of his speech!" I reassured him that was not the case – "just a minor wardrobe mishap". We made our way without further incident, handing Paul to a couple of his staff.

Paul Neville was one of the most decent men with whom I worked in parliament. Although I saw the humour in all this, I also felt sympathy for him. I left it until late the following morning before finding a pretext to go to see Paul. As always, he was cheerful. He said that the dinner had been great but he had to leave early. He had no recollection of what had happened!

The United States Secretary of State in the second George W Bush Administration was Condoleezza Rice. She arrived in mid-March 2006 for a three-day visit. From a distance, I regarded her a seriously impressive, accomplished woman.

The Department provided me with briefs, her profile, key issues and, as always, draft talking points. I always do my own research. Weeks earlier she had addressed young people at a leadership forum in Washington. The largest portrait hanging in her State Department office was of Thomas Jefferson. "I often look at him and wonder what he would think – a single black woman from Birmingham, Alabama, sitting in this office as Secretary of State."

I first met 'Condi' at the Prime Minister's Sydney residence, Kirribilli House. John Howard hosted the National Security Committee of Cabinet to meet her for cocktails. In life, sometimes you meet such people and are disappointed. 'Condi' was even more impressive than the person I expected her to be. Calm, intelligent, perceptive, personable, loyal to her country and president.

In conversation, I referred to her recent leadership speech. I told her of my admiration for Thomas Jefferson, notwithstanding his keeping of slaves, an admiration she shared. I told her of the largest photographic portrait in my office, Neville Bonner, his story and meaning to me.

The following day, I hosted Condi in Melbourne. I warned her she would be 'grilled' by Australian media. A key question would be, "What team do you support Secretary Rice?" I advised her to say, "St Kilda". When asked at Victoria Barracks, she looked sideways at me and said, "Minister Nelson recommended St Kilda, but I need to learn more about the game first."

At the end of the day, she presented me with a gift, a framed portrait of Thomas Jefferson, personally annotated by her: "To Minister Brendan Nelson, I am sure that Jefferson would have been proud of the US-Australia friendship. Condoleeza Rice."

President George W Bush, in my opinion, played a significant role in 'normalising' African American leadership. With Colin Powell and Condoleeza Rice especially, he helped make possible the election of America's first 'Black' President.

British Prime Minister Tony Blair visited Australia two weeks after 'Condi'. Another class act, Blair was also personable and possessed with a good sense of humour. When he visited our Cabinet meeting in Sydney, it was obvious that he and John Howard respected one another. At one point, Howard said, "Tony, you seem to have taken to action on global warming with great enthusiasm". Blair replied, "John, it's easy for us … Margaret (Thatcher) closed all the coal mines."

I would always think back to Blair's quip when we were being lectured by Europeans about action on climate change.

Illegal fishing in our northern waters was causing consternation. I saw an intelligence photograph of 400 boats of various sizes clustered just outside our territorial waters on the Arafura Sea. I also received reports of fishermen in the Gulf of Carpentaria arming themselves with guns to fend off these foreign fishing vessels (FFVs). Most were small timber boats owned by dirt poor Indonesian fisherman. Others were large, steel-hulled 'mother ships'. They would receive the fish caught by the small boats, processing the catches at sea.

Navy intelligence showed me photos of some fishermen on larger boats attacking our Navy personnel using large, wooden spikes. The last straw was film footage of an Australian sailor from HMAS *Bathurst* hanging onto the stern of an illegal ship as a man emerged from its wheelhouse with a machete.

I was angry.

I said to Chief of Navy, "Russ, we have Royal Australian Navy patrol boats. They have guns on them. They fire across the bow of these big ships but are ignored. It's time for us to show them we are serious. We're not going to muck about on this." In Navy jargon, what I wanted was an escalation in the Rules of Engagement. I was concerned we might have an incident in the Gulf with a civilian shooting, and injury or worse to Navy personnel and loss of public confidence in our Navy to protect the borders.

There was a lot of pushback on this but six months, yes, six months later, I had what I wanted. A series of measures were approved right up to and including authorisation to put a round into the steel-hulled vessels above the waterline in our waters should they fail to obey lawful instructions. The final request would come to the Minister for approval.

Months later I was receiving regular updates on a patrol boat tracking one of these steel-hulled, illegal fishing ships. After two days it disengaged. My 'brief' described inclement weather. I was disappointed the request had not come for direct fire. I was also suspicious. I asked my staff to get me the mobile phone number of the commanding officer of the patrol boat. I called him.

"Brendan Nelson calling from Canberra." I could sense his spine stiffening as we spoke. "Just calling to tell you I have been carefully following what you and your crew have been doing these past days. We admire all your work very much." He expressed his thanks and would pass it on to the crew. "Just one question. You didn't put in a request for direct fire. I understand the weather is pretty bad – sea state three".

He said, "No sir, the weather's fine. We couldn't fire because we don't have a gunner's mate. He had a bad back and we had to sail without him."

This and similar experiences led me to describe information getting to the Defence Minister as being "a whale carcass dragged through a pool of sharks". By the time it gets to the minister, huge bites have been taken out of it.

I made my first trip to visit our troops in East Timor, the Gulf States, Afghanistan and Iraq. Nothing has made me more proud to be an Australian than seeing these young men and women on deployment: their professionalism and willingness to place their health, safety and lives on the line. It was often put to me that we had been 'lucky'. I came to appreciate that while luck is a part of everything, it is more than luck. It is the quality of the leadership at every level of the ADF, the equipment we provide to them and the depth and breadth of training. But there is something else. Something I saw repeatedly in the Australian character.

These young Australians didn't say it, but they see themselves, not only as soldiers, but as teachers, aid workers and diplomats. Young people in their early twenties, wanting to understand and respect the culture and customs of those whom they had been sent to help. There were exceptions, but across the three services, this was my universal experience.

At that time Iraq was attracting most of the attention at home. Afghanistan was regarded as a United Nations endorsed conflict in response to the murder of 3,000 civilians. We were invited into the country by the Afghan government. We had, along with others, come out of Afghanistan in 2002, but the Taliban had returned. We went back in under a NATO-led operation in 2005, assigned Uruzgan Province in central southern Afghanistan, partnered with the Dutch.

One of the early dramas was food. Our troops, warfighters especially, were in revolt over food. The problem was the Dutch were dishing up herrings and cheese for breakfast. I called my Dutch counterpart in The Hague, Hanke Camp. After discussion of the mission, operations and construction of facilities, I told him we had to dispatch Australian Army cooks. I asked him to understand that our men were culturally ill-suited to Dutch food – breakfast especially. "They love the smell of bacon and sausages in the morning Hanke."

Having thanked me for sorting food, I learned that our Special Forces troops were being denied special allowances. Standing before them in their compound, Camp Russell, I told them I would get it fixed. Privately I was seething. These men were on the very front line of the war, highly trained, facing death and were being short-changed by God knows who. I knew what John Howard would think. "As soon as I can get to a secure phone, I will get it fixed." A voice called from the back of the crowd, "Got one right here sir". I called the Secretary. Not all ministerial visits were without meaningful outcomes!

Iraq, on the other hand, divided Australia. Toppling Saddam Hussein had turned out to be the easy bit. Without his heinous, oppressive regime, the violent sectarian disputes stemming from the 7th century caliphate erupted. De-Ba'athification of the Iraqi public service and dismantling of the Iraqi army conspired to create a violent, disorganised and dysfunctional nation. It was a mess. Our men and women were doing a superb job, in Baghdad and Tallil, in central southern Iraq. At Tallil, they were located at the huge American air base.

Aboard HMAS *Parramatta* in the North Arabian Gulf, the ship was zig-zagging at 24 knots, 24 hours a day. Busy, dangerous waterways. Boarding parties regularly took their lives in their hands, unsure of what they would find. Protecting two Iraqi oil terminals, the financial lifeblood for the traumatised country.

As a parent, I would have regarded it as 'mission accomplished' if any or all of my three had joined one of the services. Seeing these young Australians doing what they do and how, remains a lifelong source of inspiration.

I made five trips in two years to Afghanistan and Iraq. Just some of those recollections beyond meetings with the Afghan President and Ministers in Kabul, are interactions with our own people.

I started my day at 5am in Kabul, my SAS (Special Air Services Regiment) protectors in the next room. There was danger lurking everywhere, a sense of menace as we drove through the streets teeming with people, motorbikes, old cars and trucks. An electronic suppression box complements the armour plating in the ultra-heavy Toyota Land Cruiser. The two SAS troopers looking after me in the car are fully armed, the driver's weapon close at hand. We travelled in a small convoy. In the event of an attack, they literally will cover me, prepared to give their lives for mine. In the foyer of the hotel, one of our group asks one of two Afghan women if things are any better. In broken English, one replies, "They have stopped shooting women at the soccer stadium."

The Afghan defence minister was General Abdul Wardak, an ethnic Pashtun. Wardak had been a national Mujahideen resistance leader who fought the Soviet forces. Having exchanged greetings, he proceeded to remove his shirt to show me the wound in his back from which Russian shrapnel had been removed.

From Kabul meetings we flew to Tarin Kowt in Uruzgan. There we were briefed on operations, addressed and listened to our troops and then flew in our RAAF C-130 Hercules to Baghdad. Into a US Black Hawk helicopter, we flew at speed across the rooftops looking down to the potential danger of ground fire, especially rocket propelled grenades. The manned machine guns protruding from the helicopters provide a degree of reassurance. In the 'green zone' I spoke with our team embedded in the US led leadership, ranking US generals overseeing the campaign, General David Petraeus, and Iraqi political and military leaders.

We did the same at Tallil. A mounted cavalry unit and infantry had just returned from a two-day patrol. Australian flags were flying from the ASLAV armoured vehicles. A young soldier, perhaps no more than 21, grimy, tired young face, looked up from cleaning his weapon. "You know sir, what we're doing here helps. Iraqis appreciate it a real lot. They're decent people".

Just after midnight we landed in one of the Gulf States where the C-130s were based. It was bloody hot, close to 35 degrees. Standing on the flight deck between our pilots as we taxied in, I noticed the silhouette of a C-130 Hercules about 400 metres away, lights under it and light inside. I made out a couple of people under the plane.

I asked the pilot if it was one of ours. It was. Tired though we all were, I said, "Well, I better go and say hello to them". With the CDF and entourage, we set off down the tarmac. Notwithstanding the heat, I still had my tie on as Angus and I approached the aircraft. Two young men in RAAF overalls had their backs to us as they feverishly worked at something beneath the plane's fuselage. "G'day guys. What are you up to?" I asked. "What does it bloody look like mate? Fixin' the plane!" "Well, whatever you're doing, I just wish Australians could see how hard you are working in this oppressive heat. They would be just so proud of you."

With that, one glanced up. His face turned to shocked horror. The Minister and the CDF looking down. They jumped up instantly, one shouting for those in the plane to get out immediately. We had a quiet chuckle. The senior NCO explained, "Sirs, the aircraft is damaged. We're working hard to get it serviceable. The guys desperately need it." As was often the case, I was a bit overwhelmed by what I saw and heard.

Inside the transportable office we were offered a cool drink. The blackboard had a very clever chalk drawing of a cartoonish C-130 Hercules wearing a sad face. Above it, "37 Squadron Busted Arse Tour 2007." I turned to the CDF, "Angus, what is a Busted Arse tour?" He shuffled uncomfortably. The tail of the aircraft had sustained damage on take-off. It was enough for me to know. Someone had probably made a mistake, one best left alone.

Finally, just after 1am, we arrived at the hotel. The Sheraton's manager was treating me like a king. Red carpet, a room almost as big as my house, waiters, food of every imaginable kind. Exhausted and facing a 5.30am start, all I wanted was to go to bed. Nonetheless I remained polite. Was there anything "His Excellency" needed? "Sir, just an iron and an ironing board. I have to iron my shirt before I go to bed."

He was shocked, mortified, breaking into an energetic defence of his staff to the extent I relented, handing him my shirt. After 30 minutes work, I went to bed. Just before 3am I was awoken by a knock on the door. Bleary-eyed, I opened it to find a smiling man holding my ironed shirt. I tipped him some US dollars to thank him for ensuring I would feel shattered the following day. Such was the bizarre nature of the role. My day began and was spent in a war zone with Australians making immense sacrifices for me and my nation. I end up in a six star hotel trying to get an iron.

I had a few hair-raising moments on some visits. One was in Baghdad. I had just sat down for a meeting with the United States Ambassador to Iraq, Ryan Crocker. Minutes into the conversation, a loud whistling noise and then the building shook violently. Assuming it was the norm, I continued discussing the campaign, Australia's role in it, US commitments and the insurgency.

Outside the residence, getting into the vehicles, I noticed a lot of debris. "That was a close one sir", said the SAS Corporal. A rocket fired into the 'green zone' by the insurgents had just shaved the outer edge of a concrete blast wall. Just half a metre closer, we would have had casualties. These men knew who those casualties would be – them. The next time I met Ryan Crocker, he confirmed how close it had been and extent of damage.

Through the budget and having completed my first trip to our troops, a significant tragedy on so many levels, evolved in Baghdad on

21 April 2006. In Sydney, I was awoken by the CDF at midnight. Angus informed me a soldier in the Security Detachment (SecDet) was seriously wounded. A single gunshot to the head, he had been rushed to the military hospital. His name was Private Jake Kovco of 3RAR. There was no further information. He would call as things developed. I called the Prime Minister's principal private secretary, Tony Nutt, to inform him. At 3am Angus called again, Private Kovco had died. I phoned Tony Nutt.

The following morning I was due to be in Melbourne to promote an event for Defence Reserves. The media would be there in force. I spoke to Angus again to get details of next of kin, circumstances of the death and what would happen now. I asked when the body would be returned. Angus explained, "A C-130 ramp ceremony in Baghdad, fly to Kuwait, transfer to our private contractors, Kenyons and on to Australia." When pressed, Angus said it would be "about 48 hours".

I called the Prime Minister's office again, passing on what I knew and that I would front the media. General Leahy would announce an Inquiry later in the morning. I also called the Opposition Defence spokesman, Robert McClelland, of Labor Party royalty, an intelligent, humble man. I would keep him informed all the way.

Australia's first death in Iraq turbocharged those opposed to it. I knew I had to say something to the nation and answer reasonable questions. I thought as Minister that was my responsibility, rather than simply 'hide' behind the military Inquiry.

Much has been written and said about Jake's death, the hurt to so many people and the litany of errors made along the way. Some of it is worth knowing. That first Saturday morning, I said that Private Kovco had been handling his weapon in barracks. It had discharged and a single gunshot to his head had tragically resulted in his death. Months later, this was the conclusion of the Inquiry. Already beginning to lack confidence in what I was being told at times by Defence, when asked how long it would take to repatriate Jake, I replied, "around several days". The repatriation flight from Kuwait was to arrive into Melbourne after midnight a week later. Many family members lived in regional Victoria – 'battlers'. I thought it would help them if I took the Prime Minister's BBJ 737, picked them up and flew them into Melbourne. We would collect them at RAAF Base Sale.

Standing at the RAAF base in Canberra, waiting to board the plane, General Leahy took a phone call. The blood literally drained from his face. "Sir, you're not going to believe it. The wrong body has been put on the plane."

He was right. I didn't believe it. After some calls, I was satisfied the error had indeed been made. There was only one thing for it. We would get on the plane and I would tell the family what had happened. Easy though it might have been, I could not leave this to others. In flight, I called the RAAF Base Sale Commander. I asked him to have Jake Kovco's wife, Shelley, and immediate family moved to a separate room from the others on arrival. I did not tell him why. I called John Howard who had just gone to bed at the Lodge. He told me I was doing the right thing and to call if needed.

It was the most difficult thing. This family had lost a husband, son and father. Defence had now lost his body.

As I unpacked what had happened as sensitively as I possibly could, one of Shelley's brothers moved threateningly towards me. I could sense the RSM (Regimental Sergeant Major) of Army, Kevin Woods, moving closer in anticipation of what was about to happen. I said, "No Kevin. You can't blame him". I wasn't hit.

Shelley, distressed, angry and every other emotion imaginable, demanded to speak to John Howard. I decided she deserved to do so and rang him. He was asleep. I explained the situation briefly and passed the phone to Shelley. For the best part of five minutes, it was one way traffic, Shelley using choice words to vent her outrage and contempt for those responsible. She handed the phone back to me.

John Howard calmly asked if it was possible for me to speak to him out of earshot of the family. I stepped out onto the tarmac and closed the door, expecting the Prime Minister to 'download' on me. In a very understanding and reassuring tone, "Brendan, what you are going through there is awful. It must be hardest thing. If you need to call me at any time through the night, just do so." I was reminded briefly of the night he had called me when my father died, grateful to the party room and Australians for putting him in the Lodge.

After much angry outpouring, the family got on the plane to travel to Melbourne. More family and friends were waiting for the midnight ramp ceremony that would now not eventuate. I sat at the very rear of the aircraft with the Chief of Army, the RSM, Maria and Nigel. I braced myself to do it again in Melbourne.

That night was one of several in the Defence portfolio when I did not go to bed. Maria, Nigel and I were up in my hotel room working with the Secretary in Canberra, trying to piece together as much information as possible. Peter Leahy and I would front the media at 6am at the Melbourne Airport to break the news. It was ugly.

The Kovco family's pain would be prolonged over the coming weeks and months. The Brigadier hand-picked by the CDF to investigate the body bungle left the report on a disc in a Qantas Club computer. The publicly minded individual who found it passed it on to Melbourne broadcaster, Derryn Hinch. The further hurt to the Kovcos and reputational damage to Defence was significant. At the time, I was told it had been 'lost', either in a taxi or the Qantas Club. I would not know the specific circumstances until October 2008. Had I known at the time it had been left in a public computer, I would have responded by immediately briefing the family.

I was conscious of the 110 men and women in Jake's unit. A traumatic tour, they had sustained an indirect rocket attack that almost killed two members. Controversially, but lawfully, they shot and killed three members of the Iraqi Trade Minister's security team when it crossed through a convoy of ASLAVs. Then, of course, Jake Kovco's death and myriad controversies that followed. I was determined that I would get back to see them before they returned to Australia.

Having been through the Gulf States and Afghanistan, I arrived in Baghdad during the final week of their tour. The senior officer travelling with me was Major General Richard Wilson, Commander of Army Training. I told him, as I had the CDF, I was concerned for integrity of the Chain of Command coming out of the errors following Kovco's death. I had unsuccessfully tried to find out exactly what happens to a senior officer who loses a highly sensitive report in a public space. To the CDF I said, "If justice is not done and seen to be done here Angus, why would a corporal take an order from a sergeant, or a sergeant from a captain?" Finally, I arrived at the Security Detachment quarters. As always, the officers wanted my attention. Normally, I would give them all the time they wanted, but on this trip, this entire trip, my only objective was to get to the soldiers. The second in Command, Garth Callender, had survived a roadside bomb blast in Baghdad two years earlier. An inspiring and courageous man, he misinterpreted my apparent dismissiveness of the briefings as disinterest in the men. He could not have been further from the truth.

Finally, I stood before them all. Most were seated around the area and others stood at the back and sides. In part, I said, "If I personally, in anything I have done or what I have said about Jake's death and what followed, has in any way angered you or made your own grief worse, I apologise. I do so to you all unreservedly."

I opened it up for questions. A young, seated soldier looked up. "Sir, what's going to happen to that Brigadier who lost the report about Jake?" I glanced sideways at General Wilson with my best 'I told you so' look. I didn't know the answer to the question. I spoke of us all, irrespective of role and position in life, making mistakes. But that I also had confidence the military would be deal with it appropriately.

This will not happen again. With C-17 heavy lift Globemasters, we can now bring our dead back from anywhere in the world.

Jake's funeral was at his home town of Briagolong on 2 May 2006. Defence pulled out all stops, including a fly-past and a gun carriage. In the circumstances his family and mates deserved no less.

Just over a year later the Brigadier was promoted to General. I was reassured that it would not adversely impact confidence in the chain of command. On the advice of the CDF I signed off on it with the image of that young soldier in Baghdad on the page. I also knew we had an imminent election coming in 2007 which we would lose. Who was I to second guess the military on this?

I received a handwritten letter from Shelley Kovco's father, David Small. He wrote to thank me for "being the only person through all of this that was straight up with us all the time." It meant more to me than he will ever know.

My first trip to the United States had been postponed by the Kovco tragedy. The meeting with United States Secretary of Defense, Donald Rumsfeld, in late June 2006 was memorable. Secretary Rumsfeld warmly welcomed me at the steps of the Pentagon. It was soon clear that his sharp mind was matched by a mischievous sense of humour. There is something appealing about a man at ease with himself.

We entered the meeting room, signed in and sat down. I was accompanied by the Chief of Defence, Department Secretary, Australian Ambassador, my Chief of Staff Maria and Australia's Defence Attaché in Washington. As the discussion worked through terrorism, Afghanistan and American thinking on the deteriorating situation in Iraq, two advisors to Secretary Rumsfeld entered the room. The North Koreans had launched a Taepodong-2 missile. One asked him what they should do. "We're gonna nuke 'em!" Our jaws dropped. Then grinning mischievously, "Only joking!"

We moved from the meeting down a long corridor to the Pentagon Press Room. A multitude of people were talking over one other to brief the Secretary. It bordered on chaos. Suddenly, Donald turned to me. "Brendan, where are all your guys?" "Mr Secretary, I have only one advisor, Nigel Blunden." Loudly, Rumsfeld called, "Nigel, Nigel – where are you man?" Nigel scurried up, fearful he done something wrong. "Nigel, I got all these people telling me what to say. You got anything to add?" Nigel demurred with his cheeky smile.

We did the call. The last question to me was about a big Boeing project that was seriously delayed. Having met earlier with the then head of its United States Defence business and agreed on what I would say, I said that we had been let down by the company. Its response over the following two years was both swift and impressive.

We left the room. Donald Rumsfeld's minders resumed their frenetic dialogue with him. Abruptly he shouted over them, "Nigel, Nigel!" Nigel Blunden came through the crowd. "Nigel, tell me man. Anything you think I need to clean up?" Nigel reassured him there was nothing! We dined out on that for some time.

19

Some Big Decisions

The future is shaped mostly, not by what we know, but what we don't. We live in a world of fundamentalist intolerance, global economic uncertainty, sweeping technological change and strategic uncertainty. We lived then, as we do now, in vast ignorance of the long-term consequences of decisions we make and that are made for us. In this, we must be clear about who we are, what we believe and truths by which we live that are worth fighting to defend.

Loud voices were questioning our support for the 'War on Terror'.

I was strong in my conviction we were doing the right thing on the basis of what we knew, the 'enemy' with which we were dealing, our alliances and the values underpinning belief in ourselves.

The heinous 2001 attacks were the culmination of a decade of escalation: the 1993 World Trade Center bombing and terrorist attacks on the United States embassies in Kenya and Tanzania in 1998. USS *Cole* had sustained a suicide bombing in Yemen in 2000. The September 11 attacks murdered almost 3,000 civilians. A year later 88 Australians were murdered in Bali by three men who had trained with Al Qaeda under the protection of the Taliban in Afghanistan. There would be a second Bali bombing and the attack on our embassy in Jakarta.

It would have been easier to simply say that these and other terrorist attacks had nothing to do with us. Indeed, many argued that Australia was in a relatively safe part of the world and our focus should be closer to home.

Isolationism has never made us safe. It never will.

We were facing a global insurgency. Disparate groups had hijacked the good name of Islam to build a violent political utopia, fundamentalists, not only fanatically anti-American, but stridently opposed to countries whether Judeo-Christian, Muslim, Jewish or any faith that is open to others, the equal treatment of women, the liberating power of education and people of other faiths. Such countries are regarded as a threat to this ideological insanity.

I was proud to be a member of a government that regarded leaving the fight to others – the Americans and the British – as not only delusional but also irresponsible. To do so would diminish us and demean our values. I did not want to be accused through indifference of leaving the next generation hostage to a force it may never control. Nor did I want my children to look back and ask why we had not stood up to this.

This is a generational struggle between liberal values and resurgent totalitarianism, made harder by currents of moral relativism within western democracies. Where was our moral fortitude?

My grandparents' generation fought off totalitarianism in the 1930s and 40s in the form of Nazism, Fascism and a militarist, imperialist Japan. My parents' generation stared down totalitarian Communism through the Cold War. I wonder if our generation would have prevailed in earlier wars. Would we have made the sacrifices to secure freedoms that too often my generation has taken for granted?

This was a frenetic period. Counter-terrorism, Iraq and Afghanistan, North Korea, Iran and the Hizbollah/Israel conflicts. East Timor suffered a security collapse in late May 2006 requiring a major redeployment into what was an extremely dangerous environment. Commandos, infantry, helicopters, ships and planes were deployed.

Major Alfredo Reinado, along with 20 military police from a platoon under his command with riot police, defected and joined rebel soldiers fomenting a coup. They took with them two trucks full of weapons and ammunition. Though stability and peace returned, I would eventually recommend to Cabinet early in 2007 an operation to re-capture Reinado. He escaped, probably tipped off, but four of his accomplices were killed. In February 2008, Reinado finally carried out an assassination attempt on President José Ramos-Horta. Reinado was killed in the ensuing firefight.

Brigadier Michael 'Mick' Slater of the 3rd Brigade commanded our first deployment back into East Timor. The best of the Army's best, a no-nonsense, common sense, decisive 'straight shooter'. I had complete confidence in him as did the men and women he commanded. As I was about to leave Dili, having visited our troops and met East Timorese leaders, he passed me a piece of paper. "Sir, this is my wife Danielle's mobile phone number. Would you mind calling her and reassuring her I'm not as tired as I look on TV?" I accepted the note and pulled out a piece of paper, writing Gillian's name and phone number. "Mick, this is my wife's number. Could you please call her and tell her I'm not as tired as I look on TV?" He grinned as we both accepted the challenge.

Mick Slater's successor, Brigadier Mal Reardon, made an observation to me not long after he arrived in the country. "Minister, I have been in the Army for 18 years. This is my first operational deployment. Yet I have young soldiers under my command for whom this is their fourth or fifth." Mal's observation reflected the quiet 1980s and 90s and its contrast to the decade of tens of thousands of deployments. Young Australians in uniform want to be deployed. Like footy players, they want to 'get on the field'. But it also meant we were creating close to 80,000 veterans over a decade. Border protection operations, the Regional Assistance Mission to the Solomon Islands, Papuan asylum seekers, a coup in Fiji, instability in Tonga and Papua New Guinea, were just some of the challenges. Then the humanitarian crises and natural disasters.

In 2006, Defence planned for Special Forces to return to Australia in October. I was troubled by this. I had learned the vital importance of 'kinetic operations'. The strength of what SAS and Commandos were doing lay in constantly patrolling far and wide throughout the province, disrupting insurgent operations and taking out insurgent leaders.

CDF Angus Houston told me the job would be done without the Special Forces. In questioning this, I asked, "But Angus, surely this is like weed control. You can go out and kill all the weeds, but if you don't regularly follow up, won't the weeds grow back, thicker and bigger?"

I arranged to see the Special Operations Commander, General Mike Hindmarsh. He was in complete agreement with me. Emboldened, I requested a meeting with John Howard and Alexander Downer to contest the decision to withdraw Special Forces. I put my case. Angus put the ADF position to withdraw. I arced up about the security of the engineers we were about to deploy for road, bridge and other infrastructure. They were soldiers, but surely they would need protection? We decided to deploy an infantry company to support them. By March 2007, it was clear the Special Operations Task Group needed to return to Afghanistan.

Through it all though, there was governing to be done.

The way John Howard conducted himself had more of an impact on me than I appreciated at the time. He respected people that worked hard, returned loyalty and were prepared to argue their case to him directly.

In 2005, when Cabinet considered labour market reforms packaged as WorkChoices, at the third meeting he asked me what I thought. I said in part to the Cabinet, "We are not here for the sake of being here. We don't seek and hold power for its own sake. We are here to do what is right for the country based on our philosophical beliefs."

WorkChoices rationalised a myriad of awards, emphasised individual workplace agreements and reduced exposure of employers to unfair dismissal claims. It reduced the role of the Australian Industrial Relations Commission (AIRC) in setting employment conditions and resolving disputes, delivering flexibility for employers. My only reservation was removal of the 'no disadvantage' test. By the time it was put back in, the damage was done, the trust of working Australians with the government broken.

Labor was energised, backed of course by the ACTU. Its then Secretary, Greg Combet, oversaw and delivered a politically lethal campaign against us.

Returning from Jake Kovco's funeral with John Howard in early May 2006, I raised the leadership issue. Periodically Peter Costello and his backers would engineer a public discussion about transition from Howard to Costello. I told Howard I supported him and that he could rely on it. My support would transfer to Peter only when Howard decided to retire. I also told him that the large number of 'unaligned' backbenchers who had saved us in 1998 were of the same view.

Peter was admired for his intellect and work ethic. In my opinion, like Paul Keating, his brilliance in the chamber of the Parliament made him less appealing to the electorate. I also shared my experience that even after a decade in government, Peter had not built relationships – real relationships – with more than a dozen of his colleagues. It further irritated many of us that he assumed John Howard would simply 'hand' the Liberal leadership to him. There was no sense of putting his name forward to the party room, offering himself to it for leadership. He would of course receive it, but it offended the sensibilities of many of us that we were immaterial to the outcome.

Sure enough, it blew up again in July 2006. I was in the boat fishing with my brother-in-law, Bryon, listening to the radio. We learned that former Defence Minister, Ian McLachlan, had been present at a 1994 meeting between John Howard and Peter Costello. He kept a contemporaneous note of the meeting in his wallet all those years since. John Howard had allegedly told Peter that in the event of a Coalition win in 1996, he would serve a term and a half. A decade in office, Peter was understandably frustrated. Having flawlessly delivered eleven budgets, John Howard showed no signs of retiring. Peter's public positioning resembled a tantrum. He didn't have the numbers, but he did have a choice.

In the unlikely event he had asked my advice, it would have been this. He should have said to Howard, "John, it has been a privilege to serve as your Treasurer and Deputy Leader this past decade, but it is clear that you intend to continue as Prime Minister. I respect that but do not agree with you. I therefore resign both positions and move to the back bench. I will place my name before the party room for leadership in due course."

Had he said that to Howard, or words to that effect, knowing where it would end up, Howard would have done a deal, in all probability by Christmas 2006. If Peter had gone to the back bench to tear John Howard down, as Keating did to Hawke in 1991, in my opinion Peter would have been Prime Minister before the 2007 Budget. Labor switching leaders from Beazley to Rudd in December 2006 would have sealed it.

Instead, Peter said what he did publicly and continued as Treasurer. It would be another two years before Peter was fully revealed to me as the truly good man he is. I concluded he is not a risk taker. On 31 July 2006, John Howard wrote to us all, affirming his intention to stay on, praising Peter Costello as Treasurer. The die was cast. The entire McLachlan note and Peter's response to it had consolidated Howard's position with a solid majority of the party room.

We continued to bleed on WorkChoices, Iraq and the devastating drought.

I boarded a flight in Melbourne for Brisbane with my Chief of Staff, Maria. As usual, I had a briefcase full of work and was grateful for the time to get through it. Kim Beazley took the seat in front of us. As always, he was engaging. In contrast to my multiple folders, he carried only one book – *The Spanish Civil War.* I looked at Maria, "Low stress job being opposition leader."

There were big decisions to be made on defence equipment. My knowledge was limited. But it is not the minister's job to be an expert. The minister's role is to apply intellectual rigour to the process of exercising judgement on behalf of the nation, drawing on all the expertise within and outside the department.

There were two very big decisions I made that Defence preferred I did not. The first involved fighter jets, the second, destroyers.

When John Howard called in January 2006 to ask me to move to Defence, had he asked me to assess the F-35 Joint Strike Fighter (JSF) and New Air Combat Capability (NACC) plan, I would have had no idea what he was talking about. Yet, I had been a Cabinet minister in the government that had signed on for the F-35 four years earlier. I had been head down in education, these decisions made in National Security Committee of Cabinet. But, as always, I threw myself into the detail, progressively 'peeling the onion' on the NACC.

The NACC had multiple complex components, at the centre of which is the F-35 JSF. It involved a ground-based network centric air warfare system called 'Vigilare'; Airborne Early Warning Command and Control Aircraft called 'Wedgetail; upgrades to centre barrels on classic F-18 Hornet jet fighters; KC-30 Multi-Role Transport Tankers and high tech weapons. The other big unknown was the life of the F-111s. We were the only nation still flying the aging aircraft with which significant engineering problems were emerging.

Returning from Darwin in 2006 with the CDF, I told him I was not prepared to go to Washington in December to sign the Production Sustainment Follow through and Development (PSFD) MOU on the F-35 until I was satisfied of two things. The first was the Australian Industry participation package. The second was a 'fall back' option, our 'plan B'.

I was reassured that all the work was done on the latter – "Super Hornet". I was also reassured that the first F-35s would land in Australia 2012.

Prime Minister Howard was going to Washington. I asked that every Defence brief for the trip be sent to me as well. It was here I unpacked the real extent of delays to both Wedgetail and Vigilare. Both were at significant schedule risk. As F-111 issues mounted, I was still told that all would be okay.

I regarded then that the greatest risk to the plan was not the F-35 and its immense technical complexity. The real risk lay in the United States Congress and the capitals of partner countries.

A wheel fell off an F-111, requiring a 'belly landing' at Amberley, brilliantly executed by its crew. I was advised of a 'crack' in a wing and then of a fire, the crew courageously extinguishing it and landing the plane. In the space of one month, the F-111 'drop dead' retirement date shifted right, even when new problems emerged.

I was dealing with a 'conspiracy of optimism'.

Confiding in my chief of staff, this plan, the NACC, without any doubt, was the right plan for Australia. It had been in development four years. From a Defence perspective, understandably, the Minister was someone who should not be allowed to 'interfere'. He was becoming an obstacle to be overcome.

My advisors and I then took the entire plan apart piece by piece in my office. We looked at every year out to 2018. The risk of an air capability gap was not only real, in my non-expert opinion, it was highly likely. I confidentially briefed the Prime Minister, the Secretary of his department and key advisors with my Chief of Staff. Defence chiefs were not present. John Howard listened, asked many questions and finally asked, "what do you want to do?"

I presented four options. We could accept Defence advice and the risk of a gap in air combat capability. The consequences to the nation of being wrong could be potentially catastrophic. We could lease interim fighters – sub-optimal with an indeterminate end-point. We could invite the United States to increase its presence in the north of Australia. I recommended we buy a squadron of FA-18 F Super Hornets. He told me to "work it up" for Cabinet.

It was lonely at this time. There was no enthusiasm in Defence for moving from the 'plan'. However, I was convinced that the stakes were too high not to do so.

The final decision was made in March 2007 to invest $6.6 billion in 24 Super Hornets and infrastructure. I urged the Prime Minister to release the decision immediately. The Treasurer regarded it as a major announcement for budget night. I had to tell him the Defence was 'lukewarm' about the decision and it would leak. Sitting on it for two months was not real politick.

We announced it days later.

Critics of the decision were out of the blocks with rabid anger. The Super Hornet was a 'dog'. The government was wasting billions of dollars, both the Minister and Government, by-passing Defence advice and the system for making such decisions.

One criticism was that I had been 'nobbled' by former Liberal leader Andrew Peacock who was, at the time, country Vice President of Boeing Australia. The fact is that Andrew would visit me every few months. As we were finishing a meeting in my office in August 2006, I said to him as he was leaving, "Andrew, just to let you know I am concerned about a possible gap emerging in air power. You might have to sharpen your pencil on Super Hornets."

He simply said, "No problem. You know where we are if you need us." And off he went. As he did, I thought to myself, "No hard sell there."

Had the government not purchased the Super Hornet, Australia's air defence capability would have been dangerously compromised. The first F-35s landed in Australia in December 2018. The single most important capability I knew was air power, essential to ensure the free movement of Navy and Army. Sometimes you make a difference, this was a big one.

It was from these discussions around air combat capability that inviting the United States to increase its presence in northern Australia emerged. One option I canvassed was the basing of United States military aircraft in the north to 'hedge' a possible gap. Of course, that would unacceptably cause major diplomatic issues with our northern neighbours. As such it was dismissed outright. But from it, we decided to discuss with the United States the possibility of an increased presence in northern Australia.

At the AUSMIN (Australian-United States Ministerial Consultations) meeting in early December 2006, Alexander Downer and I had dinner with United States Vice President Cheney. We raised the disposition of our government to explore options for United States presence, perhaps marines and supportive infrastructure, in northern Australia. He liked the idea. John Howard and President Bush announced exploratory work on the closer ties and presence at the APEC (Australia-Pacific Economic Cooperation) meeting in Sydney, in September 2007.

There was another major acquisition process going on in Navy. It is also instructive. In selecting the design for the Air Warfare Destroyers we down-selected at 'first-pass' the Spanish Navantia F100 and an evolved American, Arleigh Burke class destroyer. It would be a competition. On the basis of what Navantia was hearing from our Navy, they believed they had little chance. We would choose an American ship. When I travelled to Adelaide in October 2006, to officially open the Air Warfare Destroyer Programme Office, I fully realised what was at stake. As a generalisation, I have found that the larger the delegation brought to a meeting, the weaker will be the veracity of the argument to be put.

Prior to the official opening I was briefed by Gibbs and Cox, designers of the evolved Arleigh-Burke. More than 20 people sat on the opposite side of the table from me, my two staff and officials. Then the Navantia team came into the room – three people.

When they left I turned to Maria, irritated: "I don't think Navantia is taking this seriously. I also think we're being spun a line by the Gibbs and Cox people." I asked for the president of Navantia to travel to Australia to see me, about nine months before the decision would be made.

While in my own mind I thought we would end up with an American ship, I said to him, "Look, of course we will rely very heavily on the advice of the Royal Australian Navy on the design we choose. But you need to know that in the end I will take a recommendation to Cabinet on this. I will not under any circumstances recommend something in which I do not have confidence, whatever our Navy says. This is how our system works – the minister persuades the National Security Committee. You need to know this is a real contest".

As the months passed, it was becoming clearer to me that Navantia had the superior design. It was also the advice of the Project Director, Warren King.

The Spanish Navy sent its warship *Alvaro De Bazan* to Australia in March 2007. I went on board at Garden Island with our Chief of Navy. I was impressed. Standing on the bridge, the Chief of Navy turned to me. "Minister, of course we will never have a Spanish ship." I was flabbergasted. "Russ, if that is Navy's view, why is Navantia in the competition in the first place and why is this the first I have heard of it? We are just months from the decision at NSC. Gibbs and Cox, despite what they're telling me, is a year away from a final design at God knows what cost. Apart from the strength of the Navantia case, if we don't sign off on this now, you may well be dealing with a Labor government next year and not get any ships!"

I was shocked and I was angry. I knew then that I was about to be snookered. John Howard would definitely not want to go against Navy's advice. The Americans were the key. I needed to know what our key ally thought. I arranged to see United States Secretary for Defence, Robert Gates, in Singapore just weeks before the National Security Committee meeting. I wanted his view. I knew what the Americans would say, but I needed to hear it and quote it to Cabinet. General Electric engines were going in the Spanish ships, so I knew the United States government would not oppose the design and offend one of its great companies. When I asked him, Gates declined to offer an opinion, deferring instead to Admiral Richard Keating, the United States Commander of the Pacific Fleet. Keating said, "The design of the ship is entirely a matter for Australia. You are proposing to put vertical launch cells into the ships. That's all that counts."

"There you have it, Brendan", said Gates. I pocketed it.

The June NSC meeting decided on $11 billion in spending. Two Landing Helicopter Docks (LHDs) and three Air Warfare Destroyers. The LHD decision was quick – Navantia. Destroyers took much, much longer but in the end it was Navantia. Announcing the decision, the next day, John Howard described the meeting as one of the best in which he had participated.

On both Super Hornets and AWDs, I feel vindicated. The 'meddlesome doctor' got some things right. Had we won the 2007 election, my plan was to acquire a fourth Air Warfare Destroyer. If necessary, I would restructure the surface fleet in the absence of more money for the fourth ship. I could envisage economies of scale and a major leap in forward force capability. It was not to be.

John Howard and Alexander Downer wanted a bigger Army. They believed Australia needed it. I certainly needed no convincing.

In surveying the future, from defence of our borders, to the South West Pacific, the Indo-Pacific and the Middle East, it was clear that the Army was going to be busy. Security, stabilisation, peacekeeping, counter-terrorism, humanitarian and disaster relief, resource security, mass people movement and pandemics. There would be no shortage of challenges ahead. We would ask our Army to do a lot more.

The 5/7th Battalion would be split and the 8/9th re-raised. The Army would increase by almost 10% over the decade at a cost of $10 billion including all the equipment and infrastructure needed to support it. At the second Cabinet meeting to consider the detail, with Peter Costello rightly working through costs in forensic detail, I was starting to doubt I would get it over the line. John Howard had been silent for quite some time when he suddenly sat forward, "Peter, I've never heard anyone complain about spending more on the Army."

This ran in tandem with a $3 billion recruitment and retention package. One idea John Howard loved was a 'gap year' in defence. If young Australians could spend a year working as nannies in the UK or working in Canadian ski fields, why not offer them a year in one of our three military services? The Gap Year in Defence was launched. It wasn't cheap but it was certainly successful. At the end of their year, 70% enlisted permanently.

Fiji had a coup in late 2006. We were concerned for the safety of Australians should widespread violence erupt. An emergency extraction may be needed. Meeting with John Howard and Alexander Downer, we decided to send two ships into the Pacific Ocean, close to Fiji. HMAS *Kanimbla* was loaded with Black Hawk Helicopters, SAS operators and medical teams. *Kanimbla* was accompanied by a frigate, HMAS *Newcastle*.

Defence's response was beyond impressive. Thirty-six hours after I walked from John Howard's office, the ships sailed. Stunning. After several weeks at sea, on 29 November, as I was about to board a plane from Shoalwater Bay in Queensland I was notified that a Black Hawk helicopter had crashed onto the deck of *Kanimbla*, catapulting into the sea. The pilot had been recovered, but could not be resuscitated. Captain Mark Bingley left a wife and son. An SAS trooper was missing. The other SAS soldiers had escaped the sinking aircraft. Tragic. We were able to retrieve the body of Josh Porter from the wreck, three kilometres down. Josh's webbing had caught on the undercarriage, dragging him to his death. Helicopters sink like a brick. How anyone gets out in the confusion is testimony to their skill and training.

Two unexpected privileges came to me early in 2007. Both changed me. The first was at Holdsworthy, the second – Gallipoli.

I met the commanding officer of 4th Battalion Royal Australian Regiment (4RAR), Lieutenant Colonel Mark Smethurst, on my first trip to Afghanistan in 2006. The SAS and Commando troops under his command were capturing and killing insurgents across Uruzgun. They were very effective. Early in 2007, Mark Smethurst invited me to 'spend a day' with 4RAR, the Commandos based at Holdsworthy barracks in Sydney, an overnight stay. I cleared my diary to do so.

Arriving early in the morning, I was 'kitted up' for a training exercise. Dressed as they were in operational cams replete with M4 Carbine, I found myself standing on the rear tray of a V8 Land Cruiser at high speed in close convoy through the streets of the replica suburb. All that held me were the arms of commandos linked around mine as we faced the front of the vehicle immediately behind. Suddenly we braked hard in front of a building. A Black Hawk helicopter hovered over the building as commandos descended from ropes onto the roof. My job was to detonate the charges on the door. The door exploded off its hinges as men rushed into the smoke-filled room. Spring-loaded life-sized 'cut-outs' of enemy combatants suddenly and randomly appeared, each instantly shot. When it was over, I entered the building. All targets had a single bullet hole – between the eyes.

Late in the afternoon, I kitted up again. We boarded Black Hawk helicopters to fly to Jervis Bay for a night exercise. On dusk, we jumped from the helicopters into the sea. I had a waterproof bag containing my weapon, boots and clothes, as did all commandos. We were picked up by inflatable boats and dropped about 100 metres off shore. The swim, pushing my bag as I swam, just about killed me. On the beach, I could barely lift my bag. Out of my wetsuit into cams, boots and camouflage paint, I crawled into an underground bunker to be briefed by two NCOs with a laptop. This was a hostage situation. My job was to accurately identify the hostage when finally recovered.

We jumped onto quad bikes, travelled some distance and then walked through the dark for half an hour. Several commandos set up mortars. I was tasked with dropping the round into the mortar. It fired off with a 'swoosh'. After 10 seconds of silence, I turned to the soldier, "It didn't go off". He whispered, "It has to travel 5 km sir."

We arrived at a clearing, two buildings in the distance. Suddenly, 50 Cal live machine gun fire. Under cover of the suppressing fire, commandos stealthily approached the buildings, surrounded them, finally fighting their way in. Eventually they dragged a life-sized dummy, roped and tied from the building. I could finally identify the hostage.

"Yes, that's him. Kevin Rudd!" We all laughed.

The Black Hawks appeared from nowhere and we climbed on board. After midnight, back in the base and a beer with the men, I had the best sleep ever.

As informative and exciting as this was, the real benefit of the visit came the following morning. Mark Smethurst gave me a DVD to watch. Over an hour of de-brief interviews recorded only 48 hours after adrenaline charged operations in Afghanistan in which they had taken casualties. In particular, the interviews with men who fought in Operation Perth in July 2006 were gripping, astounding. The raw courage, yet humility of these men. Overwhelmed and pinned down by a larger force, they had fought their way out.

One commando, in a long-range patrol vehicle, crooked his arm around the neck of the driver bleeding from a gunshot wound. As he did this, he fired the machine gun on the front of the vehicle with his free hand, cleared a stoppage and fired again until the vehicle was out of direct fire. With the medic attending the driver, he and others attacked insurgent positions.

I was emboldened to do two things. Firstly, I asked the Defence Chiefs why we were not seeing more commendations for bravery, including the Victoria Cross. In 2006 when citations came through for Medals of Gallantry, including for Corporal Ben Roberts Smith, I asked why two of the actions were less than any one of the seven VCs at Lone Pine.

Secondly, these men wanted 4RAR to be re-named 2 Commando. So did I.

There was always jostling to represent Australia at Gallipoli on Anzac Day. It had never occurred to me to even ask. I had delivered the Remembrance Day address at the Australian War Memorial in 2006 in the presence of Mr and Mrs Howard, who congratulated me. Whether that had any bearing, I will never know. But when the Prime Minister's Chief of Staff called to ask if I would go to Gallipoli for Anzac Day in 2007, I was overwhelmed in every way. I would deliver three speeches at Gallipoli: at the joint Australia–Turkey ceremony, at the Dawn Service, followed by Lone Pine mid-morning on Anzac Day. Each was to be no more than five minutes, the hardest ones.

En route to Gallipoli, I visited defence personnel across the Gulf States, Iraq and Afghanistan. On this trip, sitting in the United States Black Hawk helicopter about to take off from Saddam Hussein's palace to fly across Baghdad into the Green Zone, I was aware that the SAS trooper next to me was anxious. Unusual for these guys, I asked if he was okay. Above the roar of the rotors as the US crew checked their machine guns, he yelled, "My first flight sir".

"Your first flight on a helicopter?" "No sir. My first flight in a Black Hawk since the crash off *Kanimbla.*" I put my hand on his shoulder. Nothing needed to be said.

Gillian joined me in Istanbul and on to Gallipoli. Nothing prepared me for Gallipoli. I had often wondered why the Gallipoli campaign captured public attention when our losses, tragedies and eventual triumphs, were far greater in France and Belgium. On the afternoon of 24 April 2007, I stood silently on the beach at Anzac Cove with two SAS troopers who had come with me from the Middle East. Looking up to Plugge's Plateau, The Sphinx, Walker's Ridge and Baby 700, I was unexpectedly filled with emotion. The landscape depicted in George Lambert's masterpiece, *The Landing.* One of the soldiers broke the silence, "An amphibious landing sir, from here. To think that only six months earlier they were farm hands, bakers and clerks. You know what we can do, but a mission like this with the enemy …" He faded to silence.

My own great-grandfather had been one of them, a mechanic from Launceston.

As our guide took us through the battles, we walked into Shrapnel Gully Cemetery. A group of young people circled a grave. Spontaneously, they sang our national anthem. Just thinking of it evokes emotion.

Down on the foreshore, hundreds of Australians and New Zealanders had staked a place for the evening. Their excitement was infectious.

Booked into the only hotel then close to Gallipoli, we were under strict instructions to be on the bus by 3.30am. New Zealand was represented by Winston Peters, its Foreign Minister, accompanied by his wife. They made their presence felt by being 10 minutes late for the bus, much to the consternation of officials. Winston and his wife took their seats in the front row of the bus, immediately in front of me and Gillian. The bus made its bumpy way.

I had put a lot of effort into what I would say at the Dawn Service. I considered just speaking rather than reading it. But I thought without something to read, people would think I was paying insufficient respect to the occasion. Such doubts melted away when New Zealand's Defence Attaché came from behind. He tapped Winston on the shoulder, "Minister, I've got your speech here." Winston replied, "Yes, of course. I better have a look at that."

It was cold. After 30 minutes sitting with the wind coming off the sea, I was shaking uncontrollably. All I could think of was those young Australians 92 years earlier. Shame on me for being such a wimp. The Navy band and singer immediately in front of me were in traditional 'sailor's uniform'. I was freezing just looking at them.

The most difficult part of a speech is the beginning and the end. When my turn came, I removed my coat and went to the lectern. I looked up to 12,000 people, knowing many more were viewing it on television at home. I suddenly thought of my great-grandfather landing in the first wave in the 12th battalion. I paused to gain composure, the image of the moving scene at Shrapnel Gully prompting more emotion:

> Australians all let us rejoice, for we are young and free.
> Our anthem is a national epitaph to those whose sacrifice
> in peace and in war, gave us that freedom.

After the service, I joined the crowds rather than the 'VIP' group. In silence and early morning light, the mass of humanity slowly moved up towards Lone Pine.

At Lone Pine, I felt like an intruder into a sacred place. Here from 6 August 1915, the Australians mounted a frontal assault of the Turkish trenches. Having fought their way into them, over four days of subterranean anarchy, the fighting and dying with bombs, clubs, bayonets and teeth, a bloody victory won. At its end, 2,300 Australian casualties. Seven Australians were awarded the Victoria Cross. The site is now a cemetery and mass grave.

From freezing at Anzac Cove, now to sunscreen and hat. Stands had been erected for 6,000 people. Chairs had been laid out on the manicured lawn in front of the Lone Pine Memorial. As we sat in silence and the catafalque party mounted, two sparrows tweeted as they played in front of us. So reverential was the silence, I thought, "someone's going to have to shut those birds up". The sound went everywhere.

My turn came:

> It is with a sense of unease, trespass, humility and abiding reverence that we come to Lone Pine. Much that is precious lies here. Our past and our future.

I quoted Sergeant Lawrence, the Australian tunneling engineer who looked back from the captured Turkish trenches onto the Australian firing line:

> The whole way across is just one mass of dead bodies … beside me I count fourteen of our boys stone dead. It is a piteous sight. Men and boys who yesterday were full of joy and life, now lying there, cold, dead – their eyes glassy, faces sallow and dusty. Soulless – somebody's son, somebody's boy … The major standing next to me says, "Well, we have won". Great God, won. That means a victory and all those bodies within arm's reach. Then may I never witness a defeat.

New Zealand's finest and most tragic moment on Gallipoli was at Chanak Bair. The 852 names of their dead are on the New Zealand Memorial there. Corporal Cyril Bassett was awarded the Victoria Cross here. Embarrassed, he tried to hide the award from his family.

After the Lone Pine Service we gathered on the steep hill around the New Zealand Memorial, hundreds of young Kiwis draped in their flags – the official one and the silver fern. Winston had a bad knee. Unfortunately, the microphone was live when he finally got to it, sighing heavily, "Aaah … here we go again".

The Turks provided a military aircraft to take us to Ankara. Winston and his wife sat at the front of the plane. They were getting off at Ankara, we were flying on to Istanbul. Mrs Peters was struggling with all the suit packs. Winston strode across the tarmac to the car. "I'll take those for you Mrs Peters", for which she was grateful. Approaching the limousine, Winston turned to find me, the Australian Defence Minister, carrying his luggage. "Brendan, just put them in the boot if you don't mind."

Such was our political predicament, I was attacked by Sydney's *Daily Telegraph* for doing my job. United States Defense Secretary, Robert Gates, proposed we improve dialogue amongst nations fighting in the south of Afghanistan. We each had our own piece of the Afghan 'jigsaw', but there was little overall co-ordination. I readily agreed, having expressed similar concerns to our own military leadership. We could turn our province, Uruzgan, into a veritable Garden of Eden, futile if the rest of the country was a mess. We needed a strategic approach to the whole country.

With the CDF, Angus Houston, his considerable entourage, my Chief of Staff, ADC and media advisor we flew to Quebec. These meetings became known as Regional Command South (RCS). They would precede the eventual International Security Assistance Force (ISAF) model for NATO and its more than 20 partner countries.

It took 32 hours. We booked into the Quebec hotel just on midnight. I had breakfast with my Canadian counterpart followed by Robert Gates, then the RCS meeting before a reception with the Canadian Governor-General. We were on the 4pm flight back to Australia. Sixteen hours on the ground and 32 hours back to Australia. Foremost of my concerns were the Special Forces which we had redeployed.

Three weeks later, the *Daily Telegraph* ran my trip across its front page. I had taken a "$64,000 Junket to Canada". The entire cost of the trip and every person on it had been added up and ascribed to me personally.

USS *Kitty Hawk*, one of America's aircraft carriers, led a carrier group down the east coast of Australia in July. As the flotilla sailed to Brisbane, I was flown out to the floating city. We were met by the ship's senior command. Then, "Sir, we'll take you below and kit you up."

"Kit me up?" I asked. "Yes sir. We're going to put you up in a Super Hornet."

I had been in a Super Hornet twice previously, but at sea off an aircraft carrier! Kitted up and about to get into the aircraft, the United States Navy rating said, "Sir, this is very unusual you know. Our defense secretaries just don't do this,"

I asked why, worried I may be in breach of an order. "Well basically, they're too fat to fit in the aircraft." I took it as a compliment.

Sitting in the back of the plane as it taxied, I understood why the flight deck of an aircraft carrier is described as one of the most dangerous places on earth – planes and equipment everywhere, lots of activity all crammed into an impossibly small area. Finally, we arrived at the take-off point. The pilot went through pre-launch procedures. He asked if I was okay– "couldn't be better". I had told him earlier, he could do whatever he liked with the aircraft, I am a fatalist and had been out to 7.8 'Gs' previously. "I'd just like to return with my retinas attached."

Catapult attached, engines on maximum power, instantly we were in the air doing a barrel roll over the sea, dispersed ships and submarines. An indescribable rush. We spent 30 minutes in acrobatic flight. Coming in, I looked down at the deck and thought there was no way on earth it was going to land on that tiny piece of flight deck. Seriously unsettling! But of course, it did, once the tailhook caught the arresting wire. Exhilarating in every sense of the word.

Back in my suit, I was in the office of Admiral Rick Wren, commander of the carrier group. Discussing geopolitical and security matters, I noticed the photographs on his desk. A Harley Davidson Road King was in pride of place, with one of him and his wife behind it! "You like bikes, Admiral Wren?" He confirmed he did. "Well, you've given me a ride in a Super Hornet, why don't I give you a motorcycling experience in Brisbane? I write for an Australian motorcycle magazine. I can arrange some Harleys, riders to spend a day sight-seeing out of Brisbane."

His eyes lit up, but he declined the offer. "Minister Nelson, tragically, we've had a number of our personnel killed on rice rockets (high speed Japanese bikes) in foreign ports. So, we have issued an order that no United States navy personnel are to ride motor cycles outside the United States." Undeterred, I said, "Okay Admiral Wren, you leave me no alternative than to contact Secretary Gates and tell him that your reluctance to accept my invitation threatens United States–Australia relations".

In Brisbane we rode eight bikes up through the Glass House Mountains. At day's end he presented me with a hand-made model of a United States Navy 'Diamond Back' Super Hornet from Strike Fighter Squadron 102. It has pride of place in my office.

Saif Gaddafi is the second son of the notorious former Libyan dictator, Muammar Gaddafi. After President George W Bush named his 'Axis of Evil' backed with military action, Gaddafi had seen the writing on the wall. He rolled over into the arms of the West, welcoming Tony Blair, among others to Libya. Saif was dispatched to Australia to see me. His mission, to persuade Australia to help Libya build a Special Air Services Regiment (SASR). Australia was not going to do this.

Saif arrived at my Parliament House office with a substantial entourage. Wearing an Armani designed army uniform, he turned to his assistant for 'the gift'. From a long, ornate box he removed a jewel encrusted, gold plated sword – "a sign of respect dear minister". As he handed it to me I wondered how on earth they had got it through security. I held it, admired it, and placed it back in the box for my staff to secure.

Saif and I sat across the table from one another, exchanged pleasantries and got down to business. His father had chosen a "new path" for Libya. The Australian SAS was "the best in the world". Libya wanted to establish and build an SAS. It would pay Australia to help it do so. I diplomatically walked through the issues, explaining this was not yet something we could do. We were pleased with Libya's new direction and alignment with our allies, but helping him establish an SAS was something to which we could not commit.

He persisted. I explained it again to no avail.

In the briefing papers I received from the department, I read Saif had many female liaisons. "Saif, perhaps I can explain this in terms you might better understand. You are a very handsome man and let us imagine I am a very beautiful woman. We have just met. You like me and I like you. But if, after our first date, I told you I wanted to get married, you would be very, very nervous. Well, you are Libya and I am Australia. We have just met. We need to get to know one another, trust one another before we get married and exchange an SAS." "Dear Minister, now I understand completely!" he bellowed.

Anticipating Saif would give me a gift, I was prepared. My ADC passed me our gift. "Saif, I have something special for you. I have a set of Australian Army disrupted pattern camouflage pants, top and tee shirt. These are worn by our SAS." He was delighted.

In August 2011, an image of Saif Gaddafi went global. From the running board of an SUV, Saif exhorted his followers to fight on against the Arab spring rebels. What bemused commentators was why on earth he was wearing Australian army pants and tee shirt. When I saw the photo in London's *Financial Times,* I laughed out loud. If they only knew!

"Hot Issues Briefs" were full of surprises. Pithy summaries of incidents that should not have happened, ones that may bring unwelcomed attention from the media. One described a column of M1 Abrams tanks travelling a short distance on a Victorian public road. The column had reached a Tee intersection and stopped. A truck travelling along the road clipped the gun of the first tank. The truck driver stopped to inspect damage and remonstrate with the tank driver who had got out and walked down the road towards him. Engaged in a robust exchange, the crew of the tank checked to see if the turret was operational. The truck driver, seeing the tank's gun turning towards him, panicked, screamed and ran madly into the bush.

As Defence Minister, I had two secure cases full of briefs, documents that needed to be read, decisions to be made and information to be absorbed. After the election loss in 2007, I continued to be the Minister until my successor was sworn in. Finally, I got to the very last piece of paper I would read as Defence Minister – a Hot Issues Brief.

A Royal Australian Navy Patrol Boat had sailed into New Caledonia. The crew had put the wrong pennant on the flag pole, deeply offending the Indigenous population.

I smiled and wrote, "I'm going to miss you. I love yous all!"

I did, and I do.

20

Time to put down a much loved family pet

On 4 December 2006, the Labor Party replaced Kim Beazley again, this time, with Kevin Rudd.

We felt sorry for Kim. Rudd had conducted a ruthless campaign to bring him down. The day he lost the leadership, Kim's brother died. I arranged a RAAF special purpose aircraft to fly him to Perth.

John Howard thought that, notwithstanding his longevity, he could beat Kim Beazley. He had said of Beazley he doubted he "had the ticker" to be Prime Minister. It cut through. The electorate sensed Kim was not 'hungry' for the job. No such doubts were held about Kevin Rudd. Rudd breathed new life into the Labor Party. No media interview was beneath him, he was everywhere. He and Joe Hockey were regulars on *Sunrise,* Channel Seven's top rating breakfast show. Cabinet told Joe to pull out. He was 'humanising' Kevin Rudd, a nerd's nerd becoming likable.

Malcolm Turnbull joined the Cabinet in late January 2007, as Environment Minister. He invited Gillian and me to his harbourside mansion for Sunday lunch. A kind gesture. "Now, tell me Brendan, how are we going to win the election?" I told him broadly what I thought we needed to do, but our biggest challenge was longevity. The electorate was looking for change. It would be hard to counter.

When Gillian and I drove back across the harbour, she said, "You know, for three and a half hours, all he did was pick your brain. It was all one way traffic. No doubt a long line of your colleagues have been through there. I wouldn't trust him." As usual, she proved to be right.

When Kevin Rudd positioned himself as an 'economic conservative', the electorate heard Tony Abbott describe Rudd as trying to be a 'younger version of John Howard'– precisely what they were looking for.

This would be the year of our political death. A truism in politics is that disunity is death. Just months into the year at a Cabinet meeting, Costello remarked, "Have you noticed we're getting leaks?" I agreed, but it certainly wasn't me. Peter said, "I think it's Turnbull." I had no idea and no time to waste speculating.

I knew we were on track to lose at two junctures in 2007.

Peter Costello's 2007 budget was his best since 1996, concentrating on families, home ownership, iron clad fiscal consolidation and sovereign wealth funds. Yet Newspoll, the nation's most authoritative public poll, in the last fortnight of June when the budget had 'washed through' the electorate, gave Labor a 10 point lead. We had trailed Labor in previous election years, but not to this extent. The mood in the electorate was sombre. The grievance list was long – David Hicks, asylum seekers, Iraq, the Australian Wheat Board scandal, climate change, and refusal to offer an Apology to forcibly removed generations of Aboriginal children. The damage of WorkChoices was done. The legislation had been amended to restore the 'no disadvantage test' and Joe Hockey had replaced Kevin Andrews, to no avail.

I said to Joe Hockey in June, "They have stopped listening. People are polite, respectful but determined. It will give them no joy, but they are going to put down the much-loved family pet."

It can be the little things. At a mid-year Cabinet meeting, I listened incredulously as debate concluded with agreement for the Commonwealth to take over the Burnie Hospital. This vain attempt to hold the Tasmanian seat of Braddon would signal the government was serious about regional Australia. However, it violated the principles upon which the government had stood. I thought at the time, "It's over". shadow health minister Nicola Roxon stood in the parliament brandishing a letter from the President of the Tasmanian Branch of the AMA. When she read the description of three hospitals in north-west Tasmania within an hour's drive of one another as an 'historical anomaly' and 'waste of money', I quietly nodded in agreement. She concluded the attack as naming me as the letter's author in 1992!

APEC was held in Sydney in the first week of September 2007.

A big deal. Heads of State and major entourages from 21 countries. Memorable to me for a number of reasons.

On the first day, Angus Houston informed me of an 'incident' involving a soldier. The soldier had been to Darwin for briefings prior to deployment to Afghanistan. Having got off the plane in Sydney, the taxi driver removed him from the taxi. Angus said his bag, containing operational details for Afghanistan, was "lost".

Here we go again, I thought. "Angus, until proven otherwise, this man had too much to drink on the plane, he's upset the driver and been turfed from the taxi. We need to find that taxi ASAP. Interview the soldier, get any possible information you can. Get the spooks to look at all the CCTV. We must have some imagery somewhere that identifies the taxi. Contact taxi companies for lost property". We would try to find it before briefing John Howard and other relevant parties. I was reassured of no immediate risk to people in Afghanistan. Angus would inform key people at NATO. John Howard had more than enough on his plate without this. For four days, the feeling I had over the lost Kovco report haunted me.

President George W Bush is an impressive man. Accompanied by Condoleezza Rice, he came to our NSC meeting in Sydney. For over an hour he spoke authoritatively on any and every issue we raised across defence, intelligence, foreign affairs, trade and economic policy. Not once did he need to defer to Condi, consistent with my earlier interactions with him.

That evening, John Howard hosted President Bush to a small dinner of Cabinet ministers at Kirribilli House. We spent a couple of hours in conversation before sitting to eat. After speaking to President Bush for some time about policy matters, I made the observation that privately he is a different person from the one we often see portrayed in the media. He agreed, telling me that in his early public life he had a terrible experience with "the press". He "still gets as nervous as hell when the cameras start rolling". With that, he personally annotated for me his Address to the Joint Session of Congress on 20 September

2001, nine days after the attacks on America: "To Brendan, an ally in the cause of freedom. Thanks. George W Bush."

Three days after it was first reported to me, the soldier's missing backpack had been found, undisturbed. The taxi had been tracked down to a private residence. The backpack was in the boot. The owner driver, having evicted the intoxicated soldier from his car, drove home, parked his car in the garage and left it for a four-day break. Thank God is all I could say.

Newspoll, published on the eve of the leaders' gathering, recorded Labor holding a 14 point two party preferred lead over the coalition.

Alexander Downer sought me out. With John Howard's agreement, he was calling a meeting of Cabinet ministers to canvass views on the situation and specifically, "If Howard should go". With the exception of Tony Abbott, Helen Coonan and Mal Brough, all came to Downer's hotel room on the Thursday night. Peter Costello was not invited.

Downer, having canvassed the three not present for their views, asked what should be done. Tony Abbott had said Howard should go, but called back during the meeting to say he had changed his mind. Mal Brough believed Howard should go and Helen Coonan had asked what the problem was. Alexander told the gathering John Howard wanted our views.

I asked Downer two questions:

"Does John Howard believe we can win the election?" Downer said, "No, not likely".

"Does John Howard believe he can hold his own seat?" With hesitation, Downer said, "No – but it depends what day you ask him".

The consensus, not agreed by all present, was that Howard should go, but only if he chose to, on his own terms. I was among those that believed he should not be asked to go by the Cabinet. If he wanted to stay, then I would respect and support his decision. I told him personally early the following week.

Throughout the meeting, Malcolm Turnbull sat on the couch next to Julie Bishop. Sotto voce, he would quip, "Let's have a ballot".

At the Opera House, prior to the APEC leaders' dinner on the Saturday night, Peter Costello asked me outside, away from the drinks and canapés. We walked together alone around the perimeter of the building. Peter opened by saying that John Howard's situation was hopeless, we needed to change. He had been briefed on the Downer meeting and John Howard's response to Cabinet's advice. Having canvassed the backbench, Peter understood I had majority support to be his deputy. The election could be pushed into 2008. He and the 'new' government could reposition on a number of key issues for a fighting chance of re-election. While agreeing the proposition had merit, I told Peter that I would not be party to Howard being pushed from the Prime Ministership. His rusted on devotees would be outraged and a worse electoral outcome would eventuate. If he went of his own accord, then yes. A big if. John Howard chose to stay and fight. As Mrs Howard later said of her husband, he had never walked away from a fight before and would not do so now.

The die was cast.

The messy, dogged issue of transition carried into the campaign. Tony Abbott suggested that if the government was returned, John Howard would serve for a year, then Peter Costello for two. The voters were even less impressed with that than the multitude of spending promises. Australians had long stopped listening. But they were listening to Kevin Rudd when he said mid-campaign, "Enough. Enough of the spending. It stops now."

Campaigning in Queensland, I was booked to announce $500,000 for a set of traffic lights, with Ross Vasta, in the electorate of Bonner. Hours before the event I was told I was no longer needed. The Prime Minister was going to do it. Desperate days.

On Election Day in late November, as I made my way around the Bradfield polling booths, Liberal Party president, Tony Staley, called. Tony had been steadfast in his support of me since I was pre-selected in 1995, defending me when it was unfashionable to do so. He asked if I would stand and serve as Peter Costello's deputy in the event of the impending election defeat. Taken aback by the call, I told Tony that I just wanted to get through the day. If we did lose, I would need to discuss it with Gillian. But should she be agreeable, I would be honoured to offer myself for consideration as Peter's deputy – "We will need one another, Tony".

I did election night coverage for SKY News. It gave me a virtual 'bird's eye view' of what was happening around the country, including campaign rooms.

As friends' seats were declared lost, one Liberal member was returning to parliament with an increased majority. Malcolm Turnbull's election night event was an upbeat affair. He projected an air of great self-confidence. Celebrating the swing to him in Wentworth, Turnbull made no reference to hard working colleagues who had lost their seats. No sense whatsoever of the gravity of what was happening and the moment in history it presented to both the Nation and the Party.

John Howard later told me that as he was being driven across the Sydney Harbour Bridge to the hotel where he would concede defeat, his phone rang. Malcolm called to "detail his plans for the future". Howard told me he simply said to Malcolm, "now is not the time".

The morning following the election, I sat in the kitchen of our Sydney home with Gillian and my most loyal confidant and New South Wales Liberal Party vice president, Rhondda Vanzella. We discussed nominating for the deputy leadership, what it would mean for us and family. With Gillian's support, I would nominate.

I was literally speaking to Joe Hockey about it in the knowledge that he, and a number of others, would also nominate. Suddenly Joe stopped, "Costello's just announced he won't run for leader". We were stunned. The Liberal Party was blindsided, unprepared for a future without both John Howard and Peter Costello. A very short time later Malcolm Turnbull announced his candidacy for leader. In my opinion, he intended to run against Peter for the leadership anyway.

I was thrust into considering a tilt at the leadership. Many urged me to do so. Others knew that whoever led the party at that point would not be our next Liberal Prime Minister. A common theme I encountered was, "Brendan, we have to have the Malcolm experiment. We have to get him through the system and out of here. Let him be leader now and be done with it."

I could see the argument, but in life you have to have a go. I had also seen enough of Malcolm Turnbull in Cabinet that year to worry me. We had sustained a damaging leak against us on climate change to the *Australian Financial Review* during the second week of the campaign. The consensus was that it had come from Turnbull who had been portrayed favourably by the story.

We were a party without Howard, Costello and, also, effectively, Downer. We were about to go through a period of deep grief, anger and infighting. We needed a leadership style that would heal. One that would embrace and hold onto the Howard legacy. It would need to articulate a vision, drawing on Robert Menzies and setting markers for the future, an inclusive, consultative leadership. It would be important, coming out of government, to allow MPs to have their voices heard and let off steam in the fora of the party. It also had to accept that former ministerial survivors, soon to be opposition frontbenchers, were exhausted, convinced of years in opposition.

I was concerned that Malcolm Turnbull, at least unchallenged for the leadership, would quickly jettison much of the Howard legacy. His views on a number of the big issues aligned with Labor's. He also seemed incapable of seeing policies for an Australia beyond the Eastern Suburbs of Sydney. To the extent that I then knew him, he seemed impetuous, prone to imposing his own views on others rather than listening. The latter especially, was going to be needed in the early period of opposition. There had to be an alternative to Turnbull. Late on the Monday afternoon after the election, I announced my nomination for the Leadership.

Tony Abbott was also running, but at that stage I did not see Tony defeating Turnbull. Tony had not had a good election campaign. He had offended the dying asbestos victim, Bernie Banton; arrived late for the National Press Club debate on health and, regrettably, swore at Labor's health spokeswoman, Nicola Roxon. In defending his candidacy, Tony had described himself as having "people skills". He does. He is a good man, but timing, as I learned, is everything. Tony had six voters behind him in the race when he withdrew and put his support behind me, for which I was very grateful.

Defeat of the Howard Government had been delivered for three principal reasons.

The first was longevity. I read Liberal Party focus group research from December 2006 conducted in the electorate of Mayo. Labor had just switched Beazley for Rudd. One female participant said, "Look, I respect Mr Howard, but I am over him." In my opinion this reflected a national attitude. It gave most Australians no joy to effectively put down the much loved family pet, but they had to.

The second was overreach on workplace relations. The electorate thought we had gone too far into ideology, unconstrained by the Senate majority unexpectedly delivered in 2004.

The third was climate change. In refusing to ratify the Kyoto protocol, we had been monstered on the symbolism of climate change action. That the nation was in the grip of severe drought only escalated the issue's importance.

Labor had a strong win, but to do so, Kevin Rudd had marketed himself as a younger, modern variation on John Howard. Beyond Longevity, WorkChoices and climate change, there was not a lot in it. Simply re-starting with a completely blank page on policy would be risky. Labor won with a primary vote of 43% and a two-party preferred margin of 52.7% to our 47.3%. We lost 22 seats.

The leadership ballot was tight. Some colleagues disappointed.

Ian Macfarlane, the rugged Queenslander, simply said, "The media loves Malcolm, that's all that counts". End of conversation. Others, such as Andrew Robb, were thoughtful, having worked with Turnbull and the Packers outside of parliament, he went with him. Joe Hockey said, "We have to have the Turnbull experiment". Tony Smith came and saw me, discussing my candidacy at length. He returned the following morning to inform me he would vote for Turnbull. I respected him for doing so.

Peter Costello was very supportive of me. When I asked him why he had chosen not to run, he said, "anyone who sits in front of Turnbull doesn't stand a chance". Of course, there were other reasons, but he was right and I was about to find out.

On Wednesday morning, the day before the ballot, Turnbull was interviewed by the ABC's Fran Kelly. She asked if the Coalition should apologise to the 'stolen generations'. He was emphatic that we should. It was enough for several waiverers to lock into supporting me. It was not the issue as much as that they did not want a leader who signed them up to policy without giving them the opportunity to express their views. It confirmed my assessment that Turnbull would, unchecked, readily abandon elements of the Howard legacy he didn't like.

I knew we had to support the Apology, but I also knew we had to do so with as many colleagues on board as possible. The process was as important as the outcome. I would pay a personal price for not unilaterally committing the Coalition to the Apology, but the national interest and the Liberal Party's interests demanded that when we finally supported it in the chamber, that support would be genuine, the product of a party room process largely denied it over the preceding two years in government.

Maria Fernandez, Nigel Blunden, Simon Berger and Rhondda Vanzella helped me enormously with the leadership campaign. We worked out of a backbencher's parliamentary office I was assigned. When the ballot finally arrived on Thursday morning, 29 November, I was satisfied that I had done all that I could to put my case. I had said little publicly, leaving Turnbull to the airwaves and newspapers. As had always been the case, my support derived from all philosophical elements of the Liberal Party. However, the conservative wing was largely opposed to Malcolm Turnbull, Alexander Downer a notable exception.

Peter Costello chaired the party room meeting to determine the leadership. I sat in the front row. When the result was announced that

I had won 45 votes to Turnbull's 42, I was overwhelmed with emotions. I stood and turned to find Turnbull, seated three rows behind me, shake his hand, thank him for the contest and assure him we would now get on with it. His facial expression was confronting. It was one of shocked, menacing, explosive anger. Julie Bishop was elected deputy leader in a three-way contest. I was pleased.

Turnbull walked straight to the front of the room to harangue Peter Costello. I heard him tell Peter this was a "disaster", that "Nelson is simply not up to it". Peter told him it was a fair and clear result and should be respected as such.

After the many congratulatory handshakes, including from those who had not supported me, I stood before my colleagues. I thanked them for their support, recognising it had been a close contest, but I would lead for all of them. The ballot now over, we had many challenges before us. I thanked Malcolm for offering himself for the leadership and in doing so, giving the Party a choice. I thanked John Howard in absentia for his extraordinary leadership, prime ministership and the legacy he bequeathed to us. So, too, Peter Costello's remarkable stewardship of the economy that had put Australia in such a strong position – no government debt, a surplus and $60 billion in sovereign wealth funds. John Howard and Peter Costello had made us a "stronger nation, more confident in ourselves". I paid tribute to Alexander Downer's tireless, professional work over eleven-and-a half=years as not only Foreign Minister, but confidant to John Howard. The manner in which he had allowed Howard to come to the leadership in 1995 had laid the foundation for a remarkable government. I paid tribute to Mark Vaile and before him, John Anderson and Tim Fischer for hard work and disciplined leadership of the coalition partner. I knew that amongst other things, coalition unity would likely be another flashpoint. The Liberal members needed reminding that without the Nationals we could achieve nothing.

We had much of which to be proud. Yes, of course, we had lost the election, but that did not mean that we should jettison the Howard legacy. John Howard's longevity, WorkChoices overreach and failure to ratify the Kyoto protocol had added to the concerns of voters who had left us earlier over asylum seekers, Iraq and similar issues. As always post-election, we would review policy, but there would be no wholesale repudiation of what we had worked so hard to achieve in government. We needed to understand why we had lost, address those areas and formulate new policy.

I told them that I would articulate a vision for the nation based in our Liberal philosophy. It would be economic, social and human. We would oppose what we knew to be wrong for Australia, but we would support good policy when we saw it. I sought their consent to us supporting ratification of the Kyoto Protocol which was readily given.

At the conclusion of the meeting, I returned to my office. My team was overjoyed with the result but, like me, also apprehensive as to what it might mean. It didn't take long to get a taste of what lay ahead.

I was sitting in the office with the Liberal Party federal director, Brian Loughnane, Murray Hansen, Julie Bishop's Chief of Staff, Nigel Blunden, and my political advisor, Simon Berger. We were discussing the media conference to be held with Julie, key messages and issues.

Suddenly the door burst open. It opened with such force that it hit the door stop and began to close on the person who had pushed it. A considerable feat given the solid nature of parliament's doors. Malcolm Turnbull stood in the doorway, speaking loudly, very loudly.

He walked quickly up to me as I stood. With his index finger pointed at my chest and only centimetres away, he loudly downloaded in a menacing, intimidating, bullying tone. "That was a funereal speech to the party room. You're a wimp. Be a man. We're going to get off the mat and win the next election!"

His lower lip trembling, I was shocked. I had seen a few things throughout my AMA and political career, but I had never experienced such behaviour from an adult. That he was doing it in front of an audience was a further affront to my sensibilities.

I stood my ground and in a calm voice said,

> Malcolm, I can only imagine the emotions going through you and the disappointment you must be feeling. We have had a ballot and a result. We now need, all of us, to get on with the business of forming an effective opposition. You will have a major role in it. Thank you for telling me what you think, but I don't agree with you. Both in content and tone, I think what I said to the party room was appropriate for the circumstances. I am always happy to see you but I would appreciate it if you could make an appointment and, perhaps, knock on the door if it is closed.

He glared at me, tremulous and left without saying another word. We were all stunned. It was just the beginning, the first of such encounters with Malcolm Turnbull and his bullying, destructive behaviour.

Just three days after I was elected leader, Newspoll published a poll showing voters wanted Malcolm Turnbull as leader. I was 14% preferred Prime Minister to Kevin Rudd. Whereas normally polls would be months after an election, it started immediately and often ran weekly. The media wanted Turnbull and had predicted he would win. Turnbull had powerful media friends who readily took up his cause.

I asked Peter Hendy if he would return to be my Chief of Staff. He agreed. I knew his weaknesses and he knew mine, but I was grateful for his willingness to serve at a time when our stocks were so low. It was hard to get staff. Everyone experienced was exhausted and demoralised. I asked Brian Loughnane what his wife, Peta Credlin, was doing. He told me she had taken a job with the Australian Jockey Club in Sydney. "Do you think she might change her mind and work with me?" He suggested I call her. I did. She readily agreed to meet. I was overjoyed when she came on as my health and social services advisor, also liaising on Senate business. Andrew Hirst came to support Nigel Blunden on media. Nicolle Flint joined to work on agriculture and trade. Tom Switzer agreed to leave his job editing the opinion pages of *The Australian* to be my defence and foreign affairs advisor.

Simon Berger brought his razor smart intellect and political skills to help craft our messaging.

My loyal Chief of Staff, Maria Fernandez, decided prior to the election that she would go back to the public service. I would miss this remarkable woman. She applied to work on the Rudd Government's Defence White Paper. I called Mike Pezullo. Prior to being Deputy Secretary for Strategy in Defence, he was Kim Beazley's deputy chief of staff. "Mike, I will never ask you to do anything for me, but I am calling to ask you to do something for Maria. She has applied to work on the White Paper. You know her, she will do a superb, professional job. She has worked for me but she is not a spear carrier. If you could do what you can to see her candidacy is assessed on its merits, I will be grateful".

Mike called two days later: "I've spoken to Rudd. It won't be a problem". Maria was accepted onto the White Paper team and gave up another Christmas with her kids for public service.

I put the front bench together in consultation with the leadership group – Julie Bishop, Nick Minchin, Senate Leader and Eric Abetz, his deputy. Not an easy task!

I thought it best that Malcolm Turnbull take Treasury. As Deputy, Julie could have chosen anything, but willingly accepted Employment, Business and Workplace Relations. This would allow Turnbull to excel in what we were led to believe was his area of expertise. I asked Andrew Robb to take Foreign Affairs, unaware at the time of his inner battles with mental health. Andrew had backed Turnbull, but he was a good man, politically very smart and once ballots were over, a true team player. I thought it sensible to expand the traditional leadership group to include Turnbull in Treasury and Andrew Robb as the senior Victorian.

With the National Party's loss of two lower house seats, the Liberal and National Party ratio changed. I took the opportunity to negotiate Trade away from the Nationals to the Liberal Party, giving the role to Ian Macfarlane. I asked Tony Abbott to take up Families, Community Services, Indigenous Affairs and the Voluntary sector. He was not happy. I had to say, "Tony, I've spent the last week on the phone to our colleagues. More than a few think you shouldn't be on the front bench at all. I am going to have to defend this. You have a deep commitment to Aboriginal people. Throw yourself into this and spend a bit of time with them outback."

When Julie, Warren Truss and I held the press conference to announce the front bench, sure enough, the first question was from Mark Riley from Channel Seven. "Why is Mr 'people skills', Tony Abbott on the front bench?" I was ready. "Well, Tony is a fast bowler. We need him in the pace attack. But the price we pay is a few wides and no balls." The room cracked up with laughter.

Back at my office, I called Tony and told him what I had been asked and my reply, "Now prove me wrong Tony."

As always, there were those disappointed not to be on the front bench. Some were my strongest supporters. Knowing how hurtful it can be, I felt their pain.

Scott Morrison had been elected in Cook. His pre-selection followed the Liberal Party's New South Wales executive dis-endorsing Michael Towke in August, just months before the election. He had defeated Scott overwhelmingly in the pre-selection, but skullduggery had been afoot. Rhondda Vanzella, Jeff Selig, then New South Wales Party President, and I had agreed the Executive needed to remove him and Scott be endorsed. I was in Iraq when it happened and wrote a reference for Scott in the back of a C-130 Hercules in flight from Baghdad. He was endorsed and elected with the help of my Bradfield Liberal Party conference campaign funds.

To him, and others similarly disappointed, I said that I knew very well how they felt. I had been a backbencher for five-and-a-half years. But I had learned a lot from the experience: a better person and a better minister for it.

To several I said:

> Peter Costello did not achieve his full political potential for a number of reasons. One is that he was never on the

> back bench. He did not have to build relationships with his fellow backbenchers and appreciate what each of them had to give. He never knew what it is like to sit behind people less able, less competent and feel the frustration it brings. You need first to be the very best member for your electorate. You have only one chance to make a first impression with your own voters, make sure it is that you care and work bloody hard for them. When you do go to the front bench, they will accept your absences from the electorate and feel a sense of pride that you are making a difference to the nation.

Peter Costello made the observation that I had too many Turnbull supporters in the shadow cabinet. He was right, but I felt I had chosen the best team with all the constraints imposed upon any leader.

My first public event with Kevin Rudd as Prime Minister was the funeral of Commando Luke Worsley at St Andrews Cathedral in Sydney. Luke had been killed in Afghanistan the day before the election. The grief of his immensely proud parents was raw. Kevin brought them a small potted plant and lingered with the family long after everyone had gone.

The following day I attended the State funeral of asbestos victim, Bernie Banton, at Olympic Park. Bernie had been the public face of the campaign for asbestos compensation from the James Hardie Company. He assisted ACTU secretary, Greg Combet, in his campaign against us on WorkChoices. I respected Bernie and had met him several times. He reminded me of my father before the Labor Party left him. As Liberal Party Leader, I approached the auditorium with nervous trepidation. As I did, I noticed a lady struggling to push her husband in a wheelchair, oxygen bottle on his lap. I went over, introduced myself and offered to help. They were appreciative.

Inside, without exception, I was greeted politely and thanked for being there. It was a celebration of Bernie's life, but also of the Labor movement. In particular its victory over our workplace relations revolution.

Just before Christmas, shadow cabinet agreed to bury Work-Choices.

Most who returned to Canberra believed, with good reason, that we faced six years of a Rudd Labor Government. I wasn't so sure. By the time the parliament sat in February 2008, I was even less so.

Signing the Production, Sustainment, Follow-through and Development MOU for the Joint Strike Fighter at the Pentagon, December 2006. US Deputy Secretary for Defence, Gordon England co-signed as Secretary of State, Condoleezza Rice and Australian foreign minister, Alexander Downer, look on approvingly. At the time of signing, I had already been to Cabinet for 24 Boeing Super Hornets, convinced Australia faced a looming air capability gap.

With President George W. Bush, Kirribilli House, September 2007. I found him engaging, intelligent, principled and self-deprecating.

At the conclusion of the parliamentary apology to forcibly removed generations of Aboriginal and Torres Strait Islander children, Kevin Rudd and I spontaneously reached across and shook hands. The image is autographed by both of us.

Delivering the Budget in Reply as Opposition Leader. May 2008.

Artist and friend, Greg Wilson, presenting his portrait of me in 2008. A gifted artist and generous spirit, Greg struggled with depression all his life.

Thanking the people of Bradfield with my hand-painted sign on the Pacific Highway, leaving politics, October 2009.

Doug Thompson and Rhondda Vanzella in the Liberal Party Room at Parliament House, October 2009. A farewell event from my friends and colleagues.

British Prime Minister, David Cameron, Australian Prime Minister, Tony Abbott and Rear Admiral Ken Doolan (Retd) touring the Australian War Memorial in 2016.

21

"Kevin Rudd has just taken politics into the entertainment space, and you're now a part of it"

Kevin Rudd announced the first order of business for the new parliament: a formal Apology to forcibly removed generations of Aboriginal children. It would sit on Wednesday, 13 February. A campaign commitment, all the Labor caucus supported it.

In contrast, we in government had opposed an Apology since the recommendation to do so was delivered with the *Bringing Them Home* report in 1997. A small number of backbenchers had argued against John Howard's opposition to an Apology, but most had either supported his position or gone along with him, given the significant policy response to other recommendations.

But Australia had changed in the decade to 2007. There was a mood for change and 'Kevin 07' was the agent for it – at least for a while.

It was clear we had to support the Apology, morally and politically.

Yet, unlike Kevin Rudd and Labor, this was going to be hard for us. Support for it could not be imposed on the party room, nor on the National Party. The process of arriving at support for it, I believed, would be critical to not only the outcome but the stability and future of the Liberal Party.

About half the Liberal Party room was supportive of an Apology. About 30 per cent had reservations through to outright opposition. The remaining 20 per cent, as is often the case, were prepared to back the leadership. Malcolm Turnbull had made it clear that we should support the Apology. Like a Cheshire cat, he compared himself favourably to me by popping up everywhere in the media telling anyone who would listen.

I was conscious of the suppression of dissent to which MPs had been subjected in the final two years of the Howard Government, in the interests of discipline. This decision would be one of the party room and be settled once we had all met and heard one another's point of view. This would be important to holding things together, well beyond the issue at hand. Each one of them needed and deserved their 'day in court'.

The language of 'stolen' generations was offending the sensibilities of many of our supporters. Though recognising, in hindsight, the devastating impact of removal of these children, they resented the imputation of universally bad motives. Many younger Australians, especially, were enthusiastic in support of the Apology but less aware of the history.

One of the methods I learned over the years in bringing people to where they don't want to go, is to make sure they know that you understand and respect their view. In their heart of hearts, I knew almost all my colleagues who were opposed to an Apology, also knew it was the right thing to do. But what upset them was the shallow nature of the debate which reduced it to slogans, running roughshod over their perspective: Philberth's 'traditionalists' and 'progressivists'.

The media demanded to know the Opposition's position. For over a month, I repeatedly said that we would have a party room meeting in early February to which I would put my views along with all of my colleagues. Our position would then be determined after everyone who wanted to speak had the opportunity to do so. I knew that many frustrated colleagues were hearing this as a refreshing change. Mr Turnbull and friends, not so.

What I also did was publicly present the concerns of those within our ranks opposed to the Apology: "We look back now on these events over six decades with a sense of shame, but can our generation be held responsible for these forced removals? We are proud of what our ancestors did at Gallipoli, but we cannot claim responsibility for sending them. In many cases, the motives for removal were decimation and elimination of Aboriginal culture, but in others, the motives were to remove children for their own welfare in the belief they would have a better life."

I was criticised stridently and bled for weeks on this. But I knew that in doing so, the conservative members of the Party, significant numbers of which held that view, appreciated that I understood and respected their position. When the time came in early February to debate it, they would accept the outcome; to support the Apology.

Prior to the resumption of parliament, I wanted to return to Indigenous communities. Alan Tudge, my former schools advisor, was now working with Noel Pearson's Leadership Institute in Cape York. I had provided its initial funding and Noel was embarked on life-changing reforms to Aboriginal education, work, welfare, and nurturing young people.

Lockhart River, Mossman Gorge, Aurukun and Cairns, it was good to be with these people again. Welcoming, warm and ready to share a little of their lives, culture and hospitality along with a wish list of needs. None spoke of the impending Apology. Few seemed aware of it.

I asked Noel Pearson for his view. "Well Brendan, I worry a bit about it. I worry that white Australia will tune in for the Apology, tick that box and move on." Of course, he supported the Apology, but I shared his concerns. The nation would largely support the uplifting symbolism of the Apology but neglect the substance.

On the plane back to Canberra, I decided I would do what I had done as AMA president. On the day, I would confront Australia with the reality and existential challenges of Indigenous Australians. It would be a cathartic event. But it should also be one to jolt us into a project of national importance to improve the lives of the first Australians.

I was lobbied by many, including Mark Liebler and Father Frank Brennan SJ. I had to be guarded in what I said to both these men whom I respect. Sir Charles Court's state funeral was in early January at the University of Western Australia. At the conclusion of the service, having been in the front row, I found myself alongside Malcolm Fraser as he left the pew on the opposite side of the aisle. Only metres from the front, Fraser started haranguing me about the Apology.

When the joint party room finally convened in early February to consider the Apology, the relieved gratitude from many that they could finally have their say, was palpable. Others, led by Malcolm Turnbull, were angry that I had not locked us in weeks before.

I put the arguments before the room. The case for supporting the Apology and the case against. I then told them that my strong recommendation was that we must support the Apology. Failing to do so would be morally reprehensible and politically unthinkable. There would be no 'free' vote. We would adopt a position as a Party and as a Coalition.

The debate and contributions were thoughtful, respectful and often emotional – from both sides of the debate. After almost four hours, it was clear that an overwhelming majority supported it. Some did not and a handful said they would reserve their position. I knew who they were and would speak to them privately. When I stood to sum it up, I said I would write my speech over the weekend. When I rose to deliver it the following Wednesday, every one of them would hear something of their perspective on this. I would do my utmost to see that in turn, all Australians would not feel 'excluded' from this event of national significance.

As we broke to leave, Bill Heffernan stood: "This is the best meeting I've ever attended. I'm proud of the bloody lot of you." I quietly agreed with Bill. I was proud of them also. Even those opposed to it accepted the outcome with grace.

Within a month of assuming the leadership, I was coming to the conclusion that Kevin Rudd was not the 'real deal'. He was not the man in the pamphlet dropped into the voters' letterboxes in 2007. I told my leadership group in January 2008, "Australians have bought a Holden every year for 11 years. They have agonised over it and changed brand. It won't be until they find the 10th defect, they will throw their arms in the air and proclaim they were wrong. It will be a while, but this will turn. And it will turn quickly when it does."

Party Director, Brian Loughnane, agreed. Some listened, others simply wouldn't. They, most of the media and commentariat, were shocked, unwilling to accept that I had been elected leader instead of Malcolm Turnbull, whose first priority was removing me from the leadership. A steady stream of people in the community reported to me that meeting Turnbull, he vigorously plunged into a soliloquy of "how hopeless Brendan is". Most saw it for what it was.

New Opposition leaders coming out of government usually get a reasonable chance to settle in. Nonetheless, they are also a lightning rod for criticism of the previous government. Attacking the opposition leader helps journalists ingratiate themselves to the new government.

One of my supporters in the business community asked David Penberthy, then editor of the *Daily Telegraph,* why the paper wouldn't "give Brendan a fair go". He reportedly said, "Why should we give him a fair go when his own colleagues won't?" A fair point. But two newspapers did give me a fair go, Melbourne's *The Age* and *Herald Sun.* The editor of the latter said to me, "Brendan, we've never bought Kevin Rudd. I doubt that we will". Sydney 2GB's Ray Hadley said to me on air, "Kevin Rudd's had a long honeymoon, you haven't even had a weekend in the Blue Mountains! I don't know what you've done to upset 'em all."

I was told I should be wining and dining editors and journalists. Apart from the shallow insincerity of such behaviour, I don't understand why, in a democracy, a senior political figure has to 'schmooze' journalists simply to receive fair coverage. I always subscribed to Ida Bell's advice to the young Neville Bonner, "If you express yourself well and treat people with decency and courtesy, it will take you a long way." Naïve though it seems, I still believe it to be true.

I shared breakfast with Kevin Rudd in his office several times in the lead-up to the parliament sitting. We discussed a range of issues of national importance. With my support, he might consider formal recognition of Indigenous Australians in the preamble to the Constitution. It could be announced following the Apology. I also suggested we could begin a decade long process to review the Federation which was increasingly failing the nation. Neither suggestion got traction with him. Although I was guarded and felt somewhat awkward, I have always thought this is what prime ministers and opposition leaders should do. Robert Menzies had done so with his opposites, especially Ben Chifley whom he admired.

Rudd proposed an Indigenous 'Welcome to Country' be held the day before resumption of parliament, seeking my view. I would support it, strongly. I told him it should become a permanent feature for the commencement of new parliaments. It would run in the members' hall on the ground floor at the centre of Parliament House. It would be broadcast. Tom Calma, the Indigenous social justice commissioner, would speak, along with Kevin Rudd. The ceremony would be led by Matilda House-Williams, an elder of the Ngambri people, who have a traditional connection with the Canberra and Yass regions.

I was told by Rudd that I would have no speaking role, although all 150 Members of Parliament and 78 Senators were expected to be in attendance. I elected not to make a fuss of it, but if asked why I didn't speak, I would say so.

On the Saturday before the Apology, I sat down at our kitchen table and wrote the speech. I knew what broadly I wanted to say. I had asked my staff to gather some specific research to draw upon. It took me six hours. I went back through it several times and, though knowing it would upset some people, it had to be said. I deliberately didn't send it to anyone. These things once in the hands of a 'committee' can be neutered to the point of blancmange. I had nuanced many awkward, confronting truths, but ones in my heart I felt needed to be said. Yes, we apologise, but in doing so we also recognise the diversity of motives, the attitudes and values of the generations that oversaw it and the devastating outcomes for most who were removed. I would also paint a picture of the existential challenges facing Indigenous Australians for which my generation bears direct responsibility.

Jenny Macklin was now Labor's Minister for Families, Communities and Indigenous Affairs. She called me on Monday, 11 February 2008, to check details for the Welcome to Country the following day. I asked, "Now Jenny, just to confirm, I have no speaking role". She confirmed this was the case. Following the Welcome, Aunty Matilda would take Kevin and me through the crowd into the Great Hall for the reception.

I arrived well before 9am to meet people, a crowd of 400. Jenny Macklin confirmed arrangements and we went up onto the 'riser' for the formalities. Aunty Matilda entered the Members Hall accompanied by a didgeridoo player and one of her granddaughters, who presented Mr Rudd with a message stick.

"A welcome to country acknowledges our people and pays respect to our ancestors' spirits who have created the lands," she told the audience.

Tom Calma sat behind the lectern, Kevin Rudd next to him, Macklin between me and Rudd. Calma was introducing Kevin Rudd who was clutching his speech notes. Rudd leaned over Macklin to me, "Brendan, would you mind saying a few words when I finish?" I smiled, "Of course not Kevin". My heart raced. When Education Minister I had always, without fail, recognised the traditional owners wherever I went. Most I now knew well. I also held in my head the significance of welcome to country, key data on Indigenous health and life expectancy and the names of Indigenous people I had met, such as Rose Colless from Yarrabah when I was AMA president.

I was privileged to speak and contribute to this moment in history. I named the traditional tribes spanning the nation and, "I assure you on behalf of the alternative government … that whatever happens in future parliaments, so long as I have anything to do with it, that we will have a welcome from Ngunnawal and their descendants".

It would not be the last time I would be subject to an ambush like this.

The words of the Apology were delivered to my office later that afternoon. I suggested a couple of minor changes, but Kevin Rudd's office declined. I called Julie Bishop, Nick Minchin and Eric Abetz around to discuss it. All were comfortable with us formally supporting it. In fact, for all the criticism Eric Abetz has copped from so called 'progressives' over the years, he was a rock for me on this.

I was disappointed that on the morning of the Apology, several coalition members didn't come to the chamber. Such was their right not to do so. I was also aware of others sitting behind me, lukewarm at best. The galleries were filled with many from the 'stolen generations'. Unbeknown to me, Kevin Rudd had earlier met and been photographed with former prime ministers, including Malcolm Fraser. John Howard was not among them.

The Great Hall was filled with people and large screens had been erected in public spaces throughout the nation. Kevin Rudd spoke to the Apology and spoke well. As he did, I saw the emotion of many in the galleries and the meaning it held for them.

My turn came. What I didn't know then, but discovered the following day from ABC Canberra, was that two of Kevin Rudd's staff were in the Great Hall urging people to turn their backs from the screen before I had uttered a single word.

I acknowledged our nation crossed a threshold that day. In formally apologising to those Aboriginal people forcibly removed from their families, we were reaching from within ourselves to our past. We did so in deep understanding of its importance to our future. It was a moment in which we paused to place ourselves in the shoes of others to see the issues through their eyes with decency and respect. This chapter of forced removals in our nation's history was emblematic of much of the relationship between Indigenous and non-Indigenous Australians from the arrival of the First Fleet in 1788.

I went on to describe the Australia of the decades through which these removals occurred, its values and motives. I used the words of those who had been removed, the deeply traumatising impacts and consequences. From the National Archives oral histories, I quoted directly from those who had been removed.

Controversially – and I knew it would be – I described the circumstances in which too many Indigenous people and their children find themselves today. That more Aboriginal children are being removed today – tragically – than ever were through the period of the forced removals for which we apologised. I also reminded the Parliament and those listening, of Neville Bonner, of his life and journey as an early pioneer in the journey of reconciliation.

When I finished, there was an awkward silence. Joe Hockey started applauding as he stood. The entire chamber followed his lead with few exceptions. I stood looking at Kevin Rudd. We both simultaneously reached out over the dispatch boxes to shake hands. That image spoke to what had been achieved. I was proud of my party. I was proud of the Nationals. I was proud of what we had been able to achieve, notwithstanding the damage to me along the way.

Kevin Rudd invited me to join him in accepting a gift from the Aboriginal people present. We met those sitting on the floor of the Chamber, a number of whom I knew.

At the morning tea that followed, one of our conservative Liberal Party members, a woman not known for ever supporting me, clutched my elbow. "Brendan, thank you for what you did today. You apologised for these past wrongs and you defended our dignity. Thank you."

Later that day, when I arrived at the Canberra airport, the Qantas Lounge was full. This didn't worry me in the least. But standing just inside the entrance were five Aboriginal women. One, Nanna Nungala (Lorna) Fejo, I recognised immediately. She had featured in Kevin Rudd's speech, but I knew her from my AMA days when we met in the Northern Territory. Lorna had conceived and run the 'Strong Women, Strong Babies' programme for which she received the AMA's award for outstanding achievement in public health. We embraced and she introduced me to her four friends. They were waiting for their plane back to Alice Springs. I said I would find them a seat. Not a single person had offered to stand for these distinguished, humble women. I approached people seated in a cluster of five chairs. It appeared they were not travelling together. I introduced myself, gestured to the ladies and explained who they were. "Would you mind giving up your seats for them?" I asked.

One man looked at me, seething. “You’ve already done enough damage for one day, supporting the bloody Apology. I’ll be buggered if I’m giving up my seat for anyone, especially them.”

I was shocked, ashamed that I should live in a country with such people. The other four felt the same as me, all immediately offering to give up their seats, thanking me for taking the initiative. When I brought the ladies over, the entire area had emptied and the abusive man had disappeared.

I was accused that day of having a ‘tin ear’, delivering a bad speech. That is for others to judge. But I was determined that the nation should hear what too few ever do. I shared Noel Pearson’s concern that white Australia would ‘tick the box’ and move on. Days later I was more than willing to sign the ‘Close the Gap’ pledge in the Great Hall of Parliament on behalf of the Coalition.

Kevin Rudd wanted me to co-chair a council to oversee progress on these practical programmes. But, as was often the case with Kevin, the invitation arrived via the front page of a newspaper. I wanted Mal Brough involved. He had done so much on the practical front. That was not acceptable to the government. As Mal had led the Northern Territory Intervention in 2007, I understand why. But it was important to Tony Abbott and us that he be included. Similarly, when *The Australian* newspaper’s front page informed me that Rudd was intending to travel to remote communities with me, I felt that I was being drawn into being little more than a prop.

On the 5th anniversary of the Apology, I received a letter from a South Australian school teacher. She said that she had been preparing her Year 7 class to discuss the Apology. She confessed to being one of those who had turned her back on me on that day in 2008. However, for the first time she had read what I actually said, and was writing to apologise. I have received more than a few such letters over the years.

The new government decided that parliament would extend the sitting week to include Friday. In principle we were fine with this until we were told there would be no question time. In other words, everyone would be expected to turn up at the expense of the taxpayers, but the government would face no scrutiny. The Prime Minister would not attend.

We would dig in on this. It would require disruption of proceedings and the use of standing orders to create mayhem. But I also knew the voters would not understand why, the government easily portraying us as simply trying to avoid 'working' on Fridays. I had an idea. We needed something that would clearly say the Prime Minister was not there when he should be. I called Brian Loughnane, Liberal Party Federal director. "Brian, I've had an idea for this Friday sittings issue. We need a prop. Could you commission a life-sized cardboard cutout of Kevin Rudd? We need one like those popups you see of Russell Crowe at the movies. Make it a good image of him."

Brian was sceptical to say the least. I went on, "What we'll do is build up the case that we're all there, working hard, big issues facing the nation but where's Kevin? Where's the PM? Then, presto! We bring the cutout of Rudd in to the despatch box. There will be pandemonium, but the punters will get it." Brian liked it.

In one of the more comical moments of my parliamentary career, on the Thursday evening after the Apology, Brian arrived at my office. He had a young staffer in tow from Liberal Party HQ at the other end of a long thin object wrapped in a sheet. They looked like a pair of undertakers concealing a severely emaciated corpse. Both were sheepish but beaming.

Brian stood the object upright, pulling the sheet off in a single movement. There he was, a smiling, life-sized Kevin Rudd, one hand in pocket. Brian was ebullient. "Brilliant Brian, bloody brilliant". I called Joe Hockey to come around and have a look. Minutes later he appeared and lost it completely, belly aching laughter. He liked it and he liked the tactic.

The Leadership group had not yet been introduced to the cutout. Turnbull had proven himself untrustworthy to me and, as such, I would tell them just before the beginning of the sitting day. Everyone thought it an inspired idea. We would call divisions, create mayhem and repeatedly argue that there should be question time. By 10.30 our refrain would be, "Where is the Prime Minister?" Finally, at 11am, Luke Hartzuyker, in exasperation at the despatch box would turn to see two backbenchers carry "Kevin Rudd" towards him.

Everyone agreed it was a great tactic, except one – Turnbull. "Brendan, you're destroying our base", he intoned. As I learned with Turnbull, when seeking to summon full authority, he dropped his voice an octave and increased the volume. "Brendan, it's leadership!"

I told him that with a 20 per cent margin in Bradfield, I knew something about our 'base'. This was an important tactic for two reasons. First, without it the public would simply think we were a disruptive rabble opposed to working Fridays. The nuance of no question time and government accountability would be lost. Most in the media were hardly going to help explain it. But the second, I told them, was even more important. "If we do this well, this cardboard cutout will become a powerful metaphor for Kevin Rudd – shallow, two dimensional. He's cardboard Kev."

By 10.15am, it had gone to plan. Quorums, points of order and various degrees of disruption. Joe Hockey told me he had spoken to Laurie Oakes who was extremely unimpressed. I was nervous but still confident. Then, at 11am, Don Randall appeared with the cardboard cutout. The House went into complete uproar. 'Kevin Rudd' stood at the despatch box on our side of the chamber next to Luke Hartzuyker. To compound the government's confusion, Labor's Deputy Speaker, Anna Burke, was in the chair, "Get that disgusting thing out of here!" she yelled.

Luke asked her to confirm that she regarded the image as "disgusting". Burke shut down the House. Joe Hockey told me a short time later, "Laurie Oakes just told me we had lost him until the cutout – loved it".

On Monday the Government quietly announced that sittings would return to the traditional four-day schedule with question time. A week later, meeting Kevin Rudd in his office, he asked where the cardboard cutout was. "Joe Hockey has it in captivity in his office". Kevin said, "Oh, one of my kids said they would like it", to which I replied, "Not as much as us Kevin."

Early in 2008, I travelled up through south-west Queensland, on to Charleville and floods before going to the Cape. I spent some time with Vaughan Johnson, a man to whom I took an instant liking. No nonsense, big hat and representing an electorate the size of Tasmania and Victoria combined. One of the big issues was the future of the National Party. Some believed the coalition parties should merge. Certainly, there were existential questions about the future of 'the Nats' in a rapidly changing Australia. The Australia that had embraced Kevin 07 and his agenda with gusto. I asked Vaughan his opinion. "Mate, I reckon we're buggered. Just look at my electorate. The population is growing and the people coming here want the same things as city people. They also think the same way."

Vaughan believed a merger necessary. I did too. It was hard to see Queensland electing a National Party premier west of the Great Dividing Range. The parliamentary leader in Queensland was Lawrence Springborg, another quality man. The Nationals were the larger party in Queensland, but it was unlikely that the burgeoning population in the state's south-east would elect a Nationals premier.

Alan Stockdale was Treasurer in the Kennett Government in Victoria. Alan had, along with Jeff, saved the state after the Cain-Kirner debacle. He was tough and he knew how to count. Early in my leadership, I asked Alan if he would take up the Liberal Party Federal Presidency. Knowing how hard it would be, he nonetheless took up the role. I called him about a merger in Queensland. He understood the problem and agreed it had to be done.

As always, many in both parties immediately saw a threat to their own power. Others went into overdrive briefing the media against me and Alan – from both the Liberal and National Parties. Many in the Liberal Party Queensland division understandably felt they would be 'swamped' by the larger, more assertive National Party base. As in any merger, many harboured deep fears that their respective philosophy would be subsumed by the other.

Then there were the sitting members and senators. The only sensible thing was to 'grandfather' each one's preselection for a term. Traditional Nationals would sit in the National Party room in Canberra and Liberals with their own. Alan Stockdale invested heavily in the merger with my support. The merged Party would be the 'Liberal National Party'. It was be known as the LNP. It was another issue on which I bled. It consumed time, political capital and emotional energy. But it had to be done and well before the next election.

Coming out of government, many were exhausted. I was a bit tired myself after almost two years in the Defence portfolio, the election campaign and straight into the leadership without a break. But I had a responsibility to hold the Party together, take the blows, undertake necessary internal reform, protect the Howard legacy and get us into a competitive position. More than a few frontbenchers were going through the motions, coasting and trying to 'refresh'. I understood that, to a point.

Peter McGauran decided to pull up stumps early in Gippsland. The by-election would be in May, just after the Budget. Alexander Downer and Mark Vaile decided to leave: them playing golf during question time wasn't a good look! Two more by-elections later in the year, neither of which would be easy.

Nigel Scullion, the CLP Senator from the Northern Territory and Deputy Nationals Leader, got in early with his controversy. Just before Christmas 2007, the press reported that a decade earlier he had a big night out at a Russian strip club. A single man, Nigel had been found handcuffed to a dancer's pole wearing only his underpants. I called him early that morning. "Nigel, you need to deal with this before I front the press today. You're on your own with this Nigel." He told me he would "fix" it. I laughed out loud when, surrounded by a salivating media pack baying for political blood, Nigel spoke. Breathlessly waiting for his words, the pack was told, "Well, I've learned two lessons from this. First, make sure you always wear clean underwear as your mother told you. Second, never let anyone handcuff you to anything.".

Pat Farmer, the earthy ultra-marathon runner, represented the western Sydney seat of Macarthur. He had come in at the request of John Howard in 2001, excelling as a local member. Pat had been my parliamentary secretary after the 2004 election. A widower, he was loved by many and hung on in 2007 with a 0.7% margin. I appointed him shadow minister for youth and sport. As if my job wasn't hard enough, my media advisor called early in January: "Mate, the *Daily Telegraph* called. They want to know what our reaction is to Pat Farmer's decision to move to Mosman." I asked if this was a joke. It wasn't. Incredulous, I called Pat who confirmed he had bought a place in Mosman in 2006. The tenants had moved out so he thought he would move in and improve it. I told him in the strongest possible terms that this was a breach of faith with the electorate, damaging to him and our Party. He didn't see the problem. The *Daily Telegraph* ran the story on its front page, spilling out onto subsequent pages: a map of Sydney and a circle around Pat's home a couple of kilometres from his electorate office in Campbelltown. An arrow then tracked the 60 kilometres across Sydney to Mosman, a seriously expensive suburb. Pat had apparently explained his move in part on the basis that it "would be easier to get to the office". He would be "travelling against the traffic", and get to work more easily.

The *Daily Telegraph* headline screamed, *Go Figure*! It effectively ended his political career.

Just months into the job, I confided to Liberal Party Director, Brian Loughnane, that while I knew it was going to be hard, nothing had prepared me for this. Brian said, "Brendan, Kevin Rudd has just taken politics into the entertainment space and you are now a part of it." It was a perfect storm. Kevin Rudd was the most popular Australian prime minister in modern polling history. Peter Costello, though strongly supporting me, should have been the leader and didn't want to be. And then there was the unstoppable, all-consuming ambition of

Malcolm Turnbull. A personality that I had never encountered, and doubt I will again.

Two Sydney businessmen came to see me. I knew one of them. They described themselves as former business associates of Malcolm Turnbull. The relationship had not ended well. One proffered what he regarded as information 'damaging' of Mr Turnbull. I listened and said, "I am sorry, but that is not the way I conduct myself. I don't trade in that kind of information, especially in relation to one of my own colleagues." Somewhat surprised by my response, they stood up to leave. One turned and said, "Brendan, something you have to understand about Malcolm. If he cannot own or control what he wants, he will move to destroy it." That comment lingered with me a very long time.

In this messy, brutally gut-wrenching transition, a member of the public, a regular 'punter' summarised it in a way the professionals never could. Very early one morning I was standing in the queue for breakfast at the McDonalds Sutton Forrest. Driving to Canberra, a week after the national Apology.

As I looked to the TV screen, Channel 9's *Today Show* broadcast Newspoll. Preferred PM – Rudd 75%, Nelson 15%. The man behind me offered an assessment, "Brendan, just because we like Kevin Rudd doesn't mean we don't like you. We just put the guy in." He went on, "But I'll tell you one thing. I reckon this government is like the set of a western movie. Fake walls with sticks holding them up at the back. You wait and see."

I thought of that comment often over the coming months.

Tony Smith walked into my office one night, closed the door and said, "I was wrong about you and I was wrong about him (Turnbull). I will do whatever I possibly can now to help you." I thanked him.

Gillian and I went to Melbourne for the Victorian Division of the Liberal Party's State Council meeting on Saturday, 12 April 2008. These are important meetings at any time, but in these circumstances, critically so. The State Council comprises the leadership of the Party and delegates from all sections of it and across the state. Given powerbrokers, Michael Kroger and Senator Michael Ronaldson, were key Turnbull backers, this was my chance to speak directly to the members. I spoke to a dinner for the Party's supporters on the Friday night, which went exceptionally well.

I awoke Saturday morning to a front page headline emblazoned across *The Australian* newspaper. KEY BACKERS MOVE AWAY FROM NELSON. The story was written by the long serving Foreign Affairs editor, Greg Sheridan. I was both angry and disappointed. There could only be one person behind this. Greg does not do the 'political round.'

Thanks to this, the media pack at the State Council meeting was larger and even more aggressive. Tony Smith, Member for Casey and shadow Education Minister, introduced me to the packed auditorium of the Melbourne Convention Centre. Tony was generous in his introduction.

As I did in almost all my speeches as leader, I drew on our Party's origins and guiding philosophy. It is essential that a group of people whom you lead, never lose sight of what it is in which they believe. The past holds vital lessons for the future. It can also inspire as it points to new horizons.

Robert Menzies was a Melbournian who represented the seat of Kooyong. I reminded them that in 1942, Menzies delivered his 'Forgotten People' radio broadcasts in which he observed that big business and unions wielded power and influence. Yet the backbone of the nation was its farmers, professional people, small business owners, tradesmen and basic wage earners. In raising families, these Australians saw their greatest contribution to the nation. I spoke deliberately of Menzies' 1944 exhortation to Liberals, that we have "great and imperative obligations to the weak, the sick and unfortunate". I reminded them of my own, unorthodox path to Liberalism and that ours is a philosophy absorbed through familiarity with the idealism, hard work and self-sacrifice of people in everyday life. I reprised with pride the achievements of the Howard Government and Peter Costello's role in it. I laid out the state of the economy, emerging challenges and missteps by Rudd and Swan. I reminded them of the Cain and Kirner Governments and the role played by the Liberal Party in restoring confidence in both government and ourselves. As Kevin Rudd was then on a world trip, "Kevin Rudd has a plan for the world, but it would be good to see his plan for Australia. He is not the person Australians thought they were getting last year. This will turn, and when it does, we will be ready."

I laid out our vision for Australia and the five key challenges for the nation.

> To build and offer a level of prosperity for the next generation in which we have confidence.
>
> To begin the long, generational journey of reform of the Federation.
>
> To live not on environmental capital, but interest. Protection of the environment is fundamental, both to our Liberal beliefs and our economic future. In adjusting to the environmental deadlines being set for us and on climate change, we must act in unison with the rest of the world.
>
> To effectively defend our nation, its people, interests and values.
>
> To ensure the 'cohesion' of our nation. We would reach out to every Australian irrespective of his/her circumstances. While sound economic mangers, we are a group of men and women committed to building a better Australia that gives a sense of meaning and purpose to its citizens.

Leaders often receive a standing ovation at these events, irrespective of who they are or how impressed is the audience. I received a sustained standing ovation. I knew for most, it was genuine.

David Kemp was Victorian Branch President. A giant of Liberalism and of the Liberal Party, he delivered the vote of thanks, in part: "Delegates, you know how long I have been in the Liberal Party. I have just heard the best speech delivered by any Leader to the Victorian State Council." The audience response suggested many felt the same way. I was overwhelmed and, to this day, immensely grateful to the man.

The following day, back at our home in Sydney, Gillian called from downstairs. "I think there's a kangaroo in the garden." We lived next to bushland, Kangaroos were common but I smelled a rat. I went to investigate, finding a newspaper photographer, staked out, looking for shots of me and Gillian intended to embarrass. "Mate, what the bloody hell are you doing? Some editor has sent you out here, presumably to take photos to make me look bad for a bad story." He didn't disagree. "It's for Newspoll, isn't it?"

It was. I agreed to help him so went to the shed, pulled out the lawnmower and let him photograph me mowing the lawns.

I called Tony Abbott. Gillian thought we had a kangaroo in our garden which turned out to be a photographer! This followed from the front page story in *The Australian* by Greg Sheridan. Tony said he had ridden his pushbike from Melbourne to Sydney. He got to Malcolm's where he had dinner with Greg Sheridan. Disappointing, but unlike others, Tony was always honest. Still is.

John Button was a giant of the Australian Labor Party, a respected reformer to whom Australia owed a great deal. He modernised Australian industry through the Hawke and Keating Governments. He died on 8 April, 2008, and a state funeral was held in Melbourne six days later. I wasn't sure if I should attend. I was in Brisbane on my 'Listening Tour'. After consideration, I decided not to go. I might be regarded as an intruder into a Labor family funeral.

My assessment of Kevin Rudd was confirmed when media called seeking my response to him not attending the Button funeral. He had instead chosen to visit Cate Blanchett in her Sydney hospital, taking a toy for her newborn baby. Instead of climbing into Rudd, I simply said he would need to explain himself. I spoke instead of John Button's towering contribution to the nation.

The following weekend Kevin Rudd convened his 2020 summit. As would so often be the case, Rudd enthused people with his ambition, but failed miserably in delivery. Over 1,000 people attended, split into 10 working groups to consider multiple policy challenges. Of the 138 recommendations from the summit, Rudd rejected 135 in 2010. The Rudd model was a prescription for maximum publicity and minimal outcome. I said Rudd was "all backswing and no follow through"!

Days after the summit, appearing on the ABC radio current affairs programme, *AM*, I described Rudd as "full of it". The leadership group that morning generally agreed with the sentiment, but as always, Turnbull condemned me. As he did so, I thought, "You too, Malcolm, are full of it."

Wayne Swan, bequeathed a Budget surplus, no government debt and $60 billion in sovereign wealth funds, decided to concoct an inflation story. He criticised Costello for leaving them with an inflation problem. "The inflation genie", he claimed, "was out of the bottle". To 'fight' inflation, Kevin Rudd announced a five-point plan at a Perth business breakfast in early March. After six weeks of banging on about it, I noticed he couldn't get to the parliamentary despatch box without a pile of papers. He took a question from his backbench on the five-point plan. He spoke to the first and had to look down. I interjected, "Work force participation". When he finished, I prompted him again, "Infrastructure!" He was not across detail and 'the economic conservative' was uncomfortable with economic issues. An understatement.

As shadow treasurer, Malcom Turnbull wanted questions to Swan that appealed to an educated business audience. It was a constant struggle. I wanted cut-through to frame Rudd and Swan with mainstream voters.

Wednesday, 12 March 2008, marked the 60th anniversary of Israel's Independence. The galleries were filled with the Israeli diaspora and Jewish community. Kevin Rudd moved a motion in support of the anniversary and spoke well, reading his prepared remarks. As usual I spoke, without prepared notes, to Jewish identity, forged over a century by anti-Semitism, the Holocaust and existential threats to the very existence of the state of Israel. The state of Israel is custodian of the most fragile yet powerful of human emotions, hopeful belief in the freedom of man, freedom of speech, freedom of religion and freedom of assembly. It is home to many things that are spiritual. But it is also home to the human spirit of resilience, confidence, determination and respect for one another irrespective of political or religious affiliations. Emotionally, I described my visits to the Holocaust Museum in Washington and the sign, 'Never forget what you have seen here.'

Israel's ambassador, Yuval Rotem, wrote to me, "I was sitting in the gallery with a lot of people ... your speech, the words that were spoken and the tone in which it was delivered, caused many people to become emotional and some even to have tears in their eyes ... you made a special occasion in the history of my country, a more memorable one."

The Budget was looming large.

We had been framing Kevin Rudd around his stunts. 'Grocery watch' and 'Fuel Watch'. Petrol prices were hurting, battlers especially.

Malcolm Turnbull's behaviour at shadow Cabinet meetings was consistent with my early introduction to him. He dominated a number of submissive colleagues as he sought to dominate debate, but he also kept leaving. At one meeting Julie Bishop pointed out to me the number of times he left and returned. I quipped to Nick Minchin, "I don't think he has a prostate problem but I'm happy to check it for him."

The media would report on what had been discussed and my manifest failings. Turnbull commissioned economist, Henry Ergas, to do a Review of Taxation. Of itself, a reasonable idea. As Leader I only discovered it was being done from a media enquiry. Henry Ergas is a towering intellect, economist and to whom I would listen. Turnbull should have brought the idea to me, or Peter Dutton who shadowed Finance and the Leadership group first. Among other things, we would have set terms of reference and engaged someone to work with him. I certainly would have ruled out ideas such a cutting tobacco and alcohol taxes and pushing a flat income tax. This was my world with

Malcolm Turnbull. Completely obsessed with getting rid of me. But he occasionally offered a good idea.

At a March shadow Cabinet meeting to discuss tax, Turnbull said in passing, "Oh, you could cut petrol excise of course. That would be deflationary too." A light bulb moment. I said nothing but kept the thought. Back at the office, I raised the petrol excise cut with Peter Hendy, my Chief of Staff. An economist, Peter smiled in agreement. A good idea and good politics.

22

Watching the price of petrol does not make it come down!

The Budget was delivered by Wayne Swan on Tuesday, 13 May 2008. A real spending increase of 1.1%, failing to meet Swan's rhetoric of cutting spending to reduce inflationary pressures.

In what Australians would come to know as classic Kevin Rudd, a 70% increase in excise on Ready to Drink Mixers was applied. Assigned the name 'Alcopops', the stated objective was to reduce binge drinking. Given the budget forecast, the tax to raise $3.1 billion over the following four years, they were expecting a lot of it to be drunk. The Luxury Car Tax was increased by 30%. We coined it the 'Tarago Tax'. Aged pensioners received no increase.

The Budget-in-Reply is delivered by the Leader of the Opposition two days after the Budget. There are few such replies of merit that I could remember. I wanted to ensure ours would have impact. It had to do four things.

First, it would frame Kevin Rudd and his Government as one without substance.

Second, present some policy, notwithstanding the early months of opposition.

Third, lay out a vision for the nation upon which policy would be built.

Fourth, remind Australians and the parliamentary coalition parties of our beliefs and guiding philosophy.

I decided to go with a cut to petrol excise. It would be five cents a litre. The cost to the budget was $1.8 billion. I strategically started working my way through the leadership group and shadow Cabinet until I had critical mass of support. Word got to Peter Costello who told me not to do it. Of course, I listened carefully to his reasoned arguments about cost and damage to our reputation as economic managers. Peter had been burned on petrol excise before.

But to Peter and other sceptics I said, "Thanks to us, the budget can afford it. Australians are seriously struggling with petrol prices and the nation has inflationary pressures which a cut will help ease. Look at this Fuel Watch nonsense the government is peddling. If we announce we would cut the price of petrol at the bowser, it will demolish the stunts and expose Rudd as little more than cardboard Kev."

I unpacked it at shadow Cabinet a week out. It was agreed, with the exception of Malcolm Turnbull. The fuel excise cut would be the centrepiece. I emphasised the critical importance of this remaining confidential to shadow Cabinet, noting that backbencher, Peter Costello, raised the excise cut with me.

Tom Switzer, working with Peter Hendy, drafted notes with input from Peta Credlin and others in the office. I worked on it over the weekend before budget week. This was a high wire act. Then, on cue and intended to push me 'off the wire', an email arrived from Turnbull on the morning of the budget-in-reply speech. It stated his opposition to the petrol excise cut and for good measure, said "of course, this will inevitably find its way into the media". In other words, "I am opposed to this, I am shadow treasurer and I will see it gets into the media". My anxiety about the day skyrocketed, concerned it would leak. It didn't then, but the Sunday after the speech I read all about it in the *Sunday Telegraph.*

Kevin Rudd had all the government in the chamber for my budget reply at 7.30. All were quiet, respectful and orderly. I appreciated the gesture. I looked into the camera above the government benches for most of the speech, ensuring Australians watching knew that I was speaking to them.

Having contrasted Labor's higher taxing and spending budget with the preceding 11 years, evidence against the alcopops tax, its neglect of carers and pensioners I got to petrol:

> Before the election the Prime Minister led the Australian public to believe that he would cut the price of petrol. He has done nothing of substance.
>
> Watching petrol prices does not bring them down.

I then unpacked the five cents a litre cut in petrol excise. A real cut in taxation in the tradition of the Liberal and National parties. I knew the killer line was "watching petrol prices does not bring them down". Having delivered it with a pause for effect, I glanced at an ashen Kevin Rudd.

I set out five key challenges for the nation. These were the basis of a thematic vision for Australia throughout my leadership of the Party, as laid out to the Victorian Division. We needed to be more than critics of Kevin Rudd and his government.

Finally, I wanted to speak to our two parties – Liberal and National:

> Our beliefs are in the individual, in encouragement of, and rewards for, hard work in everyday life.
>
> We believe in family small business.
>
> We believe in families as the bedrock of the nation while respecting and reaching out to every Australian irrespective of his or her personal circumstances.
>
> We believe in choice – in health, education or membership of a union.
>
> We believe in lower taxes, sound economic management.
>
> We believe strongly in defence and security.
>
> We will be at our best as a nation if we strive to be outward looking, intensely competitive yet compassionate people, reconciled with our Indigenous history and imbued with values of hard work, self-sacrifice, tolerance and courage.

Predictably, elements of the media savaged me, presumably encouraged to do so by at least one person sitting behind me. But I knew I had skewered Kevin Rudd on petrol and his modus operandi.

Our backbench was overwhelmingly happy. Back in the office I took complimentary calls from both John Howard and Alan Stockdale. Brian Loughnane was pleased with both the speech and the strategy. But what spoke to my confidence most was a late night interaction. Gillian and I stepped into a parliamentary lift. Three Labor backbenchers stopped talking as we entered. They looked at one another, "Just talking about you. Bloody good speech Brendan."

Among Malcolm Turnbull's activities at this time was to encourage Joe Hockey and Julie Bishop respectively to leave the federal parliament and pursue political ambitions at the state level. During the budget period, Newspoll recorded Wayne Swan as better Treasurer to Turnbull – 40 per cent over 26 per cent. After the budget, Kevin Rudd took a question from his backbench about inflation. He banged on about slaying the inflation dragon allegedly created by Peter Costello. Again, he needed prompting from me to remember his own 'five-point plan'. I was suspicious, prompted by Tony Smith. I turned to Joe Hockey and Malcolm Turnbull, "I will ask the next question of Rudd. Trust me."

I got the call. "Given the Government's stated economic priority of fighting inflation and the centrality of it to its budgetary strategy, could the Prime Minister remind the House of the government's projected inflation forecast for this financial year and next?" Rudd immediately began rummaging through the rows of papers set out on the table. Flustered, unable to find it and clearly not knowing the figures, he began speaking. Before Wayne Swan could give it to him, I held up the Budget Papers, "It's not that hard – it's on page one of Budget Paper number one!" Again, he was exposed.

Just over a week from the Budget, as we ramped up our campaign to cut the fuel excise in contrast to Kevin Rudd 'watching' the price of petrol, we struck gold. Leaks from Cabinet were reported by Channel Nine: advice to Cabinet from four government departments against the Fuel Watch scheme, saying it could make petrol more expensive. Resources Minister and former ACTU president, Martin Ferguson, we learned, had opposed the scheme in Cabinet as it would "hurt battlers".

The *Gold Coast Bulletin's* front page headline said it all. I held it up in Question Time in front of Kevin Rudd who refused to look at it, "Damn you Kevin 07. It's Kevin 08 now and your job is to fix the fuel mess." The following day, Assistant Treasurer, Chris Bowen, left open the possibility of the government itself adopting the excise-cut policy. Fuel Watch was, like a number of these stunts, quietly shelved. We had made inroads.

One of the most memorably moving events of the year was held the evening before the Budget, the 40th anniversary of the Battle of Coral-Balmoral, the longest, most bloody battle Australia fought during the Vietnam War. Twenty-six Australians were killed and 100 wounded. Close to 1,000 veterans and their families gathered in the Great Hall for an official reception.

When you are in these very senior political roles, the pressure is intense. There are multiple demands, people pulling you in a myriad of directions as you jump from one issue and one event to the next. The imminent Budget was foremost in my mind. But sometimes, you suddenly find yourself in the midst of something that gives meaning to it all, a reminder of the privilege given you. The evening of Monday, 12 May 2008, was one such occasion.

Entering the room, I saw it was filled with men and women, most in their sixties and seventies. Many wore medals. Some without limbs, others pushed walking frames or supported themselves with sticks. Entertainers of the era were among them. More than a few were battlers. All were proudly dressed for the occasion. I immediately felt their reverence at being at such an event in the Great Hall of the Parliament. I sat on the stage with Kevin Rudd. He read his prepared speech which I felt lacked the emotion of the occasion.

I had thought about what I would say beforehand and shaped it once I had felt the crowd. I painted the picture of the Australia of their generation four decades earlier. The comfortable distance of our lives from their courage and sacrifices made it easy to forget the individual sacrifices made in our name, devotion to duty and to our country.

One source of national shame was the conflation by many Australians of their opposition to the Vietnam War with shunning the men and women who fought it on our behalf. In this, many in the room were denied the healing of wounds and deep, lived traumas. I told them we are as proud of them, what they did and how they did it as we are of those young men who landed on Gallipoli, struggled on the Kokoda Trail or held the line at Kapyong, Korea. The response was overwhelming, many were emotional. So was I. I knew that whatever my own considerable inadequacies, I had helped bring meaning where there had been so little.

We carried two important reforms through this period. Both were difficult.

The Labor Party wanted to abolish the 'single desk' for wheat marketing. Some things can only be done by one side of politics in government: the party of government doing something contrary to its usual beliefs but which philosophically appeals to the party of opposition. This was one of them. Belief in the single desk was an article of faith for the National Party. Some Liberals, representing regional and rural seats also harboured doubts about abolishing it. Wilson Tuckey, the irascible member for the sprawling Western Australian seat of O'Connor, was not one of them. Representing many of WA's wheat farmers, he was 'hot to trot'. It would abolish a system for selling wheat that had been in place since 1939.

I respected the National Party position and told its leader, Warren Truss, we could manage the split. "Warren, we are Liberals. Philosophically, we believe that wherever possible, the free market should operate. Growers should be free, within reason, to sell their grain to whomever they wish, when they want to at a price they negotiate." Warren understood. I told him the key was that each of our parties maintain their respective unity. The Liberals would vote as a bloc in support and the Nationals against.

Judi Moylan, who represented the WA electorate of Pearce, was almost as opposed to the abolition of the single desk as her nemesis, Wilson Tuckey, supported it. Judi, a principled woman was immovable. I didn't want to 'lose' anyone. She happened to be on an overseas delegation when the vote came up. It was a model of how to manage coalition relations on difficult issues.

Another hard one was reform of financial arrangements between same-sex couples. Of course, I had no problem with it. One of the saddest cases I encountered was in my electorate. Two sisters, high achievers, had eschewed marriage to pursue their careers as public servants at a time when women could not marry. Living together and elderly, neither could access the other's benefits. Outrageous.

Introduced in June by Attorney General, Robert McClelland, the Bill meant that 100 pieces of legislation would be amended to remove discrimination against same sex couples. It would cover public servants' pensions, defence force entitlements, Medicare, Centrelink and tax matters. I reminded our more conservative members again, that we were Liberals. These men and women, by virtue of their sexuality, living arrangements and choices made should not be denied the economic benefits of their hard work. We got there. George Brandis was superb as shadow Attorney General.

Prime Ministers commonly make 'statements' about important matters to the parliament at the beginning of Question Time. By convention, the Opposition Leader is informed two hours beforehand that a statement will be made and the topic. This allows the Opposition Leader to prepare and respond.

On 2 June, 20 minutes before Question Time, Peter Hendy walked in. "Rudd's office just called. He is going to make a statement about Iraq at 2 o'clock". We had had this treatment before, but I was livid. Peter asked me what I needed. "It's too late. Just get me what Rudd said about Weapons of Mass Destruction before the Iraq invasion. I'll have to gather my thoughts, listen to Rudd and just speak". Kevin Rudd spoke for 25 minutes. I rose to reply.

I was three minutes into it when I heard chatter above me from the Press Gallery. I thought I had made a mistake. When you give a speech without notes, you have to think three sentences ahead of where you are. I thought whatever mistake I made, I needed to fix it while still on my feet. For several minutes, as I kept speaking, I desperately and simultaneously went back over what I had said. I couldn't detect an error, so pressed on. I reminded the House of September 11, deaths in the US, the role of Saddam Hussein in two wars, the 260 mass graves, Rudd's belief that there had been WMD and, of course, what 3,700 Australian defence personnel had done on behalf of our country.

Question time followed on from the Iraq statement. As soon as it finished, I went to my advisors. "Did I say something wrong on Iraq?" Nigel Blunden said, "No mate. They just couldn't believe you were giving a 25 minute speech on Iraq without a piece of paper in front of you."

"What a relief. We might get some good press for a change". We didn't.

Scott Morrison sent me a handwritten note, "... the politicisation of the issue by the PM today was an absolute disgrace. Your comments strongly reflected my own views and displayed a knowledge and command of the issues that ensured an outstanding presentation of the Coalition's position."

The Gippsland by-election was set for Saturday, 28 June. It would test our real support in the electorate as distinct from polls and the analysis of commentators. As the sitting member had retired, the Liberal Party would field a candidate against the National Party. Some argued against it. My view is that you need to be prepared to fight with conviction. The Victorian Division pre-selected an excellent candidate – Rohan Fitzgerald, senior manager with the Central Gippsland Health Service, and based in Traralgon, a family man. The Nationals pre-selected Darren Chester, chief of staff to the Victorian Nationals leader. Darren was from Lakes Entrance. The Labor Party ran Darren McCubbin, Mayor of Wellington Shire.

I made four visits to the electorate during the campaign. We ramped up concern for the economic impact on families of Kevin Rudd's climate change agenda. I kept referring to Labor's candidate as being "a close friend of Peter Garrett". Peter was environment minister whose green evangelism scared the workers throughout the Latrobe Valley. We crafted the campaign around the hit to RTDs, the bourbon and coke mixers so loved by tradies especially. We produced '5 cents a litre off' petrol vouchers with Rohan's image on one side to promote our action plan for petrol prices crippling families. The Traralgon Post Office was slated to be closed. We hammered Kevin Rudd over it.

The Liberal Party polled 21% of the primary vote, the Nationals 39.6%. It was a 6% swing to the Coalition. John Howard called me from London, excited: "Brendan, this is extraordinary. This is the best result in a by-election for an opposition against a newly elected government since Nigel Bowen resigned in 1973. There's something going on."

I agreed. There was something going on. The swing against the Whitlam Government in Parramatta nine months after its election was 2.3%. I was convinced that having 'bought' Rudd, the voters had found their 'fourth defect'. "John, for the first time ever, we won three of the four booths in the Latrobe Valley".

On the day of the by-election, I was in Brisbane for the 'coming home' parade from Iraq. Kevin Rudd oversaw the parade at which 700 Australian troops marched, cheered on by 10,000 from families, friends and grateful Australians. Touchingly, the parade was led by 21-year-old Liam Haven from 6RAR. Blinded in a roadside bomb blast just weeks before returning, his mates guided him. Emotional stuff.

The reception was in the Brisbane Town Hall. Soldiers and their families crowded in for speeches. I had been told I had no speaking role, but I preferred to be with the soldiers anyway.

Kevin Rudd, Chief of Defence and dignitaries made their way onto the stage. I walked past the stairs to stand with the families. Defence Minister, Joel Fitzgibbon, grabbed me: "Brendan, the Prime Minister would like you to join him on the stage and say a few words."

I sat looking at uniformed men and women, families, wives, husbands, partners and children. Many held signs. Kevin Rudd addressed them and spoke well. It was appreciated. Then I was introduced. They literally blew the roof off with applause and cheers. Joel Fitzgibbon leaned over with a twinkle in his eye, "Just a bit of residual support there for you mate." Overwhelmed, I was almost lost for words. Just before I spoke, I saw a young woman holding a sign, standing at the front of the crowd. I left the microphone, went to the edge of the stage, leant over and asked if I could have the sign. She passed it up.

Back at the microphone, I said, "There is nothing I could say to you that would give more meaning to why we are here and how we feel, than this sign." I held it up to the crowd:

SMITHY YOU SEXY BASTARD

THANKS FOR FIGHTING TO DEFEND OUR FREEDOM

The reaction was rapturous. I went on to remind them of why we had gone, what they had done, what they had given and what it meant to our nation.

I don't follow cricket, but I knew that Glenn McGrath's wife had burrowed deep into the nation's heart. This remarkable 42-year-old woman had established a foundation bearing her name after her initial recovery from breast cancer in 2002. It supported women suffering the disease and breast care nurses. She died on 22 June 2008. The funeral was a sitting day, Wednesday, 25 June.

On Monday morning, I told Peter Hendy that I would attend the service in Sydney. Yes, I would miss question time, but this was important. The nation's leaders should pay their respects to a brave woman who had shaped modern Australia. I asked Peter to contact Rudd's office to see if he was going. If so, I might accompany him on the RAAF jet, returning together for question time. It wasn't until late Tuesday that Rudd's office confirmed he would go and take me. It was a beautiful, sunny day. Jane's children were radiant. Glenn was stoic. I paid my respects and stood back. I knew some of the cricketers, but didn't want to impose into the McGrath and cricketing families. The Prime Minister's presence was appreciated by everyone. We discussed a number of issues on the way back to Canberra. He was clearly impacted by cancer and wanted to use the resources of his office to advance our understanding and treatment of it.

I raised Prime Ministerial Libraries. I told him how I had covertly co-funded the Hawke Centre at the University of South Australia. The nation would benefit from an official program to establish and support a Library in honour of our Prime Ministers. Each has changed Australia, their vision, story and influence should be told, drawing on the documents, artifacts and relics of their public and personal lives. I told him I would back it and, if he felt more comfortable, it could begin with his successor whenever that time came. It didn't happen.

Alexander Downer and Mark Vaile resigned in early July, meaning two by-elections. Both would be messy. Both men had served Australia magnificently. They had earned the right, in my opinion, to leave of their own choosing. Most politicians have no choice, either the voters or the Party decides for them. Alexander's Adelaide Hills' seat of Mayo had become increasingly difficult for the Liberal Party as its demographic changed. Respect for him had held the vote. I knew we were headed into tough territory, but was buoyed by Gippsland. A lot would depend on the candidate and, as always, local issues.

Mark Vaile represented the sprawling New South Wales mid-north coast seat of Lyne. Like Gippsland, a retiring National Party MP meant the Liberal Party could field a candidate. I wanted to do so. However, the New South Wales parliamentary Liberal Party Leader, Barry O'Farrell, didn't want to upset his state National Party colleagues. The member for Port Macquarie was Robert Oakeshott. Extremely popular, elected in 1996 as a National, he had abandoned the Party to become an independent. If he ran for Lyne, he would win.

I had several conversations with Oakeshott. If the Liberal Party endorsed his close friend, a popular local mayor and Liberal Party member, he would campaign for him. This seemed like a good outcome, the Liberal Party likely to win Lyne. Barry was not for turning. The Liberal Party would stay out of it. He didn't want the Nationals provoked.

Rob Oakeshott ran as an independent and blitzed it. Given he lent his support to Julia Gillard, along with Mike Windsor, to form government in 2010, I have often wondered if history might have been different.

I didn't really get to know Peter Costello until we lost in 2007. I regret the man was not fully revealed to me sooner. Along with my colleagues, we had seen his brilliance. We had marvelled at his tactical and strategic dominance of the parliament and ability to demolish his political opponents. We saw him age as he crafted and delivered 12 budgets, guiding the nation's finances. I had also clashed with his mastery of detail in the Expenditure Review Committee.

After the loss, I was finally introduced to Peter. I discovered a man of rich intelligence, decisive, witty, deeply committed to his wife and family and imbued with solid values. But I also observed a man paradoxically somewhat shy and perhaps, risk averse. Peter came to see me in early July. He had decided it was time to go. We spent two hours talking about the political and economic environment. I told him that with two by-elections coming, I didn't need a third. Peter was writing his book. He was also supporting me.

> Peter, I can only imagine the emotions you have experienced over the past seven months. You are writing your book. That will be therapeutic in many ways. Why don't you finish the book, launch it and if you still want to go, we can have a by-election late this year or early next year? In the meantime, I'm going to have to have a showdown with Turnbull and I will need your support.

He accepted it. Both of us knew what a Turnbull leadership would mean.

As long as Peter was in the parliament there was a chance he would change his mind, return to the front bench and perhaps the leadership. Though I was determined to do my best and knew the privilege bestowed on me leading the Party, I also knew the national interest would be best served by him assuming it.

23

Climate change and other blow torches

Kevin Rudd accepted an invitation to the Group of Eight (G8) meeting in Tokyo in early July 2008. He had said he would urge the G8 nations to apply a 'blowtorch" to OPEC to increase oil production. This, he said, was the only way to reduce petrol prices. No mention of 'Fuel Watch.'

In Canberra, I called a press conference in the parliamentary courtyard to put some pressure on Rudd. He was meeting nations including the United States, European Union and Russia, some of the world's biggest greenhouse gas emitters. That 'doorstop' press conference on Monday, 7 July, would prove to be the most significant event in my leadership.

For the entirety of my leadership until that day, I had recognised the need to act on climate change, that Australia should make a proportionate, responsible contribution. We had paid a hefty political price in government for not ratifying the Kyoto Agreement. Kyoto had become a symbol for belief in climate change and acting on it. But Australians were yet to be introduced to the economics of 'action on climate change'.

In December 2007, Sydney's *Daily Telegraph* published a survey of 400 people. In response to a multiple choice question, 43% thought 'Kyoto' was something you get in a Japanese restaurant. Early in 2008, SKY News surveyed its relatively educated audience. It asked them how much a month they would be prepared to pay for climate change action. Half said they would not be prepared to pay anything. Only 5% would pay $5 a week.

Kevin Rudd's proselytising on "climate change action" played to a broader community emotional commitment to address climate change on the one hand, while exploiting its ignorance of what it would actually cost, on the other. We were being lectured by nuclear powered States in Europe, many of whom were falling short of their own Kyoto targets. As carbon dioxide doesn't respect borders, it seemed to me that without the US, China, India and Russia committed to meaningful action, Australia with 1.4% of global emissions could reduce to zero without any impact on the climate.

Fronting the media that day, I said, "Mr Rudd needs to be a human blow torch on the G8. He has to apply maximum pressure to them for meaningful action on their greenhouse gas emissions. Australia cannot alone save the world from climate change, but if we act alone, we could do irreparable damage to the Australian economy".

Suddenly, Michelle Grattan was energised, "Have you changed the policy?" Alarmed, I carefully said, "The Coalition has had the same view of this for more than a decade. We have to act on climate change, but to do so without the rest of the world, without the big emitters – China, India, the US and Russia – anything we do here will have little benefit to the climate but cause damage to our economy." Others followed up with equally aggressive questions.

Back at the office, I told Peter Hendy what had transpired. He said, "Well, let's have a look at the policy". He pulled out the coalition's 2007 election policy. One page read that Australia must "act in unison with the rest of the world". Then, over the page, "The Coalition will implement an Emissions Trading Scheme (ETS) no later than 2012". We were both incredulous.

I had been a cabinet minister in 2007 when this policy was adopted but had no recollection of any meeting at which it had been discussed and agreed. I called three former cabinet ministers, none was aware of such a policy. I phoned Peter Conran, Cabinet secretary through 2007. Sheepishly, he said, "Well Brendan, yes it did go through Cabinet but I can understand if ministers did not realise that it had". I knew what that meant. It had been 'under the line'. In other words, relevant ministers and the Prime Minister had agreed to it. The matter would have been listed for approval but not as a formal submission to Cabinet. In a sense that was understandable because then, a market-based approach to climate change was fairly 'orthodox', especially looking down the barrel of an election in the middle of a drought where our refusal to ratify 'Kyoto' was front and centre.

John Howard confirmed it was policy when I called him: "Brendan, we were facing an election and as you know, under pressure on this. Malcolm Turnbull was determined we had to do it. Shergold had done excellent work and it was agreed by Cabinet – but it wasn't a high profile."

I told him I would move to change the policy. I couldn't see the logic of us moving in front of the rest of the world. Australians were ignorant of the economic price they would pay for doing so. He understood.

There were basic principles to be followed:

> Any response needed to be truly global.
>
> Australian policy settings needed to deliver economic development, energy security and environmental sustainability. Affordable and reliable energy must be available to Australian industry and households.
>
> Australia would accept that different countries would choose different approaches.
>
> Australia would need to prepare for the inevitable impact of a changed climate.
>
> The long term emissions target for Australia must be environmentally credible and economically achievable. Any emissions trajectory should also be able to be reset if new science based technology emerged.

This seemed plain commonsense to me. However, for Malcolm Turnbull, and friends, moving from a firm commitment and timeline of an emissions reduction mechanism was heresy. By this time in July, things were shifting economically. Unease about the Rudd Government was stirring in the electorate. Australians had been subjected to Fuel Watch; Grocery Watch; Solar Panel mismanagement; students demanding their promised 'toolbox' laptops; alcopops tax, and a Toyota Hybrid car subsidy of $35 million seen for what it was – a taxpayer funded stunt.

The Roy Morgan Consumer Confidence Index for June was the lowest since the recession of 1991. The Westpac Consumer Index at 79, was the lowest level since July 1992. The Sensis Small Business Survey found only 10% of small businesses had confidence in federal government policies. Dunn and Bradstreet Business Survey of Profit Expectations found it to be the lowest level on record – since 1988. Tightening monetary policy, a global credit squeeze, a strong Australian dollar, record petrol prices and a slowing economy rounded out an unsettling scenario. I thought that imposing a complex tax on the nation for no environmental gain was bad policy and bad politics. What might work would be an ETS with a fixed negligible price for carbon. Industry could be supported in adopting the model, fix the carbon price and then wait until the big global emitters moved.

The shadow cabinet meeting was scheduled for Tuesday, 29 July, in Canberra. The weekend preceding it I did a lengthy interview with Paul Kelly, Editor at Large of *The Australian*. I outlined principles for the way ahead on climate change and where, broadly, both the nation and coalition should land on this. I knew Turnbull would arc up, but was confident of getting it agreed.

Then, on Monday night, walking through the concourse of Sydney airport to catch the plane to Canberra, my phone rang. It was Nick Minchin. He had just returned from Western Australia. "Brendan, I've been meeting large resources companies, they need certainty on climate change for investment. We have to act." My heart sank. Without Nick, I had little chance of success.

Next day at the meeting, although shadow treasurer, Turnbull assumed the role of environment spokesman from Greg Hunt. As Nick had rolled over, so too did most other conservative members of the shadow cabinet. I reiterated my views. It was John Cobb, the National Party water spokesman who backed me. "I've got to say, the most sensible things I've heard said on this whole issue was from Brendan over the weekend".

The following day, I fronted the party room at which I put the shadow cabinet position to proceed to support the implementation of an ETS. I felt humiliated, putting to my colleagues a policy that I opposed. It was clear from their reaction, though, most wanted my position. What I should have done was to tell them we had listened, that shadow cabinet would re-examine the policy. Instead, I stood by the shadow cabinet and ran it into the media. The die was cast.

For good measure, Turnbull came to see me in my Melbourne office telling me I was "a hopeless individual" and seriously deficient leader. "You are going to have to hand this over to me. You have a net negative approval rating of 17%". I sat thinking, "Well Malcolm, despite your best efforts, that's not as dire as John Howard a year ago."

As always with Turnbull, I listened, and calmly thanked him for his frank views with which I did not agree. I reminded him the Party leadership is the gift of the party room, not something to be 'handed' from one leader to the next.

Australia's Olympians were returning from Beijing early in the morning of 26 August. Arriving on a special Qantas 747 flight early into Sydney, excited, expectant families gathered in the hangar. The place was packed with media. A large set of stairs was pushed up against the plane. Kevin Rudd and I were asked to stand at the foot of the stairs and welcome them. Another privilege.

The gold medallists were first off. Understandably they were excited to be met by the Prime Minister. Libby Lenton emerged wearing her two gold, silver and bronze medals. I was surprised when she wanted to meet me. Excited, she said, "Dr Nelson, could I have my photo taken with you? My family are big fans." Kevin Rudd took the photo for her. I then said, "Well Libby, you need a photo with the Prime Minister". They stood together and I took it for her. I stayed to speak to all those who had not won medals and their families. As soon as the television cameras were gone, so too was Kevin Rudd.

Next day, the *Sydney Morning Herald* ran the photo of me photographing Kevin Rudd and Libby Lenton. The header said, "Nelson now Rudd's camera boy".

When Education Minister in 2004, I received a book with an invitation to write the foreword. *My Brush with Depression* was co-authored by Greg Wilson and Aaron Cootes. The cover spoke immediately to my taste in art – a man under a wide-brimmed hat, lugging his swag into the distance on a long, dusty road. I discovered within its pages a remarkable man. Greg had battled depression all his life, faced and barely escaped death, finding redemption in art, love and friendships. Greg had married his counsellor, Josie Adler. They lived with Aaron and his partner, Joyce Biviano. The four had an impact on me that I cannot describe, other than their friendship made me a better person. All have given themselves to the betterment of others – youth, people struggling with mental illness, and veterans. That Greg was also a country music tragic helped our friendship. John Howard, as Prime Minister, launched the book at Parliament House.

In 2005, Greg said he wanted to paint me for the Archibald Prize. I agreed, knowing that even if he possessed the skills of Leonardo De Vinci, the judges would never countenance a portrait of a Howard government minister. The portrait wasn't hung, but I treasured it. Greg shared my love of motorbikes. He painted me wearing my late brother Philip's leather jacket. Behind me was my Triumph Speedmaster. Beyond the bike was a road winding up to Parliament House. Above the road was a dove. When asked to explain, Greg said, "You love your brother and you are on a journey, trying to make the world a better place." In the bottom left hand corner of the painting was a patch of white with faint horizontal lines. I pointed to it, "What's this Greg?"

"It's an unfinished story Brendan. You have more to do."

In the midst of 2008, Greg wanted to give me the portrait. Deeply appreciative, I said, "I will hang it in the foyer of my office." Greg and Josie drove the painting to Canberra from their home at Pokolbin to present it to me. A happy day. Afterwards, as my staff admired it and I told them the story, I asked if I should hang it in the office foyer. "Will people think I am a wanker?" Simon Berger piped up, "They already do boss. Won't make any difference." Cruel but fair. I agreed we would hang it but, alongside it, Greg's story.

The following day, Quentin Bryce was sworn in as Governor General. Kevin Rudd's choice was inspired. A truly remarkable woman of substance and courage, deeply loved by her husband, Michael. To the crowd assembled for the swearing in, I said that her intellect and idealism had driven practical measures to serve the welfare of others. "You have at all times served with a grace and dignity you have worn as comfortably as a smile that will engage all Australians." Our paths would cross numerous times over the years.

I decided it was time to deal with Mr Turnbull. I also needed the authority of the party room to shift our position on climate change. I would call a spill of the leadership and re-nominate for it. If re-elected, I would deal with both. Not a single day had gone by without Turnbull actively undermining and seeking to bully me out of the job. From my experiences with him, I formed the personal opinion that he was a demanding, demonstrative, emphatic, manipulative and self-obsessed man, who used seduction and the threat of intimidation to get what he wanted from people. Others may disagree, but some will agree.

I would call it for Tuesday morning, 16 September. I told Peter Hendy only.

A dinner was held in Melbourne on Friday, 29 August, to thank and pay tribute to Peter Costello and his wife, Tanya. Media speculation was rife that he was about to resign. He wasn't, although his book launch was imminent. This man and his family had given so much to Australia and to the Liberal Party. It was an emotional evening for everyone.

The following day I headed out early to Rod Pilon Transport depot in Melbourne. Rod Hannifey was driving his B-Double truck to Dubbo. A lifelong truckie, Rod was a safety advocate. The industry was struggling, owner drivers were on their knees and reform was driven by bureaucrats. I wanted to find out first-hand what was going on. How better than to spend 24 hours on the road doing the real thing?

I learned a lot about the economics of the industry, the consequences of poorly designed road-stops, the difficulty of eating healthy food, time away from family and the importance of accessing your favourite Slim Dusty albums! The Newell Highway was unnerving at night, with its width and heavy traffic flow. At the Ben Hall Road House, we had a coffee, food and good chat with fellow truckies. I slept in the truck when we finally got to Dubbo. From the cab, I reported in to the ABC's 'Macca' for *Australia All Over*.

The by-elections for Lyne and Mayo were held on 6 September 2008. Lyne, as predicted, went to Rob Oakeshott. The Liberal candidate for Mayo was Jamie Briggs. A bright young industrial relations expert with private sector experience, he had worked for John Howard on WorkChoices. It was a big field. Burned by their Gippsland experience, Labor stayed out of it. Prominent businessman, Bob Day, lost the Liberal pre-selection and ran as a Family First candidate. Without Alexander Downer and no clear preference flows, it was tough. I knew the area well from my youth in Adelaide and felt comfortable campaigning. In the end, we sustained a 4% two party preferred swing against us. Bob Day attracted 11% of the primary vote. Jamie won with a 3% margin. Reasonable in the circumstances.

Aged Pensioners were suffering, living on $273 a week. Although the pension had increased in real terms by 24% through the Howard Government, an increase was desperately needed. My instinct was to back an increase knowing the budget could afford it. I spoke to Tony Abbott who was supportive after some encouragement. I asked Peter Hendy to arrange a teleconference of the Leadership group and Tony Abbott to consider an aged pension increase. It was scheduled for Wednesday, 10 September.

Peter Hendy came back, "You're not going to believe this – Turnbull's in Venice!"

The opposition's Treasury spokesman had so little regard for me, he had left Australia for a week without telling us. He was in Venice with his wife, Lucy, attending an architecture conference. Peter confirmed Turnbull would be back in time for the parliamentary sitting next week.

The Leadership group agreed to the increase.

I took Peta Credlin aside after the call. I told her that the following Tuesday morning I planned to call a spill of the leadership. Should I be returned, I would ask her to be my chief of staff. She had excelled and was hungry. Peter Hendy was a good man, but backbenchers found him bookish and aloof. No point telling Peter until it was over.

Jo Gash was headed to the UN for three months. In the middle of winter, she had pulled a caravan around the east coast caravan parks promoting tourism. I asked her if she could delay her departure a few days. She knew why.

On Monday, 15 September 2008, I moved a Private Member's Bill to increase the aged pension by $30 a week. The government blocked it, so I sought to suspend standing orders to prosecute the case. Kevin Rudd was away at the UN, his 16th trip as prime minister. The Parliament was sitting at a cost of $1 million a day as aged pensioners "lived on baked beans and jam sandwiches". The government was sitting on a $22 billion surplus. They increased the aged pension and, of course, took credit for it.

The issue was hurting the government, but so too was the notion of 'Kevin 747'. The feeling his interests lay elsewhere in the world was taking root. We were progressively unpacking the 'defects'.

I was in the Senate chamber listening to Helen Kroger deliver her first speech when messages arrived on the beepers of colleagues around me. The Whip, at my request, had called a Liberal party room meeting for 6pm. They would find out in the room the purpose of the meeting. I hadn't told Julie Bishop what I planned, for two reasons. First, she needed plausible deniability should Turnbull seek to exact revenge on her. Second, I needed this to be held very tightly. She was, by this time, close to Turnbull.

I rose to address them.

The past nine months have been hard. Perhaps the hardest in the history of the Liberal Party. But we are well positioned. Australians elected a government that is fast proving not to be what they thought.

We have protected and embraced the Howard-Costello legacy but listened and responded to the reasons for our defeat.

We have successfully framed Kevin Rudd.

We have begun the process of policy development and set a vision for the nation's future.

I have allowed and encouraged you all to express your views and to the extent possible, accommodate sensible change.

The first phase of this is now finished. We now have to move into a seriously disciplined phase if we are to be more than competitive in two years' time.

Financial turmoil is unfolding as we meet.

We are here to create a better Australia. Chosen by our party members and then elected by a majority of our fellow Australians, we are sent here to exercise judgement on their behalf – based in Liberal Party philosophy of hard work, idealism and self-sacrifice.

Everything we do must be motivated by the desire to make it easier for men and women to create wealth for themselves and Australia, to encourage them to raise, house, clothe and educate their families. We are here to nurture and encourage entrepreneurialism, to give people incentives to get out of bed, take risks and create a better future for themselves and our country.

But for some of you, it's not about any of this. Instead, it is a game of snakes and ladders. Some of you simply see it all as a game, the game of politics driven by self-interest, not the interests of others.

> There will be a spill of the Leadership in this room at 9 o'clock tomorrow morning. I will then be a candidate for the Leadership. Should I succeed, I will prosecute the case to you of changing our party's position on climate change. I will also be making some key changes to the front bench.
>
> I will not be working the phones overnight, nor will I have my supporters harangue or entice you to support me. Instead, I will be in my office with the door open if you want to speak to me.

Then, looking directly at Turnbull and six of the people whom I knew were working hard to undermine and remove me:

> My advice to some of you is to be up very late working very hard to persuade others not to support me. Because if I am successful, whatever you do to undermine me and the party, you will be doing from a position of considerably less influence.

I spoke for 20 minutes. They listened quietly and respectfully. It was done. I had pulled the pin on the grenade.

Turnbull and his backers did work very hard. All sorts of promises were made for preferment should colleagues back Turnbull – and worse. I had pushed reform of the New South Wales Division of the Party. Turnbull had guaranteed there would be none. New South Wales factional spear carriers, conservative and moderate, instructed a vote for Turnbull. But, as always, I didn't want to be beholden to any factional grouping. There is little point holding power if you are controlled by others. Bruce Billson, Tony Smith and Mitch Fifield publicly and strongly backed me, for which I am eternally grateful.

The following morning, a jet-lagged Malcolm Turnbull was successful, 45 votes to 41. After all his presumptive intellectual superiority and ruthless undermining, he had shifted just three votes. But it was enough.

I gathered myself and returned to the office to join Gillian. She had come down for the ballot. Our staff were emotional, perplexed. But it was done. At the packed press conference, Gillian was superb in support of her husband. She had been deeply hurt by the media portrayal of me over those nine months.

Dennis Shanahan from *The Australian* asked, "Dr Nelson, will you now show Mr Turnbull the same loyalty that he has shown you over the past year?"

"You all know me. I have never undermined or briefed you against any of my colleagues and I am not about to start. If at any time you feel that is what I am doing, please tell the Australian people. I wish Mr Turnbull well."

When I returned to my office, the packing boxes had already arrived. I spoke to the staff, thanked them all and assured them I would assist any who sought positions in other offices. I told Peta Credlin and Andrew Hirst they should accept a position with Turnbull if it was offered. "You don't work for me and you don't work for him. You work for the Liberal Party and for Australia. He will need the best people he can get." Simon Berger wanted to stay with me, and he did – right until my very last day. A more loyal man I have never met.

As I packed up the boxes, a visibly upset Peter Costello arrived. He paced up and down, "Brendan, you've got to understand, this is the worst thing that has happened to the Liberal Party in its history." "I'm pretty upset about it too, Peter." Peter had been good to me. Joe Hockey always said my "real problem was Costello". No, he wasn't. Peter's presence was used by the media, but my real problem was Turnbull and those who either could not, or would not, see the flawed character of the man. Reflecting on Peter's distress about the outcome of the ballot, packing my boxes, I wondered if he might remain in the parliament.

The media of course, heralded Turnbull's ascension to his rightful place as party leader. I was mere road-kill. But I hoped now he had what he so badly wanted, that he would do well, for all our sake. He could be assured I wasn't going to be a problem. Therein lies a difference. You could vote against me – as a number of my friends did, without retribution. But with Turnbull, many feared that with his money and influence, if you voted against him, career doors would slam shut, including in your post political life.

It was hard walking into the chamber to sit on the back bench. But it was a result of decisions I made. Still, wherever you sit in the parliament, not a day should go by when it is anything other than a privilege to be there.

Kevin Rudd was exceedingly kind to me. He came over at the end of question time and asked me to come down to his office for a cup of tea. I was touched by his generosity of spirit. I sat with him for 45 minutes chatting about many things, including the brutality of politics. His Chief of Staff, Alistair Jordan, said, "We've been waiting for Mr Turnbull. We were more worried about you getting lift-off than we are of him." I let the back-handed compliment go through to the keeper. It was the first of a number of such kindnesses extended to me by Kevin Rudd.

From its inception, early in my political career, I supported the National Student Leadership Forum on Faith and Values. Some 225 young people from 18 to 25 would come to Canberra for four days. They would be supported by an MP or Senator, be addressed by the Prime Minister and Opposition Leader, hear inspiring stories and reflect on what informs a life of value. The welcome dinner was in the Great Hall on the Thursday night. Organisers were surprised when I arrived. I met my assigned group of young people to take them to my backbench office. "This is a forum about values. I made a commitment to these young people and will honour it. It is the most meaningful thing I will do all week."

Lee Kernaghan was guest of honour, Australian of the Year. It was uplifting to re-connect with the man, already a friend and one to whom I would become even closer. I addressed the audience and introduced him.

Rhondda was devastated for me. We shed a few tears together. In the electorate office, she was overwhelmed by the mail.

Nick Minchin sent me a card expressing his gratitude, lamenting the 'bizarre' behaviour of the New South Wales right in the ballot. George Brandis' card spoke to his respect for me and admiration for what I had done and how. I have treasured both cards. You don't realise the impact you are having on people as you travel through public life. Over a thousand emails and letters arrived. Many from public figures, including Chris Bowen and Tanya Plibersek, but hundreds of everyday people. Just two from people unknown to me:

> I have just seen the evening news and am sorry you have lost the leadership of the Liberal Party. I do want to say how impressed I have been with your public speeches, delivered professionally and with sincerity ... the recent swearing in of the new Governor General, Jane McGrath's death and those who attended the 40th anniversary of the commemorations of Coral and Balmoral in May also thought the same. Thank you for your efforts in challenging circumstances. Christine Reay, Springwood, Queensland.
>
> If ever this reaches you personally, please know that there are socialists like myself who saw in you one of the examples in the Liberal Party of a concept – decency. We believe you to be a decent man. Be happy rather than ambitious.
>
> Annie Greet de Boissiere, North Balwyn, Victoria.

Turnbull called me on the Friday morning at Joe Hockey's urging, to offer a front bench position. I declined for two reasons. First, it would be hypocritical in the extreme to serve as a loyal front bencher to a man whose behaviour I regarded as reprehensible. Second, I was tired. I needed time to think and reflect.

I had been hurt by the leadership experience. What I didn't appreciate was the impact it had on Gillian, seeing me so treated and portrayed as the person she knew me not to be. She said I could of course remain in parliament, but she didn't ever want to go through "that" again. If I stayed, it would be for another tilt at the leadership if the opportunity arose. From what I had seen and now knew of him,

I thought Turnbull would fail. Not for lack of ability, but for flawed judgement. I laughed out loud when, several years later, Turnbull blamed me for his failure as leader, asserting he had "not been ready for the leadership when Nelson called the spill".

The Coalition Christmas drinks for Members and staffers was in the parliamentary courtyard in early December. I happened to be in what would become the 'front row' when formalities began. Standing right in front of me, Malcolm Turnbull spoke of his gratitude to Julie Bishop, various front benchers, staffers and the party secretariat. As usual, he was buoyant about our electoral prospects. No mention of me. It was National Party Leader, Warren Truss, who said, "Thank you to Brendan for getting us off the mat, holding us together through a tough time and for all his hard work." The contrast between the two men was stark.

President George W Bush was completing his second and final term in the presidency. A veritable conga line of people were lining up to attack him. Sitting in my backbencher's office, I pulled out a sheet of paper and wrote him a letter. I had told my children that, by virtue of the office I had held, I knew that thanks to his leadership, heinous acts in the world had been prevented. That he had led from principle and, unlike others, been prepared to acknowledge mistakes. In the long term, I believed history would judge him well.

I put the letter in an envelope and posted it to President George W Bush, The White House, Washington DC, USA. In late January 2009, a man appeared at my parliamentary office door from the US embassy. "Sir, I have a letter for you from the President of the United States of America."

I opened it. A handwritten letter from President Bush, written from the Oval Office. He thanked me for my note which "meant a lot" to him. He and Laura were about to head back to the ranch with his "head held high". He would "always remember the friends who had been steadfast through the tough moments". This small act spoke to the character of the man. Most Australians would be lucky to get an acknowledgement note from their departing Member of Parliament were they to write. Yet, here was a retiring president writing personally to a relatively minor political figure on the other side of the world.

I took soundings from people whose views I respected. One, Paul McClintock, said "Brendan, I don't think you are mad – or bad enough, to be Prime Minister." One of the thematic criticisms of me was I was "too nice" and "not enough mongrel". Much of what I experienced was dismissed as, "politics".

It's not actually. It is reprehensible, unethical and unacceptable behaviour in many instances. But, as Paul observed, you have to be 'mad'. Being Prime Minister is your life, 24 hours a day. Few people want that, let alone are suited to it.

When John Howard encouraged me to stay, I thought his perfect day would be sitting in front of the TV at Kirribilli House watching a cricket test. Janette would be nearby, reading and chatting to family members by phone. During the ad breaks, he would enjoy speaking to backbenchers. In contrast, my idea of a perfect day is sitting in my boat fishing with my son, Slim Dusty quietly playing. I enjoyed V8 Supercars, and admire Mark Skaife. I went to his last race at Oran Park with the Holden Racing Team on 7 December. As he roared towards to finish line, the team held the board over the track rail, SKAIFE. THANKS FOR THE MEMORIES.

After the crowds had gone, I found myself in the pits alone with Mark, his wife Toni and son Mitch – a privileged moment to be with a man who had given his all to the sport. After some special photos, I left thinking that at the end of it all, what truly counts are those whom you love and who love you. Kevin Fagan was right.

The moment had an enduring impact on me and what I would do next.

24

THANK YOU – do you like cold weather?

Liberated form the pressures, with time to think, re-engage with my family and friends and take soundings, I came into 2009 accepting I had run my race. I could stay, and was open to doing so but knew my family would pay too high a price. It was time.

On the evening of Monday, 16 February 2009, I told members of the Liberal Party in Bradfield that I would not seek pre-selection for the next election. I felt I was letting them down. More than a few had given their all for me to be successful in 1995. We had been through a lot together. After their initial shock, they accepted it and inevitably, thoughts turned to the next member for Bradfield.

Dr Ken Rowe, the man whom I so admired in educational leadership, was tragically killed in the Marysville bushfire tragedy. I was afforded the privilege of speaking at his funeral in Melbourne the following day. On my way to the Sydney airport, I called Malcolm Turnbull just after 6.30am to formally advise him I would not stand again. He was chipper, "the right decision Brendan".

At 6.45 am my phone rang, "Brendan, Kevin Rudd. I am very disappointed that you have chosen to leave the parliament. You will be a loss." I was taken aback by his generosity. After 15 minutes of conversation he asked what I was doing that night. I was on my way to Ken's funeral and would be back in Sydney to speak to an electorate Rotary dinner. "What are you doing after that?" As it was Rotary, I told him I would be finished by 8.30pm. "Well, come down to Kirribilli House and have a beer". Given he was the Prime Minister, I felt I should accept, notwithstanding the late hour.

In Melbourne, Minister Jenny Macklin greeted me, kindly asking if I was okay. I was and I wasn't. "That we are here at Ken's funeral speaks to true perspectives in life."

A long, emotional day, I arrived at Kirribilli just after 9pm. Kevin welcomed me. He was alone. I told him that whatever the purpose of the invitation, I was happy to speak about anything other than the Liberal Party and Malcolm Turnbull.

I had accepted Bruce Shepherd's challenge to take up the cause of newborn deafness. One unresolved issue was that not every newborn had their hearing tested. Yet if deafness afflicting 600 babies born every year in Australia could be diagnosed just after birth, early intervention delivered stunning results. I told Kevin that early diagnosis, cochlear implant and intensive audio-verbal therapies, made these children better that hearing children by age five. Kevin Rudd said, "Okay, this will be my political gift to you. We will mandate universal newborn screening for deafness."

I then raised the report on Teaching Reading produced by Ken Rowe from the 2005 National Inquiry. I told him that for $64 million, we could rectify the defects in the teaching of reading, thereby liberating children to be their best and lift the nation's productivity. He said he would seek advice and think about it.

We spoke about Australia's place in the world, the Global Financial Crisis, the challenges of climate change and of political leadership. He thought it important that irrespective of which side of politics, good people should be put to use for the national interest. I strongly agreed and still do.

It was after a surreal two hours of conversation, interrupted occasionally by the lady offering a drink, I suggested it was time for me to go: "Kevin, you're a very busy man". Driving home, I was grateful for his kindness but wondered if he was lonely. It would be some years later that we learned he was barely speaking with many of his own cabinet ministers.

When Parliament resumed after the winter recess, I was watching Darren Chester in the chamber and thought what an asset he was to the National Party. Renewal in Gippsland had been good. I thought it time for Bradfield to also have a new member. I had run my race and would not be returning to the front bench. It was time to go.

I went to Peter Costello. As I thought would be the case, he said, "Well, if you're going, so will I. You announce first." On Tuesday, 25 August 2009, outside my electorate office, with considerable emotion, I announced I would resign from parliament. Peter did so in early October.

The following Saturday night at home, Kevin Rudd called. He asked if I could come and see him in Sydney on Tuesday afternoon. "Kevin, I know you're the Prime Minister, but I promised my brother-in-law that I would take him fishing. He's a school teacher and has just three days off. I have to get the boat in the water." "Okay, I've got a bit on, but could you come into the Sydney office about 10.15?"

I arrived at the office just after 10am to a media frenzy. I quickly pushed my way through the madness and into the lift. Kevin's personal assistant greeted me: "The Prime Minister is doing a press conference Dr Nelson. I'll put you in his office." I sat, surrounded by Cabinet papers, classified documents and sundry sensitive papers. I asked to be moved to another room. A short time later Rudd walked around the corner with Al Gore. Smiling, he introduced me to Gore as "a misguided friend – from the other side". He invited me in. Gore asked me what I thought we should be doing on climate change. I was explaining my views when Kevin suggested we change the topic.

When Gore had gone, Kevin asked, "Do you like cold weather?" Unsure where this was going. I said I preferred it to hot weather. "Well, that's good. I would like you go to Brussels as our ambassador to the European Union and NATO". He went on, "The world has changed and it is going to change a lot more over the coming decade. We've spent years fighting the EU. I want to send a signal to the Europeans that we seek a broader, deeper engagement by sending someone they will take seriously. In relation to NATO, I intend to appoint you as our first ambassador. I need someone that can break down doors and get us to the table. We need influence."

I had not expected this nor sought it. I told him I had been speaking with Medicines Australia about leading it. "Who are they?" he asked.

I would also be Ambassador to Belgium and Luxembourg and Special Envoy to the World Health Organisation in Geneva.

I never saw myself in the 'Gin and Tonic set.' Had we been in government, I would not have sought a diplomatic post. What attracted me to this was NATO. We were in a NATO-led war with little influence. This was another way of helping our troops on the ground. Gillian was supportive. She also thought it a good thing for me to spend time out of Australia. I had resolved not to fall into the trap of so many former political figures, constantly turning up in the press commenting on the performance and failures of their successors. How you are regarded in the long term is determined by how you leave politics. This posting would impose on me the discipline to uphold the public silence to which I had committed.

I went back to Rudd and accepted the role. He would announce it "in due course".

My last party room meeting was Tuesday, 15 September 2009. I urged my colleagues to "stand for something". Malcolm Turnbull was lining the Coalition up to support Labor and, in doing so, we were at risk of being 'intellectual lemmings'. It would put higher costs on energy, travel and households for no environmental gain. Our response, I said, should be "proportionate" with the rest of the world. What Turnbull wanted to back was "a new tax". Applause followed and a long line of speakers in support.

My valedictory speech coincided with the first anniversary of my losing the leadership on 16 September. I invited a small number of close confidants to the gallery. Gillian sat proudly amongst them in the front row. The Labor Party suspended standing orders to allow me to speak for as long as I wished. An immense privilege. Kevin Rudd and almost all his front and back bench attended. Most of my friends and colleagues came to listen. I wrote the speech. I did so because this would be the record of my service and gratitude expressed to those who made it possible and who worked to make me better than I deserved to be.

Emotion suddenly overcame me when I received the Speaker's call. I needed to quickly settle, so departed from the speech with an impromptu explanation about my earring: why I got it in the first place, the Bradfield ladies so offended by it in 1995, and why I removed it in 1999. It did the trick.

Whatever Australians thought of me, Gillian would have made an outstanding first lady. The House broke up when I told them Gillian had described politics as "not a positive working environment". I summarised my contribution over more than 13 years, but also spoke to young Australians, urging them never to abandon their idealism. You can make a difference to your community, your country and to your world. The way each of us lives impacts our world; you can choose to live in a way that changes it.

Kevin Rudd responded with generosity in every sense of the word, including humoring Bruce Shepherd sitting in the Gallery. I finally understood how much my gesture of reaching out to him after his mother's death on Election Day 2004 had meant to him. When it finished they stood and applauded. Sitting behind me, Wilson Tuckey, was especially emotional.

Later, having dinner with Gillian and friends, Kevin Rudd called. He wanted to announce my diplomatic appointment the next day. He had "another appointment and wanted to do them together". I thought, Kim Beazley.

I was due in Kevin Rudd's office at 9.30am. I called in to Malcolm Turnbull's office at 9am. He came out and I told him that I was accepting an offer to be Australia's Ambassador to the EU and NATO. Surprised, he appreciated the courtesy, wished me well and off he went. As things were unravelling for him politically, he had other things on his mind.

As I was ushered into Kevin Rudd's office, Kim Beazley beamed warmly at me. Foreign Minister, Stephen Smith, joined us, having already met me to seek my agreement to represent Australia to the Humanitarian Dimension of the Organisation for Security Co-operation in Europe. When I saw Kim, I felt sympathy for him. This was a very big day for him – Australia's Ambassador to the United States, and he had to share it with one of his former political adversaries. Some accused Kevin Rudd of deliberately wanting to diminish Kim's day. Even if it did, to some extent, I thought back to Rudd's earlier idea of wanting "good people from both sides". He saw this as powerfully saying to the nation he was 'above' petty partisanship. His earlier appointment of Tim Fischer to the newly created Vatican post, spoke to this ambition.

Some Liberals criticised me for accepting the posting from a Labor government. Former New South Wales Labor minister, John Aquilina, said: "Brendan, don't listen to these critics. You are not working for the Rudd Government. You are working for the people of Australia and I know you will do us proud."

I noted with irony that a year after Turnbull defeated 'hopeless' me, the Liberal Party primary vote was lower (35%) and he had a net negative approval rating of minus 29% (AC Nielsen). And all that without ruthless undermining from behind.

The field for the Bradfield pre-selection in late September was big. A number of my friends and local party members were candidates. I refrained from endorsing anyone. Party members need to have their own say and choose their preferred candidate without being told what to think by people like me. One of the reasons I lost the leadership was over that very principle. It underpinned the reforms I supported and had been rejected by the factions.

Paul Fletcher was successful, backed by the 'moderates' and gaining a good cross-section of support from unaligned members. It was a very good choice. Tennis great John Alexander was unsuccessful, but I had already suggested to party HQ that he would be ideal for Bennelong. As the outgoing member, I did what I could to help Paul. Early morning train stations, meeting community leaders and locals. I wanted to write to every resident. Thank them for the privilege they had given me, reflect on what we had achieved and urge their support for Paul. The letter would be funded from my electoral entitlements (taxpayers). As a team player, I sent it into the Liberal Party director for approval. It was returned with myriad changes. I looked at it and said to Rhondda, "This is now meaningless propaganda. I'm not going to insult the intelligence of the electorate by charging them to send out this nonsense."

There must be another way. At home, I grabbed two of my campaign corflutes, taped them together and pulled out a can of paint. In bold letters, I simply wrote, THANK YOU. The next morning, at 6am, I set myself up on the Pacific Highway, outside the Lindfield train station. With a campaign poster image of me on an A-frame, I held up the sign. Cars slowed, tooted, people waved. Some threw obscenities. Others took photos. The first television crew arrived an hour later. Filming, the Channel 9 cameraman asked, "So who are you thanking, Dr Nelson?" "Certainly not you people in the media!"

The following morning, I repeated the exercise on the other side of the electorate. Lots of well-wishers and tooting horns. An abusive woman emerged from the house behind me. "You are creating a disturbance. The sooner you're gone the better." But it was done. I had thanked these wonderful Australians in a simple but powerful way.

Rhondda was planning a tribute dinner in late October. As always, it would double as a party fundraiser. I was humbled when both John Howard and Peter Costello accepted the invitation to attend and speak. It was the first time since the election loss they had come together publicly. Alan Jones agreed to emcee the evening and Ray Hadley to run the auction. Lee Kernaghan sang, *Put him in the long yard.* Rhondda arranged personal tributes from people as diverse as President George W Bush, British Conservative Leader, David Cameron, John Anderson, Father Chris Riley, Jesuit priests, colleagues and members of the public. Among the many messages received from members of the public, which she printed in the testimonial book, one meant so much.

> "If John Howard was our Rock, you were our soul."(Lynn Pinsuiti, Turramurra).

Liberal Party President, Alan Stockdale, wrote me a letter I treasure. In part:

> In an environment where many see success as dependent on manipulation and an ability to dodge the facts, you always presented what was real to people. Where many are content to devote their careers to managing the spin, your focus was on what really impacted the lives of people … you were a driver of change. Your personal integrity was always a hallmark of your approach to public life. In the long run, I believe your inclusive and consultative approach to leadership is one that builds real and lasting commitment to what is best for our nation and its people.

In his address, Peter Costello referred to the infamous protest against Paul Keating that I led at the Toorak bookshop in 1993. I sat wondering where it was going.

> We got word that Keating was going to be at this bookshop in Toorak. I told Tony Smith and a bunch of young Liberals to get down there and give Keating hell. Later in the day, Tony called. He described a bunch of medical people already there running a full-on protest. One guy with a megaphone was really dishing it out to Keating and the union heavies. In the middle of it he screamed he had never voted Liberal in his life. Tony said it was pure genius!

Hand on my shoulder, Peter said he had to "correct the record".

Malcolm Turnbull finally imploded, replaced by Tony Abbott in early December. Turnbull had sought to sign the Coalition on to Kevin Rudd's Carbon Pollution Reduction Scheme and falsely impugn Rudd in a Ute scandal.

The Bradfield and Higgins by-elections were held four days later without Labor candidates. Paul Fletcher and Kelly O'Dwyer, both had a two party preferred swing to them.

When the 'sticks' holding up the façade of the Rudd Government fell down late in 2009, the Liberal Party galvanised behind Tony Abbott. The unplanned transition was complete, with another election in sight.

25

Your Excellency, 'Lady' Nelson and their 'rescue' dogs

It was snowing when Gillian and I arrived in Brussels. Kevin Rudd had been right about cold weather. We were collected by the Australian mission's deputy, Rhonda Piggott. Typically DFAT, Rhonda was smart and helpful in every way. When the Belgian driver, Raphael De Becker, said, "Welcome, your excellency", I almost corrected him but thought better of it. Something I would have to accept.

We arrived at the Australian official residence, a gated community at the end of Avenue Louise, the Square du Bois with a magnificent early 20th century residence. There were high ceilings across four floors above a basement, a grandeur to which we were unaccustomed, while a large official area and dining room looked out onto a terrace and beautiful lawn. Behind the residence was a large forest. We met the domestic staff and looked forward to our personal effects being delivered the following day. I went to the airport with one of the embassy staff to collect our dogs, Jack Russell terriers 'Sniff' and 'Lucy'. Strange, after two hours of paper work, to see two little dogs in their cages being delivered on a forklift. After two minutes of great excitement, both collapsed in exhaustion.

I had done the pre-posting course, familiarising myself with the history, politics and substantive issues in the bilateral relationships. It was a little daunting coming into the diplomatic world. But I soon learned that while they had skills and knowledge I never would, I possessed a unique skill set that would complement theirs.

My first day at the embassy, I addressed all the staff: the Australians and the locally engaged Belgian staff. I could only imagine what they were thinking. An ex-politician and doctor, Brussels being first such appointment. No doubt they had heard horror stories of lousy political appointments. I set out our vision for the key relationships, especially with the EU and NATO. We would move beyond the traditional conflict with the EU in trade and market access to a broader, deeper engagement. The changing world demanded it be so.

> After 30 years of hitting the EU on the back of the head over agricultural tariffs and quotas, we have achieved nothing other than a recent small increase in our premium beef quota. I imagine my predecessors have hammered the European Commission daily, retreating to the residence for a Gin and Tonic at 5pm, satisfied in a job well done. We are now taking a different approach.
>
> Australians are fighting and dying in a NATO-led war in Afghanistan. Our ambition and responsibility here is to get to the NATO table. We have to deliver influence to those men and women whose lives rely on us shaping decisions made here.

Having gone on in a similar vein, I thought it time to lighten things up. "There is something quite sensitive that I need to raise with you. It is my wife". DFAT people are serious types. Taking notes, many sat forward to hear what was coming. With the straightest face I could muster, "I have heard some of you refer to her as Mrs Nelson, others are calling her Ms. Adamson or Madam. I have even heard her called, Gillian. But on the continent here, she is known as Lady Nelson." Days later, Gillian said to me, "They're very nice at the embassy, but gee, they are very formal."

At the first meeting of the embassy leadership Anzac Day loomed large. I asked what the arrangements were. The day started at 9am at Zonnebeke (Flanders) with a wreath laying followed by a mayoral morning tea. From there, wreath laying at the Tyne Cot Cemetery and on to Ypres (Ieper) for a Belgian wreath laying and ANZAC service at the Menin Gate. This would be followed by a reception with speeches in the magnificent Cloth Hall.

"No dawn service?" I asked. I was told there is a Dawn Service at the Buttes Cemetery at Polygon Wood but, "we have nothing to do with it. It's driven by competitive tourism with Ieper". I couldn't believe what I was hearing. I would travel to Flanders, meet all the players and visit the cemeteries and memorials before Anzac Day.

I was booked to meet the President of the European Commission, the enormous bureaucracy that runs the EU and sets its agenda. As a non-professional diplomat arriving in Brussels early in 2010, it seemed a sound basis for diplomacy would be trying to see the world through their eyes. Brussels has over 220 diplomatic missions. It is not easy for a country like Australia, notwithstanding being a G20 country, to get attention. That we were largely Eurosceptic made the task even more difficult. The European Union had just published its EU2020 vision. Its stated ambition was for a "Smart, Sustainable and Inclusive Europe". One of the proposed ways of achieving this was to lift EU investment in research and development to 3 per cent of GDP.

When fronting for a meeting it is important to have something on the agenda that is a priority for the other party. As I thought about the fifteen minutes I would have firstly with the President of the European Commission and then the President of the European Council, I asked myself how Australia might advance its own interests while also helping the Europeans meet theirs. Research co-operation seemed a strategic area for discussion.

At the time we were also contemplating our bid for the Square Kilometre Array (SKA), the world's largest radio telescope. Simply saying to the bloc's leaders that Australia should be awarded the SKA on the basis of its scientific research quality, seemed likely to have negligible impact. We needed to position ourselves as being helpful to Europe in the field of science and demonstrate the strength of Australia's research output.

Presenting credentials to President Barroso, a former Portuguese prime minister, I went with four issues. He listened carefully to the first three with the polite air of a seasoned politician with a busy day ahead. Then I got to science. I told him I had noted the ambition set out in the EU2020 agenda for a 3 per cent R&D spend by 2020. Agreeing that was one of the levers the EU could pull to lift itself from the enveloping economic crisis, it was nonetheless unlikely to be achieved. "A number of finance ministers are publicly stating they could not – and would not, invest more in research. You won't get there, Mr President", I boldly said.

He leaned forward. I went on to explain that Australia produced 3 per cent of the world's intellectual output. In some disciplines, much higher. I reminded him of our Nobel Prize winners, members of the Royal Society and citation rates. To go further, we needed to substantially lift our levels of international collaboration. If the EU was to get anywhere near its 3 per cent target, one device for doing so would be collaboration. I had his attention.

I proposed that Australia and the EU pool some of our research money into joint projects. This could be at both the researcher and institutional level. The specific projects to be funded would be selected on a peer reviewed basis by our respective scientific communities. We could jointly nominate areas for research collaboration. I suggested water resource management, agricultural productivity, energy efficiency, renewable energy and human adaptation to new and emerging technologies. Such a model would not only deepen co-operation between my country and the EU, it would leverage up our respective research spend. Though Australia's research budget was small in comparison, such a model applied to similar 'like-minded' countries, would be a 'win-win'.

He got it, telling me with some enthusiasm that he saw considerable potential in this idea. He instructed his staff to arrange for me to see the EU Commissioner for Research. Given the EU nations produce 38 per cent of the world's scientific papers and the European Commission has a budget for research and innovation exceeding 120 billion euros, the potential for Australia was – and remains – significant. When I debriefed our embassy staff, Dr Martin Gallagher, our indefatigable science counsellor, said, "Brendan, excellent science diplomacy". A new expression to me, but it sounded good.

When I arrived early in 2010, the EU's Lisbon Treaty had just taken effect. The European Parliament, an endless talkfest, now had teeth. It had power in almost 90 new areas. The EU now had a department of foreign affairs, the External Action Service. The first foreign minister was a former British MP, Catherine Ashton. The EU also had a seat at the G20 and speaking rights at the United Nations. Australia's 30 year approach to the EU was no longer tenable. As Kevin Rudd had said, we needed to engage.

Consistent with the strange way the EU works, it has two parliaments – one in Brussels, the second in Strasbourg. Once a month I flew to Strasbourg for the sittings, making sure I was in business class on the Monday morning flight. Almost always I was sitting next to a European Commissioner, the equivalent of a minister, establishing relationships. Having identified key parliamentarians, committees and office bearers, I met them all. I learned three things. Ambassadors paid little attention to them and they appreciated someone doing so. As I was a former politician with an impressive CV, they freely opened up to me. Australia was universally liked.

I found amongst these members of the European Parliament, those with distinguished careers in their home country. Some wielded immense influence in their nation's capital. It was an opportunity to skilfully shape thinking back from Brussels to Paris, Berlin, Rome and elsewhere. The best illustration of the strategic value in political appointees to diplomatic posts came in my quarterly visits to Luxembourg. The Prime Minister, Jean Claude Junker, had been in office for 15 years when we first met. An engaging man and heavy smoker, he gave me an hour in which I passively smoked the equivalent of two cigarettes. The things you do for your country!

Jean Claude Junker was also the Chairman of the Eurozone countries, those whose currency is the Euro. Europe was in meltdown in a financial crisis, Greece and other member states in serious, existential trouble. He said, "Brendan, I don't treat you like a diplomat. I treat you as one of us." At the end of the hour, back in the car I would immediately write down what had been discussed, turning it into a cable back in Brussels.

I similarly worked through the key ambassadors to NATO, very much enjoying my interactions with the United States Ambassador, Ivo Daalder. As a consequence of the Australia-US Alliance, Australia's role in Afghanistan and my relationship with Ivo, I frequently found myself at the United States NATO residence with the most senior people in the Obama administration. We could effectively get an insight into United States thinking and help shape it.

Our Defence Attaché was Major General Brian Dawson. Absolutely 'solid', ex SAS, straight as a gun barrel and possessed of a dry sense of humour. Brian did with his military counterparts what I did on the political side. We were an effective team. We could be more influential in shaping thinking in many European capitals from Brussels than in the member countries themselves. Those sent to NATO were the best their country had to offer at the highest political and military level.

Early in my Liberal leadership, I had told my colleagues things would turn against Rudd, and quickly when the electorate discovered the "10th defect." In my opinion, the 10th came in October 2009. A ship, the *Oceanic Viking*, carrying 78 Sri Lankan asylum seekers was effectively held hostage, moored off Indonesia. The month-long negotiations were shambolic, revealing inconsistencies as Kevin Rudd said he had "infinite patience". Then, in the middle of it all, on national television, Rudd said he wanted "a big Australia of 50 million people". Things were unravelling. The mining tax and obvious dysfunction of the government were exacting a heavy toll.

Former United States Secretary of State, Madeleine Albright was leading a group of experts developing a new Strategic Concept (White Paper) for NATO. It was difficult to get direction from Canberra. I made the decision there were three things Australia needed from NATO.

> First, we needed NATO to take a global approach to Euro-Atlantic security. The re-emergence of China into the Indo-Pacific and its strategic competition with the US, a region replete with deep, unresolved historical enmities,

> demanded NATO regard threats to its own security coming from anywhere.
>
> Second, we needed NATO to develop a template for immediately and easily engaging partner, non-NATO countries in its operations.
>
> Third, NATO needed a significant civilian capability. Whatever the Alliance did would require meaningful engagement with non-government bodies.

My deputy cautioned me against advocating any of this without direction from the Australian government. One of the enviable things about not caring if you are sacked, is that you can exercise your judgement. And I did, advocating this formally to the NATO leadership.

A month after our arrival, we had an unexpected drama. One Saturday morning, I returned to the residence from the supermarket. The front door was open and Gillian was highly agitated. I walked up and asked what the problem was. "The dogs are on the roof!" Incredulous, I laughed. "How on earth could the dogs get on the roof? Don't be bloody ridiculous". She led me down the stairs to the access road in front of our house and pointed up.

My God. Four floors up, standing on a small semi-circular 'roof' over the dining room balcony windows was Lucy. Her paws were at the edge as she looked down at us. Sniff was nowhere to be seen. It beggared belief. I asked Gillian how she knew they were there. She said there had been a knock on the door. A man from the top floor apartment on the other side of the street asked if we had two little white doggies. He told her they were up there.

It turned out they had got onto a back balcony from which they had run up a narrow access corridor onto the roof, five floors up. They then charged onto the steeply sloping front roof, fell off and landed on one of the small, semi-circular roofs above the Juliet balcony at the front. We then learned that in Belgium the fire brigade does not rescue animals. Nor is there a dedicated animal rescue service.

In the end I got a ladder. On the small Juliet balcony, it was close to vertical. I asked the chef, Peter, to hold it, very tightly. Without daring to look down I slowly made my way up. Lucy, the short-haired Jack Russell and smarter of the two, knew there was a 'problem' and fully co-operated. I grabbed her skin behind the neck and passed her down to Gillian. Sniff, however, was petrified. She was jammed up against the house, out of reach. I asked Gillian to pass up meat. I placed it half way across, within reach. Sniff didn't budge. "Pass me up a tablespoon of Peter's chicken liver pate". Gillian passed it up. I placed it again, half way across. Sure enough, Sniff edged out to the spoon. I left it until she was well into it and made my move. I knew I would only get one crack at this. I quickly reached out and grabbed a handful of loose skin on her back. I was resolute, prepared, for her to bite me but not to let go. I passed her down.

Slowly, step by step, I was back on the balcony. By this time, people were looking from windows opposite. A crowd had gathered at the gates. They cheered. I took the moment to raise my clasped hands to the appreciative audience. Our neighbours opposite came over to express their admiration. Jacques said, "We have photos of the rescue." I panicked, "Yes Jacques, but please tell me no social media!" He said he didn't know what that was!

As planned, I went to Flanders before Anzac Day. It would become the most spiritually meaningful part of my three years posting. It would provide the most hauntingly beautiful memories of my time serving Australia in Belgium. It would also inspire my next job.

Many people think Flanders is in France. It isn't. In this part of Belgium are buried 13,500 Australians killed in the First World War. Half have no known grave. Their names are etched into the Menin Gate, that magnificent, towering archway column built on the medieval wall of Ypres. I met the mayors and local officials, those who conduct services and commemorate the dead.

Ploegsteert is a Belgian village in the municipality of Comines-Warneton. It is the most westerly settlement of Wallonia. It was here I discovered a small cemetery where a year later I would have an epiphany. We went to the Prowse Point Cemetery, then a short distance on the narrow dirt road to 'Mud Corner' Cemetery. A truly Anzac cemetery, 84 Australians and New Zealanders are buried here.

We got out of the car and walked down a narrow country lane. In a lightly wooded forest, a Commonwealth War Graves cemetery appeared. The Toronto Avenue Cemetery. The shards of spring light pierced the trees onto 78 graves. All Australians, they had been killed over three days in the battle of Messines in June 1917, probably gassed. I resolved then that next year we would hold an Anzac Day service here in the late afternoon.

At the Buttes Cemetery, where the "tourism motivated' Dawn service was held, I walked up onto the Butte. This man-made 'hill' was constructed in the late 19th century. Originally used by the Belgian military for shooting practice, its height made it of critical strategic importance during the First World War. With much bloodshed, it had been taken by the Australian 5th Division on 26 September 1917. Standing beside the 5th Division's memorial, I surveyed the 1,700 headstones below of which 564 were Australians. Beyond the graves stood the New Zealand memorial, honouring 378 of its missing.

The following week at the embassy leadership meeting, I said, "Look, you're not going to like this. I am going to the Dawn Service at Polygon Wood. I will just go as myself and take Lady Nelson, but I'm going. I am not lying in bed on Anzac Day having someone else commemorate our war dead – as an Australian, let alone the Ambassador."

Straight away, "You can't go as a private citizen, you're the Ambassador. If you go, the Kiwis will have to go". "It's done then. I am going as the Australian Ambassador and you are all welcome to join me. I'll call the Kiwis." Richard Palk, the senior administrative officer who had been posted with me, ex-army, said, "Brendan, thank you".

I called the New Zealand Ambassador, Peter Kennedy. A career diplomat of the old school variety: "That's okay Brendan, I knew we couldn't hold out forever".

Just two days after an emotional Anzac Day, Kevin Rudd announced he was deferring his Emissions Trading Scheme. I was genuinely shocked. He had famously described it as "the greatest moral challenge of our generation". He had a double dissolution trigger he chose not to pull. Tony Abbott was doing a relentless job as Opposition leader pulling it apart, but Rudd walked away from what we understood was a 'core' belief. A million voters walked away from him.

Senator John Faulkner was Minister for Defence, one of the best and most respected. We were in the car headed out to NATO headquarters. He asked my opinion of the political environment at home.

> Well John, I'm not one of your voters. But for what it's worth, it would be madness to dump Rudd. You need to do a mea culpa on the mining tax, clean up the internal workings of the Cabinet processes, get your climate change story straight and put some people with grey hair into the PM's office. Presumably you will spend your war chest demonising Tony. Do all that and I think you'll win. If you dump Rudd now, you will alienate and outrage the people who love him.
>
> I'll tell you what your problem is. Two weeks ago, a couple of tradies arrived from Australia to work at the embassy. They walked into my office and were generous to me and then said, but as for your mate Rudd, never again. He's your classic home handyman. He's started a hundred jobs, he hasn't finished one of 'em and he's bullshitting to his missus about what's goin' on.

John said nothing, He didn't need to. Uncontested, Julia Gillard assumed the Labor leadership and became Prime Minister on 24 June.

The Last Post is played and wreaths are laid at the Menin Gate in Ieper (Ypres) at 8 o'clock every night. A few months into the job, my deputy came into my office and closed the door. A serious sign. "Brendan, I think we have a problem. You're going to the Menin Gate a lot. You have spent as much on wreaths in several months as your predecessor spent in three years":

> So, Rhonda, you think we might have a controversy? If so, let's hope it's tabloid, front page. Australians are rightly concerned about how their taxes are spent. But they like visiting the Menin Gate and seeing those beautiful green and gold flowers with the sash, *Laid on behalf of the people of Australia*". If I went to the Menin Gate every night for the three years I am here – and I wish I could – I would still only cover less than a third of the Australians named on the Menin Gate.

I kept going and I kept laying wreaths.

The European Parliament, like ours, displays artworks. I noticed a preponderance of theirs related to human rights, injustice and Europe's many dark historical chapters. Until you live in Europe, you don't appreciate how much war, especially the Second World War, is never far from the surface of political and social discourse.

When I arrived, there were three 'head turners' for the EU and Australia: Kevin Rudd's Apology to the 'stolen generations' of Aboriginal Australians; his new commitment to climate change action; and, Australia's engagement with China.

I proposed to Denis Richardson, Secretary of DFAT, that we gift the European parliament a large parchment displaying the words of the Apology. We could 'twin' it with a substantive piece of Aboriginal art. Both could hang in a prominent place in the Brussels chamber. He liked the idea and agreed to fund it.

The European Parliament was challenging. There was a push to ban the import of kangaroo meat. Cars commonly display signs with a joey in its mother's pouch to depict 'baby on board'. The culling of kangaroos was equated by some with the clubbing of seals in Canada. I worked the Parliament feverishly with our superb Agricultural counsellor, Matt Koval. To one meeting, I said, "There are 23 million people in Australia, but 50 million kangaroos. We have to cull them and are encouraged to do so at times by the RSPCA. They are also the most greenhouse gas friendly meat on earth". Axel Voss, a German centre-right MP piped up, "These kangaroos are like deer on springs then? You have to shoot them." The tide turned.

Having concluded a wine agreement, we moved on to a Passenger Name Record Agreement. The privacy committee of the Parliament had to approve it and, of course, we had to negotiate it with the European Commission. This is information collected about passengers at intervals just before they fly. It detects pedophile sex tourists, drug traffickers, terrorists and other criminals. The EU's negotiator was Reinhard Pribe, a German national and jurist. An hour into one of our meetings I kept probing him on Australia's compliance responsibilities. He stopped: "Ambassador, I have been negotiating agreements for the European Commission for twenty years. We are not accustomed to parties actually intending to do what they sign up for." To which I replied, "Well, we're Australians. We say what we mean and we mean what we say."

Within months, I could see a way through with the EU. The only language everyone spoke in Brussels was Treaty with a capital 'T'. I recommended we negotiate a Treaty Framework Agreement. Apart from formally setting out areas of common interest and rules by which each party would engage, it was an essential precondition for a Free Trade Agreement. My advice was accepted and I co-drafted the cabinet submission.

We would expand our relationship into five key areas: Defence – Security and Intelligence; Trade – Economic and G20 issues; Aid and development assistance; Environment and climate change; Research, technology and innovation.

Julia Gillard scraped back into government with the support of the two independents in the August 2010 election. She came to Brussels in October for the Asia Europe Meeting (ASEM). The Treaty Framework Agreement scoping study and negotiations would be announced.

She was impressive. On our way to NATO to meet the Secretary General, I told her what was not in her brief. Post Albright, I had been pressing NATO to adopt a global approach to Euro-Atlantic security along with the partners' template and civilian capability. She agreed it made sense. At the meeting she raised these issues with Rasmussen who agreed. "Your Ambassador has proposed these", he said. When Gillard spoke to it at the joint press conference, I turned to our DFAT staff, "you've now got the policy".

Julia Gillard did nine bilateral meetings with heads of state in different parts of Brussels in a day. The official ASEM meeting was at the palace. The side meetings were in one of the large ballroom corridors, impromptu lounge chairs and couches arranged a little like an airport lounge. The French President, Nicholas Sarkozy, walked towards us at the assigned time for our meeting. Wearing an unhappy face, he abruptly diverted away to a window, engaged in deep, animated conversation. I left Gillard and our group to investigate.

The chief of staff explained that President Sarkozy was very unhappy with the arrangements. He thought that meeting like this in a corridor was beneath the two leaders. Given German Chancellor Angela Merkel had just met us, I didn't see the problem, but I could see what was at stake, headlines – "Australian prime minister snubbed by French president".

I brushed past the chief of staff, directly to Sarkozy. I introduced myself, "Mr President, I appreciate that this is not an ideal ambience, suited to a meeting for someone of your standing. But as a man, I ask you please not to disappoint a lady, my prime minister." I could see his mind ticking over as the translation went through. He smiled, "Oui!" The two had a very agreeable meeting.

Julia Gillard asked me what the diplomatic job was like. "It's like politics without party branch meetings, fund-raisers, backstabbers and the media". She thought it sounded, "Pretty good." She also asked me if I had any advice to offer. I told her the 'home handyman' story in relation to Kevin Rudd. I said, "You need to decide three things you want to do for Australia and govern like you've got a twenty seat majority. What you want for Australia will not be what I want, but if you've got more than three priorities, you don't have any".

After two days of frenetic work and having personally thanked all our staff for their work, she changed into casual clothes. At my suggestion, she walked to the magnificent Grand Place, medieval square. She was photographed buying frittes (chips) and, for it, hammered by sections of the Australian media for having a holiday.

The Toronto Avenue Cemetery, Flanders (Belgium), Anzac Day 2011. The Federation Guard stands at the stone of remembrance, the crowd lining the perimeter of the small cemetery. All 78 of the men buried here are Australians, killed over three days in the battle of Messine in 1917. Peter Pickering, who drove the commemorative crosses programme, stands wearing the AIF First World War uniform at the rear, closest to me. Peter died three years later. I told him three days before his death, “Peter, your legacy will live. I have ordered 100,000 crosses for the Australian War Memorial. Inscribed by students, they will be placed on Australian graves in 39 countries.

At the Menin Gate with Gillian, October 2018, and the Last Post Association and Buglers. The evening honorary citizenship of Ieper (Ypres) was conferred. Many of the most moving experiences of my public life I had here.

My great friend, Lee Kernaghan, with the Wolfe Brothers in the cloisters of the Australian War Memorial next to the Roll of Honour. An emotional tour of the Memorial in June 2103. The day the Spirit of the Anzacs was conceived.

With two men I greatly admire, Ben Roberts Smith VC MG and Kerry Stokes AC, in the commemorative area of the Australian War Memorial 2014.

With Mark Donaldson VC in 2014 front of the Afghanistan panel which I had just relocated onto the 'main wall'. A true hero, the Roll of Honour and mates named on it, means more than anything to him.

The opening of the First World War Galleries, Australian War Memorial, 2014. Explaining the powerful symbolism of Gilbert Doble's 'Winged Victory', to former Prime Minister, John Howard, Governor General, Sir Peter Cosgrove, and Lady Lyn Cosgrove.

Introducing John Schuman and Hugh Macdonald to perform 'I was only 19' in the Hall of Memory to 103 Vietnam veterans, 17 August 2016. Desperately ill, it was Hugh's final public performance before his death.

At the launch of the Afghanistan Exhibition, Australian War Memorial, August 2013. My wife Gillian, Opposition Leader Tony Abbott, Prime Minister Kevin Rudd and Therese Rein, all of us laughing. Chief of Defence, General David Hurley, following my address in which I said that the nation would soon need to make a generational investment in the Australian War Memorial to create the space to tell the stories of a young generation of veterans, responded by saying, "Well Brendan, you'll have to get in line for funding behind me".

26

An Epiphany – "you cannot imagine my emotions"

Months into the posting, a letter arrived under the letterhead, *Sons of the British Empire.* The author, unknown to me, was Peter Pickering. An occupational therapist at the Royal Hobart Hospital, he described how he and volunteers made wooden crosses in their sheds and garages. They would dress in First World War uniforms, visit senior primary school students and speak of young Australians who fought and died on the Western Front. Each student would be given a wooden cross upon which they would write their name and school on one side and a commemorative message on the other.

Mr Pickering asked if I could help. The Department of Veterans Affairs had declined any assistance and the Tasmanian government had advised him it was 'broke', unable to support a $500 grant. In my reply, I offered to become patron of the group, should it be helpful. I also enclosed a personal cheque for $500 and told him that if he sent the crosses over, we could have them placed on Australian graves during major commemorative events. He accepted all three offers on behalf of his members with much enthusiasm.

I was better prepared for my second Anzac Day in Flanders. The ceremonies began at Polygon Wood and Buttes Cemetery with the full Australian and New Zealand contingents present for the Dawn service. Peter Pickering and his fellow volunteers were present in their First World War, AIF uniforms. Several had come from the UK. The evening before they lovingly laid out 564 poppy crosses inscribed by Australian children on the stone of remembrance. The service was conducted on the lawn around the stone, 350 attendees gathering around it, serenely standing among the headstones.

As the sun pierced the darkness and backlit the 5th Division memorial above the Buttes, I returned to the microphone. I explained the crosses laid on the stone of remembrance and invited the Australians present to come forward, take a cross and place it on an Australian grave. It was intensely emotional. In the early morning light, through a faint mist, as three Defence Force singers sang *The Green Fields of France* and *The Band Played Waltzing Matilda,* they wandered, each carrying a single cross through the cemetery. I saw some spontaneously weep reading the child's inscription. Having found a grave, many took a photograph to send back to the school in Australia.

The power of simplicity.

As I had committed, we held an afternoon Anzac Day service at the small, all Australian Toronto Avenue Cemetery. The Australian ceremonial Federation Guard had come from France, supported by local Belgian veterans groups. About 150 pilgrims gathered around the perimeter on a beautiful spring day. Again, Peter Pickering's group had provided 78 crosses to be placed on each grave in this all Australian cemetery.

The most important things in life seem to be funded by cake stalls and raffles. One such group I discovered when Minister for Defence, 'Families and Friends of the First AIF' (FFFAIF). With no minister attending Anzac ceremonies in Flanders, I would deliver the address. I wrote to the FFFAIF asking if one of its historians could send me a profile of six men buried at Toronto Avenue Cemetery. I chose one, largely because it was an unremarkable, typically Australian story:

> John Stannon Luff was born in 1887 in Fremantle, Western Australia. A gardener for the Fremantle municipality, in 1908 he was appointed caretaker of the Fremantle Oval. He married the love of his life, Ruby McLaughlin, in 1911. They lived under the grandstand at the Fremantle Oval (Victoria Pavilion), producing three children – Eric, Ron and May.
>
> John Luff enlisted in the AIF in March 1916. He would fight in France and Belgium, writing eleven letters home to Ruby.

> John Luff was killed on 7 June 1917. He was thirty years old.
>
> The Ugly Men's Association volunteers built Ruby a house. She moved into it with the children in July 1918 and lived there until her death on 26 May 1968.

So, on Anzac Day 2011, at this first service at Toronto Avenue, I told John Luff's story. But I also had a photograph sent me by the FF-FAIF – John Luff in his uniform and Ruby in her 'Sunday best' with children Eric, Ron and May in front of them.

I enlarged and laminated the photo, inscribing the rear:

> To Jack and Ruby.
> In immense admiration and appreciation.
> Brendan Nelson
> Australian Ambassador. Anzac Day 2011

I placed the photograph on the grave next to the commemorative cross, and we left.

Three weeks later I received a letter from Mr Roland Rayfield, of Bicton, Western Australia, written just after Anzac Day.

> Dear Dr Nelson,
>
> My wife and I are pensioners and have not been overseas before. I wanted to visit my grandfather's grave before I die. We were in Belgium recently. We went to the Toronto Avenue Cemetery on Sunday the 8th of May. For the first time I visited the grave site of my grandfather, John Stannon Luff. It was an extremely emotional moment. What we saw on the grave completely blew us away. You cannot imagine my emotions approaching my grandfather's grave to find on it a photograph of my grandfather, grandmother and their three children, one of whom is my mother. On the reverse is a hand written note from yourself. To find something like that placed on the grave site was totally unexpected and enormously enhanced the emotion of our experience. Of course, we left the grave as we found it.

To the letter he attached a photo of himself and his wife holding the photograph in front of John Luff's grave. Overcome, I immediately phoned Mr Rayfield at home in Western Australia. Having forgiven me for waking him, we both emotionally discussed his grandfather, mother and the extraordinary serendipity of what had transpired. Our paths would cross again.

In 2011 I was invited to address the NATO leadership conference at its facility in Oberammergau, Germany, a high-powered lineup of NATO leadership and partner countries. I decided to tell them what they needed to hear. Australia's history, who we are, sacrifices made in Europe across two world wars and the values that inform and define us. I was often asked why Australia was "so committed" to the Afghanistan campaign. In short, the murder of 3,000 people on September 11, then 88 Australians murdered in Bali and our view that leaving the fight to the US, British and a handful of others would be delusional, an abrogation of our responsibilities to fight radical fundamentalism.

I also criticised NATO. Australia, a non-NATO member, was doing more in Afghanistan than more than half the NATO members. Yet we were often denied a place at the decision making table. I prosecuted the need for NATO to see that trouble coming from the Indo-Pacific would threaten Euro-Atlantic security. Word got out that the Australians were not happy campers.

The Russian ambassador to NATO, Dimitry Rogozin, called. He invited Gillian and me to his residence. We arrived at the stately residence for dinner a couple of weeks later, the only guests. He and his wife, Tatyana, were charming. We accepted the shot of "Russia's best vodka" before dinner. Fortunately, the diplomatic scene makes you a seasoned drinker, so we managed a couple of glasses of wine as well. We discussed geopolitical issues, including Russia's Kuril Islands dispute with Japan. Then Tatyana sang for us with recorded musical support. She was good. Dimitry then showed us a You Tube video they had recorded on the grounds of the residence. It had to that point received 35,000 views. Filmed at night with Tatyana singing, ringed by exploding fireworks, Dimitry was dancing around behind her with an AK-47! We loved it.

Not being enthusiasts for New Year's Eve parties, we wanted to do something meaningful in 2011, so we went to the Menin Gate. It was eight degrees below zero, a still, starry night. There were only 20 people at the Last Post Ceremony, half of them from Western Australia. Afterwards we had a glass of champagne with the buglers and officials under the Gate. I slowly walked along the panels bearing the names of the 6,192 Australians, paying my quiet tribute.

Kevin Rudd was now Julia Gillard's Foreign Minister. He had come to Brussels for a meeting of the Friends of Democratic Pakistan in October 2010, just before Julia Gillard's visit. He seemed despondent, struggling with loss of his prime ministership. But, as always, he worked hard. I felt a little sorry for him. He and his Chief of Staff, Philip Green, had got off the plane in Paris and driven to Brussels via the cemeteries in Flanders. By January 2012, when he came to address the political and military leadership on Asia-Pacific issues, he was energised. We went to NATO headquarters. He had written a speech and asked if he should read it or simply speak. I suggested a bit of both. I sat next to him at the head of the table, sixty chiefs of defence, ministers and NATO ambassadors seated with their contingents.

Kevin Rudd spoke and took questions for an hour. Sitting next to him as he authoritatively spoke to the rapidly changing Indo-Pacific, China's rise, US-China relations, ASEAN, Australia's concerns and why NATO needed to turn its attention to the region, I was proud to be an Australian. Rudd was not just good, he was stunningly impressive. Our DFAT security counsellor said to me the next day, "It's a pity you can't keep him in a cupboard and just take him out and point him when you need to." How true.

Several years later, when he was bidding for UN Secretary General, I publicly supported his ambition. I had seen what he could do. He always had a plan for the world.

The EU's 'foreign minister', Catherine Ashton, came to the residence for a one-on-one dinner with me. An intelligent, hard working woman with no sense of self-aggrandisement, she recognised the increasingly important role Australia played in the Indo-Pacific. The EU wanted membership of the East Asia Summit. Australia was not supportive of this and she wanted to know why. The United States, Russia and China are members.

The EU loves membership of multilateral fora. It was already a member of the ASEAN Regional Forum (ARF) but rarely turned up at the most senior level. To put it delicately, I said, "Catherine, diplomacy in Asia is like marriage – making it work is hard. But like marriage, one of the essential pre-conditions is you have to turn up".

She raised another sensitive issue, Foreign Minister Kevin Rudd. "Brendan, Kevin calls me a lot. He often rings late at night, on the phone for a very long time covering all kinds of issues". I was Australia's ambassador, chosen by Kevin himself. It was not my job to undermine confidence in my minister. How could I put this in terms she would understand?

"Catherine, you are a former politician, you understand these things. Kevin Rudd was, and remains, the most popular prime minister ever in Australia's modern polling history. In less than three years his own colleagues removed him from the job before he could face another election. That takes a lot of skill." She reflected on that through a long silence.

NATO was a constant battle, to ensure we were included in key Afghanistan meetings. In the lead-up to the 2012 NATO summit in Chicago, at a March meeting of ISAF, the full 49 countries fighting in Afghanistan discussed arrangements for the meeting. I listened carefully. The 'Stans' nations surrounding Afghanistan were to be invited along with Russia. NATO needed co-operation from Afghanistan's neighbours and Russian facilitated land access. That made sense, but I was suspicious. I pressed my 'call' button.

"Secretary General, while recognising the reason for inviting those countries to the summit, could you please confirm that there will be a meeting for only the leaders of the ISAF nations fighting in, and contributing to the Afghanistan campaign?"

The answer was evasive. I pressed my button again. I asked the same question. This time, he awkwardly confirmed there would be no separate meeting – all nations would attend and address the one meeting only.

> I pressed my button.
>
> Secretary General, I wish to record Australia's strongest possible opposition to the proposed arrangements for Chicago. We are not a NATO member, yet we are the 3rd largest Special Forces contributor, the 9th largest overall contributor to the war. We are fighting and dying in the south and we have committed over a billion dollars for building Afghan forces and development assistance. When the Australian Prime Minister goes to Chicago, the Australian people expect she will be able to speak openly and directly to the leaders of nations that are actually fighting.
>
> We are pissed off!
>
> By the way, I thought Russia was a bit of issue for NATO.

You could hear a pin drop. I glanced to the booths where interpreters were pushing my words out to ambassadors. Ambassadors looked at one another and at me, more than a few in delighted approval. I turned to Brian Dawson, "Mate, can you call the PM's office? Tell them what I've said, why and ask for instructions." Brian returned and passed me my instructions from the PM's defence and security advisor. I pushed my button again and waited for the call.

"Secretary General, just to reinforce and be clear about Australia's position, my specific instructions from Canberra are to, and I quote – *keep sticking it into the bastards!*"

At the meeting's conclusion, we were overwhelmed with ambassadors, especially but not only from Eastern Europe, offering support. In Chicago, NATO had a discussion only for leaders of countries fighting in Afghanistan.

We were the first non-NATO country to negotiate a High Level Political Declaration, the Secretary General coming to Australia in June 2012 to sign it. This formally recognised the co-operative relationship extending through military, intelligence and security dimensions. To the National Press Club, Anders Rasmussen said:

> Geography and distance no longer protect us. No country or continent can be insulated against global challenges – or deal with them on their own. So, NATO-Australian cooperation … makes perfect sense. We are like-minded and we are single minded when it comes to security.

We had achieved what I had set out to do.

Early in 2012, two years into the posting, the Gillard Government felt me out about an extension of my three years to four. I was very appreciative. I enjoyed the job very much, but felt that if I did four years I would just be doing the third year again. It would be time to go home.

I was regularly being asked what I would do when I returned to Australia. I didn't know, but said to Gillian, "Whatever I do when I go back, I want to do something meaningful. The medical profession and taxpayers have invested a lot in me. I just feel I have more public service in me."

Just weeks later, in March 2012, I received a call from Ross Bain. A Labor-oriented public servant, Ross was Chief of Staff to Veterans Affairs minister, Warren Snowden. A good man I had worked with previously, he wanted me to look after a VIP on Anzac Day. We went on to discuss other portfolio issues. I asked how Steve Gower was, Director of the Australian War Memorial. I knew his wife was ill. Ross became animated. "Have you read *The Canberra Times?*"

"Ross, I don't read the bloody *Canberra Times*, and certainly not from Brussels."

He went on. "There's a lot of controversy about Steve. He's retiring and we've advertised the job. We're happy to appoint a non-military, non-historian as director and all these people are angry about it." I digested what he was saying. "A non-military, non-historian?"

He confirmed it. When I hung up, I immediately googled the job application and filled it in.

Peter Costello asked me how I got the job at the Australian War Memorial. "Peter, a very strange and novel experience. I filled in an application, went for an interview and they rang three weeks later to tell me I got the job." I did, but there is more to the story.

I had two conversations with the head hunter engaged to find the new Memorial Director. At the end of the second, she told me that I was "not likely to get an interview as there was a high quality field." I had no experience in the cultural sector. My first reaction was disappointment, then annoyance. Why couldn't she have avoided wasting my time and hers by just tell me straight up? I moved on from hoping I might be considered for the job at the Memorial. Then, at the NATO summit in Chicago, Julia Gillard said, "Brendan, I just want you to know that I'm very happy about the Australian War Memorial."

I had no idea what she was talking about. I thought it referred to ideas I had proposed for the centenary of the First World War and started talking about Menin Gate Lions. She looked at me perplexed, "No, Warren (Veterans Affairs Minister) told me you applied for the job. I just want you to know I am happy about it."

A week later, the departmental secretary called and asked if I would come back to Australia for an interview. Something had happened, I had obviously been added to the shortlist.

Not everyone was happy. One person closely associated with the process asked, "Dr Nelson, do you know much about museums?" I said that I didn't, but had visited a few. He asked me if I had ever run one. Of course, I hadn't. I could see where it was going.

> If you are looking for an expert for this role, my advice is not to. As I understand it, there are 300 people who work at the Australian War Memorial, all experts who have forgotten more than I will ever know. But I have learned something about experts, from my time in the medical pro-

> fession through everything I've done since. They see the world through a straw.
>
> This job as I understand it, and I have been in this position before, is to not only manage the Memorial, but also to be a leader of it and ambassador for it.
>
> The key task in these roles is to remain true to its vision, to apply intellectual rigour to the process of exercising judgement, drawing on all the expertise both within and outside the institution.

Chaired by the Public Service Commissioner, my name was recommended by the selection committee to Cabinet.

Like Roland Rayfield approaching his grandfather's grave at Toronto Avenue Cemetery, you 'cannot imagine my emotions' when the Secretary called to offer me the job. Before the appointment was publicly announced, I confided in a small number of close friends.

Rhondda Vanzella by this time was planning the re-enactment of a First World War recruitment drive through regional NSW – the Kangaroo March. She was exhilarated. Doug Thompson literally cried with joy. Bruce Shepherd on the other hand said, "What? You're going to run the Australian War Memorial. You're wasting your life. You've got far more important things to do for Australia than rearrange its history." I was hurt by this, but that was Bruce. "Bruce, if you can find something in life that you love and get paid for it, surely that's mission accomplished. More importantly, the world is changing very quickly in uncertain ways. This has more to do with our future than it does our past. We have to be clear about who we are".

I travelled to Afghanistan in October 2012 with the NATO Secretary General. An Australian soldier said, "Sir, thanks for lookin' after the family jewels". I correctly interpreted this as referring to my appointment to run the Australian War Memorial. "I take my son to the War Memorial when I'm home. I can show him what his great grandfather and grandfather did, but why can't I show him what I'm doing?"

I didn't know, but undertook to find out.

I was especially humbled when I left the embassy for the final time. The Belgian staff lined the foyer and clapped me out in gratitude. Simply wonderful people who had supported me and worked so hard for our country.

On our last night in Belgium, Gillian and I went to the Menin Gate. It is here that I had the most meaningful experiences of my posting. The 10 Scottish pipe bands playing *Highland Cathedral;* six female students from Goondiwindi High School reciting the Ode in unison – each with a relative named on the panels; the girl who bought an old bugle and taught herself to play the Last Post – which she did at the Menin Gate; the Australian national anthem sung by three female uniformed Defence Force singers on Anzac Day, so many memories.

As the ceremony was about to commence and as I looked across to the Australian panel, Chairman, Benoit Mottrie leaned over: "Ambassador, this is your 74th visit. We didn't count at first, but we noticed you coming more often than any ambassador ever."

I whispered, "Benoit, if the Menin Gate was in Brussels instead of a 90 minute drive to Ieper, I would have come every night." I would return again and again in the years to come.

27

Thank you for making my son's life mean something

I arrived at the Australian War Memorial the week before Christmas 2012. Two assistant directors welcomed me. The third, responsible for the national collection, resigned effective the day before I started. Chairman of the Council, Rear Admiral Ken Doolan AO (Retd), also came in to welcome me. A tall man of impeccable integrity, Ken retired from a life of service to the Navy as its Deputy Chief. He was also the national president of the RSL (Returned and Services League of Australia) and one of the finest men with whom I would ever work.

My predecessor, Steve Gower, was less than enthusiastic about my appointment. "You've never done any project management, have you?" He shot at me. "No, I haven't … but I have had to clean up after people who have", I replied dryly.

A Vietnam veteran, Major General, historian and engineer, Steve Gower had towered over the Memorial for 16 years. He had run it in a military fashion, overseen construction of the Hall of Valour and Anzac Hall, secured the money and commenced early planning for the First World War Gallery redevelopment. Early in his tenure, he sorted out the Memorial's finances. For this and more, I admired him. But when I arrived, it was a very quiet pond.

I made my way from the administration building to the Memorial. Some history is important. What many don't appreciate is that the Australian War Memorial has three primary functions.

It is a Memorial, with the pool of reflection, cloaked by bronze panels in cloisters, listing the names of 102,800 Australians whose lives have been given for us in war and now also, peacekeeping and humanitarian operations. Beneath the byzantine inspired dome above the Hall of Memory, since 1993, has been interred the Unknown Australian Soldier.

It is also a museum: galleries filled with artefacts and relics, from deeply personal possessions to planes and a ship's bridge, telling the stories of those who have given their all for our nation.

And it is an archive: letters, postcards, maps, documents, photographs and much more are conserved and stored in the research centre, housed in a cavernous library.

Australia's First World War official correspondent was Charles Bean. He landed on Gallipoli on 25 April 1915 and stayed with the Australians at the front through to the Armistice in November 1918. Wounded three times, he refused evacuation.

At Pozieres, France, in July and August 1916, he was witness to 23,000 Australian casualties in six weeks – 6,800 dead, five Australians awarded the Victoria Cross. "No place on earth", he wrote, "is more thickly sown with Australian sacrifice". It was here that a mortally wounded Australian asked of Bean, "Will they remember me in Australia?" From there he conceived and resolved that at the war's end, he would build the "finest memorial and museum to these men of the AIF and the nurses".

The Australian War Memorial officially opened on 11 November 1941, with a second, even greater cataclysm unfolding. Bean articulated his vision for the Australian War Memorial in 1948:

> *Here is their spirit in the heart of the land they loved, and here we guard the record which they themselves made.*

I stood in the commemorative area looking up to the Dome above the Hall of Memory. I asked the retiring infrastructure manager, "Do you think it possible to project names at night onto the horizontal beam just below the Dome?" He thought so.

I walked up to the Roll of Honour and remembered something haunting from the Tyne Cot Cemetery in Flanders. There I had heard a young woman's voice reciting names of the dead. Slowly passing the rows and rows of names on the Roll of Honour, I pondered the possibility of similarly getting children to record these.

The bronze place names of where Australians have fought ended with Vietnam. I imagined the impact on young servicemen and women visiting to place a poppy on the Afghanistan, Iraq or East Timor Roll of Honour. The Afghanistan Roll of Honour was not on the 'main wall', but behind one of the pillar arches.

I made my way into the museum to contemporary conflicts. I asked a guide, "Where do I find Afghanistan?" She said there was no exhibition. With the soldier in Afghanistan's words ringing in my ears, I was deflated to find the only item – albeit impressive, was a long range patrol vehicle used by the SAS that had been hit by a bomb. I placed myself in the shoes of these young Australian veterans, near nothing of their stories told.

I looked at the Peacekeeping gallery. Close to 40,000 Australians had served in 64 peacekeeping missions. Some, such as Rwanda and Somalia worse than wars, yet the space was less than a standard 7-11 store.

A Last Post Ceremony was held at the end of the day in the commemorative area. I went across. Behind a lectern at the pool side, a staff member read the history of the Last Post which was then played. I had an idea. We could do something substantial and meaningful with this.

The following day, I met the managers and Assistant Directors. "When are we doing Afghanistan?" I asked. A prolonged silence was broken by one of the then assistant directors. "Director, it will be at least a decade, probably more. We have no money, we have no space. We have to wait until the war is over and all the troops have returned."

I couldn't believe what I was hearing.

"We've got 30,000 young Australians coming back to a country that's got no idea what they have done and the impact it has had on them. They can't explain it to their families, let alone the rest of Australia. We have to tell their stories and we have to do it now."

"If we'd told the story of the Vietnam War broadly and deeply in the late seventies, perhaps some of those men might not have suffered as much as they have."

I was on a mission.

I didn't have a holiday that year. Instead, I spent January in my office, poring over the financials, staffing profiles and thinking about the year ahead. The commemorative role of the Memorial needed to be turbocharged, the First World War Galleries shaped into something truly special and come hell or high water, an Afghanistan exhibition.

Walking into the Memorial in late January, an irate woman accosted me. "Dr Nelson, I want to report a girl doing handstands and cartwheels along the Roll of Honour". I could see a pair of legs moving just behind the 'Northern France' arch. Resisting my school prefect instincts, I gently said to her, "Madam, I think that all those young men whose names she is passing would smile with delight to think there is youthful joy here. It is an age appropriate way to celebrate life denied to them but for which they gave theirs." She said nothing and turned away.

It was on this day I made two discoveries.

I had been passing a table with six folded 'blankets' on it for weeks. Just inside the entrance on a table, I thought they were nurses' blankets. I stopped to inspect them, surprised when I touched one. Sculptured marble funeral shrouds. Each bore the name of an Australian killed in Afghanistan, an artwork by Alex Seton, inspired by a news headline, *Six more killed in Afghanistan.* When I realised this, I asked the staff to commission one 'shroud' for every Australian killed in Afghanistan.

Entering the Hall of Memory I noticed, hanging on the wall just outside the entrance, a framed poster, Paul Keating's poignant "Eulogy for the Unknown Australian Soldier", delivered at the interment in the Hall of Memory on Remembrance Day, 1993. It looked shabby, like something stuck up in a teenager's bedroom. This year would mark the 20th anniversary of the eulogy. We should do something special to mark it, to give reverence and permanence to arguably the nation's most towering piece of oratory.

Sarah Hitchcock was the Head of Commemoration and Visitor Engagement. Like people from regional Australia, she was organised and down to earth. Amidst a myriad of things, she and her team spend all year planning Anzac Day. She briefed me on the plans. I asked who was giving the Dawn service address. "Oh, the RSL always invites the padre to do it. The ceremony is run by the ACT branch of the RSL."

I was surprised. The National Memorial provides the venue for the televised service but did not control the content. Although I had attended Anzac Day services all of my life, never one at the Australian War Memorial. I asked Sarah for a video to watch. I arranged to meet the padre giving the Dawn Service address to get a 'feel' for it. For the national ceremony mid-morning, which included the march, Sarah said the choice of speaker was mine. She told me I should do it. I would check with Ken Doolan.

I watched a video of the 2012 ceremony attended by 25,000 people. I canvassed views. When the third person said, "Brendan, we stopped going because our kids are just looking at someone's bum", I knew it was time for change.

I met the padre. His speech was already written. He would speak about Australians captured by the Turks. "I have a great story about two Aussies picking over 200 body lice from one another". My heart sank. As delicately as I could, I said, "Look, we invaded Turkey at the behest of the Brits, it turned out to be a disaster for which the Turks have forgiven us. But dredging over these things might not be the best approach. Perhaps Padre, a focus on families?"

I then thought how to enhance the service.

The first thing to do was get screens erected so that people could see what was actually going on. As people were arriving from 2.30am to 'get a good spot', having uniformed personnel read excerpts from diaries and letters to the crowd would create an emotional, meaningful ambience. We would start at 4.30am. Australia had four living Victoria Cross recipients. I would invite Ben Roberts-Smith to read reflections from 5am until 5.15 when all the lights would go down into silence until the service commenced at 5.30am.

I asked Ben to canvass those serving in Afghanistan or recently returned for their reflections. He also asked Keegan Locke and Elle Lou Diddams whose SAS fathers respectively were killed in Afghanistan.

Looking at the Memorial's façade, it could be used as a canvass. We could project images from the archive onto the front of the Memorial all night. From the Boer War to Afghanistan, these evocative images would provide a rich visual sense of sacrifice and purpose.

The Memorial Council liked all of this. When announced, though, many expressed outrage, ventilating their condemnation through *The Canberra Times,* social media and letters to relevant ministers.

In January, sitting in my office looking across to Parliament House, I was thinking about the resumption of parliament. The events that preceded it included an ecumenical service. I had always attended, but wondered how Julia Gillard, an avowed atheist, would deal with it. Another idea.

I immediately wrote to Julia Gillard and Opposition leader, Tony Abbott. I proposed they attend the Australian War Memorial and symbolically lay a wreath together at the Tomb of the Unknown Australian Soldier. Both readily accepted. We did not promulgate what was happening. When Julia and Tony arrived, walked up the steps of the Memorial together, people spontaneously applauded. Such is the uniting power of the Memorial and the belief of the average Australian in it. The great privilege, opportunity and responsibility bestowed on me in leadership of the Memorial was laid bare.

The only space for an Afghanistan exhibition was one being used by volunteers. Using desk-top computers, they helped members of the public research their family history. From this area, people walked into the cavernous research centre and professional staff. I was warned that moving the online gallery volunteers would not be easy. It wasn't. There was stout resistance. "I have been doing this for ten years", one said, "and not a single person has ever asked me about Afghanistan". Letters again to the local paper and ministers.

Weeks after raising an Afghanistan exhibition, I was told it would take three years and several million dollars. Surely it could not be this hard. I was new to all this and remember saying in response, "Karen Middleton is at SBS. The executive producer says, Karen, we want to do a story on Afghanistan. You've got two researchers and we go to air in three weeks. I sit down to watch it, impressed. Why does it take so long here?"

The reason is that the exhibitions were, as Bean himself envisaged, based entirely on the collection. It took time to find and choose artefacts, get the human stories, select artworks, design and build cases.

Frustrated, I reached out to acclaimed journalist, Chris Masters, who had done a lot of work in Afghanistan. He came and worked with our professional staff, a perfect marriage. "I want you to interview young veterans across three services, DFAT and AUSAID staff, widows and families. In this exhibition, I want them to see, hear and feel something of themselves. We will use artefacts, relics and artworks to round it out". I asked DFAT officers in Afghanistan to record Afghans speaking to what the Australian presence meant to them.

To present the central issues, I commissioned a 10-minute piece explaining why we went to Afghanistan, why we stayed and were so committed to the war. I particularly wanted film footage of Prime Minister Julia Gillard saying, "This is a war with a purpose and a war with an end."

One of the curators came to me, "Director, we found the Gillard footage you want but we can't use it". Thinking this madness, I asked why. "The only footage is from the ABC's *7.30 Report* and, of course, we can't use that". "Of course, we can. I'll call Mark Scott (managing director of the ABC) and ask him". "No director, we only use material in our collection or borrowed from another institution. We can't use footage from public television".

I asked who had decided that. She told me it was "Director's instruction". I said, "Okay, you've got a new instruction. We're going to use whatever we need from whatever source to tell the stories of Australian service and sacrifice. This is a new world."

We needed money. I asked the country president of Boeing, Ian Thomas. “Ian, we desperately need an Afghanistan exhibition and I need money, half a million dollars”. He said, “I’ll need to get my boss out”. He did, and Boeing made the exhibition possible.

One of my first tasks was to write a foreword for the Ben Quilty catalogue. Ben had deployed to Afghanistan for a month in October 2011 as the Official War Artist. His commission was not to paint the battlefield, but instead depict the impact of the war on those sent to fight it. It was a transformative year for him, having won the Archibald Prize earlier in 2011.

I looked at the images of his paintings. They looked like nothing normally associated with the Australian War Memorial. I asked, “What do the subjects think?” I was reassured they “loved” them.

I went out to our storage facilities to meet Ben and show some of the works before they went to Sydney. The opening was at the National Art School in April 2013. Ben looked like he was straight out of 2 Commando – tall, bearded and fit. He lacked the airs and graces of many in the art world. Down to earth. I liked him. Afghanistan, the men and women he painted, had changed him in ways he was only beginning to appreciate. I naively asked why the Quilty exhibition was opening in Sydney, touring through a myriad of small regional galleries before coming to the Memorial three years later. When I was told it was a ‘space’ issue, I blew my top, threatening to bring my own tools in to “clear a wall in a morning”. I couldn’t believe it. I later discovered reluctance at the leadership level to hang the confronting works at the Memorial. The tour was ‘renegotiated’ and *After Afghanistan* came to the Memorial a year later.

The opening in Sydney was packed. A number of the subjects were present – soldiers, a badly damaged SAS Sergeant and an Air Commodore living with PTS. The family of a young soldier had driven from Townsville. Proud, they had shown courage in allowing themselves to be so painted. Quilty had asked them to remove their clothes for the sittings, to ‘fully reveal themselves’. Ben kept contact with his subjects, going on to mentor and support others, especially commandos. He changed them and they changed him.

We filled the assistant director position for the national collection in March with Tim Sullivan, CEO of the Sovereign Hill museum. I wanted someone from outside the conventional museum sector. We needed to get the flat-lined, visitor numbers up. Tim embraced the role with reformist gusto.

By March 2013, we were well advanced in progressing the Last Post Ceremony. Like pretty much everything, I had an idea but no money. Seeking a financial partner for something as sensitive as a Last Post Ceremony is no mean feat. I wanted to install and operate a webcam to stream the service.

I approached the New South Wales RSL and Services Clubs. They would be recognised in the introductory script and, of course, they could broadcast the ceremony into their clubs. They embraced it immediately. RSL Queensland and RSL Victoria came on board. These three groups made it possible. To them Australia owes a great debt.

We started 'softly' in late March and 'played around' with it until satisfied with the content and order. When I was comfortable we had it right, the date was set for the first official Last Post Ceremony to which dignitaries would be invited.

I chose the first story to be a much loved, Canberra-born soldier, Private Robert Poate. Robert had been killed in Afghanistan the year before, along with two other Australians, by a rogue Afghan soldier. His parents, Hugh and Janny, accepted their son being the first. A soldier killed in Afghanistan would prompt Australians to realise that a real war was being fought in which Australians were dying.

Three hundred attended that first night, including the Poate family and friends, General David Hurley, Chief of Defence, Service Chiefs, Australia's four living Victoria Cross recipients, RSL leaders, veterans and members of the public.

It is a moving service. Everyone sings the national anthem. The emcee reminds the crowd of the origins of the Memorial and vision of its founder, Charles Bean. A piper and a bugler emerge simultaneously from the Hall of Memory and stand either side of the entrance. The piper plays the lament as wreaths and floral tributes are laid. Standing at the base of the pool is a large framed photograph of the person whose life is being honoured, having been on display all day at the Memorial entrance. Then, a uniformed serviceman or woman reads the story of just one of the 102,800 named on the Roll of Honour – who they were; where they were born and grew up, went to school; who they loved and who loved them; how they joined the military; what they did and how they died. The Ode is recited, the Last Post is played and visitors are left with the words of Charles Bean:

> Many a man lying out there at Pozieres, or in the low scrub of Gallipoli, has often thought in last moments, well … well, it's over. But in Australia, they will be proud of this.

Deep emotions that first night. To Hugh and Janny I said, "Another step on a very long and painful journey. Another step forward."

I managed another major reform in March – Peacekeepers and the Roll of Honour.

When I arrived late in 2012, controversy raged over the proposed addition of Australians killed in peacekeeping operations to the bronze panels of the Roll of Honour. Only upon my appointment did I discover it was not the case.

Private Jamie Clarke was 21 years old when he was killed in the Solomon Islands in 2005. Fully armed, he was looking for weapons caches when he went down a mining shaft and was killed. His mother Avril pointed to the Vietnam Roll of Honour and asked, "Why is my son's life worth less than any of them?"

In 1988, Captain Peter McCarthy was in an Australian uniform wearing a blue beret, a UN peacekeeper in Lebanon. He drove over a landmine and was killed instantly. His daughter, Sarah, asked me, "Why can't I put a poppy next to my father's name?"

The Air Force and Navy Chiefs accepted the arguments and agreed to change. Army needed a little more persuading. When I went to see the Chief and RSM, I was well armed.

> General, the families of this nation give their sons and daughters to you with pride but also sense of ambivalence about what might happen. Should they be killed or die, Defence has no greater right to determine how they are commemorated than the nation from which they come.
>
> Of the 521 names on the Vietnam Roll of Honour, 106 died in the following circumstances: knife fights with South Vietnamese soldiers in bars; misadventure; suicide and alcohol induced trauma; and six were murdered by other Australians. A reflection of the nature of the war. Every single one of them should be on the Roll of Honour. But how am I to explain to the mother of a soldier killed peacekeeping in the Solomon Islands or the daughter of an officer blown up by a landmine that they should not be so honoured?
>
> Death is coming to us all. For your people it is front of mind more often than for the rest of us. Why not ask your own people? If they are killed on a non-warlike operation, should they be on the Roll of Honour?

He agreed to do so. The response was overwhelmingly supportive. The Memorial Council unanimously accepted my recommendation to change the policy. I called Sarah McCarthy to tell her she would be able to place a poppy next to her father's name. We both shed a tear.

Come Anzac Day, I was nervous about the new elements, mindful of the criticism unleashed in advance of the day. Others asked why we didn't have a 'welcome to country' at Anzac Day ceremonies. At the Australian War Memorial, all are equal in death – no rank, no military honours, race or religion. Another idea.

I asked Gary Oakley, more than 20 years in the Navy and the Memorial's Indigenous liaison officer, if we could get a uniformed Indigenous serviceman to play the didgeridoo from the parapet to begin the service. The powerful symbolism would say everything without saying a word.

Gillian and I arrived at 4am. I made sure I was on the steps for the commencement of readings at 4.30. The crowd was already big with people streaming in. Quietly they stood listening to the words of the letters, diaries and last testaments of Australians over a century. Ben Robert-Smith VC MG was imposing behind the lectern, backlit by the uniformed Army band and images on the Memorial's façade. He struggled emotionally at times reading the reflections he had collected.

Just two:

Trooper F, of the Special Air Services Regiment, describes his last mission in Afghanistan:

> For a split second as I was crawling forward on my hands and knees, towards my wounded mate, I couldn't help but think, 'this is *déjà* vu' … the same situation occurring again, just in a different Afghan valley.
>
> Five years ago, I battled to save, but in the end had to watch a mate die – my heart had broken. Four years ago, I reassured and held the hand of a mate who had his legs blown off – my heart shattered. And only three years ago, it was happening to me, as I found myself staring down at my own lifeless bloodied limbs after two machine gun bullets ripped through both my legs.
>
> And here I was today, watching another mate, another brother, suffer this indescribable pain.
>
> Soaked in mud made wet from his own blood and the hot sand around us, and still receiving heavy fire, we did all we could to save him.

SGT C Fallon, Ordinance Corp, Rotary Wing Group Kandahar:

> At this moment I am proud, proud of my wife and her efforts back home, proud of my country, proud that I am serving my country, proud of my mates' service and proud of the sacrifices we all make in order to serve.

> As the unmistakable thud of the 'chook' taking off resonates around the airfield, I close my eyes and say a little prayer for the team heading out and wish them well as they head into the darkness.
>
> I will catch a couple of hours sleep and do it all over again, because this is what I do, and where I want to be.

Then, at 5.15am, complete silence.

At 5.30am Flight Lieutenant Tjapukai Shaw of 22 Squadron RAAF broke the silence with the didgeridoo. It brought a shiver up my spine, the rich sound reverberating through the crowd, a welcome like no other.

It went superbly, the staff and volunteers making it a moving, dignified event which brought to life the meaning of sacrifice. The crowd of 35,000 was up 40% on the previous year. We had found a way to bring the service to a modern Australia.

When researching the Peacekeepers and Roll of Honour, I discovered that one name had not been added to the Vietnam Roll of Honour. Dal Abbott was 21 years old, fighting with 1RAR, when he was killed in Vietnam at the battle of Balmoral on 30 May 1968. A conscript, he was second man on a machine gun that sustained a stoppage. He went forward to help Private Bob McLean clear it when he was shot and killed instantly.

At the time of his death, Abbott's sister was protesting the Vietnam War. His whole family opposed the war. Two days after Abbott's death, his parents went into the media, describing his death as state-sponsored murder. His father had fought in the Second World War and his mother served in the Army. In 1973 when the Memorial's staff rang to check details for the Roll of Honour, his family didn't want him on the Roll. Abbott's sister wrote to the Minister for Veterans Affairs regularly over the years, seeking assurances he would never be added.

I wondered why Dal Abbott was buried at the Terendak Cemetery in Malaysia, and not in Australia. The family had declined his repatriation. The Regiment's chaplain was told that as Australia had killed Dal

Abbott, Australia should "keep him". I encountered suffering Vietnam veterans who served with Dal Abbott. Some badly so. They were with him when he was killed. Their wounds, when I met them, still raw. Bob McLean returned from Vietnam, basically drinking himself to death with guilt over Abbott. I recommended to the Council that his name be added to the Roll of Honour. This was now more about the living than the dead.

I tracked down Abbott's sister and called her on 22 May 2013. I told her his name would be added to the Vietnam Roll and why. She was very angry. The following day another family member called, equally distraught. I learned something else. Dal had been named after his father's brother. The first name on the Roll of Honour under HMAS *Perth*, sunk in the Sunda Strait in March 1942, is Abbott DSN.

Dal Abbott's name was added the Roll of Honour on 30 May 2013. A dozen emotional Vietnam Veterans were waiting for the gates to open and pay their respects to him after 45 years. Before the Vietnam panels, veteran, Garry "Pepe" Prendergast wept in my arms.

Afghanistan: The Australian Story was officially opened on 6 August. The entrance was between two blast walls, stencil artwork of soldiers with weapons done by a serving soldier, a Boeing ScanEagle drone used in Afghanistan suspended from the ceiling, a map of Uruzgan, personal uniforms, log books, Improvised Explosive Devices, a 'sound shower' and film explaining the war, the crumpled storage box from a Bushmaster infantry vehicle hit by a bomb and one of Ben Quilty's paintings of an SAS Captain were superbly displayed and provenance described.

At its heart was a twin physical and emotional multimedia soundscape: rich vibrant images and film of men and women, Afghans, the landscape, naval operations, schools, road building, airlift, fighting, dying, ramp ceremonies, grief, coming home, PTSD and more.

The courage of Elvi Wood. Her husband Brett, a commando and Medal of Gallantry recipient, was killed in Afghanistan:

> I woke up because my phone was ringing and it was Brett's best friend and it just didn't click because I just didn't understand why he'd be calling me at 5 am … when I went to pick up the phone I heard the door bell ringing at the same time so I just went downstairs, tuned on the light and opened the door.
>
> You read about it in books and you see it in TV shows and on movies, where someone opens the door and there are men and women there in uniform. But to actually have it happen, I – I can't even put it into words.

The official opening was attended by Governor General, Her Excellency Dame Quentin Bryce, Prime Minister Rudd, Opposition Leader Tony Abbott, Chief of the Australian Defence Force, General David Hurley, uniformed men and women, diplomats, families and veterans.

Included in my remarks: "This nation is going to have to make a generational investment in the Australian War Memorial to create the space necessary to tell the stories and do justice to the 100,000 veterans we have created over the past twenty years."

Speaking, General Hurley turned towards me, "And on money Brendan, you're going to have to join the queue behind me!" The crowd erupted in laughter. But I had laid a marker for what would lay ahead.

In the Afghanistan gallery is what I regard as one of the five most important relics in the Memorial's collection. Mounted behind glass, the cowling from the US Blackhawk helicopter in which one American and three Australian commandos were killed in June 2010. It was used as a stretcher to bring out our dead and dying.

Pam Palmer's son, Scott, was one of them. She embraced me, buried her face in my shoulder and wept, "Thank you for making my son's memory live and his life mean something."

It isn't possible to explain to those who don't or won't understand, the importance of these stories being told. A Navy Officer wrote, "Thank you for telling my 11-year-old son in words I never could, why his father has spent so much time away from home." An Air Force Officer: "Sir, thank you for the Afghanistan exhibition". I reassured her that it would be more commensurate with what they had all done once we had more space.

She went on: "Sir, you don't get it. One of the guys I work with flies C-130s. He's been flying across the Middle East for over three years. His wife hates the military. She hates the air force and hates him being away. He took her to see the Afghanistan exhibition. She broke down and said, I'm sorry. I get it."

28

It's not about war, but love and friendship

Thinking how to get the story to an international audience without spending money, the History Channel seemed an ideal vehicle. Foxtel agreed, sending the Scottish archaeologist and historian, Neil Oliver. He came and went with his 'fly on the wall' crew for nine months. Staff were apprehensive. We were redeveloping the First World War Galleries with behind the scenes 'creative tensions'. The five-part series covered all the dramas of moving sacred relics like the Gallipoli landing boat and dioramas.

Filming included historian, Ashley Ekins, rowing a boat pre-dawn onto Anzac Cove for the Gallipoli section. I was filmed in a barnyard at a dairy farm at Bullecourt, discovering the rusting remains of a British Mark V tank which the owner was gifting to our new exhibition. Oliver went to the Adelong tip. A couple discovered in fossicking, precious, discarded letters from a soldier burying the dead at the Adelaide Cemetery, France, in 1919, the cemetery from which the Unknown Australian Soldier had been exhumed.

Other stories included a man handing to the Memorial love letters his mother had received from her champion rower fiancée, Tom Whyte. He was mortally wounded rowing ashore at the Gallipoli landing. The dramas around KNOWN UNTO GOD on the tomb of the Unknown Australian Soldier: Cameron Baird's parents Doug and Kaye, the day after receiving their dead son's Victoria Cross, standing in the Hall of Valour presenting it to the nation. Doug emotionally saying, "Tell your kids you love them … because you don't know what's around the corner."

They filmed me lying on my stomach cleaning the Tomb, after which political leaders and MPs regularly came and cleaned it. In doing so, you look straight down Anzac Parade to the Parliament. A deeply humbling experience.

Months into the project, Neil said, "Brendan, I've done many of these projects. This is the most emotional, but I don't know if it's about war".

"Neil, I have already concluded after a year it is about love. Love for friends and between friends, love of family and of our country. We honour men and women whose lives are committed not to themselves but to us, and their last moments to one another."

"That's it. Love and friendship." And with those words, he stood in twilight darkness in the commemorative area next to the flame of remembrance to end the final episode.

I had thought a lot about the "Eulogy to the Unknown Australian Soldier". In the end, we settled on striking it in bronze and mounting it at the entrance to the Hall of Memory.

The front of the Tomb was inscribed, *He symbolises all Australians who have died in war.*

Those words gave us information. But the brilliance of Paul Keating's eulogy is that it gave us both information and understanding. I recommended it be replaced with the key phrase from the eulogy: *He is all of them, and he is one of us.*

In those words, he represents the 62,000 killed in the First World War and the 41,000 killed since. There is a direct link between him, his sacrifice, whom he represents – and us. Almost all of those listed on the bronze panels were not professional soldiers, sailors, airmen or women, they were everyday Australians just like us.

Charles Bean had been adamant that there should never be religious symbols or language in the Hall of Memory. But, in 1999, six years after the Tomb was installed, the words KNOWN UNTO GOD were inscribed at one end. The Memorial's attempt to return to Bean's vision by replacing it with the opening line of the eulogy was dropped after strident criticism. It was to have been: *We do not know this Australian's name, and we never will.*

I went up to Sydney to see Paul Keating to explain what we planned. I spent an hour with him.

> Brendan, I was Prime Minister, I was pretty busy. Don (Watson) and two guys were writing speeches. We discussed this one, I emphasised the gravity of the occasion. They came back a couple of weeks later with a speech. A lot of strident criticism of incompetent British generals. I told them while I agreed with every word, this was not the occasion for such a speech.
>
> This should be the speech given at the funeral on Tuesday, for a man killed by a bus last Thursday.

Amidst the controversy, I said to Les Carlyon, icon of Australian journalism, "Les, I must be missing something. I regard Keating's "Eulogy to the Unknown Australian Soldier" as one of the greatest speeches given by any prime minister on any topic". "No Brendan. You're wrong. It is the greatest."

As provenance would have it, Lee Kernaghan called in early June: "Mate, we're doing a show in Canberra in a couple of weeks if you and Lady Nelson would like to come." Of course, we would. He asked if I could show him and the Wolfe Brothers around the Memorial.

We stood in the Hall of Memory before the tomb. I gestured to the freshly engraved words from the eulogy. "Lee, by 2015 the nation will be looking for an anthem for the centenary, and I reckon that's it."

Lee returned weeks later with Garth Porter. Ex-Sherbet, Garth had produced and co-written Lee's material for twenty years. A man of extraordinary talent and a sensitive humility. I introduced them to the archive, providing them with letters, diaries and stories. Garth phoned countless relatives to make sure he had facts right and families were comfortable with stories becoming songs. I would regularly take a call from either of them checking something or testing words for lyrics. Late in 2014, Lee called: "Mate, sometimes you aim for the moon and hit the stars. We've done it – *Spirit of the Anzacs*. He sang the chorus. I could barely speak.

The Spirit of the Anzacs was the biggest selling Australian album in 2015. All the proceeds from the song were donated to Legacy and

Soldier On. The song was sung by Lee, Jessica Mauboy, Shannon Noll, Jon Stevens, Guy Sebastian, Sheppard and Megan Washington.

The chorus, *He's all of them, he's all of us, born beneath the Southern Cross.* In the dome above the Tomb, in gold leaf, is the Southern Cross.

At the Australian Record Industry Association Awards (ARIAs) in 2015, I was asked to speak about the Anzacs and present the outstanding achievement award to Lee. On stage during the ad break, nervously looking towards the partying audience, I thought this a tough gig. Behind were enormous images from the *Spirit of the Anzacs* video.

I had 60 seconds to capture the moment and significance of the award.

The emcee introduced me. The instant I said 'Anzacs', the room went to complete silence:

> The Anzacs gave their all at Gallipoli.
>
> 102,000 Australians have since given their lives for us and our freedoms.
>
> Their poignant last letters and diaries are held at the Australian War Memorial.
>
> From Gallipoli to Afghanistan, they speak to us of love and friendship.
>
> They have given us a greater belief in ourselves and a deeper understanding of what it means to be – Australian.
>
> Every nation has its story.
>
> Anzac is our story.

I glanced down at a tearful Jessica Mauboy as I spoke.

I brought Peter Pickering's 'Poppy Crosses' idea from Flanders to the Memorial. I asked Sarah Hitchcock to ensure all Year 6 students received a cross to inscribe. Peter Pickering, Ron and Andrea Gerard made the crosses, sent them to us and once inscribed, DFAT sent them to Turkey, France and Belgium in the diplomatic bags.

Peter Pickering died on 18 January 2014, leaving a wife and two boys. I called him three days before his death, "Peter, your legacy will live. I have ordered 100,000 crosses for the Australian War Memorial. They will be placed on Australian graves in 39 countries from all conflicts. You have achieved more in your four decades of life than most people will do in ten." I have a treasured photograph of us shaking hands on Anzac Day 2011 at the Toronto Avenue Cemetery in Flanders.

Thanks to use of the ABC's 35 regional studios and Google who built us an App, school students recorded the name and age of death of the 62,000 names on the First World War Roll of Honour. When people walked along the First World War Roll of Honour, they would hear these young voices simply saying the names and age of death.

To coincide with the centenary of the commencement of the First World War, we launched the recordings of the names of our dead and the nightly projections of names.

At the launch of the 'Voices' in the heart of the commemorative area, my task was to interview James Martin. He was unaware that the youngest Australian on the First World War Roll of Honour is James Martin – 14 years and 9 months when he died at Gallipoli. I asked James what the project meant to him. "I now know they were real people just like me and not made up."

At night, in letters a metre high on the horizontal beam beneath the Dome, were projected the names of our 62,000 First World War dead. Each name was up for 30 seconds. People can go to the Memorial's website, put in the name of the person they want and the specific date and time comes up. People stood out there in the early hours, just waiting for a name. Some drove from as far as Adelaide and Townsville, such is the meaning of this simple act.

Now a permanent feature, there were two motives for it. First, it is very tempting, human beings that we are, to settle for the headlines, broad brushstrokes and popular imagery of our history. Our comfortable lives breed easy indifference to individual sacrifices made in our name, devotion to duty and to our country. Second, in a world of uncertainty, emerging, unseen and threatening horizons, we have to be clear who we are, in what we believe and the truths by which we live. We need to be reminded that there are some things worth fighting to defend, politically, diplomatically and, at times, militarily.

Early in 2014, I stopped to look at 'The Queen's Tree'. The plaque beneath it told me the Queen had planted the tree in 1954. I don't know much about trees, but it looked sick. Back in the office, I asked staff to get an arborist in to inspect all the trees. The report confirmed my suspicions. The Queen's Tree was close to dead. The Lone Pine Tree, grown from a pine cone retrieved by a soldier from the epic battle and sent to his mother, had perhaps only another decade of life in it.

This would be sensitive. I told the team to quietly remove The Queen's Tree early one morning and replace it with an identical, mature specimen. Water and fertilise it vigorously. Days after the job was done, a letter arrived from the President of the Remembrance Driveway Committee, Air Commodore Ian Scott AM (Retd).

In 1954, The Queen planted two trees. One was in Macquarie Place, Sydney, the second at the Australian War Memorial. Trees were then planted along the Highway from Sydney, creating a 'Remembrance Way'. A number honour our nation's Victoria Cross recipients. The committee wanted to mark the 60th anniversary of the planting of The Queen's Tree at the Australian War Memorial with a ceremony and plaque dedication. Panic.

It suddenly got worse. The Palace contacted me. The Duke and Duchess of Cambridge would be visiting Australia in April. They would like to attend the War Memorial on Anzac Day. Ye Gods, I thought. Of course, the Remembrance Driveway Committee would rightly expect an event at The Queen's Tree.

An idea. The Lone Pine Tree was a decade away from demise. I asked the team if we had some young Lone Pines propagated from it. We had three! So, on Anzac Day, we would invite their Royal Highnesses to ceremonially plant the 'new' Lone Pine thereby drawing any attention away from The Queen's Tree.

The story of the Lone Pine Tree is powerful. In August 1915 at Lone Pine, Gallipoli, after four days of subterranean anarchy, Australia was victorious. The price was high, 2,300 Australian casualties. Seven Australians were awarded the Victoria Cross. At its end, Private Benjamin Smith of the 3rd Battalion went in search of his brother, Mark, who had gone into the attack with the 4th Battalion. He scoured the captured Turkish trenches for signs of his brother, but after three days could find no trace of him. From one of the pine logs covering the Turkish trenches, Benjamin took a pine cone. He sent it to his mother, Mrs. Ida McMullin, in memory of her dead son. She germinated several seeds and sent one to the Yarralumla Nursery in 1929, intended for the Australian War Memorial. She wrote to the Memorial's director, John Treloar, every six months to ask of "her son's tree".

In 1934, Prince Henry, Duke of Gloucester, visited the grounds of the Australian War Memorial when only its foundations had been laid. Treloar invited the Duke to officially plant the Lone Pine sapling. From that planting our nation has this magnificent Lone Pine Tree, sadly nearing the end of its natural life. Given the Duke of Gloucester is Prince William's great, great uncle, the synergy was perfect.

Ben Roberts Smith VC MG delivered a superb Dawn Service address to 50,000 people that Anzac Day. I was standing with their Royal Highnesses, who were clearly moved. Later, at the conclusion of the National Service in the Commemorative area, I presented them with a photograph of the Duke of Gloucester planting the Lone Pine in 1934, framed in timber from the same tree.

The final event that day was the planting of the 'baby' Lone Pine by Prince William and Kate. By this time, Gillian and I knew we were in the company of two very special, down to earth people. After the planting, we took them to the plaque.

"Your Royal Highness, your grandmother planted a tree in front the Memorial during her visit in 1954. I probably shouldn't tell you this, but it died. I had it removed a few months ago and replaced."

Startled, he looked at the newly planted Lone Pine and smiled, "Well, make sure you water and fertilise this one well". We both laughed. As they were getting into the car, Prince William turned and said, “Dr Nelson, I won’t tell Her Majesty about the tree”.

The Remembrance Driveway Committee was very happy. No mention of a ceremony at The Queen’s Tree.

On my first day at the Memorial in December 2012, I was at the front steps with the assistant director. In search of a coffee, we headed to a building on the eastern side. “Where are we going Rhonda?” She gestured to a building with a terrace along it, “The Terrace café restaurant”. It looked like a library. “The architects designed it so it wouldn’t be noticed”. “Mission accomplished. But aren’t you trying to run a business here?” The building seemed well designed and modern, but completely soulless. The furniture was of the Coles Cafeteria, white plastic on steel frame genre.

My instructions to the creative designers were to “create soul. People have to feel that they are at the Australian War Memorial, not the tea room at the High Court”. A stunning result. Bright, modern furniture, timber inlays, soft lighting and across three sides in the loft space, huge, blown up images of young Australians across the three Services. Screens ran continuous film footage of events and displays at the Memorial.

I told the staff we would rename it *Poppy’s,* in honour of trooper David ‘Poppy’ Pearce. Killed in Afghanistan on 8 October 2007, he left a widow, Nicole, and two daughters, Stephanie and Hannah. The young soldiers called him ‘Poppy’ because at 41 years of age, he was a father figure. When David was killed, two sappers made a timber sign *Poppy’s.* They placed it on the recreation centre at our Afghanistan base at Tarin Kowt.

I met Nicole when Defence Minister at David’s ramp ceremony and again at his Brisbane funeral. I called her early in 2014 to explain the idea as a tribute to a deeply loved and missed husband. Also battling breast cancer, Nicole didn’t say a word as I unpacked our vision for *Poppy’s.* After a long silence, she said “That’s the best news I have had since David died.”

I was then told by senior staff that the architects who designed the building were not happy with any of this. In particular, I wanted to put a large, polished metal sign on the concrete façade – *Poppy's*. "Moral licence", I was told.

I said, please pass something on to the architects before they reach for their lawyers. "The taxpayers have paid for the building and own it. We are giving soul to something that has little. All we want is to put the nick name of a dead soldier whom we are honouring onto the concrete outside. If they want a bloody war, they'll get one – me, Nicole Pearce, her girls and a large group of grieving soldiers against them".

Prime Minister Tony Abbott personally brought the *Poppy's* sign back from Afghanistan with the big red kangaroo from the recreation centre. He officiated at the opening of *Poppy's* in July 2014.

Two more precious items arrived from Afghanistan. The Camp Holland and Camp Russell Memorials. Services were held at them after the deaths of our men in Afghanistan, conceived and constructed in theatre. The Camp Holland memorial was on the parade ground. Services for those killed from the International Forces, including Australians, were held at it.

The Camp Russell memorial was for Special Forces, named in honour of Sergeant Andrew Russell, the first SAS soldier killed in Afghanistan. One of our operatives who oversaw the construction of the marble memorial said it had come from Pakistan.

Before moving them to their final resting place on the western side near the Lone Pine Tree, I wanted to send a clear message to young servicemen and women, veterans and families, of our pride in them, a message to those resisting what needed to be done to make the Memorial relevant to a new generation of veterans. I asked that both Memorials be placed on the forecourt of the War Memorial, facing down Anzac Parade to the Parliament. They stood there for two weeks.

The First World War Galleries finished under budget and on time. Bryon Cunningham did much of the exhibition design. I called him the guy with the black skivvy. A gifted genius, working with our team, they produced an exhibition worthy of our nation and the sacrifices made.

At the base of the bullet ridden Gallipoli landing boat, we placed Charles Bean's summation of the entire war. Having written and edited the 12 volumes of the official history, Bean found the words to sum it all up:

> What these men did, nothing can alter now. The good and the bad, the greatness and the smallness of their story, it rises, it always rises, above the mists of ages. A monument to great hearted men, and for their nation, a possession forever.

In the penultimate room, we wanted to reflect victory but also the price paid for it. Our staff finally found what we needed in the storage shed of Marrickville council. 'Winged Victory' had been created for Marrickville in 1919 by artist, Gilbert Doble, a statue of the Greek Goddess, Nike. She held the sword of victory aloft in one hand, the laurel wreath of loss below in the other, the face of a grieving mother. For decades she had stood proudly above the 450 names of Marrickville's war dead until repeated lightning strikes left no choice but for her be taken down.

Staff carefully removed the top from waist up. Magnificently mounted, she sits in the centre of a semi-lit room in which six stories are told. One is that of John and Ruby Luff, the photograph I left on John's grave in 2011, one of his letters to Ruby and the house Ruby lived in with their three kids.

We flew Roland Rayfield, grandson of John, over for the opening. He and his wife were photographed in front of it with the Governor General. The circle was complete.

I was proud of the very final reflections space. As images of First World War Australian soldiers and nurses appear and morph into the earliest ANZAC Day marches, on through generations of marches to today, you hear Beatrice Tucker. Then aged 16, she simply sings the song she wrote of her grandfather, a Second World War spitfire pilot:

There was a man among the soldiers, but not upon the fields
He flew up high, in the sky, as a moving defence shield
When he went to war he risked his life, without a family or a wife
He was brave, honest and always true
There was a man among the soldiers
Arthur Tucker was his name
My gaffer he has gone now
But I love him just the same

Hauntingly beautiful, the moment I heard it, I said "That is going in the galleries".

I asked Lee Kernaghan to record a slow refrain from *Tom Traubert's Blues*, to the tune of *Waltzing Matilda*, ... "Good night Matilda, too".

The obvious choice to officially open the new galleries in February 2015, was Council member and wordsmith, the great Les Carlyon AC:

> The Great War galleries now unfold as a seamless narrative -- story after story ...
>
> Stories that tell us where we came from ...
>
> Stories that give us reference points as a nation ... stories that tell not so much of heroes, as of great-hearted men who kept going back and back.

A small incident spoke to the significance of it all. I saw two women in full Burqas with young children standing in front of *Winged Victory.* I introduced myself and thanked them for coming. "Where are you from?" I asked. One replied, "Auburn, Sydney. We came to Australia from Pakistan eight years ago". Then the other, "We love it here. This is our third visit. This is where we learn to be Aussie".

The rich multicultural profile of visitors suggests that many others share that ambition, learning 'to be Aussie'.

Anzac Day 2015 marked the centenary of the Gallipoli landings.

The Memorial was teeming with people on the eve of Anzac Day. Now chairman, Kerry Stokes, and I walked among the crowds. One man had driven his caravan, family and mother from Townsville. "If we can't go to Gallipoli, then this is where we want to be". Others had crossed the Nullabor plain: "This is the most significant cultural event in my lifetime".

Gillian and I pulled out of our Canberra apartment at 3am straight into a traffic jam. The usual 10 minute drive took close to an hour, with people everywhere. In solemnity, columns of people of all ages, slowly but determinedly made their way to the Australian War Memorial.

Among the arrangements in place to record the event, a giant cherry picker at the top of Anzac Parade, two of our photographers perched atop. It was not until the break of dawn from the dais in front of the Memorial, that I fully appreciated the enormity of the event. I couldn't see the lake for people. The official count was 128,500 people.

Here they had come in the dark and the cold. No movie star to see. No free food or drink, just words of their fellow Australians who had served, suffered and died. Gunggandji man, Boatswain's Mate, Alan Patterson, broke the silence from the parapet with the didgeridoo. Hymns sung, a dedication, prayer, two wreaths laid – by the Australian and New Zealand Chiefs of Army. The ode recited and Last Post played. An address from the Chief of Army and the national anthem sung. Thousands silently made their way into the commemorative area to place a poppy on a name and visit the Tomb of the Unknown Australian Soldier.

I was proud of my country, proud of my fellow Australians and proud of our Memorial staff.

My best friend, Doug Thompson, has three passions in his life beyond family: Slim Dusty, those who wear our uniform, and dogs. I had seen the work of the explosive detection dogs in Afghanistan. Without these remarkable dogs, the Afghanistan Roll of Honour would list many more names. I suggested to Doug a sculpture honouring the dogs would be a powerful enrichment of the stories told at the Memorial. He agreed to provide the funds to make it happen and worked with his late wife, Monique, to choose the design. We settled on Melbourne sculpture artist, Ewen Coates. Standing proudly just outside Poppy's, *Elevation of the Senses* was dedicated in October, 2015.

In bronze, the military dog handler looks eye to eye at the dog which lies on rough terrain. They have returned from a mission as the handler lovingly removes the dog's harness. There are several bombs beneath the dog on one side of the plinth, reflecting the dangers they both face. Two smaller plinths, again with roughened bronze surfaces, stand separately in line behind the main one. The effect of a long tunnel is provided by the three, speaking to the tight confines into which the dogs go. On the ground behind the soldier's feet is his bag, on top of which sits a ball. The ball is the dog's reward.

The dedication was done by treasured TV vet, Dr Harry Cooper OAM. He spoke authoritatively and emotionally about dogs. The Army's Explosive Detection Dog Section attended in force with more than a dozen of them and their dogs lined up with the RAAF Explosive Detection Dogs. Tania Kernaghan sang, *Rusty it's goodbye.*

I have a number of photos displayed in my office. From the many accumulated throughout my career, these mean the most. One is of two soldiers sitting, resting against a concrete slab in Afghanistan. Between them looking straight at the camera is a dog, 'Herbie', a collie-cross. Herbie's handler is an Army engineer, Sapper Darren Smith. Alongside both sits Sapper Jacob Moreland. Jacob's mine detector rests on the concrete just behind him. Not long after the photo was taken, all three were dead. Darren was 25, Jacob 21.

The main plinth of the sculpture has a smooth surface. I said, "Let's engrave the names of the dogs killed and missing in action onto the front of the sculpture. Of course, we will put Darren Smith's name next to Herbie's". I was told it wasn't appropriate to have a man's name here to which I replied, "You're missing the entire point of the sculpture – equality of service and in death, between dog and handler". Undeterred, I called Darren's father Graham in Adelaide. He listened quietly. "Brendan, before they deployed, Herbie had a hindquarter problem. Darren slept with that dog at the vet's for three nights. My son and Herbie fought together, they were killed together and they are buried together. You put my son's name next to Herbie's on that sculpture."

At the Last Post Ceremony, the night of the sculpture dedication, we told the story of Darren Smith. The photo of Darren and Herbie was displayed. The handlers lined either side of the pool with their dogs, wearing their ceremonial red coats, medals attached.

Some things are funny but not funny.

On the evening of Thursday, 18 February 2016, approximately three hundred people, including veterans and children, gathered in the commemorative area. I always attended the Last Post and was standing in the middle of the crowd. Having just heard the story, the Army officer began to recite the Ode when a drone appeared over the crowd. Hovering throughout the Ode and into the Last Post, it was low, noisy and unsettling those present.

From the corner of my eye I could see staff moving quickly outside to find the operator. The four prop drone then went up over the dome towards Anzac Hall behind the Memorial.

Outside, mixing with visitors, I kept looking up but it seemed to have gone. After 15 minutes, I walked back up to my office in the admin building. One last look. There it was, high above Anzac Hall. I watched it slowly descend and hover around the bridge of HMAS *Brisbane*. If it got any lower, I might be able to catch it. When it got to the top of the rosemary bushes, I sprinted. Drawing on school AFL skills, I caught it. You bloody beauty. I turned it upside down and looked into the camera, "Got you, you bastard. Now come and get it!"

A man arrived five minutes later at the back of the building to claim his drone. Unapologetic, all he wanted was his drone. What I said to him before security got his details and returned the drone cannot be printed. He was heavily fined by CASA. I wrote to his employer.

I was privileged to address the National Press Club each year through my tenure at the Memorial. The Memorial's historians provided me with what I needed. I read the historical documents and then letters and diaries given me by the research centre. Chris Widenbar, my executive officer did superb research for me. So often I felt like I was walking through a field finding diamonds.

The two Press Club speeches I found most emotional were 2016 which covered Fromelles and Pozieres, and the following year, Passchendaele, the latter even more so as I had spent so much time in Flanders. I am regularly stopped by strangers thanking me for both speeches to which I reply, "Not about me, it is about them. Please urge others to watch the YouTube videos or read them".

Fromelles was Australia's worst day ever. In 24 hours, 5,533 casualties, of whom 1,718 were dead. At Pozieres, 23,000 casualties in six weeks. Two excerpts from that speech:

Major Geoffrey Gordon McCrae of Hawthorn, Victoria, wrote his last letter home before leading the 60th Battalion into withering machine gun fire at Fromelles:

> Today I lead my battalion in an assault on the German lines and I pray God that I may come through alright and bring honour to our name. If not, I will at least have laid down my life for you and my country, which is the greatest privilege one can ask for. Farewell dear people, the hour approacheth.

Private Walter 'Jimmy' Downing of the 57th Battalion described the 15th Brigade's carnage:

> Hundreds were mowed down in the flicker of an eyelid, like great rows of teeth knocked from a comb … men were cut in two by streams of bullets … swishing in a flat lattice of death …

McCrae's 60th Battalion was annihilated crossing open ground in full view of German machine gunners. Geoffrey McCrae was killed leading his men. He was 26 years old.

Victorians of the 15th Brigade suffered mightily in their assault on the German Sugar Loaf. Their commanding officer, Brigadier Harold

"Pompey Elliott", a much loved and respected veteran of the Boer War and Gallipoli, had vented opposition before the attack.

Lieutenant John Schroder was in brigade headquarters with 'Pompey' when his 15th went 'over the top':

> Pompey got tired of sitting in advanced brigade headquarters, and took me up the line with him ... it was impossible to walk far without falling over dead men ... there must have been dozens of German machine guns operating ... Pompey never thought of ducking, but went on right along the line. A word for a wounded man here, a pat of approbation to a bleary-eyed digger there – he missed nobody. He never spoke a word all the way back ... but went straight inside, put his head in his hands, and sobbed his heart out.

At Pozieres on the 31st of July, Charles Bean narrowly missed death getting to the front. On his return, he simply wrote:

> Everywhere were blackened men, torn and whole – dead for days.

Lieutenant John 'Alec' Raws had been a correspondent for *The Argus* on enlistment. He abhorred the 'absurdity of war' but felt a duty to serve. Then self-described as a man who could not 'tread upon a worm', he documented the suffering and courage of his men of the 23rd battalion who would dig the new front line for the 2 August assault:

> We went in single file along narrow communication trenches ... shelled all the way up, but got absolute hell when passing through a particularly heavy curtain of fire which the enemy was playing on the ruined village of Pozières ...
>
> I would gladly have shot myself, for I had not the slightest idea where our lines or the enemy's were ... shells were coming at us from three directions.

Aghast, Bean wrote of Pozieres:

> The men are simply turned in there as into some ghastly mincing machine.

It was an especially emotional speech. Among the several hundred letters and emails that arrived after that speech, was a hand-written card from an elderly lady in a Brisbane retirement village:

> Dear Mr Brendan,
>
> I listened to your address to the National Press Club last week. My father fought at Pozières, shot in the hip. As you said, none of the boys escaped – many killed & wounded. Others suffered in their later years.
>
> My dad ended up taking his own life and our mother's.
>
> We were young and knew nothing of "mental illness" and wondered 'why'.
>
> I was so impressed with the authenticity and depth of feeling expressed by you.
>
> One of my sons rang me asking if his grand dad was at Pozières.
>
> I told him of your association with the "War Memorial" and had given a graphic account of the battle.
>
> If it is permissible, I would dearly appreciate a copy of your address. Would be happy to pay any cost incurred.
>
> Yours sincerely,
>
> (Mrs.) Mary O'Neill

The impact of that card will remain with me until my own death.

Australians fought many battles during the Vietnam War. Victory at Long Tan, its courage and casualties captured public admiration. The 50th anniversary of the battle of Long Tan was commemorated on 18 August 2016. I was determined it would be both special and memorable.

From dusk to dawn on 17, 18 and 19 August, images from the Vietnam War were projected onto the façade of the Memorial. The key theatres of the war scrolled alongside the name and age of death of the 521 Australians killed in Vietnam.

On the afternoon of 17 August, John Schumann and Hugh Macdonald performed *I was only 19* in the Hall of Memory. They did so in front of the Tomb of the Unknown Australian Soldier to 100 Vietnam Veterans, including nurses. I told them there was no more powerful way of us telling them how highly we valued their courage and sacrifices than to give them the song of their generation in that most sacred of places.

In choosing the story to be told at the Last Post Ceremony that night from the 18 Australians killed at Long Tan, I thought back to Mount Gravatt in April 2006. As Defence Minister I was walking through a shopping centre. A man clutched my elbow and said, "Dr Nelson, my best mate was Kenny Gant. He was killed at Long Tan. Do what you can to remember him". As if to explain his dishevelled appearance, "I was run over by a tank". He melted into the crowd and was gone. I told the staff we would honour Ken Gant.

I received a call from a man in Brisbane. He introduced himself as a friend of Ken Gant's from school. "Did you know that Ken fancied himself as a singer?" I reassured him there was reference to it in the Last Post script. He went on, "the day before he deployed, Kenny hired a recording studio. He recorded four songs for his mother. I've had them put onto a cd. Would you like me to send it down, might be useful?" Days before the service, the cd arrived. I put it into my computer. A scratchy, vinyl record sound. Then, the beautifully haunting voice of a young man, unaccompanied, singing *Danny Boy.* I sat at my desk, tears streaming down my cheeks.

Several hundred Vietnam veterans supported by family and friends packed into the commemorative area for the Last Post Ceremony, joined by 600 visitors. Kenny Gant was a member of 11 Platoon. He was one of those found and so described by Private Robin Langdon "Pom" Rencher of D Company the morning following the battle:

> I came to the 11 Platoon position. My mates were lying in an arc, facing outwards, with rifles still in the shoulder as if they were frozen in a drill and it only needed a touch to bring them back to life again.
>
> They hadn't been touched by artillery, thank goodness, and the rain had washed off any blood.
>
> They looked very peaceful and dignified, dying in place, doing their duty. And that's when the tears started. I don't suppose anyone was dry-eyed. I know I wasn't.

Ken Gant was 21 years old when he died. When the story of his life and death was finished, his voice filled the Memorial. Sweeping over the crowd, it took us to a very emotional place. *Danny Boy* brought us all to tears before the Ode was recited.

The Last Post Ceremony on 18 August featured the life and sacrifice of Lieutenant Gordon Sharp. He had led 11 Platoon into the battle of Long Tan; one of our nation's true heroes.

The Afghanistan exhibition proved to be as popular as it was powerful.

I walked in one day to find four teenaged girls sitting on the floor watching the visuals, listening to the interviews. Two women were talking loudly behind them about inane daily trivia. It was at the point Elvi Wood tearfully describes being told of her husband's death, "You see it on TV, in the movies and the papers …" Abruptly, one of the girls turned to the women, "Mum, this is really important. Can you either shut-up or leave!" The look I gave the girl's mother reinforced the point.

I asked Chris Masters back to record more interviews, including Special Forces, and add another 10 minutes to the exhibition. We produced a powerful documentary, *Afghanistan: The Australian Story.*

Special Forces Engineer, Dan Costello, having worked all night with Brett Till clearing mines for a convoy of commandos, sees Brett killed alongside him. "I said 'what do I do now?' You know, like I've never done this before. Who prepares for this sort of stuff?"

Captain Nick Perriman describes Lance Corporal Andrew Jones dying in his arms as the helicopter comes in, “Don’t leave me Jonesy, don’t leave me”. He goes on to explain his decision to visit Andrew’s mum when he returned to Australia. “It was the right thing to do”.

Kerry Stokes assumed chairmanship of the Memorial Council in 2015. Another extraordinary man, Kerry’s commitment to the Memorial, love and respect for those who serve and have died for our country, are exceeded only by his generosity to causes in support of them. His efforts in acquiring the nation’s Victoria Crosses for the Memorial are well known. But his help in many other ways is beyond words, unknown but to a handful of people. We screened the Afghanistan documentary for him. We were all emotional, again.

He turned and quietly said, it should be televised. It was, Channel Seven ran it without advertisements, Sunday night. Kerry Stokes introduced it himself. It should be seen by every Australian.

Back in 2011, I wrote from Brussels to the Minister for Veterans Affairs suggesting initiatives for the centenary of the First World War. The Menin Gate Lions could be loaned by the Australian War Memorial to the city of Ieper (Ypres) in 2017 to mark the centenary of the battle of Passchendaele. A letter returned telling me the Australian War Memorial was opposed to the idea: the Lions are “too fragile”. I was miffed at the time but, of course, had no idea then what my next job would be.

Two ceremonial Lions were made in 1822 from Belgian marble for the base of the ornamental staircase at the Cloth Hall in Ypres. In 1856, they were relocated to the medieval wall around the city. The Lions stood either side on the bridge, the ‘Gate’ having been removed. The road leading from Ypres to Menin does so through the Menin Gate. For almost every Australian leaving to fight and die on the Ypres-Salient, those Lions were the last sign of civilisation.

In 1935, Australia’s High Commissioner in London saw the Lions in a stonemason’s yard in Ypres. He suggested to the Burgomeister (Mayor) that they be gifted to Australia in recognition of the sacrifices made for them by our countrymen. They were loaded on the train in Ypres, big crates marked 'AWM Canberra'.

In the late 1980s, the Australian War Memorial restored them to their original form, placing them at the entrance. When I arrived at the Memorial as director, I said, "The Lions are going back in 2017". I was presented with all kinds of contrary arguments – can't be in the weather, too fragile, a car might run into them. To this I responded, "They were in the weather for 90 years. They went through a bloody war! If a truck runs off the road into one of them, we'll put them back together. You only get a centenary once in a hundred years, we're sending them back."

Next were the Belgians. The *In Flanders Fields Museum* in Ieper (Ypres) fell into the same line, insisting the Lions go into their museum in the Cloth Hall. I went to Ieper and met them. "I will be absolutely clear about this. If the Menin Gate Lions come, there is only one place they are going, and that is to the Menin Gate. We are not going to ship them half way around the world from one museum to another. They're going home – and I mean home."

They knew I wasn't mucking about. I went to the Commonwealth War Graves Commission leadership in Ieper and London. They agreed to build tall plinths for them in front of the Menin Gate as you drive into the city. The RAAF agreed to fly the Lions, packed up in a C-17 to Brussels. There, the Belgian military gave them a ceremonial welcome and transported them to Ieper. The Lions sat proudly on those plinths for nine months. So beautiful did they look, I suggested we commission replicas from the original quarry south of Brussels. We contracted a Flemish master artisan. Those Lions on plinths now permanently welcome people to Ieper as they did in the 19th century. Our Lions returned safely. The film about their journey is poignant.

I was awarded honorary citizenship of Ieper a year later in the Cloth Hall. In his address, the Burgomeister said, "Dr Nelson, you are the 10th person in our history to be so honoured, and we have a long history." More emotion.

Back home, an equally meaningful award was given me, honorary life membership of the RSL.

It troubled me that with six million Jews murdered by the Nazis during the Holocaust, only seven small references to it were contained in the Second World War galleries. We would appropriate a small temporary exhibition area next to the Second World War galleries for a permanent Holocaust exhibition. The subject matter was important enough to crash through any resistance, of which there was some.

Working with our limited collection, and loans from the Jewish Holocaust Museums in Melbourne and Sydney, our staff designed and built a remarkably powerful exhibition: "Witnesses and survivors", focused on those who had survived and came to Australia, telling their stories. It included the Wannsee Conference of 1942.

Not everyone agreed with the Holocaust exhibition. One regular visitor to the Memorial told me emphatically that she was opposed to this exhibition. "This has nothing to do with Australia and the Australian War Memorial", she said. She would never walk through it.

It has everything to do with us, for we are a part of humankind.

In a world grappling with the mass movement of people; the persecution of political, religious and ethnic minorities; euthanasia and a generational struggle against resurgent totalitarianism in the form of those who have hijacked the good name of Islam to build a violent political utopia, we must remind ourselves of the depths to which human beings are capable of descending in certain circumstances.

One of the most memorable experiences of my life occurred in the very room in which the Holocaust exhibition was placed. In 2013 we had hung the works of Alan Moore in that space. Alan Moore was commissioned by the Australian War Memorial as an official war artist during the Second World War. He deployed to the South West Pacific on New Year's Day 1944, drawing and painting. He went on to Europe and was there with the British at the liberation of the Bergen Belsen death camp in April 1945. As I wheeled him along the wall, in his late nineties, he looked up at the works he had not seen for decades. We stopped in front of a drawing of the SS guards removing the bodies of the dead women and children from the railway carriage. He whispered, "The Welsh guard … the Welsh guard. As I was drawing this, the Welsh guard told me that no one would believe it. He was right, so I went and got my camera and took photos as well."

We paused again at a drawing of clearly nondescript buildings and a perimeter fence. There were objects of some sort on the ground and a man standing in their midst. Alan said, "The blind man … the blind man with the stick. He was walking amongst the dead and did not know it". Two generations ago, the leadership of the Australian War Memorial had refused to hang his works, telling him, "No-one is interested in the Holocaust". I am proud that has now changed.

In the permanent Holocaust exhibition will be found our own sense of morality. It reminds us of the difference between right and wrong and the consequences of allowing currents of political and social thought to head in certain directions.

The service of Aboriginal and Torres Strait Islander Australians to our nation also needed more focus, although much had been done to recognise them through the galleries. We named the area used for events and temporary exhibitions, the Captain Reg Saunders Gallery. A Gunditjmara man, Reg fought in North Africa, Greece, Crete and New Guinea. His brother was killed on the Kokoda Trail. Reg went on to fight in Korea, heroically so at Kapyong. No other person has been so honoured within the Australian War Memorial.

We built an exhibition, "For Country, For Nation", working with Indigenous curators to tell their story. Indigenous artist, Daniel Boyd, was commissioned to create a sculptural work and pavilion for the grounds. "For Country" has at its centre a fire pit and soils collected from traditional lands throughout the nation.

I noticed a painting for auction by acclaimed Aboriginal artist Rover Thomas. I asked our art curators to "take our cheque book to the auction". We were successful. It would be the first in a series of such acquisitions and commissions. *Ruby Plains Massacre 1* is part of a series by Thomas about the 'Killing Times' in the East Kimberley region of Western Australia from the 1880s to the 1920s. It tells the story of several Aboriginal men killed by a station owner after they had killed a cow. Aboriginal stockmen were drawn to the crime by birds circling around decapitated heads placed in a tree trunk.

When challenged on why we would hang such a work, I said, "Context is everything. Everyone is equal here – no rank, race, religion or politics. Within that framework of equality, a special place is accorded Aboriginal Australians. Only four or five generations after the First Fleet arrived, with all they had endured, including 20,000 dead in dispossession, they denied their Aboriginality, kinship and family in a desperately unequal Australia to enlist, serve, fight, suffer and die for the young nation that had taken so much from them."

I also wanted to commission a major work by Indigenous artists to hang at the entrance of the Memorial. It would be one that would depict the importance of country, defence of it and our common land, Australia. In consultation with our head of art, we chose artists from the Anangu Pitjantjatjara Yankunytjatjara (APY) lands in remote, north-west South Australia. Not only is their art vibrant and expressive, it is accessible to broad audiences.

Early in 2017, we brought seventeen APY artists to Canberra from their lands, from young men to several in their late 70s and early 80s, extending back to first contact with Europeans. Almost all had never been to Canberra. Our Indigenous liaison officer, Michael Bell, hosted the group. At the First World War Roll of Honour, we told them of William Punch, thought to be a Wiradjuri man. His family from Bland River in New South Wales was murdered for having killed a cow. An infant, William was found suckling on his dead mother's breast. The Siggs family of Goulburn adopted and raised him. Educated, an athlete and musician, Punch enlisted in late 1915. He fought in France and Belgium, was wounded and finally died in England.

Surrounding the Tomb of the Unknown Australian Soldier, the men spontaneously held hands. They began speaking in traditional language, several were crying. When finished, I asked their art manager, Sky O'Meara, what had happened. "They said a prayer for the Unknown Soldier. Rivers of blood have been shed, Aboriginal blood and non-Aboriginal blood together".

They went back to the APY lands and painted the work in four days, *Kulatangku angakanyini manta munu Tjukurpa* (Country and Culture will be protected by spears), 19 senior male artists from 10 communities.

Frank Young, chairman of the APY Executive Board, travelled with young men to Canberra for the unveiling in late 2017. We hung the painting at the entrance to the Memorial, deliberately and directly opposite the most precious symbolic relic of our nation's birth rites, the Gallipoli landing boat.

The painting, over 5 metres long and 2.5 metres high, tells the story of Aboriginal people protecting their lands with spears, environmental conservation, education and passing skills to protect land to the next generation. A rich tapestry of trees and waterholes, it has written across it, "*Wati Tjilpie Tjutaku Angakakanyilpai Manta Munu Tjukurpa*", translated, "the many men and old men hold and protect Country and Culture".

In front of the painting, Mr Young said:

> When I'm in here, I feel my spirit is with them … We will cry together.
>
> An ocean of blood has been lost for Australia, we are very pleased and very proud to come here … and to remember our people who fought for our Country.
>
> It is one of the most important responsibilities: looking after Country, protecting Country, and keeping Country safe. The ancestors handed down this responsibility, and it is as important today as it was hundreds of years ago.
>
> Together we are remembering and thinking about the soldiers, the Indigenous and non-Indigenous soldiers who … shed their blood … who died to defend our County. And

> we remember them. We remember them with a little bit of a sorrowful heart, but we remember them.
>
> It's a story about Australia and all of our stories … We sometimes get sorry about what people did – it makes us cry – but we can think about not only our people, but white people who fought for our Country ... white and black together.
>
> It is a particular man that will risk his life for Country. Since the Boer War Aboriginal soldiers have fought alongside so many non-Indigenous soldiers, together with one goal, to protect this Land.

They were worried we may not like the painting, so had done a second one. Of the same dimensions with similar storyline, equally breathtaking in symbolism and art form. They wanted to give it to us. I insisted on buying it. Today, at my instigation, it proudly hangs in the entry foyer of Defence Headquarters in Canberra. Hundreds pass it every day.

I regard the five most significant relics held at the Australian War Memorial as being the Gallipoli Landing Boat; the Lancaster Bomber G for George; Nurse Vivian Bullwinkel's uniform from the Banka Island massacre; the cowling from the Blackhawk helicopter used as a stretcher to bring our dead from it in Afghanistan; and the Long Tan Cross.

Veterans Affairs Minister, Dan Tehan, called from Beersheba, in Israel, in late October 1917. The Vietnamese Government had decided to gift the Long Tan Cross to Australia. Could we pick it up from Sydney airport in a couple of days?

On 6 December, in the presence of the Prime Minister, Opposition Leader, Military Chiefs and Vietnam Veterans, we were presented the Cross. It now had a home at the Australian War Memorial. We would create a 'chapel-like', semi-lit room for its permanent display.

Neil Rankin was the Platoon Sergeant of 10 Platoon D Company. He fought at Long Tan in 1966. In 1969, he was sent out in an Armoured Personnel Carrier to find the right spot for the Cross. He said that he looked for 11 Platoon's position, commanded by Gordon Sharp and Bob Buick. Of 28 men, 13 had been killed, Gordon Sharp and Ken Gant among them.

Neil told us in 2012:

> With the heel of my boot, I marked the site where the cross was to be erected. Where I put that cross – 11 Platoon's position, I knew it was the blood of that platoon. It was important to me that was where the cross stood.
>
> I hope when you look at the Long Tan Cross you will see it with a different view, by having the knowledge of where this cross once stood – in the blood soaked earth where so many young men paid the ultimate price for what they believed.

From then, I have always seen it with a different view. Now permanently resting behind softly lit glass, stand, reflect and be moved as you look upon it.

29

"Fear is infectious, but so too is courage"

The pressure for more space was growing. Not only space for exhibitions to tell the stories of the 100,000 veterans created in 20 years through Afghanistan, Iraq, East Timor and the Solomon Islands, but for Peacekeepers. The Memorial also needs to tell the story of what our nation actually does to prevent war in the first place, our diplomatic efforts and achievements. I learned the power of art to heal and, in it, a gallery for art produced by veterans. There was also not a single place for quiet reflection for distressed visitors, let alone veterans. Nowhere, not even a broom cupboard.

Early in my tenure, I realised the power of the Memorial to both hurt and to heal. I could see that it is very much an integral part of the 'therapeutic milieu', enabling veterans and families to come to terms with what they have done and the impact on them. Whether in the galleries or the Roll of Honour, people break down, often falling into the arms of a staff member. I put everyone through Lifeline's 'Accidental Counsellor' program – a first aid certificate for someone having a psychological crisis in front of you.

Kerry Stokes saw it and understood the desperate need for space as did the Council. Kerry, at his own personal expense, had preliminary conceptual plans developed by our architects in 2016. We produced introductory materials for key stakeholders, including a video. Veterans spoke to what the Memorial means and why the project had to be supported.

One we recorded, on Anzac Day 2016, was Milton Cottee. He had flown aircraft in the Second World War, Korea and Vietnam. In July 1950, he was reported missing in action flying with 77 Fighter Squadron in Korea. Proudly wearing his extensive medal set, Milton stood before the 340 names on the Korea Roll of Honour, reaching up to touch it:

> Every time I come here, I have a little ritual. I touch the names of these two men and I hold them. They weren't just mates. We went to school together, we flew together. They died together … to me, this place, the Australian War Memorial, has little branches reaching out all over Australia to the memorials and cenotaphs all over the country.

I was filmed standing in the exit corridor at the rear of the Memorial which we used to tell more of the Afghanistan story. The photograph of Sapper Darren Smith, his Explosive Detection Dog, Herbie, and Jacob 'Snowy' Moreland, looks out at me. Jacob's destroyed mine detector, sits behind the photo. A short distance away, Sapper Curtis McGrath's first prosthetic legs are displayed after his had been blown off. Losing consciousness and being put into the helicopter, he said to his mates, "Guess I'll see you at the Paralympics".

In these Middle East Galleries – the corridor – we placed replica blast walls with the 'Welcome to Tarin Kowt' sign, returned from our base in Afghanistan. Anyone who served signs the 'wall'. Much emotion is revealed here as veterans either sign or read the names of those who did. On one occasion, I observed a young man kneel, touching a name for a long period, in tears. It was the signature of a mate who had subsequently suicided.

So too, the peacekeeping area approximating the size of a corner store. Yet East Timor was the most significant thing we had done in a generation. I stood in front of the line of 41 carved funeral shrouds sitting on the long bench in the exit corridor to the shop: "We owe them better than this".

Early in 2017, Kerry and I started briefing key ministers. Such was the power of the video, one ashen minister asked, "Who's seen this?" Kerry reassured him only Max Uechtritz who had made it, the interviewees and "a couple of people at the Memorial". The minister asked that we not show it around. When we left, Kerry said, "Brendan, we'll keep that one in the vault, just in case. Very effective".

Finance Minister, Mathias Cormann, was supportive from the outset and then Treasurer, Scott Morrison, committed the $5 million we needed for an Initial Business Case (IBC). Once completed, later that year, the government budgeted $11.4 million for the Detailed Business Case (DBC). We were on our way. We briefed Opposition Leader Bill Shorten who was equally and steadfastly supportive.

From an initial 18 ideas, four major options were developed by the expert consultants working with us and our staff. Each offered different designs, additional space and at differing cost. The key was to retain a connection to the heritage building and commemorative area. The architects recommended demolition and rebuild of Anzac Hall. They persuasively argued that the most valuable land we had was that on which Anzac Hall stood behind the heritage building. The lowest risk to the Memorial itself and best value for money was to bring it down and build a larger, deeper, wider building with scope for further development by subsequent generations. The Memorial's then management in 1999 had chosen the design which did not allow for future, architecturally sensitive expansion.

Both Malcolm Turnbull and then Scott Morrison as prime minister backed the project and understood the need for it. Morrison strongly so. Turnbull asked if we could co-fund it from private fundraising. Kerry agreed we could and if that was the government's intention, he would donate and spearhead fundraising. But companies would want their names on exhibitions and in galleries.

I said, "Malcolm, we will raise money as we do now, to enhance what we offer, but this is a primary responsibility of government. As one visitor said to me, you tell them we've already paid – in blood".

We established a jury of eminent architects led by Professor Daryl Le Grew, an internationally recognised researcher and architect. He had been the Vice Chancellor of Tasmania University when I drove the Higher Education reforms. He was Dean of architecture at Melbourne University when I called to ask him to oversee the choice of designs for the Memorial.

The designs chosen for the new Anzac Hall and underground, southern entrance are seriously world class. That and the other features cost $550 million over nine years, the amount of money Australia spends on defence in four days. Primarily for veterans and families, it adds to the $12 billion spent annually supporting them.

Critics argued that the young veterans' stories could be told at the storage facilities on the outskirts of Canberra. Just read that again and reflect on the insult. No need for more space, they argued, to display large objects. Apparently it is quite acceptable to have a Lancaster Bomber, Iroquois Helicopter, Gallipoli Landing Boat and the Bridge of a Vietnam era destroyer at the 'main' Memorial, but God help us if the young ones have their Chinook Helicopter, Bushmaster or FA-18. The storage facilities, of course, have no connection to the heart of the Memorial, the commemorative area and the tomb.

Typical of the correspondence coming in from young veterans was a letter from Colonel Mick Mumford. In 2006, through Jake Kovco's death, he had been commander of 3RAR:

> I and many other veterans appreciate what you have done and what you have put in motion for the future of the AWM … last year as I was standing at the Roll of Honour brushing Jake Kovco's name a little cleaner, one of the soldiers from 3 RAR back in 2006 approached me and introduced himself … I asked him what he thought of the new exhibits and he waved an arm at the WWI Roll of Honour wall, "This place used to belong to them, but now it feels like it belongs to us."

The sheer power of the Memorial to heal, its 'therapeutic value', was exemplified with the visit of the Australian INVICTUS Games team after the Toronto Games in 2017, many wearing medals, carrying their physical and psychological injuries, gathered in the Commemorative area. In a group photo, I was standing next to Gary Robinson. A decorated commando, who had fought in the epic 2010 battle of Shah Wali Kot, Gary had been seriously injured in the Blackhawk crash in

Kandahar ten days later. From his wheelchair, he looked up, "You've got my photo on the front of the War Memorial".

At first, I didn't know what he was referring to. Then I remembered. We had the exhibition "Special Forces – From the shadows". I had chosen an image for the giant banners to hang on the vertical pillars either side of the entry. It was a tall, strong, bearded commando, his M4 carbine resting in front of him, the harsh Afghan landscape backdrop. Gary could have jumped out of his wheelchair and run 10 kilometres.

My revelation came in 2014, standing with Ken Doolan in front of HMAS *Brisbane*, Australia's first Guided Missile Destroyer. When I look at it, I see a warship. But he and those who served in it, see something completely different. Ken had commanded HMAS *Brisbane*. "Brendan, when I look at this ship, it all comes back. I think of those with whom I served, my responsibilities to these young sailors to get them home alive. I think of my wife, the sacrifices she and my family made."

Whether a ship, plane or tank, what they see framed is their life of service, reminders of sacrifices and lives given – for us.

The heart of the Memorial, Hall of Memory, Tomb, Commemorative area and heritage building remain untouched in the redevelopment.

Milton Cottee had given me another idea. When he spoke of the Australian War Memorial as having tentacles reaching out to those across the nation, why not bring that to life? These cenotaphs and memorials were for many, surrogate graves. They are repositories of love, places of commemoration and daily reminders for us to strive to be a people worthy of such sacrifices. Why not invite the public, schools, veterans groups, local government and anyone to photograph every one of them? The uploaded images could be consolidated into a single site. When the new galleries are built, onto a giant screen will be scrolled "Places of Pride". Like Peter Pickering and his crosses, Milton Cottee's legacy lives.

The 100th anniversary of General John Monash's leadership of the Australian Corps approached. By any standard, Monash is one of the greatest Australians ever. His leadership of the Australian Corps and its 5 Divisions led to a series of stunning victories. We commissioned a statue of Monash for the Memorial grounds. The dedication was 4 July 2018, the 100th anniversary of Monash's stunning victory at Hamel. He had used infantry, aircraft, artillery and tanks to deliver a victory planned in 90 minutes. He also had, for the first time, 1,000 American troops under his command. It was done in 93 minutes.

Charles Robb and Sarah Holland-Batt did a superb job with the sculpture. As we are Australians, we wouldn't have a uniformed general on a horse with a sword. I proposed Monash circa 1924 in a suit, wearing his medals and the RSL badge he proudly wore every day. Monash stands on tiered, stylised concrete, reflective of his engineering skills. He holds a book in one hand – education. Looking determinedly into the distance, vision.

For all that Monash did during the war, perhaps his even greater contribution was in the decade that followed. Victorious but inconsolably mourning 62,000 dead, Australia emerged from the First World War more divided than at any time in its history. Principally, but not only, around the conscription referenda, politics and religion. Monash was the most widely respected Australian. Jewish, of Prussian descent, he was regarded by the everyday Australian as an 'outsider', not of the establishment, honest and intelligent. In the depths of the great depression, the fascists sought to enlist Monash in an insurrection against the elected government. Repudiating them, he said, "The only hope for Australia is in the ballot box and an educated electorate." I insisted that on a steel band around the base of the sculpture, these words would be inscribed.

Capital 'P' politics jumped back into my life in August 2018. Malcolm Turnbull's tenure as prime minister was coming to an end. He had called a shock spill in the Liberal party room on Tuesday morning, 20 August. From a standing start, Peter Dutton polled 35 votes.

Several ambassadors wanted to see me 'urgently', not to discuss commemorative events.

I told them that although Mr Turnbull had survived, he was now "a destroyer that had taken two torpedoes mid-ships". Still afloat, he would sink by week's end. They should also expect the person to replace him would not be Mr Dutton, notwithstanding my personal respect for him, but most likely, Scott Morrison. As pressure grew over the next few days, Malcolm Turnbull insisted that those who wanted another spill should sign a letter requesting it. He wanted to see the names of the 43 party room members necessary to pull the trigger.

By Thursday afternoon I received several texts, "Brendan, have you seen what Entschy has done?" Warren Entsch called. "Mate, you're gonna like this. They came to see me with their letter. They had 40 signatures. I told 'em, when you've got 42, come and see me. A couple of hours later, they were back. I wanted to sign it as number 43. I wrote after my name, for Brendan Nelson."

"I don't forget what Turnbull did to you and no one else should either."

A true and loyal friend.

The Last Post Ceremony exceeded all expectations in its impact on individuals, families and the nation. By 2017, we thought the ceremony worthy of a book. The stories are powerful, but so too are the backstories of the services. For our historian, Emma Campbell, the book was a true labour of love. Two stories touched us all deeply.

We will never forget Roma Page. Her husband, Robert Page, was a member of 'Z Special'. He participated in the Jaywick raid to Singapore Harbour in 1943. They married ten days after his return. He was beheaded by the Japanese on the second disastrous mission.

On their 70th wedding anniversary in 2013, we told Bob's Last Post story. Roma made her own wreath, placing the flowers from their wedding cake in the centre.

Corporal Luke Gavin was killed in Afghanistan in October 2011. We told his story in the presence of his young widow, Jacky, and their three children on 10 November 2016. The President of Hungary and his wife were visiting that night. As I stood at the base of the pool of reflection, Jacky and her children on my left, Luke's father wearing his son's medals and the President's wife on my right alongside her husband, we listened to Luke's story. Gazing at his photograph, we learned of his life, meeting and falling in love with Jacky at St Claire, love of his family and country, Army service, and death. As the story was told, I could hear and feel the Hungarian president's wife sobbing. At the end of the service, Luke's youngest daughter Olivia, only six years old, pointed to her. "Is that the president?" she asked. "No darling, that is his wife". This little girl then rushed to her, wrapped her arms around her legs and looked up, "It's okay to cry. I cry about it a lot too".

As the centenary of the end of the First World War approached, we planned an exhibition, "After the War". It told the stories of war ending, the aftermath – broken people, lives and families, from the First World War to Afghanistan.

The National Press Club not only agreed to have me speak again, but to broadcast the address from Anzac Hall: "We're all Australians now; 1918 and the War that changed us."

Australians, disturbed by alleged actions of Australian Special Forces in Afghanistan, might reflect on a passage from this speech:

> The Australian National Memorial in France rises above a hill north of the village of **Villers-Bretonneux**.
>
> From its tower, pilgrims survey the key Australian battlefields.
>
> The town's school is named in honour of the Australian state of Victoria. The playground bears a sign exhorting children to, *N'oublions j'amais l'Australie* (Never Forget Australia).
>
> This is why.
>
> Sergeant Walter Downing of the 57th Battalion wrote:
>
> … houses burning in the town threw a sinister light …

> it was past midnight. Men muttered, "It's Anzac Day"... there was nothing to do but go straight forward and die hard.
>
> And die hard they did.
>
> *The whistle of bullets became a swish and patter ... boys fell all round me ... without a sound.* They went forward, many straight into the face of machine guns.
>
> Some in the 57th Battalion began yelling, their screams heard across town above the deafening noise
>
> Downing wrote:
>
> *The yelling rose high and passed to the 58th and 60th Battalions. Baying like hell-hounds, they charged.* Oblivious to their losses, they attacked with bayonets and grenades backed by machine guns,
>
> Their blood was up.
>
> Lieutenant Clifford Sadlier of the 51st Battalion won the Victoria Cross that night and Sergeant Charlie Stokes a Distinguished Conduct Medal. Carrying bags of grenades ('bombs'), they boldly led their platoons against at least six enemy machine gun posts.
>
> Stokes later confided to his youngest daughter that the morning after Villers-Bretonneux, when he saw what he had done to other human beings, he wept like a child
>
> Days later, Downing wrote to a friend: ... the killing went on, I was mad ... I had blood all over my rifle, bayonet and hands ... we had avenged Fromelles ...

So too, from that speech, to a modern Australia grappling with the aftermath of wars to which we send young Australians, context for modern controversies:

> Private Richard Williams had fought on the Somme and Passchendaele. The end of his war was a taste of things to come.

> Just hours from Fremantle on the morning of the Armistice, he killed himself by jumping off the ship. He had told Chaplain Wilson Smith that "he would rather do anything than go back to Australia".

Two women, Margaret Knight and Lynn Berry, set out to crochet 120 poppies to 'plant' at the Shrine of Remembrance in Melbourne for Anzac Day 2013. They wanted to honour their fathers. By Remembrance Day that year, the 120 poppies had turned into 5,000. They were supported by award winning landscape architect, Philip Johnson, in designing a display for the Chelsea Flower show in 2016. Gillian and I saw it, breathtaking, sweeping across the grounds in front of the Chelsea Hospital. Deeply moving. When I returned to Canberra, I suggested we invite them to design a display of 62,000 knitted poppies across the grounds of the Memorial for the centenary of the Armistice.

Margaret, Lynn and Philip worked tirelessly with a small army of volunteers to lay the poppies out. They swept from the General John Monash sculpture down to the Lone Pine Tree, around back up to the Flanders Memorial Garden. The display would be there for a month in the lead-up to 11 November.

We put the call out for knitters – 62,000 poppies were needed, representing our First World War dead. Over 400,000 knitted poppies were sent, including yellow and black, in recognition of Aboriginal sacrifice.

A year out from this, in October 2017, we held a 'test run' one night of the various planned features. A light beam from the parapet of the Memorial down Anzac Parade to the Parliament. It would symbolise the link between exercise of our democratic freedoms at one end, and those who underwrite it with their life at the other. The light would go from white, to pink and crimson, back to white again.

We projected images of soldiers onto the trees. Breathtaking.

The team placed 3,000 knitted poppies on the grounds with the lighting and classical music. Again, I could sense the power of what together we were creating. Then the kangaroos arrived as they do every night. Packs of 20 raced in at speed. I could see that 62,000 knitted poppies on sticks wouldn't survive the onslaught.

The staff consulted animal experts on how to deter kangaroos. I thought there must be a sophisticated technology. When they came back, I was told, "Dingo urine keeps them away, Director". "Dingo urine? How on earth do they collect it? We'd need thousands of dingoes with weak bladders for this job".

We needed guards. For good measure, guards with dogs. I was thinking Jack Russells, something that barks.

The installation was complete and open to the public on 5 October 2018. I walked back from the Last Post Ceremony at 6 o'clock. In the car park were several vehicles with dogs in the back, trained guard dogs, big – you wouldn't mess with them. The first guard introduced his dog, "Killer". I asked if they were ready for the kangaroos. "Yes sir. We've been in each night this week. About 150 of the bastards wait over on Campbell High School oval. We detect another 150 out on the eastern side of the grounds. We have a plan. They won't get near the poppies". Impressed, I said thank you.

"This is war sir, and we know how to win". Unsettled, I went off to view the display.

Another animal was at work. Up at the Tomb of the Unknown Australian, another 'war' was ongoing – pigeons. The staff were battling to keep them and their droppings to a minimum. I was taking a group on a tour when a pigeon landed on the surface of the Tomb. It picked up a poppy and flew off with it. I looked up to the base of a stained glass window to see it was making a nest from the poppies on the Tomb.

Reporting it to Dave, our maintenance man, he said he would get it down immediately. "You most certainly won't Dave. This is an uplifting story of joy, especially with the commemorations coming". That pigeon built a large nest and produced a baby. The staff took photos from a cherry picker that went global.

Over 130,000 people came to see the field of Poppies. Families had picnics around them, little girls did their handstands and cartwheels.

The British High Commission was hosting a dinner in the Great Hall of Parliament House for the evening of 10 November, with Governor General, Prime Minister and a multitude of dignitaries. Conflicted, I decided to stay at my post. Kerry Stokes felt the same way. "Kerry, we will, as for Anzac Day 2015, have many everyday Australians from all over the country at the Memorial; the light beam down Anzac Parade, projections onto the trees and Memorial, the poppies and soundscape. The Roll of Honour and Tomb will be open. I want to be here with them." Kerry smiled, "So do I".

It was a night to remember. Over 10,000 people packed the grounds. Quietly, sombrely, they walked through the poppies, crowds, mesmerised by the light beam and images of our war dead brought to life on the trees. The commemorative area was packed, yet quiet. They milled around the Tomb. "We have done them proud, Kerry".

The following day, Prime Minister Morrison delivered a superb address, Opposition Leader Bill Shorten read epitaphs from headstones and Lee Kernaghan and John Schumann performed *Tom Traubert's Blues/Waltzing Matilda* and at the conclusion, *Spirit of the Anzacs.*

Since 2013, the Last Post Ceremony on Remembrance Day features the "Eulogy for the Unknown Australian Solder". A fitting conclusion.

By 2019 I was very proud of what we had achieved over those six years and looked back with pride.

The "*Spirit of the Anzacs* Centenary Exhibition" was one. When I had arrived, the plan was to haul two 12 metre long electronic walls around the country. Madness. I was new to all this but wondered why people would get excited by two huge iPads. Surely they would want to see real things from the Memorial collection with technology used to draw out the stories. And they did. Alison Creagh, Brian Dawson, and the genius of Heath Campanaro from *Imagination,* pulled it off.

Many Vietnam Veterans carried deep, understandable bitterness towards their treatment, none more so than in relation to herbicides and diseases contracted during their service in Vietnam. Their hurt had been compounded in the 1990s when the official historian, Professor F. B. Smith, denied any diseases linked to herbicides. Worse, he accused them of being motivated by opportunism and greed. In 2016, the Memorial commissioned Dr Peter Yule to research and write a new volume on all the health legacies of the war. This would be informed by 30 years of new knowledge, understanding and interviews with veterans themselves.

The Veterans Affairs Minister, Michael Ronaldson, was not supportive. He could see the incendiary politics of 'pulling the scab off this wound'. Although he couldn't stop me, he knew I had no chance of securing the $1.5 million needed for the five year project. A week after Ken Doolan and I briefed him, I was told by our Chief Finance Officer, "Brendan, we've just received a bequest for $1.5 million." Divine intervention.

Both the process, and the book when published in 2020, were appreciated deeply by these veterans. Not all lived to see it. For some over many years, the pain had been too great. Phil Thompson had given his all for this, including his own life in 1986. John Schumann paid tribute to him with *Safe behind the wire.*

In 2014, Ken Doolan and I told Prime Minister Abbott we had to begin the process of writing the official histories of East Timor, Iraq and Afghanistan. "Tony, even if Cabinet made the decision today, it will be a decade before these veterans and scholars will be able to read the first page. He accepted and funded it. Dr Craig Stockings was appointed, building a first rate team. Another war began to get access to the records needed to write the histories. Within the decade, veterans will be reading them.

I brought Ben Quilty back with another commission in 2016. To paint the impact of war on three women. He painted Lisa Kwok who lived with husband, Jamie suffering severe PTSD, and their five kids; Elvi Wood, commando husband Brett killed in Afghanistan; and, Elle Lou Diddams, 20 years old when painted, her SAS dad having been killed when she was 15.

Standing before the works with Ben, Lisa and two of her kids, I asked about her red dress. "That's my Legacy dress, it gives me the courage to speak about our challenges". I then asked Quilty what the small meteor-like balls were coming across from the left side of the painting. Lisa's son jumped in, "They're mum's stress bullets".

Elvi Wood stood diminutively in her portrait. Ben picked up on her feeling that with Brett's death she was 'an actress reluctantly pushed onto a stage'. Of her red, knitted top, I asked Elvi if it was a poppy knitted into it on the left side. "It's a floral element. I've only worn it twice – for Brett's funeral and for the sitting."

Elle-Lou Diddams was wrapped in a dark shawl. She said she had been "shattered", her whole world falling apart, when her father was killed in 2012. "I wore that shawl the first Anzac Day after Dad was killed. I felt really bad. The only other time I wore it was for the painting."

One ongoing controversy was the commemorative approach to suicide. The Memorial's Council grappled with a number of these during my tenure. The critical point is that the suicide relates directly and predominantly to operational service as determined by Defence and independent medical advice. Some families actively seek such recognition, others don't.

In 2018, I suggested a sculptural work and pavilion be commissioned for the Memorial grounds, the working title, *The Sufferings of War.* Such a work would encompass all suffering – physical and psychological, at the extreme end of which is self-harm. It would also reflect the suffering of families. As a pavilion, it would offer a place of quiet contemplation at which people could gather.

Following my Press Club address for the end of the First World War, I was approached by Mike and Kate Ribot, generous supporters of the Memorial. "Brendan, if we funded it, could you make a film about the Hall of Memory and values? It should go to as many Australians and schools as possible".

The Hall of Memory is at the heart of the Australian War Memorial within which, since 1993, has been interred the Unknown Australian Soldier. Above him stand silent sentinels, fifteen stained glass windows depicting Navy, Army and Air Force servicemen and a nurse in the uniforms from the First World War. At the base of each window is a single word.

Charles Bean and John Treloar, a veteran of Gallipoli and France and the Memorial's longest serving director, asked themselves a very important question: "What are the essential personal, social and battle qualities we saw in these men and women?" They probed the foundation of character. 'Character' derives from the Greek word meaning the impression left in wax by a stone seal ring. The Greeks called it "the stamp of personality".

Character makes and breaks people. Informed by worthwhile intrinsic virtues, character transcends everything else in life – rank, power, money, influence, looks, talent and intelligence. Some people with immense ability never achieve their potential for deep character flaws. Others, with modest natural attributes, go a long way for strength of character. They settled on fifteen values:

> RESOURCE – look for every human and material resource that may be available to help you achieve your goals.
>
> CANDOUR – be open, honest.
>
> DEVOTION – completely subsume yourself to the people and causes to which you have committed.
>
> CURIOSITY – ask questions. Don't uncritically accept what you are being told, interrogate the facts and the motives of others. Successful people are curious.
>
> INDEPENDENCE – know when to stand aside from a mob, maintain your orientation in the face of uncertainty. In the worst of all circumstances, you have one thing left – the power to choose how to respond.
>
> COMRADESHIP – 'mateship': that spirit that binds us in the face of adversity, no matter what.

ANCESTRY – never forget from where you came, who gave you what you have and made you who you are.

PATRIOTISM – support for, and belief in, your country.

CHIVALRY – the chivalric codes of medieval knights: courage, honour, integrity, courtesy, a sense of justice and a willingness to help others, no matter what the cost to yourself.

LOYALTY – be faithful to your cause and to others.

COOLNESS – remain calm, clear-minded in the midst of turmoil.

CONTROL – restraint, knowing when not to speak or act is often more important than the alternative.

AUDACITY – courage. Nothing of value in life is achieved without taking a risk. Moral or physical, the spirit that challenges doubt, imposes will, advances values and allows us to break through fear.

ENDURANCE – keep going, you never give up.

DECISION – in the end, we have to make decisions and to be responsible for them.

The result was powerful. Max Uechtritz filmed it. Garth Porter wrote and produced the musical backdrop. Any parent, teacher or leader in any capacity will be enriched by watching it. (https://www.youtube.com/watch?v=lMxsogyys1c).

Young Australians in search of belonging, meaning and purpose, values for the world they want as distinct from the one they think they are going to get, need look no further than these.

Les Carlyon AC lived these values. He died on 4 March 2019. With him went one of our greatest storytellers. Husband and father, writer, journalist, newspaper editor and author, Les made an impact on me and the lives of those whom he touched, in ways I wish I could describe. A heavy smoker who loved the majesty of horses and racing, he offered a rare wisdom of life. A dry sense of humour, impeccable judge of people, he was blessed with a rarely found understanding of the everyday Australian. His love of Denise was deep, a true team. He twice won the Walkley Award for Journalism and, in 1993, the Graham Perkin Australian Journalist of the Year Award. Yet none of those and many other awards speak to his influence and legacy. When Les spoke, you listened. Kerry Stokes' regard for him was visceral.

Les' two books on the First World War, *Gallipoli* and *The Great War,* tower above all others. He and Denise invested their lives in researching and writing these two great gifts to the nation. He absorbed the terrain, where they lived, laughed, fought and died. He immersed himself in their diaries and letters, distilling the humour and the horror in ways that academics never could.

Les was dying in early March. Those who knew this asked me to pass on to Denise and her family the respect they held for him. On the morning of 4 March, with Denise's blessing, I flew to Melbourne to say goodbye and tell him in my own inadequate way, what his life, his work and legacy meant to our nation.

When I arrived, I felt like the intruder I was, but Denise and Patrick welcomed me. I spoke to Les as if he was hearing me. "Les, you brought them to life. Through *Gallipoli* and *The Great War,* you brought meaning to their sacrifice. You made us think, gave us understanding and a legacy that will outlive us all." I thanked him and Denise for the privilege of being there on behalf of so many Australians who, like me, knew we owed him a great debt, one we couldn't put into words.

On the plane back to Canberra, all I could think was that a unique part of Australia was leaving us. When I landed, Les had died.

The vision for the Memorial's redevelopment includes telling the story of what we do to prevent war, the tireless work of our diplomats. In the meantime, we could use our temporary exhibition space to shine a light on these remarkable men and women.

'The Courage for Peace' was opened by an emotional Foreign Minister, Marise Payne, in October 2019. It honours all those who work for peace – public servants, non-government organisations, police, military and people who have put their lives on the line for peace. These are special people. They find themselves with a constant tension between conflict and compassion, in circumstances where there is capacity for atrocity. It takes a lot of courage to fight wars. It takes as much to fight for peace – political, moral and physical courage. These people have the capacity to dream of a better world and do whatever they can to make it happen.

Visitors were confronted by an enormous window, smashed. It was retrieved from the 4th floor of our Jakarta embassy. A piece of steel went through it, narrowly missing our ambassador, David Ritchie, when a bomb exploded in September 2004. Nine people were killed that day, 150 wounded. David Ritchie's posting included the two Bali bombings, the Marriott Hotel bombing and the 2004 Boxing Day Tsunami. He, our diplomats, military, federal police and so many others placed our interests and that of victims ahead of their own.

Then think of 'Black Jack' John McEwen, Minister for Trade and Industry. Only 12 years after the defeat of Japan, McEwen spearheaded trade ties, signing the Australia–Japan Agreement on Commerce and Trade. Most Australians were still at best untrusting of Japan and others, outraged by war atrocities. Many opposed the move. Yet that leadership laid the foundations for our economic development and a modern relationship with a democratic Japan and friend.

The enigmatic, gifted artist, George Gittoes, has seen the best and worst of human beings. He has built an extraordinary body of work depicting suffering and man's inhumanity to man. The Memorial houses some of his most evocative works. Arguably the most recognised is the photo, now also a painting, of SAS Trooper Jon Church carrying a child to safety during the Rwanda massacre.

When George Gittoes described the action of Captain Carol Vaughan Evans MG at Kibeho, Rwanda, as "the bravest thing I have ever seen", I paid attention. At the Kibeho refugee camp in southern Rwanda, they witnessed the Rwandan army carry out a revenge attack on Hutu refugees. The Australians could not stop the massacre, but they courageously continued life-saving work under fire. Innocent people were dying in their thousands as the international community did nothing – carnage, death and dying everywhere, and powerless to stop it.

Despite the gunfire and stampede, the Australian medical team, led by Captain Carol Vaughan-Evans, continued to work. She called in medevac helicopters, took the wounded under gunfire to be evacuated and then shielded them while waiting. They went to the hospital repeatedly, despite being told they would be killed. She tended to a child, bullet-ridden as the killing went on around her. She was one of four Australians awarded the Medal of Gallantry. Sergeant Kevin O'Halloran said of the events and her leadership, "Fear is infectious, but I did not realise until Kibeho that so too is courage."

Members of 2RAR stood among the bodies of the massacre. Corporal Jake Blake said, "Everything and everyone changed that day. We never looked at anything the same way again."

Imagine the toll on these men and women, confronting, beyond our comprehension – the anguish of a professional soldier, unable to stop people being murdered in front of you. Their stories need to be told at the Australian War Memorial for ours and future generations. Those critics of expanding the War Memorial to allow these and many more stories to be told, who denigrate the idea of it being "part of the therapeutic milieu", lack understanding. Post-Traumatic Stress is compounded by meaninglessness – the sense that what you did doesn't matter, that no one knows, let alone cares.

I wanted a service dog buried on the grounds of the Memorial. The installation of the Explosive Detection Dog sculpture reinforced my instincts on this. There always seemed to be some reason why it couldn't happen. I kept saying to senior staff, "Normal people love this sort of thing. There is a bond between dogs and their military handlers that transcends understanding. Normal people get that and need a place here where they can reflect on what these animals have given for us."

Finally, in 2019, we had movement. Artist Steven Holland was commissioned to produce a work that would honour all military working dogs. He went to the Army dog unit at Holsworthy. A handler held his dog by the lead as it walked on a plaster cast, circling until it laid down. The dog's paw prints were then cast and carved into stone to produce a beautiful circular memorial – *Circling into sleep.* The remains of explosive detection dog, 'Aussie', are interred in a steel canister at the centre of the memorial where a circling dog would sleep. His handler, Sergeant Alistair Le Lievre, did multiple deployments with 'Aussie', a yellow Labrador. There is an inspiring photo of 'Aussie' with Alistair in Afghanistan, wearing goggles as dust swirls around a Chinook helicopter.

When a little boy jumped on the monument to walk in the paw prints of the dog, I smiled.

30

You don't realise what you're learning when you are learning it

The most significant thoughts and ideas, that challenge, shape and transform your thinking, often come when least expected. In random moments of quiet revelation, you can find yourself excited by an idea.

I was lying on my stomach, cleaning the Tomb of the Unknown Australian Soldier. Alone with my thoughts in the early morning light, I looked from the Tomb down Anzac Parade to the Lake and Parliament beyond. Reflecting on the vista and man buried beneath me who had given his life for what it represented, I pondered an Australia he would now not recognise.

There was a confluence of issues: a growing controversy around Australia Day; more calls for the recognition of violence perpetrated against Aboriginal people in the colonisation of Australia; the long overdue repatriation of Aboriginal remains to Australia from mainly British museums – what to do with them?

An idea.

That vista before me is arguably the most powerfully symbolic our nation has to offer: from the Australian War Memorial to Anzac Parade lined with memorials honouring our most significant moments and people; across Lake Burley Griffin to our first Parliament, now the Museum of Australian Democracy and, rising behind it, our Parliament with, at its pinnacle, the Australian flag.

The symbolism is deliberate, compelling us to remember who we are and what we hold dear.

From the parliament in which we exercise our political, economic and religious freedoms, our political leadership has a direct line of sight to the Australian War Memorial. Some decisions, we are reminded, come at a heavy cost. The Australian War Memorial honours those who underwrite those freedoms.

The most sacred place within the Memorial is the Hall of Memory. Beneath its Byzantine inspired dome lies the Unknown Australian Soldier. We don't know who he is. He is definitely not a General or an Admiral. He is certainly of the lower ranks – a private, corporal, sapper, sergeant or junior officer. He could be an Aboriginal Australian. We will never know. We revere the idealism and heroism of the everyday Australian.

Aboriginal people recognised that they needed a presence here. Decades ago, in 1972, the Aboriginal Tent Embassy was established on the grounds in front of the first parliament. It seeks to visibly focus the nation's leadership on the injustices endured by Indigenous Australia. It is time for Indigenous presence here to be formalised in a way that advances understanding of and respect for the first Australians.

Decades of hard work, seeking to repatriate the remains of Aboriginal people from British institutions, has finally come to fruition. Taken as trophies or objects of scientific and cultural curiosity, Aboriginal remains stored in the vaults of British museums are slowly being returned.

Where the origin of those remains is known, they are returned to their traditional lands. But in many cases ancestral origin is unknown. Thousands of remains already returned are stored most inappropriately, in multiple places. They are owed better than this.

The area in front of the first parliament, just up from Lake Burley Griffin, is known as Reconciliation Place. It lacks a presence commanding the respect its purpose deserves, obscured in the vista from both Parliament House and the War Memorial. It could be developed as a dignified precinct, honouring Aboriginal custodianship, culture and history. It would appear to emerge out from the Lake. At its centre would be an Ossuary of significant proportions. Into it would be solemnly placed the remains of Aboriginal people repatriated to Australia, centuries after they were taken.

The symbolism would be powerful.

It would not impinge upon the Tent Embassy in any way, being distant from it.

At one end of Anzac Parade is the Unknown Australian Soldier.

At the other end before our Parliament would effectively be the Tomb of the Unknown Custodians. Contemporary thought is 'The Resting Place'. That is a matter for Indigenous people. Whatever the name, it must be on the centre axis with visible presence.

The precinct would be inlaid with granite, marble and stonework from regions right across Australia. It could list in stone the tribes, nations and languages and use some common languages for curation. All of it would need English curation.

It would tell the story of Aboriginal presence from its known origins, history, culture and customs. It would mark European arrival, what occurred with contact and what followed. It would tell dispassionately of the devastating impact of European colonisation on the first peoples and key milestones in this journey. From the beneficent, awkward relationship to dispossession, violence and Indigenous war service for Australia. Significant Indigenous Australians might be profiled. The 1967 referendum, 2008 Apology and other major milestones could be documented in our journey of Aboriginal Reconciliation.

The Ossuary, or Tomb, would periodically see the ceremonial interment of repatriated remains. It would have a presence above the ground and visibility in the vista.

The entire area should have a spiritual ambience of reflection and sanctity, being the destination for pilgrims in search of knowing more of Aboriginal history and paying respect to it. A visitor welcome and interpretive centre could be established from which groups could be taken to the Tomb and precinct. The construction of an Ossuary or Tomb in such a Memorial precinct would complete the 'picture' in our nation's capital. From the Australian War Memorial or the Parliament, we would look upon and be reminded of the first peoples, their culture, sacrifices and contributions to the nation.

It would also provide a practical yet spiritual solution to the destination for repatriated remains. Having such a place would help leverage negotiations with British institutions. In the journey of Reconciliation, this would be a major step likely to be supported by the overwhelming majority of Australians.

If such a significant site were to be so developed and curated, it would also provide a national focal point and new structure for Australia Day. Irrespective of whether the date is moved from 26 January, that day remains the most significant day in the most significant year of this nation's history. On that day, Admiral Arthur Phillip sailed 11 small ships carrying 1,450 people into Sydney Harbour, half of them convicts. It was the event that would devastate millennia of rich Aboriginal history, custodianship and culture. But that day, and all that followed, marks the origins of the Australia we now are and the people we have become.

Keeping Australia Day on 26 January compels us to reflect on the impact those events had on the first Australians. But it needs structure beyond citizenship ceremonies, barbeques, fireworks and parties.

A major national event could be conducted at the Tomb early on 26 January. It would reflect upon millennia of rich Indigenous history on the threshold of the arrival of the First Fleet. It would mark the last hours of undisturbed Aboriginal isolation on the cusp of upheaval beyond our modern comprehension. The ceremony would evoke feelings of a commemorative event that celebrates all this continent was, those who cared for it to sustain life and a unique culture. It would also reflect on endurance in the face existential adversities.

It should be a major, nationally televised event attended by the nation's leaders, Indigenous and non-Indigenous. The centrepiece would be the ceremonial interment of remains repatriated over the preceding year.

Those events would precede a day of common celebration of who we now are, the people we have become and restate our aspirations for a common future; a celebration of Australia and Australians, Indigenous, non-Indigenous and immigrants.

Placing the First People in front of the Parliament in this way is likely to receive broad and deep support. The Commissioning event, when it is completed, is likely to be one of the most significant practical and symbolic acts of reconciliation this nation has seen.

I was overwhelmed when, in 2022, the Australian government announced $300 million to fund the project.

The war in Afghanistan has many ongoing impacts.

I stood in support of Ben Roberts-Smith VC MG against the attacks on him by elements of the Australian media. I still do. War is a messy business, none more so than Afghanistan. It is a miracle he is alive. There are many men with whom he fought who returned to their families thanks to his courage. Already the recipient of the Medal for Gallantry, at Tizak in 2010, he demonstrated the rarest of courage. With his patrol pinned down under intense enemy fire from three elevated machine guns, he deliberately exposed his position, finally charging and taking out two of them. He then went on to assault further enemy positions in the compound. "Extreme devotion to duty and the most conspicuous gallantry", the Victoria Cross citation reads. Damn right I support this man.

The 'Brereton Inquiry' into alleged war crimes by Australian Special Forces found that 26 soldiers may justifiably have to face civil court proceedings. I told the most senior political and military leaders that if the wrong thing has been done by some, two groups bear responsibility. The first is the politicians, including me. We sent them to Afghanistan repeatedly. We gave them lists of bad people, insurgent leaders to kill or capture. That they did, very effectively.

The second responsible group is the military chain of command. It is their job to ensure soldiers are 'swimming within the flags'.

The fall of Kabul in 2021, the manner of the United States withdrawal and collapse of the Afghan security forces was sickeningly confronting. Its impact on those men and women who gave their all for our nation over two decades, is beyond my comprehension. Forty-one sons, brothers, husbands and fathers were killed in Afghanistan. In our name, in our uniform and under our flag, lives given for all we hold dear. Many more have taken their own lives since, their lived traumas too much to bear. In many, many households is a pain that cannot forget. The pain, the healing of these deep wounds, is hardly helped knowing that after twenty years, the Taliban resumed control. Indeed, many wounds will have reopened.

The truths by which we live, the values that define us, demanded we contribute to a better world after the events of 11 September 2001. As a result, there was not a repeat of the heinous events of that day, the planning and execution of which had come from Afghanistan.

Of course, mission objectives achieved is one measure of success at a national and international level. But there are others. The service, professionalism, courage and willingness to protect and change the lives of Afghans by Australians made a difference to them. It literally changed lives. Young Afghans have seen a better future. They have seen girls and women respected, work, receive education and learn of another world. Roads, bridges, public buildings and more were built and given them by proud, brave and generous young Australians in the service of their country.

The Afghans saw Australian soldiers fight a brutal, unforgiving enemy, killing and capturing many who terrorised and killed at will before we were there. The collapse of the country was not of Australia's doing. We did more than was asked of us. Our Defence Forces were widely regarded as the best in country, Special Forces especially.

Whatever substantial difference these 35,000 Australians made in Afghanistan, they made a difference to us. We are immensely proud of what they did and how they did it. Their stories will be told in the new, expanded galleries at the Australian War Memorial. For generations, their memory will live long after the rest of us are forgotten. My respect for these extraordinary young Australians, and the families from which they come, is immense. They have given me a greater belief in my country and what it means to be an Australian.

Veterans and families grappling with all this should know there is something else intangible, yet powerful, they have given us.

On 3 June 2017, three terrorists weaponised a van on the London Bridge. Their intention was to kill and maim as many people as possible. A panicked melee of humanity ran screaming from the carnage. But one young woman, an Australian, ran in the opposite direction.

Kirsty Boden was a 28-year-old nurse from Adelaide. Her last words were, "I am a nurse. I have to go". Her concern that day was not her own welfare and safety, it was the safety of others. She was one of eight killed that day, fatally stabbed in the chest. A year later she received The Queen's Commendation for Bravery and, later, the Florence Nightingale medal.

But what really moved me was, two days after her death, Kirsty's family went into the Australian media, describing their much-loved daughter as "selfless, caring and brave".

I asked myself, what is it that makes some among us "selfless, caring and brave?" Genes and a family upbringing; a values-based education, in her case, Immanuel College.

But there is something else. It is a social milieu that places a value on those who manifest these qualities.

When I look at the faces of the 41 young Australians who died in Afghanistan, the wounded, those who served, fought and suffered, I see men and women inspiring us to be a people who are "selfless, caring and brave". A truly priceless gift.

I loved my tenure at the Australian War Memorial. Beyond budgets and staffing, every day brought unexpected, lifelong memories and emotions. By 2019, I found myself often consoling visitors who felt compelled to tell me their stories and those of family sacrifice.

We had secured the money for the expansion, built the project team, chosen the new designs and commenced preliminary works. Young veterans could be confident their stories would be told. The First World War commemorations had been delivered and Indigenous service to Australia had its rightful, proud place at the Memorial.

When most of what I am doing this year is what I did last year, it is time to look for another challenge. When people want you to stay is also a good time to go. I felt my time had come and, with it, opportunity for renewal, a new set of eyes and ideas. My successor, Matt Anderson, was a superb choice.

When Boeing approached me to lead the company's presence in Australia, I knew immediately this was what I would like to do. It was one of the world's great companies with a diverse portfolio of research and technology-based businesses advancing humankind. Its support for the Australian War Memorial, when we most needed it in 2013, is something I will never forget.

When President of the AMA, the doctors in training invited me to their annual conference to speak about success. I now have a better idea and advice for young people.

Leadership is not something that can be taught, but it can be learned. The qualities that inform leadership can be discovered in observation of, reflection upon and absorption of the leadership qualities we see in others. To understand the purpose leadership serves is to know it.

Vision differentiates leadership from management.

Management is about emptying an inbox or in-tray, making day to day, week to week decisions.

Vision offers a comprehensive sense of where we are going and why we want to get there. It inspires people to lift their horizon, to rise above their own narrow self-interest and strive for a common cause. People need to be reminded constantly of what binds them and in which they believe.

True leaders are at ease with themselves without any sense of self-importance, clear-minded, ethical and decisive, motivated by service to others. The people I admire take their work seriously but not themselves. They treat people well, making those with whom they work feel a reverence for themselves. Every person is important, irrespective of position or role.

Never stop believing you can make a difference – to your community, to your country. The most powerful, yet fragile of human emotions is hope. We all have to believe that tomorrow will be better than today, next week better than this and next year better again. Hope and idealism are most sustained by men and women who reach out in support of one another.

In driving change, never lose sight of the conservative 'traditionalists'. It is essential to understand and respect in any organisation those whose values underpin it. Once they are reassured that you respect them and will build on those fundamentals, they will support you in building that future.

To achieve your potential, learn how to communicate effectively. Public speaking is hard, but whether it be to five people or 500, learn how to do it. The key is to provide meaning and context. Speak to people in terms you would like to hear if you were in the audience. Tone, how you speak, is often as important as content. People will often remember little of what you said, but they will always remember how you made them feel. The fewer notes and slides, the better. Leaders need to communicate in ways that are authentic and compelling. You need to take the 'risk' of revealing something of yourself to those whom you lead. The power is in the story.

Politics is one of the most powerful ways of effecting change. The best preparation for it is life.

Join the political party that most aligns philosophically with your view of the world. Be prepared, in doing so, to meet a range of personalities of diverse backgrounds and views. Seek the counsel of others. But should you seek a parliamentary political career, don't think about it until you are in your thirties. It is what you do before you enter this unreal world that anchors you. Life experience provides perspective and context to the myriad of competing demands that constantly threaten to erode your values. Irrespective of your level of education, it is important to know what it is like to find and keep a job, start a business, pay a mortgage and, perhaps, support a family. It is the joys and bitter disappointments of life that most equip you for what lies ahead.

Sadly, too many governing us today have experience of little other than the 'game' of politics.

Neville Bonner was not one of them. In his address to the graduates at Griffith University in 1994, on the occasion of him receiving an honorary doctorate, he spoke to a life changing incident:

> Once when I was a skinny-called (sic) black youngster, living in a humpy on the outskirts of Lismore, NSW, a shopkeeper gave my grandmother a packet of porridge peppered with weevils. Wow, we thought! We are going to eat breakfast like the white fellas. As the adults went out soaking the porridge to enable the weevils to float and to be tipped away, I remembered white people had milk and sugar on their porridge. Every morning. Every morning ... thought I'd just nip up the road and ask the farmer living reasonably near for some milk. I greeted the stern-faced farmer with the astonishing announcement: We're having porridge! Could I have some separated milk? I literally hit the ground as he screamed "He'd need his milk for his pigs, and not for some little black me".
>
> I tell you this story my sons and daughters, to illustrate not discrimination or cruelty, but how I came to my goals. For right there and then, I determined someday I would have all the porridge, sugar and milk I could eat. And for as long as I wanted to eat it! Oh yes, I achieved this special goal, and more.
>
> I firmly believe that Northern Rivers farmer planted my little black feet steadfastly on the rocky road leading to Australia's Senate. I travelled on ready to accept each and every discomfort, savagery and racial hatred felt by refugee Aborigines in that era and turn it into yet another determined goal.
>
> If I achieved goal after goal, so perhaps can you ... my ambition for my people and myself was planted by that farmer, watered by the one year of formal education, but nurtured by the skills I acquired along the hard road.

Turn setbacks, failure and pain into new goals and determination to achieve them.

The keys to ‘success:

Keep an open mind. Be open to new ideas and people that are different. We all have our own inherent biases and prejudices. We tend to think we are right about everything, but we aren't. The age of social media and algorithms reinforcing our own prejudices in everything from politics to culture threatens you fulfilling your own potential. Those who close their mind set themselves up for failure.

Nurture and protect the inner integrity of your intellect. Your ability to think, articulate ideas, to challenge and change the attitudes of others, is critically important. Make time to reflect and read. Be interested in the world and make yourself interesting to others.

Build and develop your character. It transcends everything. Embrace values for the world you want. The most important changes begin with just one person. Lead not only from position, but principle.

Imbue yourself with the capacity to see the world through the eyes of others. Understanding how people think is more important than knowing what they think. Wise people penetrate the character of people and the circumstances in which they find themselves.

In the end, we are all remembered not for what we are, but who we are. Irrespective of the wealth you accumulate, the spectrum of friends you have or power you wield, you will be remembered for the way you treated others.

Each of us has only one life. It goes quickly. Squeeze every last drop from it.

As Thomas Wolfe wrote in *Of Time and the River:*

> *Man's youth is a wonderful thing. It is so full of anguish and of magic.*
> *Yet he does not know it until it has gone from him forever.*

Index

www.ingramcontent.com/pod-product-compliance
Lightning Source LLC
Chambersburg PA
CBHW060837100426
42814CB00016B/409/J

* 9 7 8 1 9 2 2 8 1 5 2 3 1 *